图书在版编目（C I P）数据

2017 中国设计红星奖年鉴 / 中国设计红星奖委员会主编 . — 北京 : 中国书店 , 2017.11
ISBN 978-7-5149-1854-0

Ⅰ . ① 2… Ⅱ . ①中… Ⅲ . ①工业产品－造型设计－中国－ 2017 －年鉴 Ⅳ . ① B472-54

中国版本图书馆 CIP 数据核字 [2017] 第 287130 号

2017 中国设计红星奖年鉴

中国设计红星奖委员会 主编
责任编辑：木洛

出　版：中国书店
社　址：北京市西城区琉璃厂东街 115 号
邮　编：100050
印　刷：北京朝阳印刷厂有限责任公司
开　本：850mm×1168mm　1/12
版　次：2017 年 11 月第 1 版第 1 次印刷
印　张：24
书　号：ISBN 978-7-5149-1854-0
定　价：298.00 元

12th 2017 中国设计红星奖

CHINA RED STAR DESIGN AWARD

设计让生活更美好

Design makes a better life

红星奖荣誉宣言

“公平、公正、公益、高水平、国际化”是中国设计红星奖所代表的原则。

评审标准、评审程序均面向参评者和社会公开。评委按照评审标准所规定的指导原则对参评者所提交的资料和实物进行评审。为确保评审公平、公正和不受外界干扰，评审现场不对外开放，评委对产品进行试用和评估，以评委的独立判断为评审的最终结果。

评委代表着奖项的高水平，来自多个国家，包括资深设计师、院校教授、媒体和经济界人士，他们均在本领域有出色的表现并同意遵守评审的荣誉准则。奖项还不断地邀请新的专家加入评审，以其专业知识丰富决策，对于设计超越文化、国界，实现基于文化多样性的设计创新极具意义。每年的评委主席由著名的专家轮流担任。

红星奖是国家级的政府公益奖项，不向任何参评企业和个人收取报名费、评审费和宣传费用。同时，奖项还通过颁奖典礼、电视转播、网络新媒体、全球巡展和年鉴出版等形式，为参评者和企业提供尽可能多的宣传推广机会。

为保证红星奖的声誉和社会公信力，红星奖自创立之日起，评审结果就不受政府官员、红星奖主席、执行主席等奖项组织者的影响，今后也将一如既往。

中国设计红星奖委员会

Red Star Honorary Manifesto

Fairness, justice, commonweal, top-level and internationalization these are the principles that China Red Star Design Award stands for.

The evaluation criteria and procedure is open to the participants and public. The jury board will evaluate the material and object of each individual entry based on the principles of the criteria. To ensure the process of screening is fair, impartial and undisturbed, the screening on site does not open to the public. Furthermore, the jurors would test and assess the products independently, and give the final results based on their own judgment.

The invited jurors represent the top-level of the event, all of whom are qualified designers, college professors, media and business experts from international range. They all perform outstandingly in professional fields and promise to abide by the code of honor during the screening. The event will continually invite new experts to join the jury committee with their participation can enrich the decision making, which is of great meaning for design to go beyond culture and nations, and to realize the design innovation based on culture diversity. Every year, the chairman of the juror committee is held in turn by experts on reputation.

China Red Star Design Award is a national award that is public welfare and supported by government. Therefore, the fee for entry, screening and promotion from individuals and businesses is not requested. And at the same time, the event will provide extra chance for publicity and promotion via the award ceremony, television relay, online media, world tour exhibition and the yearbook publication.

To ensure the reputation and credibility of Red Star Award, since Red Star's establishment, the fact that the competition result absolutely keep the impregnability from government side, the chairman of the award, executive chairman and the organizers. And we insist that we will always keep this belief.

China Red Star Design Award Committee

2017
2th
2017

12th

至尊金奖

Best of the Gold Prize

2017

niu

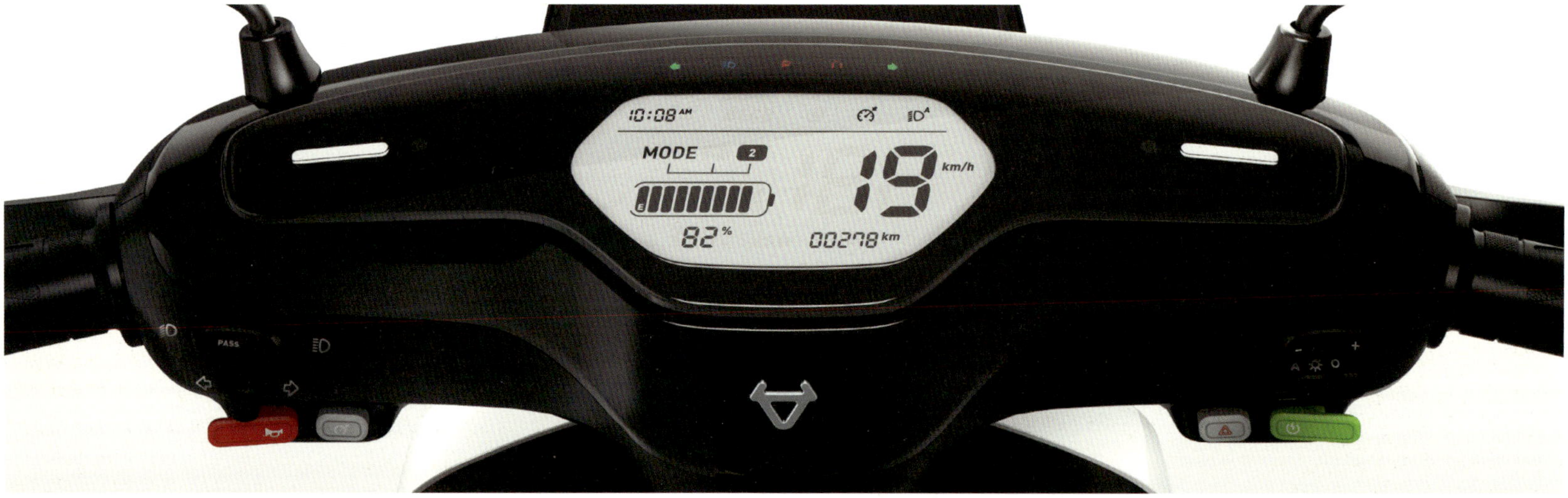
10:08 AM
MODE
2
19 km/h
82%
00278 km
PASS

小牛电动 M1
Niu M1 smart escooter

此款小牛电动车让科技与交通完美融合，满足了都市短途出行的需求。产品设置 360 度灯光识别系统，实现双闪警示灯、自动转向灯回正等功能，安全无死角。产品与手机应用软件的搭配使用满足了消费者对及时掌握车辆位置等信息的需求。电池轻便易拆卸，兼顾美观性与操作性，解决充电问题。产品重视人机工程，设计了启动时需停留一秒的按键开关和放下时自动进入停车挡的边撑开关，提高易用性和安全性。结合摇篮式和弯梁式车架优点，设计了适合都市出行的桁架式车架。铝钛合金后摇臂轻巧坚固又具科技感，搭配中置斜拉避震结构设计，减轻车体重量又使操作富有乐趣。整车线条流畅，车身主要部分由三块大型塑件组成，体现一体成型的视觉美感。该产品重新定义了电动出行的智能生活形态，为消费者提供更好体验。

This is one type of Niu electric vehicle, having a perfect fusion of technology and transportation, to meet the needs of urban short-distance travel. We have incorporated 360 degree all around lighting system, achieving several functions, such as double flash warning lights, automatic turn signal back to positive, so that our riders can be safe riding in all conditions. With the use of product and mobile phone APP together, it can meet the needs of consumers to grasp the vehicle location and other informations. The battery is light and easy to disassemble, taking into account the aesthetics and operability, to solve the charging problem. The design values ergnomics, we design a button switch must be held for 1 second before the bike is fully started,also design a side stand switch when the switch down, the vehicle can enter into the parking file automatically, which improve the convenience and security. Combined with the advantages of cradle and curved beam frame, the design is as a truss frame, which is suitable for urban travel. The aluminum and titanium alloy after the rocker arm is light, strong, rich in a sense of science and technology, with the design of the center of the cable to avoid vibration structure, to reduce the weight of the body and make the operation enjoyable. The whole streamline is smooth, the main part of the body consists of three large plastic parts, reflecting the formation of a visual beauty.The product redefines the intelligent life of intelligent travel patterns, to provide consumers with a better experience.

设计
DESIGN

小牛电动创新研发室
Niu Innovation Lab

江苏小牛电动科技有限公司
Jiangsu Niu Electric Technology Co.,Ltd.

生产
MANUFACTURE

12th

2017

金奖
Gold Prize

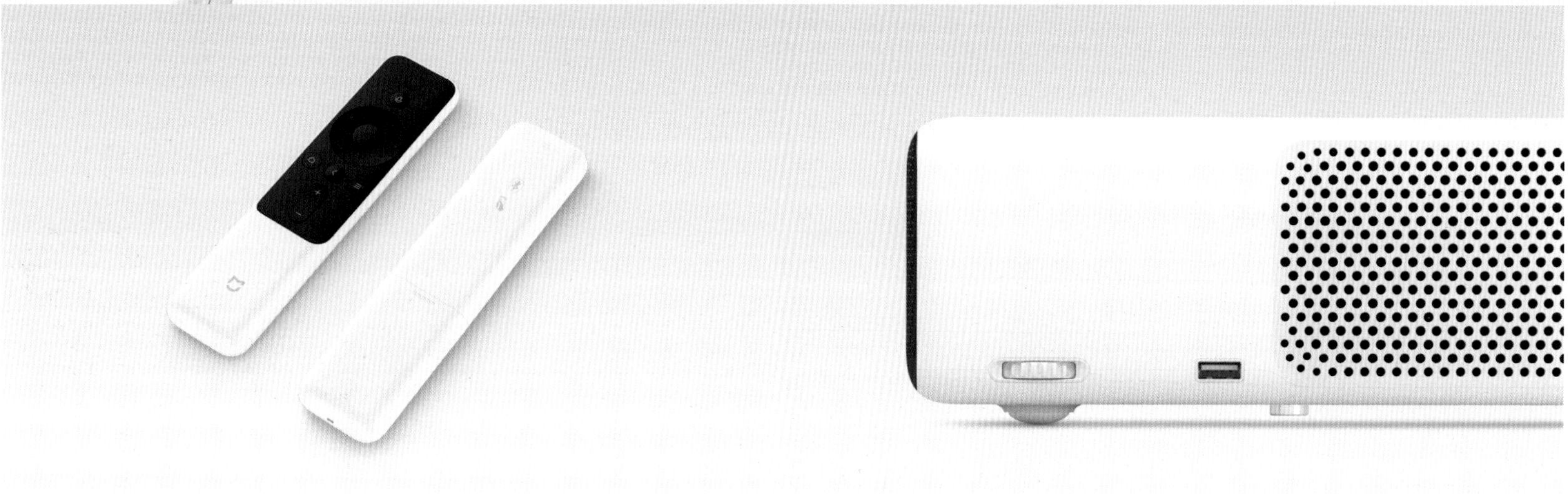

米家激光投影电视
Mi Laser Home Cinema Projector

米家激光投影电视是全球首款采用先进激光荧光粉显示技术和影院级激光照明技术而设计研发的家用超短焦投影设备。这款紧凑型家庭影院将提高生活质量，150 寸的投影画面和清晰的画质将会改变视觉体验，提升家庭和朋友之间的关系。定制支持杜比音效的音响系统，渲染出更逼真的临场感，令使用者在家中也可享受影院级视听体验。用户在任何地点甚至狭小的空间均可使用该产品。主机配套 12 键蓝牙全功能遥控器，支持用户在房间内任何角落对主机进行控制。这款投影电视设计紧凑、价格亲民，将引领生活趋势，极大地改变使用者的生活方式。

Mi Home Laser Cinema is the world's first household ultra-short throw projector, its design and R & D featuring advanced laser phosphor display (ALPD) and theater-level laser lighting technology. This compact household theater will improve the quality of life,it creates a cinematic viewing experience with up to a 150 inches of picture in Full HD quality, which enhance the relationship between family and friends. The custom-tuned sound system with Dolby Audio render a more realistic telepresence, so that users can enjoy the theater-level audio-visual experience at home. Users can use the product in any location or even small space. The host is equipped with 12 keys Bluetooth full function remote controller, which enables the users to control the host at any corner of the room. The design of this projector TV is compact, and the price is close to the people, which will lead the trend of life, greatly changing the user's way of life.

设计
DESIGN

小米生态链工业设计团队
Mi Ecosystem Industrial Design Team

峰米（北京）科技有限公司
Fengmi (Beijing) Technology Co.,Ltd.

生产
MANUFACTURE

机器人行李箱 R1
Cowarobot R1

该产品是一款机器人行李箱，融合了现代行李箱和现代科技技术。将射频跟踪定位技术、激光测距技术、避障与导航技术、人工智能技术形成模块，集成到拉杆及底座，实现自动跟随及自主避障功能，释放双手，提升出行效率。产品创新使用飞机起落架原理，实现自动和手动模式的瞬时切换。应用 GPS 全球定位系统，使用安心。产品不仅应用了先进技术，也兼具了美观的外形，仿照汽车流线设计，增加横向扩散线条，既表达了速度感又增大行李箱空间。机器人行李箱开启了新的产品类别，并将启发更多产品为人们创造更简洁和舒适的生活。

The product is a robot suitcase,combines modern suitcase and modern technology. The RF tracking and positioning technology, laser ranging technology, obstacle avoidance and navigation technology and artificial intelligence technology are formed into modules and integrated into the rod and base to achieve automatic follow and independent obstacle avoidance function, releasing hands and improving travel efficiency. The innovative use of aircraft landing gear principle achieves instantaneous switching of automatic and manual mode. The application of GPS global positioning system reassures users. This product not only uses the advanced technology, but also has a beautiful appearance,it imitates car streamline design, increases the horizontal diffusion lines, expresses the sense of speed and increases the luggage space.This robot suitcase opened a new product category, and will inspire more products for people to create a more concise and comfortable life.

设计
DESIGN

黄定
Daniel Huang

安徽酷哇机器人有限公司
Cowarobot Co., Ltd.

生产
MANUFACTURE

比佛利净饮机
Beverly High-End Gas Water Dispenser

比佛利净饮机兼顾美观性与实用性，细心考虑到各种用户使用场景。产品具备提供煮水、泡奶、泡茶等功能。机器下半部分内置冰箱，方便储存红酒、罐装饮料、茶叶、牛奶等物品。此款净饮机采用敞开式的接水平台，可以更灵活地匹配不同类型和容量的容器，提高接水的舒适性。产品设置智能触摸交互界面，可将饮水机运行状态更直观清晰地呈现给使用者。产品采用一体化滤芯和快速接口技术，不但把体积控制到最小，也减少不必要的材料浪费，更加环保。白色外观搭配木头质感纹理，让产品具有别致感和亲和力，适用于办公、家居等多种环境。

Beverly High-End Gas Water Dispenser takes into account the aesthetics and practicality, consider carefully the use of different scenes to a variety of users.This product can provide users with hot water, milk, tea or other different operation modes.The down part of the dispenser has refrigerator storage function and it's convenient to store red wine, canned drinks, tea,milk and other items.The open form water platform can match more flexible for different types and capacity containers, and make you feel more comfortableto take water. Intelligent touch interface presents a better operation state of the dispenser to the users in a more convenient and more intuitive and clearer manner.Products uses a integrated filter and fast interface technology, it not only can control minimizely the volume, but also reduce the unnecessary waste of materials, more environmentally friendly. The white appearance with wood texture, the product has a sense of chic and affinity for office, home and other environments.

设计
DESIGN

美的集团热水器事业部工业设计部
Industrial Design Center of Midea Group Water Heater Appliances

生产
MANUFACTURE

美的集团热水器事业部
Midea Group Water Heater Appliances

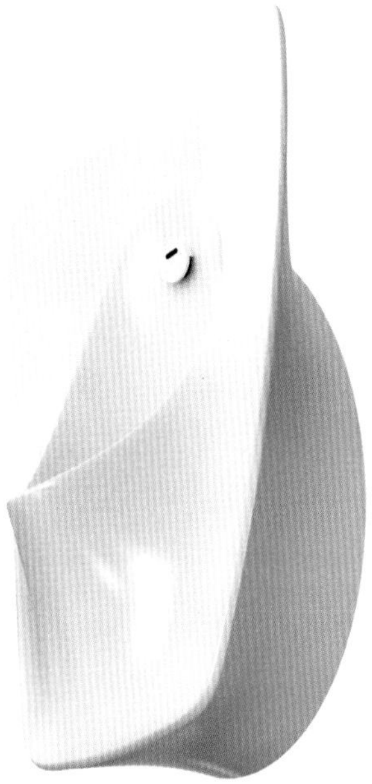

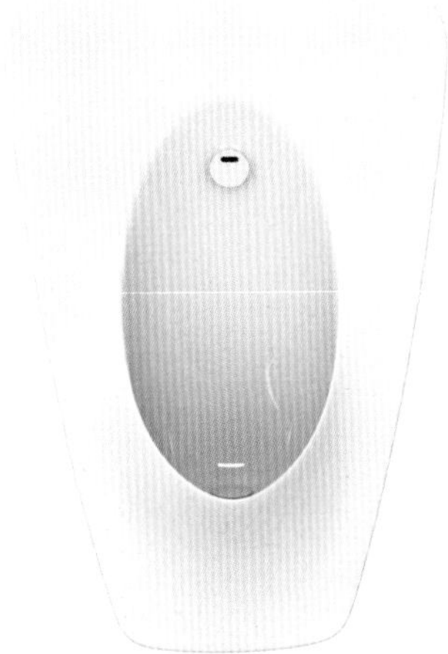

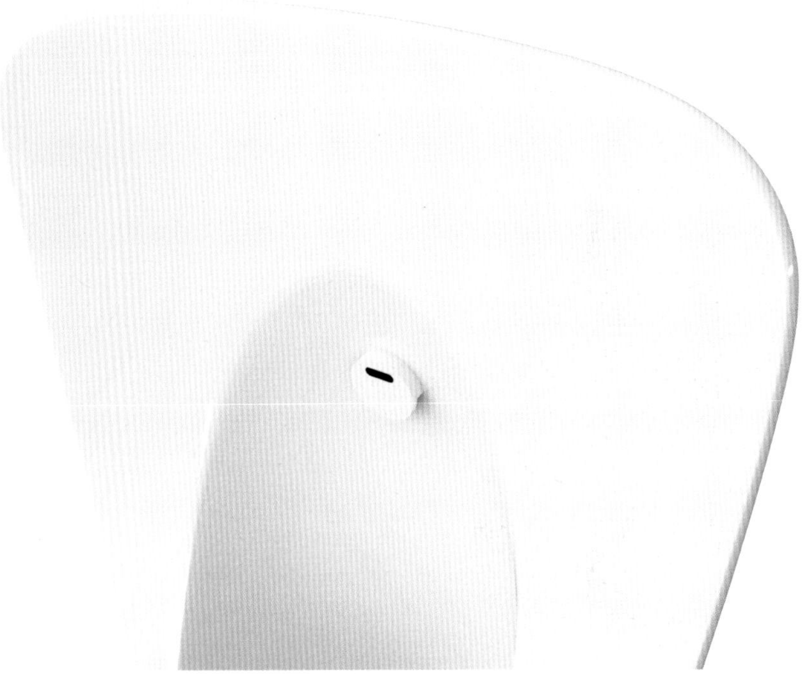

超薄小便器
Urinal

该超薄小便器是一款兼具外形美观与使用人性化的产品，有效保护了用户的隐私和尊严。超薄元素展现陶瓷艺术魅力，45 度斜角设计节省了昂贵的分隔板，能够更好地优化空间。超大弧形陶瓷面，有效保护个人隐私，减少了使用过程中的尴尬。产品采用一体造型设计，圆滑无死角，易于清洁并节约水资源。产品的整体性较强，与不同的卫浴环境配套协调。内部配件使用标准化设计，有效控制成本。可回收工程材料的应用，提高了材料利用率和环保性。产品采用超薄陶瓷工艺，经过 1200 摄氏度以上高温烧制，经久耐用。

This ultra-thin urinal is a product with both beautiful appearance and user-friendly feature,can effectively protect the user's privacy and dignity. The ultra-thin elements show ceramic art charm,the 45-degree angle design can save the expensive divider board, can better optimize the space.And the large arc ceramic surface effectively protect personal privacy,reducing the embarrassment during the using process. It adopts an integrated mould and round design without dead angle to make cleaning more convenient, and the overall integrity is compatible with bathroom environment. Internal accessories use standardized design for effective cost control. It uses recyclable materials to improve material utilization and environmental protection. The product uses ultra-thin ceramic technology made by high temperature firing above 1200°C and it is durable and practical.

设计
DESIGN

舒曼先生、刘惠锋
Schumann, Liu Huifeng

九牧厨卫股份有限公司
Jomoo Kitchen&Bathroom Appliances Co.,Ltd.

生产
MANUFACTURE

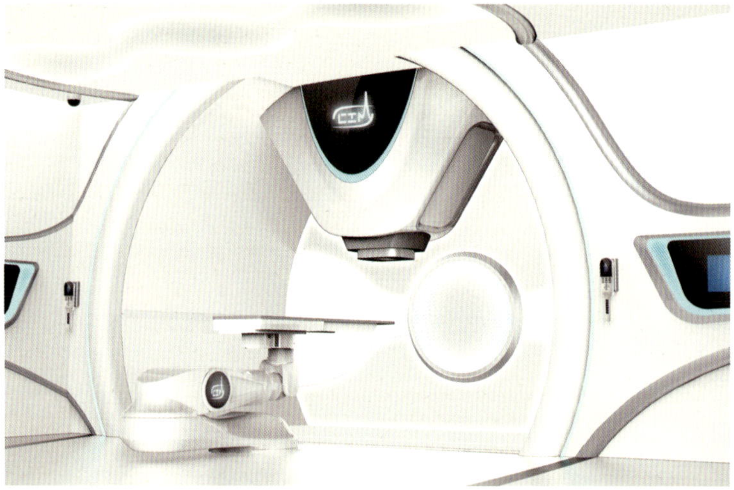

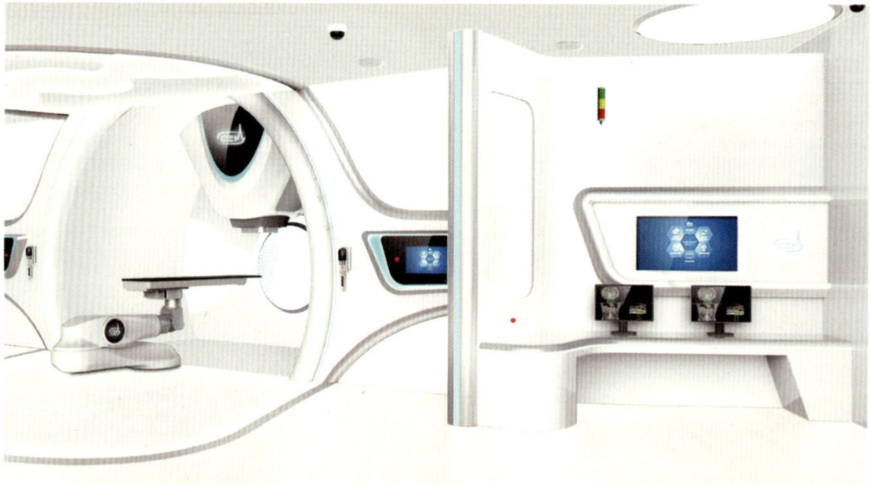

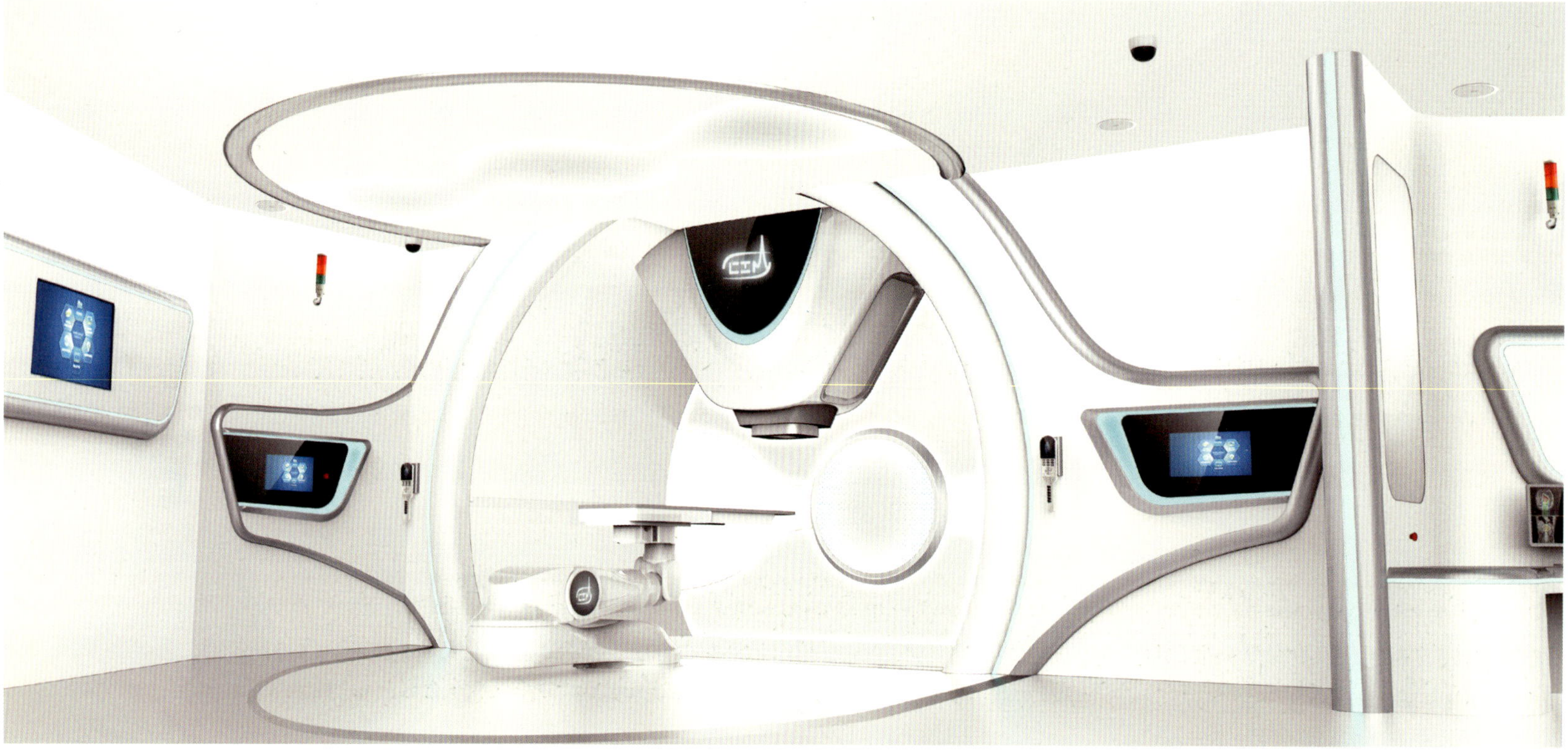

质子治疗系统
Proton Therapy System

该产品是由中国自主开发的第一台质子治疗系统装备，打破欧美对该行业设备的垄断。产品采用质子射线治疗，更安全，治愈率更高，并且减少医疗垃圾的产生。产品采用防辐射材料，最大程度防止射线对医生和患者的伤害以及设备外壳老化问题，节约成本。这款质子治疗系统不但功能强大，设计方面也具有创新性、操作性、经济性并兼具美观性。同时，在设计上也考虑到了患者情感上的需求，为患者带来希望和关怀。设计理念来源于“化茧成蝶”，治疗舱室造型像温暖的蚕蛹，主体采用温暖的白色，通过此理念给癌症患者带来希望。

This product is the first Chinese independent development proton therapy system equipment, breaking the monopoly of the Europe and the United States for the equipment in this industry.This product uses proton ray therapy in the treatment, which is safer and has higher recovery rate,and reduce the generation of medical waste. The product uses radiation protection materials, it can reduce radiation's damage to the doctors and patients to the maximum and prevent the device from being aged by radiation, in the end saving building and maintenance costs. This proton therapy system not only has a powerful function, but also has a design innovative, operational, economical and aesthetic. At the same time, the design also takes into account the patient's emotional needs for patients with hope and care. The idea of the design is derived from the image of butterfly spreading wings, and abstracts the concept of "cocoon forming and butterfly", the whole treatment cabin on modelling is like a huge, warm silkworm chrysalis,hoping to bring hope to cancer patients through this design concept.

设计
DESIGN

北京智加问道科技有限公司
Beijing ZCO Design Co.,Ltd.

合肥中科离子医学技术装备有限公司
Hefei CAS Ion Medical and Technical Devices Co.,Ltd.

生产
MANUFACTURE

魔碟灶
Rotatable-Burner Stove

华帝魔碟灶的翻转炉头给燃气灶市场带来了创新。该款煤气灶采用行业首创的可翻转炉头，将炉头及锅的支架结构整合为一体，安装在悬臂上。产品采用电机驱动炉头上翻或下降，为现实问题提供了巧妙、科学的解决方案。灶具面板无须开孔，无安装结构。烹饪结束可将炉头上翻，一体化的钢化玻璃台面干净整洁、易于清洁，减少了昂贵的厨房工作台面面积，有效利用空间，优化了厨房的空间结构。该产品设计不仅具有创新性，同时也具有良好的可操作性。黑晶钢化玻璃面板采用触摸设计、火焰动态显示环及白色数字屏幕，给使用者以清晰、直观指引。

Vatti rotatable-burner stove has brought innovation to the gas stove market. This gas stove is the first to adopt rotatable burner in the industry,the burner and pot stand structure are integrated into one and then mounted on a cantilever. A motor is used to drive the burner to rotate up or down, providing a clever, scientific solution for practical problems. The stove panel does not need to open a pore or install a structure; after cooking,turn up the burner rotates, a clean, tidy and dirt-free integrated toughened glass top appears and it is very easy to clean; and it also saves much space for storage in the kitchen; this product utilizes effectively the space and optimizes the kitchen's spatial structure.The design of this product is not only innovative, but also has good operability. The design of black crystal toughened glass panel,touch control,flame dynamic display ring and white digital screen provides a clear and direct-viewing guidance to consumers.

设计
DESIGN

何伟坚
He Weijian

华帝股份有限公司
Vatti Corporation Limited

生产
MANUFACTURE

小米 MIX 手机
Mi MIX

小米 MIX 是全球首款全陶瓷机身的智能手机，并且采用最高屏占比设计，拥有 6.4 寸超大屏幕，以全面屏、全陶瓷保持着极简纯粹的几何形态和高度统一性。全面屏为消费者带来更好的视觉体验，修长机身更适合人手握持。应用压电陶瓷声学系统代替普通听筒，通过微振点击的方式带动手机中框共振传递声音，从而取消了正面玻璃的听筒开孔。内置辅助定位系统解决手机通过隧道时失去卫星信号的问题，实现持续导航服务。虚拟按键栏可以下滑隐藏，也可以快速切换至悬浮球，使全屏操作更加简单方便。小米 MIX 是一款极具创新性的手机，为用户创造了全新的体验。

The Mi MIX is the first smartphone with full ceramic body in the whole world. And its design has he highest proportion of screen on a 6.4 inch ultra-high display. It keeps pure geometric form and highly uniform with an immersive full display and ceramic body.The full screen brings a better visual experience for consumers,a slender body is more suitable for hand gripping. The product is equipped with a piezoelectric ceramic acoustic system instead of the ordinary handset, through the micro-vibration click mode to drive the phone frame resonance transmission sound, thereby canceling the opening of the earphone of the front glass. Mi MIX packs internal auxiliary GPS technology, solving the unstable satellite networking problem in tunnel and implementing continuous navigation service. The virtual button can be lowered and hidden, and can also be switched to the suspension ball quickly, which makes the full screen operation easier.The Mi MIX is a very innovative mobile phone, creating a new experience for users.

设计
DESIGN

小米科技有限责任公司
Xiaomi Inc.

生产
MANUFACTURE

小米科技有限责任公司
Xiaomi Inc.

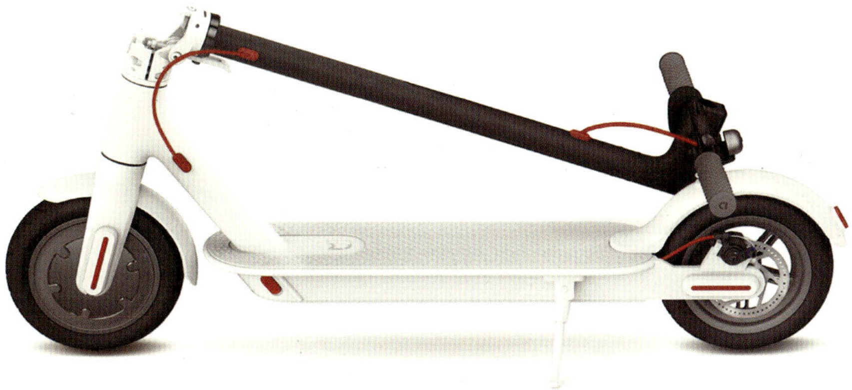

小米米家电动滑板车
Mi Electric Scooter

该产品是一款融实用、结实和时尚动感为一体的滑板车，解决了城市短程代步问题，提升了用户乘用体验，并体现了小米产品的一贯质量和设计语言。该产品采用创新折叠设计，将折叠锁扣与铃铛挂钩结构结合，整合了琐碎配件同时避免安全隐患。产品采用动力型锂电芯，续航里程 30 公里。前后轮设有双重刹车系统，按压刹把时即点亮尾灯，多重措施保障安全。支持定速巡航模式，减轻驾驶者持续手部操控造成疲劳感。踏板边缘采用圆角设计，避免撞伤脚踝。产品可连接手机应用，查看当前骑行速度、剩余电量等信息。该电动滑板车对于缓解交通压力、提升人们出行效率有很大帮助。

The product is a scooter, integrated the practicality, burliness and dynamic fashion into one, to solve the problem of short-range urban travel, enhances the user experience, and reflects the Mi product's quality and design language,like it always does. The innovative design of folding combines folding lock with bell hook, integrating the trivial parts and avoiding hidden dangers. The scooter adopts dynamic lithium batteries to extend mileage to 30 km.The front wheel the rear wheel are outfitted with double braking systems,and when you press the brake lever when the taillight lights, there are multiple measures of security.The product supports the cruise control mode, which reduces the fatigue caused by the continuous hand manipulation of the driver. The pedal edge is designed with rounded corners to avoid bumping the ankle.If you connect the scooter into your phone's APP, you can check the current speed and remaining battery level and other information. The scooter helps a lot to alleviate transportation pressure and enhance people's travel efficiency.

设计
DESIGN

小米生态链工业设计团队
Mi Ecosystem Industrial Design Team

纳恩博（天津）科技有限公司
Ninebot Inc.

生产
MANUFACTURE

小牛电动 U1
Niu U1 smart escooter

该款电动车造型设计轻巧秀丽、质朴典雅，具有高超的制造工艺、轻便的重量和方便的折叠功能，美观易用且节省空间。通过手机应用软件进行实时定位，及时掌握车辆位置等信息。产品搭配无钥匙启动方案及电子引擎锁，能够通过遥控器或车身按键迅速启动车辆，也能在检测到异常状态时锁死。产品打造了灵活的平台，用户可以根据自身需求加装不同配件，让车型和功能更加符合自己的使用。该款电动车轻便的锂电池、结实的铝质框架、先进技术的应用等充分满足了都市人群对品质耐用、防盗报警和置物空间的要求，为生活出行带来了实用和便利。

The design of the electric car is light and beautiful, simple and elegant, with superb manufacturing process, lightweight and convenient for folding function, it is beautiful and easy to use and can save space.Through the mobile phone application software, we can make real-time positioning, timely grasp the vehicle location and other information.Products with keyless start-up program solution and electronic engine lock, through the remote control or body buttons to quickly start the vehicle,it can also be detected in the abnormal state locked.This product creates a flexible platform, the user can install according to their own needs different accessories, so that models and features more in line with their own life style. The electric car's light lithium battery, solid aluminum frame, the application of advanced technology to fully meet the urban population's demand on the quality of durable, burglar alarm and the requirements of the space, whcih has brought practical and convenient for the living trip.

设计
DESIGN

小牛电动创新研发室
Niu innovation lab

江苏小牛电动科技有限公司
Jiangsu Niu Electric Technology Co.,Ltd.

生产
MANUFACTURE

银奖
Silver Prize

管家机器人
Unibot

管家机器人为现代家居智能化家电，具有净化清洁、加湿空气、互动娱乐等功能。其创新之处在于通过其模块化组合，使用激光定位扫描系统和全局规划系统，通过自主巡航绘制家居平面地图，形成家庭移动控制中枢。用户可通过手机应用软件远程遥控，设定家电控制点，实现开启、暂停、关闭功能，并可定时定点进行巡逻拍照或视频记录，与家人实时互动娱乐。产品模块可自由组合与扩展使用，用户可根据实际情况配置，形成实用高效的家庭控制体验。产品外观设计简约兼具时尚科技感，且制作材料采用免喷涂注塑工艺，减少生产中的环境污染。

Unibot is a modern home intelligent household appliance, having the function of purifying, humidifying the air and interactive entertainment. The innovation lies in the combination of modules,it uses LDS laser positioning scanning system and the global planning system, and it draws the home plane map through the autonomous cruise, and forms the home mobile control center. The user can remotely control and set control point of the household appliance through the mobile phone application software to achieve functions of open, pause and close, and patrol camera or video recording on schedule, interact with families in real-time. Product modules are open to free combination and expansion, forming practical and efficient home control experience.The design of this product is simple and stylish sense of science and technology, and the production of materials uses spray-free injection molding process to reduce environmental pollution in the production.

设计
DESIGN

科沃斯机器人股份有限公司
Ecovacs Robotics Co.,Ltd.

生产
MANUFACTURE

科沃斯机器人股份有限公司
Ecovacs Robotics Co.,Ltd.

XCA550 全地面起重机
XCA550 All Terrain Crane Truck

该产品是一台全地面起重机。首创的单发动机系统，降低了整机重量，提升了吊装性能，节省了维修成本。新型节能液压系统大幅度降低了油耗，节约能源，更加环保。该产品独创的智能臂架技术，提高了起重机的稳定性，其自拆卸技术，效率远超于同行业水平。其立体式风道、平台折叠梯等方面设计更为人性化，提升了用户体验感。产品通过模具化方式生产，降低了成本。该产品反映出中国重型装备制造企业的问题意识和解决问题的能力。该产品整体达到国际领先，改变国内依赖进口的局面，实现占有率 60% 以上，体现中国工业实力。

This product is an all terrain crane truck. It firstly creates a single motor system to reduce the machine's weight, improve hoisting performance and save maintenance costs. New type of hydraulic system can widely decrease oil consumption,saving energy resources, more environmentally friendly. The original big load transverse arm can enhance stability. With its self-disassembly technology, the efficiency exceeds its industrial counterpart. Humanity design such as stereo air passage and platform folding ladder can improve user experience. The modular production of the crane truck will reduce costs. The overall level has reached international leading position, the actual share accounts for over 60% , and changing the domestic situation of relying on import.

设计
DESIGN

徐工集团 徐州重型机械有限公司 工业设计所
XCMG Xuzhou Heavy Machinery Co.,Ltd.Industrial Design

徐工集团 徐州重型机械有限公司
XCMG Xuzhou Heavy Machinery Co.,Ltd.

生产
MANUFACTURE

微单 V1 锂电折叠自行车
V-danci V1 Lithium Folding Bike

微单 V1 锂电折叠自行车是一款智能操控、便于存放的绿色交通工具，解决了城市短途代步的问题，拥有比自行车速度更快，比普通电动车更轻便、可折叠的优点。车架、把手、车梯、曲柄等采用铝合金三维一体锻造工艺，提高了车架强度，简化结构并且不留焊道，使车架结构设计更简洁、美观。产品实现折叠器隐形、车梯隐形、前后轴紧固螺丝隐形，避免螺丝对人体造成伤害。产品辨识度高，采用高亮橙红色圆环设计，体现能量与动感。汽车级金属漆面喷涂的微曲折面车架和极简的车体线条，彰显速度感，是一款具有未来感的专业代步工具。

V-Danci V1 Lithium Folding Bike is a green vehicle with intelligent control for easy storage, solving the problem of urban short-distance travel,it has the advantages of faster than the bike, lighter than ordinary electric cars, and it can be folded.The products uses aluminum three-dimensional forging process in the frame, handles, ladder, crank, etc, to improve the frame strength, simplify the structure and do not leave the weld, so that the design of the frame structure is more concise and beautiful.The product achieved in the invisible of folder, stairway, front and rear axle fastening screws,to avoid the screw on the human body accidental injury.This product is highly recognizable, with bright orange-red ring design, reflecting the energy and dynamic.The micro-curved frame with car-level metal paint spray and the minimalist body line can highlight the speed sense, which is a futuristic professional means of transport.

设计
DESIGN

北京洛可可科技有限公司
LKK Design Beijing Co.,Ltd.

天津微驰科技有限公司
Tianjin V-Danci Co.,Ltd.

生产
MANUFACTURE

康复理疗车
Rehabilitation Wheelchair

该理疗车是为了满足残障人士生活自理需求而开发，其核心在于增加了电机驱动行驶功能，可以实现遥控站姿与坐姿行驶方式的自由切换，以高度人性化的界面方式解决了残障人士自主出行、参与社交生活的需求。理疗车遵循着向用户传达心理安全感的原则，使用特色的双电机驱动，电机不易发热且节能高效，寿命长，续航能力强。康复理疗车顺应国民养老政策，改善残障人士生活质量，惠及未来老龄化人群，更好地满足残障人士生活自理需求，使残障人群出行轻松自如，生活更加充满自信，身心健康。本产品具有良好的市场前景、商业价值与社会效益。

This rehabilitation wheelchair is designed to better meet the self-care demand of people with disabilities. Its core is to increase the function of driving motor drive, and free switch of remote control of standing and sitting position, and other functions to help the disabled's need in independent travel and social life. This rehabilitation wheelchair follows the principle of conveying the sense of psychological security to the user. The adoption of dual motor drive makes the motor not easy heat and energy efficient, long life and a strong endurance.The rehabilitation wheelchair conforms to the national pension policy, improves the quality of life of the disabled, benefits the future of the aging population, and better meets the needs of the disabled, and makes their travel easy and enjoyable.This wheelchair makes their life more confident and healthy, and has a good market outlook, commercial value and social benefits.

设计
DESIGN

杭州瑞德设计股份有限公司
Hangzhou R&D Design PLC

浙江旺得福车业有限公司
Zhejiang Wangdefu Motor Co.,Ltd.

生产
MANUFACTURE

传祺 GS8
Trumpchi GS8

传祺 GS8 是一款旗舰级豪华七座运动型多用途汽车，外观大气硬朗。产品采用独特外轮廓的矩阵式 LED 大灯，呈现纵横交叠的不规则特性。中央的凌云翼与侧面腰线紧密地联系起来，凸显整车的高贵与威猛。产品采用双 U 型隧道式 LED 组合尾灯，与前灯呼应，具有立体环状观感。车型轴距 2800 毫米，后排乘坐空间最大化且具有多模式大空间布局。采用传祺第二代 320T 发动机，动力强劲，节省油耗。内饰设计不仅整体上豪华舒适，细节上也精致动感。前后排及车门位置的储物空间进行了植绒处理，美观又最大限度减震防噪。优化座椅填充物厚度，使座椅更具舒适性。

GS8 is a flagship like luxurious seven seats SUV.The appearance is generous and tough. It adopts matrix full-LED headlights with unique outer contour,showing the irregularities of vertical and horizontal overlap.The vehicle is more closely linked between the central Lingyun wing and the side of the waist line, highlighting the vehicle's noble and mighty.This product uses a combination of dual U-type tunneling LED and taillights, echoing with the headlights, with a three-dimensional ring view. With a wheelbase of 2800mm, GS8 has a multi-model and large space layout. The product adopts the Trumpchi second generation 320 torque supercharged engine, with powerful dynamics and is more energy saving. This interior design is not only reflected in the overall luxury and comfort, but also in the details of the exquisite dynamic.We carried out flocking in the front and rear row and the storage space in the position of door, it is beautiful and maximum shock and noise control. Its seat filler thickness is optimized and it is more comfortable.

设计
DESIGN

广州汽车集团股份有限公司汽车工程研究院
Guangzhou Automobile Group Co., Ltd. Automotive Engineering Institute

广州汽车集团乘用车有限公司
Guangzhou Automobile Group Motor Co.,Ltd.

生产
MANUFACTURE

米家全景相机
Mi Sphere Camera

该产品采用折返式镜头设计，在有限的空间里实现体积紧凑、防水防尘，使用户携带方便，更加人性化。小巧设置兼顾电池续航能力，依赖于对内部零件排布的仔细推敲以及创新的防水结构设计。采用整块铝合金打造金属中框，切割工艺让边缘的过渡顺滑贴合，表面材质经过喷砂处理，产品工艺优良。使用激光镭雕工艺处理产品表面，前、后外壳喷涂纳米防污亲肤手感漆，温润防滑，镜头的黑色高亮 CD 纹，准确地传达出该产品是新型全景相机这一理念。外观设计简洁，将所有功能浓缩成三个物理键，并能够一键拍摄 360 度全景画面，提供用户更佳的使用体验。

The product features reflex lens design to achieve compact size in a limited space, waterproof and dustproof,so that users can easily carry, it is more humane.It is small and flexible,taking into account the battery life, depending on the layout of the internal parts carefully examined, as well as innovative waterproof structure design.The metal center piece is made from a whole piece of aluminum alloy. The cutting process makes the edge quite smooth. The surface material is treated by sandblasting,the product process is excellent. It uses the laser engraving process to handle the product surface. The front and back shell is coated with Nano paint for smooth touch,it is gentle and non-slip. The black CD pattern around the lens conveys the idea of a brand new version of sphere cameras.Its design is simple, all functions are condensed into three physical keys, and can use a key to shoot 360-degrees panoramic picture, providing users with a better experience.

设计
DESIGN

小米生态链工业设计团队
Mi Ecosystem Industrial Design Team

北京疯景科技有限公司
Fengjing Techonolgy Co.,Ltd.

生产
MANUFACTURE

ARJ21 国产支线喷气式客机
ARJ21 Regional Jet Plane

该产品是我国自行研制的具有自主知识产权的国产新型涡扇中短程支线客机，座级为 78—90 座，填补了中国国内民用飞机的空白。该产品采用了国际先进技术和机载系统，发动机、航电、电源等系统通过竞标在全球范围采购，其中许多系统部件、产品在中国制造，体现中国制造的综合国力。客机驾驶舱采用了 6 块双曲面风挡设计，使外形更加流畅，在降低阻力的同时给驾驶员更大视野。产品采用轻质材料，减轻自身重量，提高飞机航程。该产品是多学科、多工种、多领域融合、交叉的成果，体现了中国设计与中国制造的能力和水平。

ARJ21 Regional Jet Plane jet plane is self-developed independently by China, with independent intellectual property rights,a China-made new turbine mid-range and short-range regional aircraft, with 78-90 seat classes. This plane fills the domestic gap of civil aircraft. This plane adopted international advanced technology and airborne systems, through the global bidding to purchase engines, avionics, power and other systems, among them, many system components and products are made in China, reflecting the comprehensive strength of manufacturing of China.The flight deck has six multi-curved wind shield, which make the shape more smooth, reducing the resistance and also providing a better view for pilots inside. The plane uses lightweight materials to reduce weight and improve aircraft range. The product is a cross result of multi-disciplinary, multi-species, multi-field integration, reflecting the capacity and level of the Chinese design and manufacturing in China.

设计
DESIGN

上海飞机设计研究院
Shanghai Aircraft Design and Research Institute

上海飞机制造有限公司
Shanghai Aircraft Manufacturing Co.,Ltd.

生产
MANUFACTURE

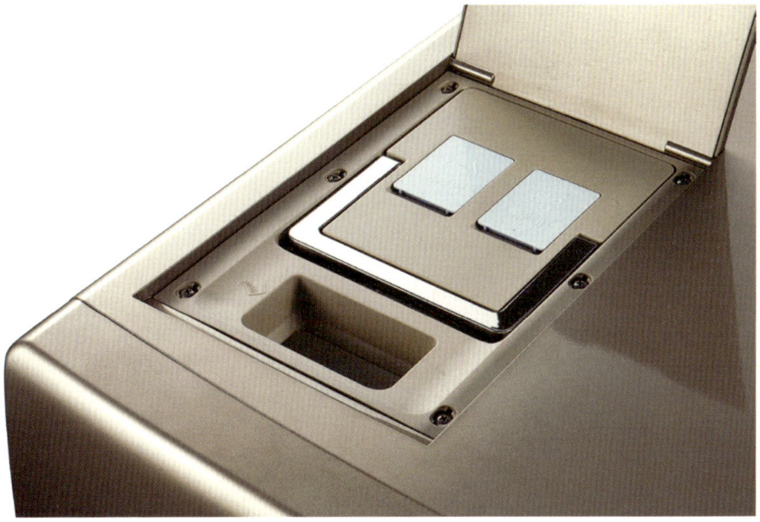

光芒系列洗衣机
Radiant

此款洗衣机行业首创在洗衣机门上做隐藏式智能彩屏，除简洁的外观设计之外，还提高了用户使用的便捷性。开关门采取了最大限度的开合角度，使用户在放置和收取衣物时更加方便。基于安卓系统的用户界面，可在无线网络环境下更新操作系统，与谷歌合作开发的具备高度智能化、人性化的学习型交互体验，可按照用户的操作使用习惯自动设计并生成最佳洗涤程序，并保留在云端，使用户使用习惯得到优化，同时节省水和清洁剂。依托目前的硬件平台和可在线更新的软件系统，未来将不断植入诸如声音控制、手势控制等前沿科技，进一步丰富洗衣体验。

This washing machine made a hidden smart color screen in the washing machine door, which is the first time in this industry. The design of the appearance is simple, it also can improve the user's convenience. The switch door takes the maximum opening and closing angle, allowing users to place and receive clothing more convenient.The user interface is based on Android system, and it can be upgraded when connected to Wi-Fi. Working together with Google, we developed the smart and user-friendly interaction experience, and the system will utomatically design and generate the optimal washing procedure based on users' habits, and data is stored in the cloud,optimizing the user's habits, while saving the use of water and cleaning agents; It was based on the current hardware platform and the developing software system, more functions will be developed, including voice and gesture control and other cutting-edge technologies in the near future to offer better washing experience.

设计
DESIGN

惠而浦（中国）工业设计中心
Whirlpool (China) GCD

惠而浦（中国）股份有限公司
Whirlpool (China) Co.,Ltd.

生产
MANUFACTURE

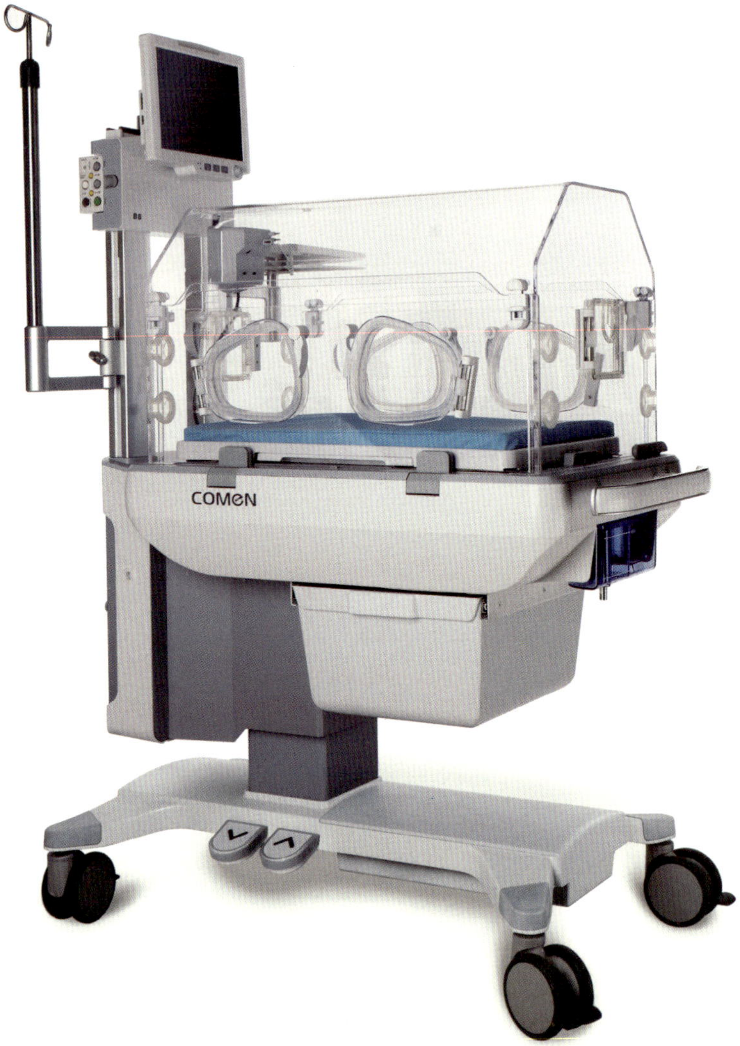

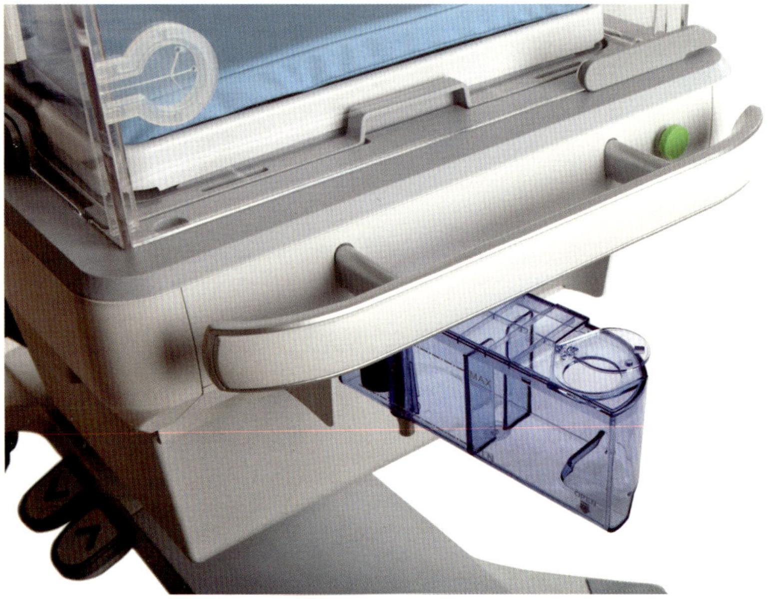

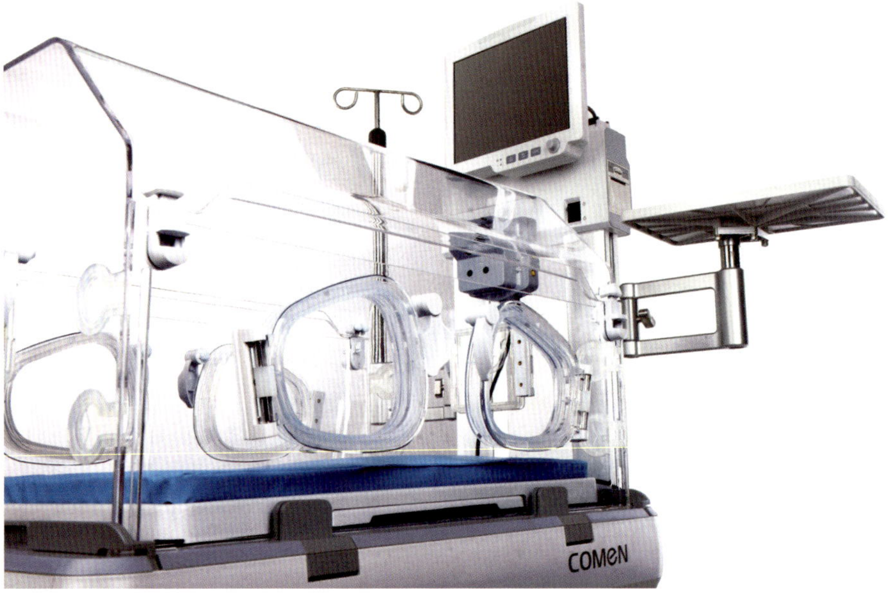

婴儿培养箱
Neonatal Incubator

该产品设计深入、细致，充分考虑了婴儿的病理需求与生理需求，解决了原来需要监护仪和育婴箱两个设备才可以完成的护理需求。该培养箱集成监护功能和远程探视功能于一体，让家长可以远程了解患儿的康复过程和康复情况，体现人文关怀，减少家长的不安和焦虑情绪。查房系统可以使医护人员在电脑前查看到每个患儿的病情，减轻医护人员的工作量。该婴儿培养箱整机塑胶外壳采用了钢模注塑工艺，婴儿仓采用的是进口食品级的有机玻璃材质，该材质具有高透光效果，并且耐摩擦，使婴儿仓内做到无死角消毒。

The product is a neonatal incubator,the product design is thorough and detailed.It fully considered the baby's pathological needs and physiological needs of infants, solving the situation that people had to buy a monitor and infant incubator in the past. It integrated function of monitoring and let the parents know the recover process of infant through long distance, showing humanistic care and reducing anxiety. The system can view each child's condition in front of the computer and reduce the workload of the medical staff. The plastic shell uses steel for injection mould. The baby warehouse adopts imported food grade organic glass which has high transmittance effect and bear friction. The infant room can be sterilized with no dead corner.

设计
DESIGN

钟琳琳
Zhong Linlin

深圳市科曼医疗设备有限公司
Shenzhen Comen Medical Instruments Co.,Ltd.

生产
MANUFACTURE

12th

最佳团队奖
Best Team Prize

2017

小牛电动创新研发室
Niu Innovation Lab

小牛电动创新研发室专注于品质化、智能化的电动车整车产品研发与工业设计。坚持原创设计，力求制造出世界上先进的个人载具以及电驱系统，从而改善个人出行体验。小牛电动创新研发室 2015 年成立，成员来自 Frog Design、Designworks、Idea Dao Design 等国际知名设计公司。三年内，先后完成了小牛电动车 N1、M1、U1 等车型的研发与设计，创下国内众筹最高纪录，并荣获多项国内外设计大奖。小牛电动创新研发室拒绝简单的代工模式，秉承坚持原创的精神和不断创新的信念，在延续家族式极简设计语言的同时，不断以设计提升产品价值。其设计的“小牛电动 M1” 让科技与交通完美融合，兼具美观性与操作性，满足了城市短途出行的需求，荣获 2017 中国设计红星奖至尊金奖。

Niu innovation lab focus on Research&Development and industrial design of quality and intuitive intelligent electric vehicle whole product. We emphasis original design and hope to provide the most advanced transport products as well as electric drive system to enhance the user experience for our consumers. Innovation lab has been established in 2015, its members came from Frog Design,Designwork,Idea Dao Design and other internationally renowned design companies. And we have currently accomplished the Research&Development and design of our N1, M1, and U1 products with in the 3 years time since it has been established.We made the highest crowd funding record in China.Our design has also been recognised by many top domestic and international design awards.Niu innovation lab refused to simple foundry model, adhering to the spirit of insisting on the original principles and innovative beliefs. It continued in the family minimalist design language, at the same time it continued to design to enhance product value. The design of the Niu M1 smart escooter is the perfect fusion of technology and transportation, taking into account the aesthetics and operability, to meet the needs of urban short-distance travel, which win the best of the gold prize of China Red Star Design Award in 2017.

12th

最佳新人奖
Best New Designer Prize

2017

赵自然
Zhao Ziran

男，2013 年本科毕业于清华大学美术学院工业设计系，获得“清华大学优良毕业生”荣誉，并保送研究生。2015 年至今在小米生态链工业设计部门担任工业设计师，参与设计的米家车载空气净化器、小米无线鼠标、小米米家电动滑板车等项目荣获国内外知名设计奖项。个人作品“Life Passageway”获得 2012 年 iF 概念奖，设计研究论文《城市轨道交通车厢内部空间人性化设计》发表于核心期刊《装饰》2015 年第 4 期。其设计的“小米米家电动滑板车”兼具美观性与实用性，解决了城市短途代步问题，提升用户体验，并体现了小米产品的一贯质量和设计语言，荣获 2017 中国设计红星奖金奖。

Mr. Zhao Ziran, graduated from Department of Industrial Design, Academy of Arts & Design of Tsinghua University in 2013, he was awarded "Outstanding Graduate of Tsinghua". In 2015, he graduated with a master degree from Tsinghua University and has been working in Xiaomi Ecosystem as an industrial designer since then. He have participated in the design of Mi Car Air Purifier, Mi Wireless Mouse, Mi Electric Scooter and some other Mi products, some of which have won world-known design awards at home and abroad.His personal design project Life Passageway is a winner of "iF Concept Design Award" 2012. His paper Humanitarian Design in the Inner Space of Urban Trail Transport was published in the CSSCI journal of Zhuangshi (No. 4, 2015). Mi Electric Scooter takes into account the aesthetics and practicality, to solve the problem of urban short-distance travel. It enhances the user experience and reflects the consistent quality and design language of Mi products, which win the Gold Prize of China Red Star Design Award in 2017.

设计的过程是在充分地理性思考下对产品本源的表达。
Design is an expression of product nature under rational thinking.

2017

12th

红星奖
Excellent Prize

2017

安旅盒子
Hotel Security Equipment

该产品是一款协助酒店进行旅客信息确认的安防信息终端。不同于传统产品的安装烦琐费用高昂，该产品集成操作系统和相关业务软件，无须专业人员上门安装，接通电源连接显示器即可使用。该产品与当地公安部门的安防系统结合，无须酒店服务人员便可自助完成入住手续办理。产品简洁有张力的造型配合素材本身的亚光面处理结合凸显了强烈的设计感。

This product is a security information terminal to assist Hotel passenger information confirmation. Different from the traditional product cumbersome installation costs, operating system and related products of the integrated business software, without professional installation, just plug and play. The device lineups with the local public security system for the hotel passenger's ID information confirmed.Customers could complete the formalities without hotel service personnel. The simple styling design with its matte treatment brings out a very strong of design looks and feels.

设计 DESIGN 浙江公共安全技术研究院 Zhejiang Province Public Security Institute of Technology

七百设计（深圳）有限公司 700 Design (Shenzhen) **生产 MANUFACTURE**

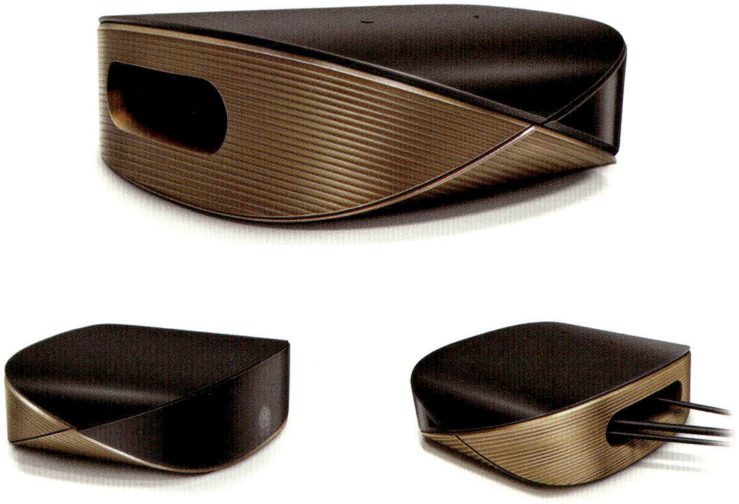

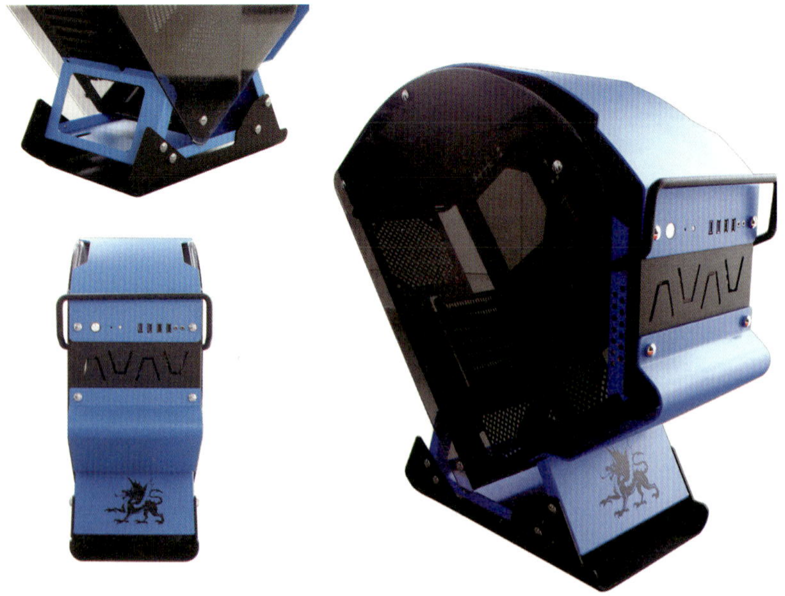

火麒麟电脑机箱
Fire Kirin Computer Case

该产品是一款为电竞设计的电脑机箱，为电竞提供了酷炫的硬件支持。它改变了传统机箱方形的外形，以巨大的铝合金脚架支撑整个塔形主体，前面板提手设计灵感取自重机枪造型。区别于传统机箱开模注塑的工艺，只对金属进行切割折弯即可完成生产，减少成本的同时获得良好的市场反应。

This product is a design for the e-sports computer chassis and should be cool for e-sports hardware support. The computer case is no longer a square of boring box, with aluminum alloy huge tripod to support the whole tower body. The handle of the front panel from the inspiration of heavy machine guns and creation. Other process is different from the traditional injection mold machine box. This module is to cut the metal bending can complete the production, reduce the cost and obtain a good market response.

设计 DESIGN 广州耀众电子科技有限公司 Guangzhou Yaozhong Electronic technology Co., Ltd.

东莞市尚同工业设计有限公司 Dongguan Shangtong Industrial Design Co.,Ltd. **生产 MANUFACTURE**

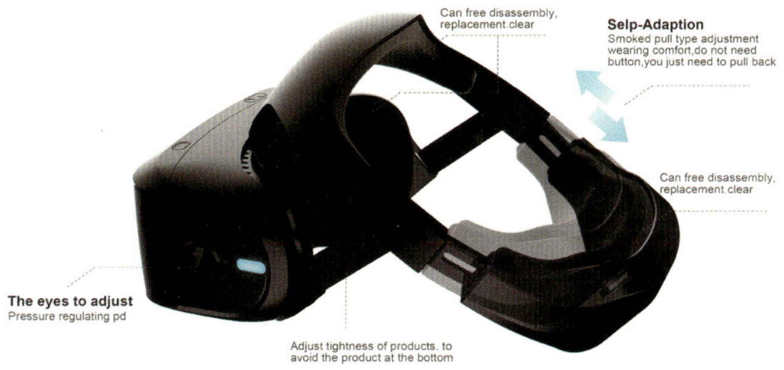

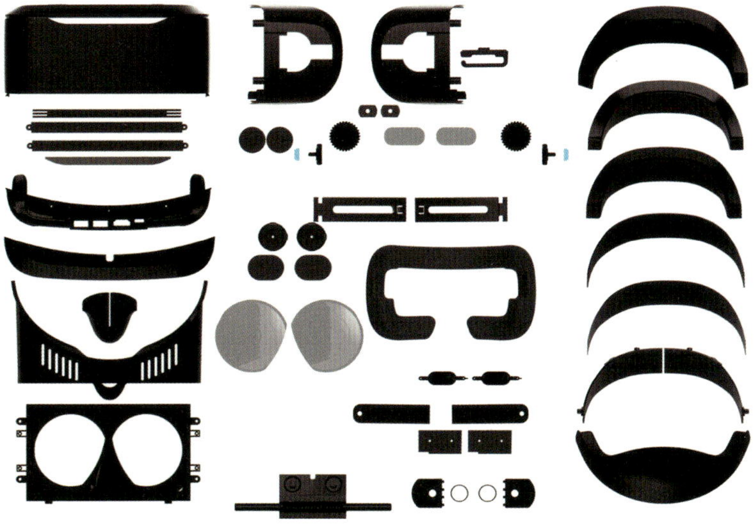

背包式 VR 一体机
Venus

该产品是全球最小的背包式虚拟现实一体机，自动识别手势动态与方向，设备主机可以放置在口袋、背包里，采用一根线连接虚拟现实设备的方式，增加手势感应功能，让用户可随时随地体验。为了减少消费者的佩戴重量，整机只有 400 克，用户可以长时间佩戴而不觉得疲惫。结构创新的一体式抽拉头戴方式让用户更容易佩戴。

The product is the global minimum one-piece backpack VR with automatic identification signal dynamic and direction. The host devices can be placed in pockets or backpacks, adopting the way of a thread connection between a host and increasing the gesture sensing function. Users could use PC anytime and anywhere. To reduce the carry weight, the machine is only 400 g, allowing the user to wear for long and don't feel tired. Venus by way of one-piece smoked pull head, through the way of structural innovation, make the user more easy to wear.

设计
DESIGN
何海洋、刘汶涓
Ocean He, Liu Wenjuan

浙江大华技术股份有限公司
Zhejiang Dahua Technology Co.,Ltd.
生产
MANUFACTURE

"天鹅"智能云 POS
"Swan" Smart Cloud POS Equipment

该产品是一款高性能硬件结合智能操作系统，设计师将银行卡支付、二维码支付、会员卡管理、头像采集、票据打印、商品库存管理、消费数据采集等功能集成于一体，将售卖与后台及云端连接，为零售行业提供一站式信息化支付解决方案，使支付活动变得异常简洁、高效，并可随时掌握产品销售情况及库存数量。设计灵感来源于天鹅，造型简洁、优雅。

The product is high performance hardware, equipped with intelligent operating system. Designers integrate bankcard payment, QR code payment, membership card management, head portrait collection, bill printing, merchandise inventory management, consumption data collection and other functions together. The POS equipment links the front end selling with big data at back end and cloud database, thus providing an one-stop information payment settlement scheme for the retail industry, which makes the payment become extremely simple and efficient. The sale and inventory of products can be viewed anytime at the device. Inspired by the swan, the style is simple and elegant.

设计
DESIGN
胡源
Hu Yuan

东软集团
Neusoft Corporation
生产
MANUFACTURE

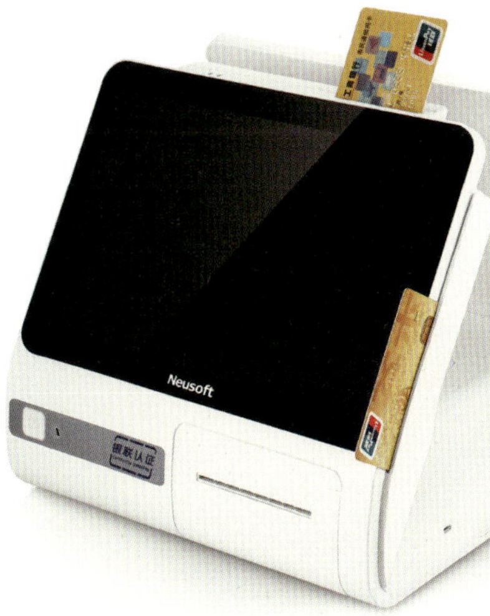

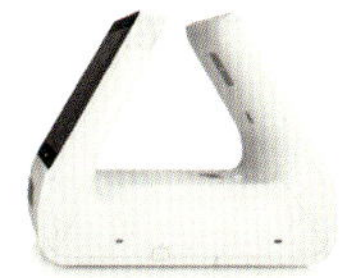

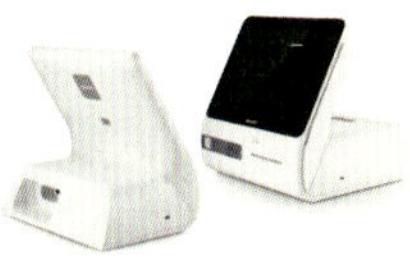

4G 智能执法记录终端
Video Speaker Microphone

该款智能 4G 执法记录终端从设计上融合国内外先进理念，外观设计上强化了其摄像录像功能，按键位的设计也充分考虑到使用者的人机交互体验，在辨识度、手感、防误触等细节加入了大量的设计元素。除强化摄像拍照功能外，还加入实时图传、外设备拓展、远程定位、快速充电等实用功能，帮助警务人员更好地完成出警任务。

The product is an independently developed 4G single police enforcement recording terminal which encompasses various advanced technology. The appearance design highlights its video recording function. The design of the push buttons has also taken into consideration of the users' device-human interaction experience and added numerous design elements such as resolution, touch and feel as well as avoiding mistouch. This device boasts not only the video and photo function improvement but also the live transfer of these digital data, external devices application, remote location positioning as well as some practical functions such as quick charge, all of which can assist police force to better achieve relevant police tasks.

设计
DESIGN
深圳意云科技有限公司
Shenzhen Eevin Technology Co.,Ltd.

深圳意云设计有限公司
Shenzhen Eevin Design Co.,Ltd.
生产
MANUFACTURE

HPC 高性能服务器机柜
HPC Server Cabinet

该款产品定位于关键行业的信息化装备，在设计上遵从了科技感、稳定可靠的设计理念。造型以硬朗语言为主，给人以安全、可靠的印象，结合灯光的运用，突出科技创新感 。与国外同类产品相比，具有明显的性价比优势。产品在设计理念上突出绿色、人性化等特性，为高端服务器的创新设计打造了新的设计标杆。

Products are mainly located in the key industries of information technology equipment, so in the design to comply with the sense of science and technology, stable and reliable design concept. Modeling, line and plane combined with tough language, to people in a safe, reliable impression; combined with the use of light, feeling to the science and technology innovation. Compared with foreign similar products, it has obvious cost advantage. Products in the design concept to highlight the characteristics of green, humane, innovative design for the highend server to create a new benchmark for the design.

设计
DESIGN
浪潮电子信息产业股份有限公司
Inspur Electronic Information Industry Co., Ltd.

浪潮电子信息产业股份有限公司
Inspur Electronic Information Industry Co.,Ltd.
生产
MANUFACTURE

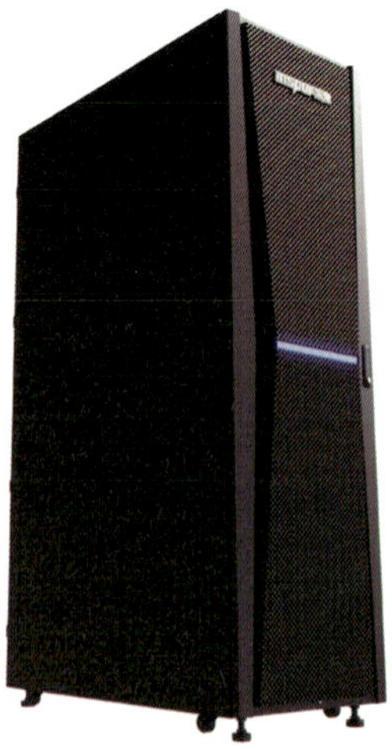

华号智能安全路由器
Beacon Tower Intelligent Security Router

该产品是一款安全智能路由器，响应国家反恐法在满足智能上网和快速组网的同时，为中小企业、政府、学校等公共场所提供更安全的网络，保护内网不受黑客和不安全因素侵害。产品设计结合了中国古代烽火台的形象，表达出硬朗、智能、安全的寓意，整体呈现硬朗有力的设计，四立柱包裹着主体使产品辨识度很高。

The product is a security intelligent router. It is in accordance with national anti-terrorism law to satisfy the meet of intelligent internet access and fast networking and provide more security net for enterprises, governments and schools and other public places. It is also used for protecting intranet from hackers and unsafe factors. Design combined with the ancient Chinese beacon of the moral, to express the tough, intelligent and safe. The overall presentation of tough design. Concise form has more details of the embodiment of the four pillars wrapped in the main form of the whole product looks like a high degree of recognition, while the meaning is also on behalf of the defense, security. Reflect the security and network security.

设计
DESIGN
大庆华号科技有限公司
Daqing Huahao Technology Co.,Ltd.

深圳市佳简几何工业设计有限公司
Shenzhen XIVO Design Co.,Ltd.
生产
MANUFACTURE

糖猫儿童手表 M2PRO
Teemo Children Watch M2PRO

该产品是全国首款双摄像头智能 4G 电话手表，双摄像头设计解决了儿童佩戴手表后摄像头只能单一方向拍摄的问题，使儿童可以随时拍摄或录制视频与家人分享。产品通过内部程序优化实现极低功耗待机，最长待机时间能够达到一周时间，为目前所有同类产品之最。外形设计传递出一种多彩、运动的产品气质，更能满足青少年爱时尚、爱运动的心理需求。

The product is the country's first smart 4G phone watch for young people with dual camera. The dual camera design solves the problem of single-way shot after wearing. Users can take pictures or videos and share with families at any time. We adjusted internal program and firmware to optimized standby signal policy to reduce power consumption for standby, after calculating, the longest standby time can reach one week, it is the longest standby time in all children watches in the market. The colorful design with sporty feature is better to meet the children meet who love fashion and sports.

设计
DESIGN
深圳比亚迪股份有限公司
BYD Company Limited

北京搜狗网络技术有限公司
Beijing Sogou Network Technology Co.,Ltd.
生产
MANUFACTURE

按键式加密 U 盘
Touch-Tone Encrypted USB Disk

该产品是一款加密 U 盘，可保护政府机关文件、公司机密、财务资料、个人隐私等信息。一体化设计使整体圆润无瑕，首次将布料这种柔软材质运用于这类产品，采用金属加工成型，装配精密。布料作为表面材料与金属的质感形成非常强烈的对比，柔软质感与刚硬融为一体。同时创造性地采用圆球包塑钢丝绳作为盖子防丢失设计。

The product is an encrypted u disk which play a very important role in protecting file for the government, company secrets, financial information, personal privacy, and so on . Its fuselage adopts integration design to make the whole mellow and flawless. Applying the soft cloth material to encrypted U disk is the first time. As a surface material, the cloth forms a very strong contrast with the metal texture, and the soft texture combines with the rigid one. It is made of metal processing molding, assembly into a very sophisticated products. It is creatively using wire rope as a loss prevention design.

设计
DESIGN
深圳市艾尔卡特电子科技有限公司
Shenzhen Arycarter Electronic Technology Co.,Ltd.

深圳市点臻设计有限公司
Shenzhen a.Cus Design Co.,Ltd.
生产
MANUFACTURE

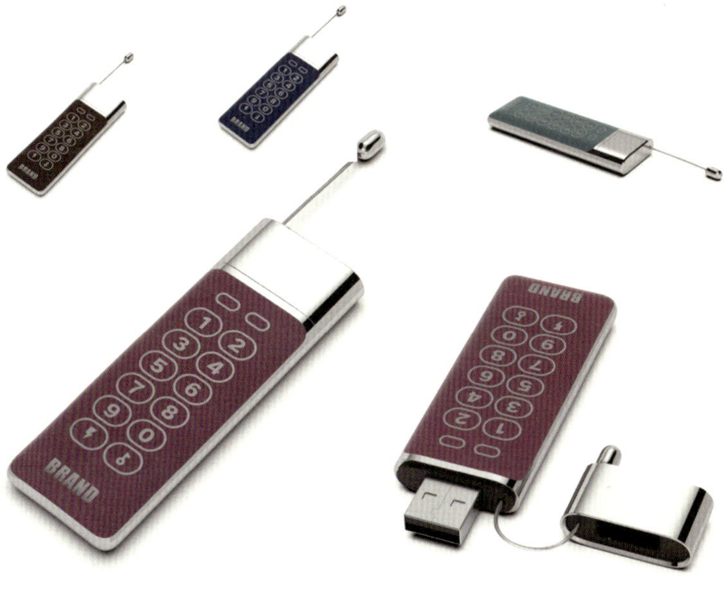

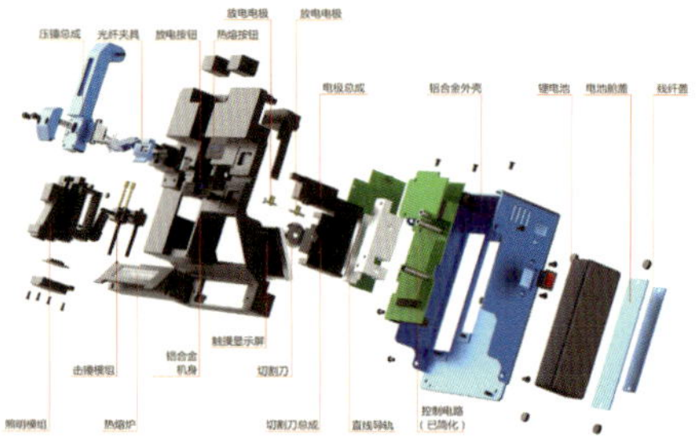

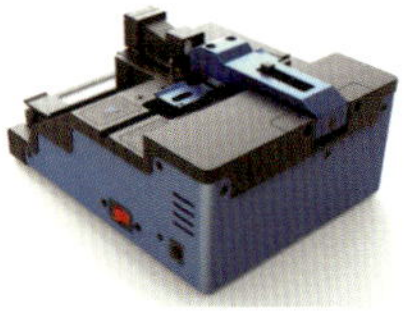

切割定位式光纤熔接机
Cutting and Positioning Type Optical Fiber Welding Machine

该产品是全球首款切割定位式光纤熔接机，突破现有光纤熔接机的使用形式及光纤对准原理，具备同时完成两根需接续的光纤切割功能，利用光纤本身的应力，切割后光纤恢复到自然状态并在光纤定位总成中彼此对准且位置唯一，对准后放点熔接。本产品精简了设备结构，无须另配切割刀，缩小了体积，简化了光纤熔接的操作流程，由原来耗时 2 分钟缩短至 30 秒。

The product is the first cutting and positioning type optical fiber welding machine in the whole world. We have broken through the existing form of optical fiber splicer and the principle of fiber alignment. This product has optical fiber cutting function, and at the same time to complete the 2 fibers cutting, Using the stress of the optical fiber itself, optical fiber can return to its natural state and in the optical fiber positioning assembly aligned with each other after cutting, and position is unique, then discharge welding. This product does not need to be provided with a cutter, simplifies the equipment structure and reduces the volume. It simplifies the process to 30 seconds from previous 2 minutes.

设计 DESIGN
成都捷康特科技有限公司
Chengdu Jiekangte Technology Co.,Ltd.

成都思睿工业产品设计有限公司
Chengdu Sirui Industrial Product Design Co.,Ltd.
生产 MANUFACTURE

多功能声级计
Multi-Function Sound Level Meter

该多功能声级计是采用数字信号处理技术的新一代噪声测量仪器，采用分辨率为 480×800 的彩屏显示器，界面直观。超宽的线性测量范围适用更多的噪声环境。32GB 大容量多点触量存储可作数字记录仪和精密录音仪。可做声学的各种分析，快速设置功能帮助用户一键设置相关标准要求的分析仪模式和参数。产品用模块化设计手法，用户可以根据需要选购相应的模块。

The multi-function sound level meter is a new generation of noise measuring instruments, using digital signal processing technology. It is equipped with a resolution of 480×800 color display, and intuitive interface. It uses ultra-wide linear measurement range for more noise environment and 32 GB large capacity multi-touch storage, which can do digital recorder and precision recorder. The product can do acoustics of the various analysis and has a unique quick set function to help users "a key" set the relevant standards required for the analyzer model and parameters. Product is equipped with modular design techniques so that the user can choose the appropriate module.

设计 DESIGN
杭州爱华仪器有限公司
Hangzhou Aihua Instruments Co.,Ltd.

杭州领跑者工业设计有限公司
Hangzhou LPZ Industrial Design Co.,Ltd.
生产 MANUFACTURE

苹果手机 U 盘 U365
iPhone USB Flash Drive U365

该产品是专为解决苹果手机无法扩容内存而设计的 U 盘，它通过与苹果手机相连安全自动备份照片从而快速释放存储空间，令使用者可随时随地观看视频，无须电脑即可处理文档。使用可回收环保铝合金材料，电子零件及外壳不含铅、汞等有毒有害物质。采用金属压铸一体成型工艺获得更好的强度和小巧的外观。金属旋转盖帽美观小巧，双向旋转使用方便。

The product is designed to solve the problem that iphone can not expand memory shortage. It can automatic backup photos with iphone to quickly release storage space so that users can watch the video whenever and wherever and process documents without computers. It uses recyclable aluminum alloy materials. All electronic parts and shell does not contain lead, mercury and other toxic and harmful substances. Metal die-casting forms a better strength and compact appearance.Metal rotary cap is beautiful and small, easy to use two-way rotation.

设计 DESIGN
爱国者电子科技有限公司
Aigo Electronics Technology Co.,Ltd.

杨晔
Yang Ye
生产 MANUFACTURE

FPV 航拍微型摄像机
FPV Aerial Miniature Cameras

该产品是一款航拍微型摄像机，体积小，重量轻，便于隐藏、携带，可以防逆光、去黑影，可以满足各种不同的特殊拍摄角度和环境。微型摄像机主要测清晰度和色彩还原性、照度、逆光补偿，其次是测其微型摄像机失真、耗电量、最低工作电压等。内置 OSD 功能菜单，支持多功能设置；支持数字宽动态、数字降噪、背光补偿。

The product is an aerial miniature camera with the feature of small volume, light weight, easy to conceal and carry. It can prevent light and shadow and meet various special shooting angle and the environment. Miniature cameras mainly test definition and color reducibility, intensity of illumination, backlight compensation, followed by measuring its miniature camera distortion, power consumption, the minimum operating voltage and so on. The built-in OSD function menu supports multi-function settings, digital WDR, digital noise reduction and backlight compensation.

设计
DESIGN
深圳市金标源创工业设计有限公司
Shenzhen King-Bill Design Company

生产
MANUFACTURE
深圳市三锐智能技术有限公司
Sree Technology Co.,Ltd.

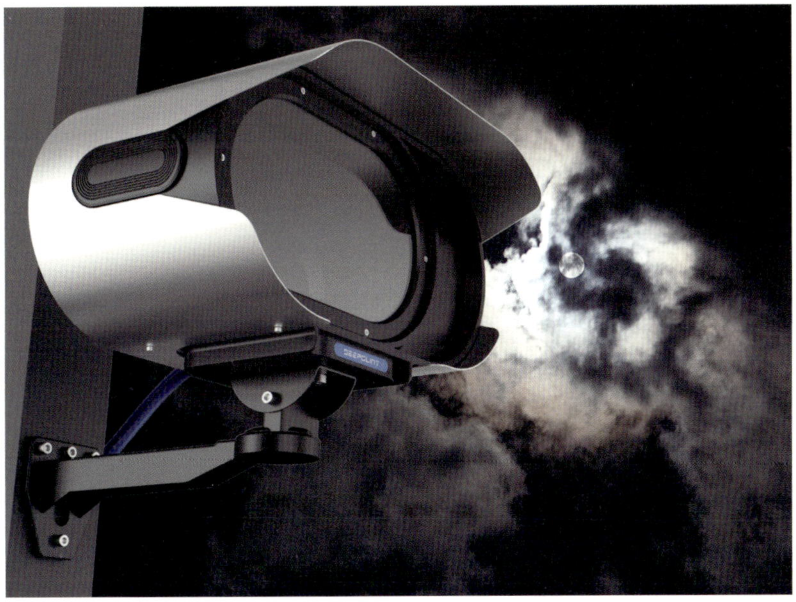

深瞳人眼摄像机
DeepGlint Foveacam

该产品是一款人眼仿生摄像机，采用独创的像素动态瞬时分配技术，瞬间将局部画面的有效像素提升百倍以上，整体画面可以达到数亿级等效像素，50 米内展现清晰的可识别人脸，100 米内看清全身特征。基于前端抓取的高质量图片可极大地提高后端识别任务的准确率。拥有自动和手动两种模式，配备星光级传感器保证全天使用，可应用于室内室外所有场景。

The product is biomimetic eye camera. Its patented Dynamic instant pixel allocation (DIPA) technology can dynamically increase the pixel density in a local image region and instantly boost the effective resolution of that area by over 100 times. Based on the images enhanced by DIPA Technology, faces up to 50 meters and bodies up to 100 meters away can be reliably recognized. High quality images based on front-end capture can greatly improve the accuracy of back-end recognition tasks. All FoveaCams equip with two working modes: auto mode and manual mode. Equipped with star-light sensor, it works not only during the day but also at night and fits almost all indoor/outdoor surveillance scenarios.

设计
DESIGN
成都意町工业产品设计有限公司
Chengdu Iding Industrial Design Co.,Ltd.

生产
MANUFACTURE
北京格灵深瞳信息技术有限公司
Beijing DeepGlint Technology Limited

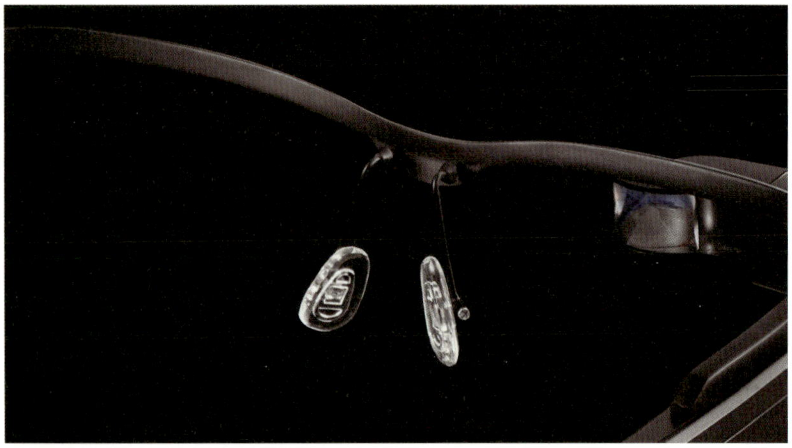

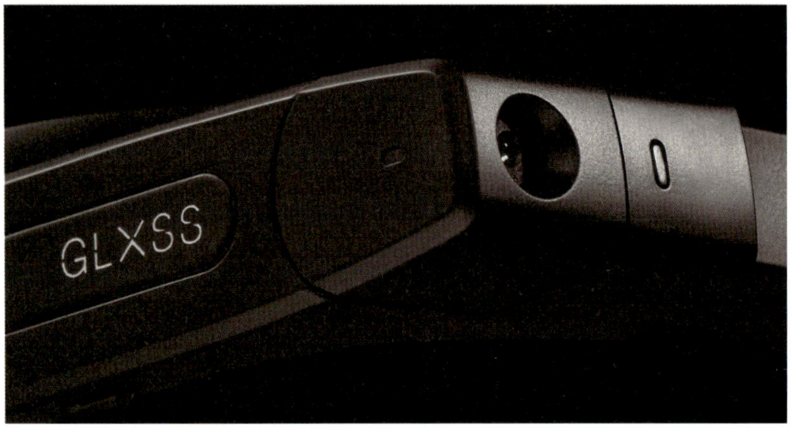

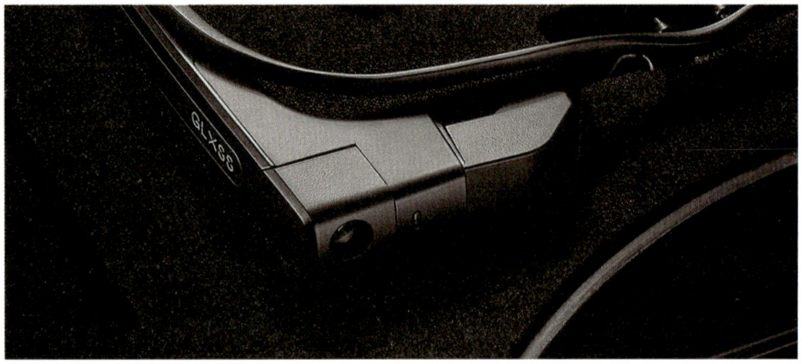

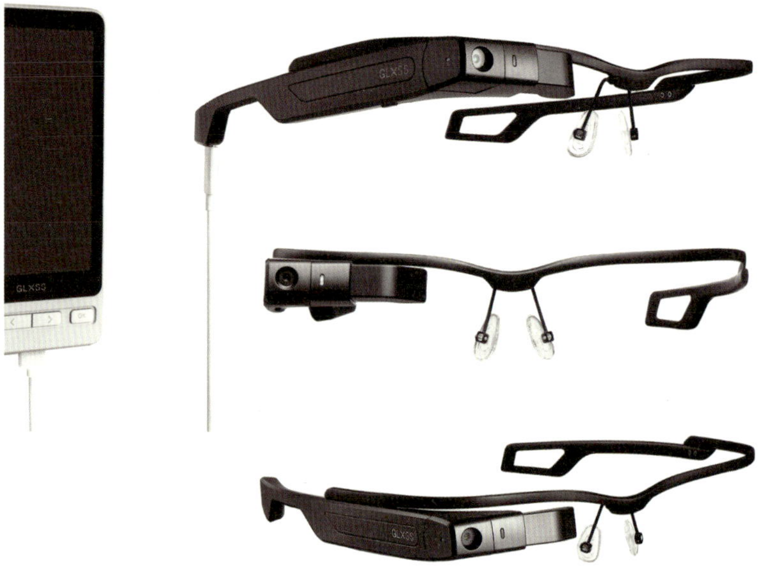

GLXSS Pro 智能眼镜
GLXSS Pro Smart Glass

该产品是全球最轻的智能眼镜，其分体式设计将计算、供电和存储模块设计成独立佩戴的主机，眼镜部分仅保留必需的功能模块，减重的同时降低眼镜发热。出色的光学设计与业内首屈一指的加工精度将树脂自由曲面显示的畸变控制在肉眼不可察觉的范围，图像边缘拥有极高的解析力。超声波焊接技术可在不使用挥发性胶水的同时减轻重量，兼顾了美观与环保的要求。

The product is the lightest smart glass in the whole world. "Split Type" design means keep only the necessary components on smart glass, while packs computing, power and storage modules in glass host. Not only over heat issue is solved, but also the weight of glass is reduce. Top notch optical design and manufacturing precision, bring down the distortion to unnoticeable level, while keeps very high resolution from corner to corner. The ultrasonic welding brings lightweight to the product without using glues, which takes both the beauty and environmental protection requirements into account.

设计
DESIGN

杨金超
Seed Yang

北京亮亮视野科技有限公司
Beijing LLvision Technology Co.,Ltd.

生产
MANUFACTURE

红米 Note 4X 手机
Redmi Note 4X

红米 Note 4X 搭载了 MIUI 8 系统，提供“隐私双系统”功能，照片、应用、数据独立保存，更有效保护隐私。拥有 4100 毫安大容量电池，超长续航，可连续看书 22 小时。整体设计圆润，其全对称设计强调纯粹的美感，与此前版本相比机身换用了三段式设计，采用金属冲压成型减少浪费，提升运输效率。多彩的金属机身带来了科技感与未来感。

Redmi Note 4X equipped with MIUI 8 system, offering privacy dual system function to keep photos, apps and data independently. It is more effective in protecting privacy. With 4100 Ma large capacity batteries, it could give you 22 hours of continue reading. Adopting a compact design, its symmetrical design emphasizes pure beauty. Compared to the previous version, Redmi Note 4X adopted 3 stage design on its metal body to reduce the waste of raw materials after stamping. The colorful metal body brings a sense of science and future.

设计
DESIGN

小米科技有限责任公司
Xiaomi Inc.

小米科技有限责任公司
Xiaomi Inc.

生产
MANUFACTURE

10G-PON 智能网关
10G-PON

该产品是一款应用光纤接入技术开发的商用无线高性能智能网关，具有国际专利的 100G TWDM 光传输技术，可提供高达每秒 10G 的网络传输速度。产品具有广覆盖、高互通、节能、部署灵活、兼容、智能、全业务的特点，可以满足 4K 高清、VR/AR 业务的快速发展，可以兼容各种运营商标准。外置天线、功能按键、导光机构与机身融为一体，整体简洁明快。

The product is a commercial WIFI high-performance intelligent gateway developed from the fiber access technology, with an internationally patented 100G TWDM optical transmission technology, and can provide the network transmission download speed up to 10G/S. Wide coverage, high interoperability, energy saving, flexible deployment, compatibility, intelligence and full service are key factors of this design. It can meet the rapid development of 4K HD and VR/AR business and be compatible with various operators standards. The external antenna, function keys and light guiding mechanism are integrated with the fuselage, forming simplicity of the product.

设计 DESIGN
烽火通信科技股份有限公司
Fiberhome Telecommunication Technologies Co.,Ltd.

武汉栎维道创意科技有限公司
Wuhan Liweidao Creative Technology Co.,Ltd.
生产 MANUFACTURE

生物指纹终端采集器
Biometric Fingerprint Acquisition Termina

该产品是一款生物指纹终端采集器，可广泛应用于公安、民政、银行、酒店、证券、交通管理等行业。考虑到识别指纹和证件信息 的采集过程均是以一对多，因此设计了手持、悬挂、桌面摆放的方式，可达到高效采集的效果。产品具备手机通讯功能，拥有 7 寸显示屏幕，200 万像素前置摄像头，LED 补光灯，4500 毫安电池，内置双 SIM 卡槽。

The product is a biometric fingerprint acquisition termina, which could be widely used in the fields of public security, civil affairs, banking, hotel, securities, traffic management and other industries. AS for the collection method is one to many during the collection course of fingerprint acquisition and ID card, the product use the way of hand hold, suspend and desktop to collect the Identity information efficiently. It has the function of Mobile communication and the features of 7 inch screen, 2 million pixels of front camera, LED fill-in light, 4500mHA battery and Built-in dual SIM card slots.

设计 DESIGN
深圳市白狐工业设计有限公司
Shenzhen Bifoxs Industrial Design Co.,Ltd.

深圳市白狐工业设计有限公司
Shenzhen Bifoxs Industrial Design Co.,Ltd.
生产 MANUFACTURE

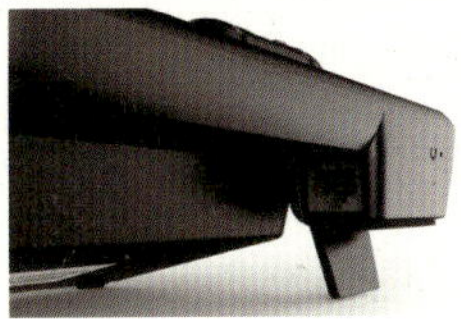

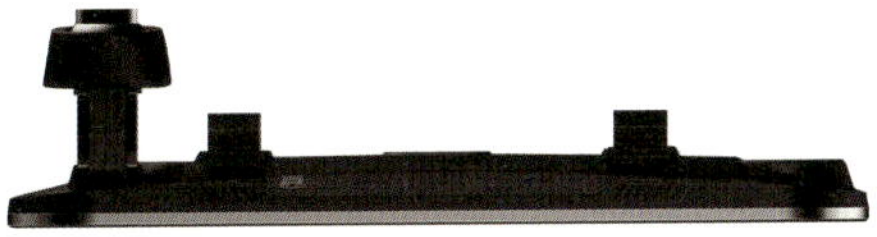

车喵 H8 智能后视镜
Carmew H8 Intelligent Rearview Mirror

该产品为一款智能汽车后视镜，相比普通智能后视镜所具备的在线导航、蓝牙、在线音乐等附加娱乐功能，该产品还集成了行车记录功能、智能辅助驾驶功能和儿童镜功能，提供前方碰撞预警、车道偏离预警、前车启动提示以及观察后座儿童等创新体验。产品采用高度模块化设计，其中配有模块化的专车支架，方便匹配不同的车型安装。

The product is an intelligent rearview mirror. Compared to the online navigation, bluetooth, online music and other entertainment functions of the traditional intelligent rearview mirror, it integrates driving record function, baby mirror function and intelligent auxiliary driving function, providing users "front collision warning, lane deviation warning and the car before the start prompts and other innovative experience function. The product uses a highly modular design, which is equipped with modular car bracket, easy to match the different models installed.

设计 DESIGN
北京高科中天技术股份有限公司
Itonology Co.,Ltd.

杭州领跑者工业设计有限公司
Hangzhou LPZ Industrial Design Co.,Ltd.
生产 MANUFACTURE

远云网络云储存
Yuanyun Network Cloud Storage

该产品是一款家庭数据云存储中心，用户可方便地将手机、平板电脑和电脑内的资料存储在时尚精致的家庭数据云存储中心里面，便捷的免工具硬盘替换功能，轻轻一按即可弹出内部硬盘。秉承极简主义的工业设计风格，运用航空铝质拉丝，以匠心独具的模块式抽屉设计，巧妙植入神秘的摩斯电码元素，将数据安全与时尚外观完美结合。

The product is a cloud storage center for home data. Users can share data in phone, panel computer or computer through the fashion family information cloud easily. It is convenient to change the hard drive by push only one button with tool-free hard disk replacement function. With the minimalism design style, high quality aluminum material, clever design of drawer and the elements of Morse code, data security and stylish appearance are perfect combined.

设计 DESIGN 广州远云网络科技有限公司 Guangzhou Yuanyun Network Technology Limited Company

广州大业产品设计有限公司 Guangzhou Daye Industrial Design Co.,Ltd. **生产 MANUFACTURE**

联想 ideacentre 620s 型号计算机
Lenovo ideacentre 620s Mini PC

联想 ideacentre 620S 是首次集成智能语音交互技术的台式机产品。其超小型设计，极大地节省了使用空间。独特的云声音识别技术，让用户直接与该计算机对话。产品有针对性地提供了图片、音乐和视频编辑等功能，并实现了快速个人云存储。产品仅重 2.25 千克，便于移动使用。其隐藏式散热开孔设计和解决方案，使产品噪音小、温度低，为用户带来更好的体验。

Lenovo ideacentre 620S is the first desktop to integrate intelligent voice interaction technology. Its ultra small design greatly saves space. It is equipped with voice control function that allows the users truly communicate with the PC. The product is targeted to provide a picture, music and video editing functions and is able to provide fast personal cloud storage. It weighs only 2.25kg for use. The concealed radiating hole design makes the product low voice and temperature for better user experience.

设计 DESIGN 联想集团 Lenovo Group

联想设计 Lenovo Design **生产 MANUFACTURE**

中兴锁屏系统应用
ZTE Locker System APP

中兴锁屏是一项基于智能手机的图片推送应用。设计师把景点、美食、活动等图片制作成适合锁屏展示的图片上传到服务器，标注其地理位置信息和活动链接。客户端通过 GPS 定位获悉用户的位置信息后发送到服务器，服务器端将位置信息和图片位置标签进行匹配，筛选出位置一致的资源，将其推送到该客户端。用户即可收到附近的景点、美食、活动等图片推送。

ZTE Lock screen is an APP for picture push based on smart phone. The designer would polish photos of attractions, food, activities and so on into a screen wallpaper and upload to the server, with the locations and links. Users location will be found by GPS and sent to the server by client, then all the related pictures or located information will be matched through server. Then they would be sent to the terminal equipment and users will receive all the nice photos about landscapes, restaurants and events.

设计 DESIGN 中兴通讯股份有限公司 ZTE Corporation.Shenzhen,China

中兴通讯股份有限公司 ZTE Corporation.Shenzhen,China **生产 MANUFACTURE**

指纹识别笔记本
Lockbook

该产品是全球第一款利用指纹加密的笔记本产品。将传统的电子锁结构小型化与指纹识别技术结合，形成专属于笔记本产品的指纹锁加密设备。指纹识别模块采用更大的识别面积进行360度全方位感应，对干湿手指识别有更好的效果。材料采用通过德国认证的皮料制作，达到亲肤品质，纸芯可更换，同时采用回收的废旧纸浆制作包装。

The product is the world's first innovative lifestyle product that equips a fingerprint senor. the mechanism of the traditional electronic lock is minimized and combined with the biometric technology and together a customized device for the notebook is created. A larger module for the scanning is designed to provide a more reliable unlocking experience from every angle even when the finger is wet. Lockbook uses the leather that has passed the Oeko-Tex Standard 100 test. The paper core can be replaced and the recycled waste paper pulp can be used for packing.

设计 DESIGN
深圳指尖儿科技有限公司
FPlife Technology Co.,Ltd.

生产 MANUFACTURE
深圳市麦锡工业产品策划有限公司
Maxypro Industrial Product Scheme Co.,Ltd.

小米米家对讲机
Mi Walkie-Talkie

小米米家对讲机是一款创新型对讲机产品，它内置蓝牙芯片，配合手机应用可在没有手机信号的野外进行队友间位置共享，满足多种场景下的通话需求。采用极简交互设计，正面仅五个按键，按键对应界面文字提示可快速上手使用，可通过手机应用快速设置频率、进行固件升级。外观由纯粹的几何形态元素构成，功能元素布局合理，有很强的对称性、统一感。

Mi Walkie-Talkie is an innovative walkie talkie product. The built-in Bluetooth BLE chip enables real-time location sharing among teammates even when network connection is lost. It could meet the call demand in a variety of scenarios. Minimalist design with just five buttons on the front and its corresponding prompts on the screen creates an intuitive user experience. Quick frequency settings and firmware upgrading through app are available. Employing mainly geometric forms, the product has logically arrange functional elements and address the sense of symmetry and unity.

设计 DESIGN
西安蜂语信息科技有限公司
Xi'an Fengyu Information Techonolgy Co.,Ltd.

生产 MANUFACTURE
小米生态链工业设计团队
Mi Ecosystem Industrial Design Team

CP200pro 老人定位手机
CP200pro The Aged Positioning Mobile Phone

该产品是为 65 岁以上轻度限制行为人群设计的养老智能硬件，它为老人及家属提供定量快捷亲情通话按键设置、SOS 一键呼救、语音提醒与推送、子女端手机应用精确定位老人位置、长时间待机和底座充电等功能。整合社会资源参与服务运营，使老年人能够获取社区医疗、家政、出行等服务，也帮助老人的亲属能时刻掌握老人的具体位置信息，必要时获得救助。

It's an exclusive intelligent hardware equipment which provides necessary services for more than 65 years old persons with mild limited capacity. The quick call keys could be used to call families with one key. There is a SOS key which is used for emergency call. The equipment could remind and push sound information for elderly to solve their problems. It is easy to locate the elderly by using a specific APP which is installed on their relatives's mobile phones. The battery of the equipment supports charging through cradle and could last long. The product integrates social resources and service operations to satisfy the elderly's service demands, so that it's more convenient and safe for the elderly to obtain community health care, housekeeping, travel and other services. The elderly's relatives can also easily locate the elderly to prevent them lost. And when an elderly is not well or in an emergency, the product ensures he or she obtains help promptly in order to take care of the elderly.

设计
DESIGN

四川长虹佳华信息产品有限责任公司
Changhong IT Information Products Co., Ltd.

生产
MANUFACTURE

四川长虹佳华信息产品有限责任公司
Changhong IT Information Products Co.,Ltd.

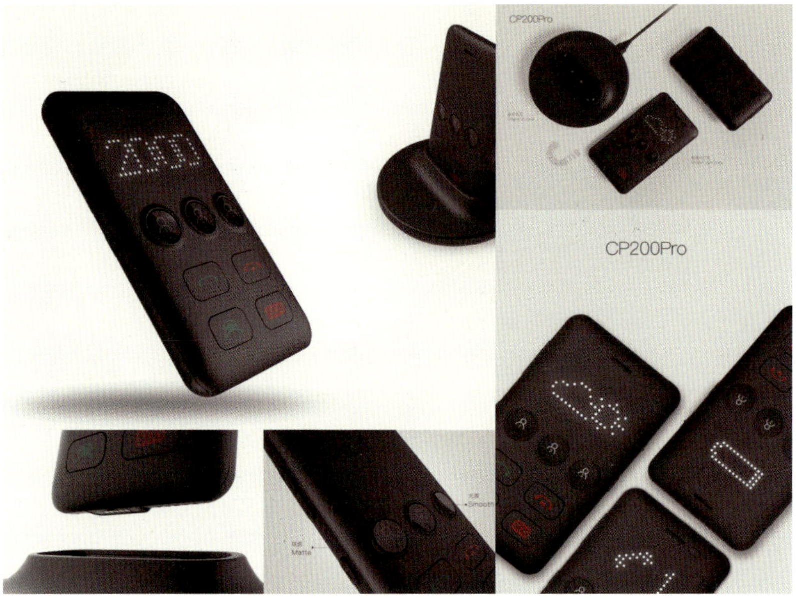

飒途 600B 卫星通信系统
Sattour 600B Satellite Communication System

该产品是一款国际领先的卫星通信产品，将卫星应急通信系统中的多台设备集成，突破了以往分体形式设计了大量快卡、调节及折叠结构，使未经培训的用户可在 5 分钟内完成安装及对星连接。系统重量从 20 千克降到 7.5 千克，适合野外作业。在无手机信号环境下，可与卫星连接建造一个可传输视频等急速宽带信息的无线环境，并在紧急情况下快速向外界求救。

The product is an international leading satellite communication product which integrated research of multiple devices in the satellite emergency communication system. It breaks through the form that the antenna and function units are separated. The system has a lot of rapid assembly structures, adjusting structures and folding structures which have been analyzed and verified. So the untrained users can complete the installation and connection of the star in five minutes. The system weight is reduced from 20kg to 7.5 kg, which is more convenient for carrying and suitable for outdoor camping expedition and exploration. This system is available for providing a WIFI environment for your personal mobile electronic devices while your cell phone signal is zero with the connection of satellite. Also, you can achieve communication and contact with the outside world in an emergency situation.

设计
DESIGN

航天恒星科技有限公司（503 所）
Space Star Technology Co., Ltd.

生产
MANUFACTURE

毕朝瑞、李志中
Echo, Dr.Lee

生活防水携带式硬盘
Diamond D30

该产品是一款防水便携硬盘，可以随时随地进行快速安全的资料传输。特有书签造型的滑盖设计可对硬盘进行保护，只要盖上盖子就能够有效防水防尘，已通过 IPX4 防水标准。表面采用激光立体纹路设计，不仅美观具有质感，更能有效降低刮纹。该硬盘分为 2TB 和 5TB 两种大小，2TB 可选择超薄外形，5TB 可选择强壮坚固外形。

The product is a waterproof portable hard disk, which can be used for fast and safe data transmission anytime and anywhere. With a sliding cover in the shape of leaf, the D30 is perfectly protected against water splashes (IPX4 rated) and dirt. Fast secure data transmission has been through the IPX4 waterproof standard. The special rhombus design pattern not only looks good, but also helps to avoid scratches and fingerprints.The hard disk is divided into two sizes: 2TB and 5TB. 2TB can choose ultra-thin shape while 5TB can choose strong appearance.

设计
DESIGN
邱美玲、王钟纬
Qiu Meiling, Wang Zhongwei

生产
MANUFACTURE
广颖电通股份有限公司
Silicon Power

5G 通讯基站
5G Base Station

该产品是全球首款 5G 高频段通讯基站，采用 5G 核心技术，利用多天线多用户空分技术成倍提升无线频谱效率，较传统 4G 通讯基站提升 10 倍以上，创频谱效率新纪录，已具备商用能力，对推动 5G 通讯时代的到来具有里程碑意义。5G 基站带来更高的速率、更宽的带宽并且可靠性更高，满足智能制造、虚拟现实、自动驾驶等行业应用的特定需求。

The product is the world first 5G high band base station. Compared with traditional 4G base station, it has 10 times spectrum efficiency improvement by adopting Massive MIMO 5G key technology and multi-antenna multi-user space division technology. It creats new record of spectrum efficiency. It is capable of commercialization now and surely the milestone for the coming 5G era. The 5G base station brings a higher rate, wider broadband and higher reliability, which can meet the intelligent manufacturing, virtual reality, the automatic driving and other industrial specially applications.

设计
DESIGN
中兴通讯股份有限公司
ZTE Corporation.Shenzhen,China

生产
MANUFACTURE
中兴通讯股份有限公司
ZTE Corporation.Shenzhen,China

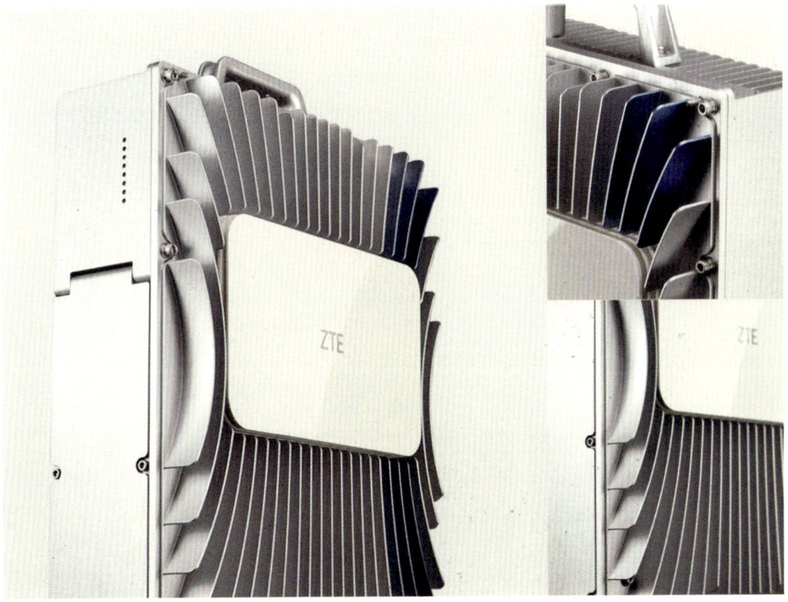

小米电视 4
Xiaomi TV 4

小米电视 4 被设计为一个整体系统，包含了音箱、低音炮和电视。它搭载了杜比全景声，内置人工智能系统，其屏幕画质、音质，丰富的内容库以及人工智能系统能够满足一切家庭娱乐的需要。产品采用分体设计，主机从电视移到了音箱上，因此无须购买昂贵的电视，无须更新包含主机的音箱即可升级。超薄机身，超窄边框，鹿角底座让电视简洁又富有细节。

Millet TV 4 is designed as a whole system, including speakers, subwoofer and TV. It is equipped with Dolby Atoms, built-in artificial intelligence system. Its screen quality, sound quality, rich content database and artificial intelligence system can meet the needs of all family entertainment. The product adopts the split design, with the host shifting from TV to the speaker. So there is no need to buy expensive TV, but only to update the speaker which includes the host. Slim, ultra narrow frame and antlers base make the TV concise and of rich details.

设计
DESIGN
王川、李宁
Wang Chuan， Li Ning

生产
MANUFACTURE
北京小米电子产品有限公司
Beijing Xiaomi Electronics Co.,Ltd.

M1E 蓝牙运动耳机
M1E Sport Bluetooth Headset

M1E 耳机特殊形态舒适便携地贴合任何耳朵形状，引导音频进入耳道并提供出色音质体验，人机工程学设计，保证运动时不会滑落。M1E 耳机所采用的高质量材料可确保耳机的耐用性和舒适性，并且环保可回收。流线型设计，独具创意的造型设计，令使用者在享受流淌着的美妙音乐之余，同时享有赏心悦目的视觉感受。

The M1E sports HiFi Bluetooth Earphones design is based on the human ergonomics. The professional earhook shape make you feel comfort for any ear shape. The unique earplug design allow sound slip into the ear and provides excellent bass experience, It will be comfortable and won't slip out during sports.High-quality materials are used in its construction for maximum comfort and extra durability. It is also environmental friendly and recyclable. This unique and innovative smooth design not only bring you the excellent sound, but also exhilarating and delightful visual enjoyment to the eyes.

设计
DESIGN
深圳市科奈信科技有限公司
Shenzhen Cannice Technology Co.,Ltd.

生产
MANUFACTURE
深圳市科奈信科技有限公司
Shenzhen Cannice Technology Co., Ltd.

VR 电脑
VR Computer

此产品是一款把虚拟键盘、光触板应用、win10 系统及投影技术融为一体的创新产品。键盘及屏幕均在开机后展现，设计轻量化，便于携带移动，可完全手势操作，并拥有 14—100 寸的多种尺寸画面，可满足办公娱乐多种需求，并最大限度地减少蓝光对用户眼睛的伤害。体积小巧，造型简洁，工艺精琢，使用可回收材料，包装更加环保。

This product is an innovative product which has integrated virtual keyboard plus light touchpad, win10 system application and projection technology. Both keyboard and screen are displayed with the starting up and it is designed to be lightweight and easy to carry, also it can be operated with gestures completely and the screen can be any size between 14 inch and 100 inch, which could meet various office and entertainment needs. Meanwhile, the way that the Light Computer displays reduces the harm of blue ray to eyes as far as possible. With small size and concise and elegant appearance, the product uses recoverable materials and environmentally friendly packing.

设计 DESIGN 北京有初科技有限公司 Beijing Yochu Technology Co.,Ltd.

北京有初科技有限公司 Beijing Yochu Technology Co.,Ltd. **生产 MANUFACTURE**

智能集尿器
Intelligent Urine Collector

智能集尿器是一款家用高科技小便护理产品，适用于卧床患者或行动不便、夜间小便频繁人群。用户可独立操作，上下组件模块化设计，产品结构紧凑、体积小巧、提携便捷。依照人体工程学，分别设计了男女分体式机尿杯，尿液无侧漏，使用安全舒适。大容量储液桶设计，无须频繁清理。一键式排污设计，避免细菌感染。自动检测小便，及时触发并启动。

This intelligent urine collector is a household high-tech urine care product, suitable for bedridden patients or people with inconvenient for mobility,frequent urination at night. Users can operate it independently, the upper and lower components are design as modulars,the structure of product is compact, easy to carry and convenient. In accordance with ergonomics, it was designed separately for men and women with different urine cups, without side leakage for urine, the use is safe and comfortable.It has a large capacity storage design, do not need frequent cleaning. One-button sewage design, can avoid bacterial infection. It can automatically detect urine, timely trigger and start.

设计 DESIGN 宁波新海医疗科技有限公司 Ningbo Xinhai Medical Technology Co., Ltd.

慈溪大业工业设计有限公司 Cixi Daye Industrial Design Co.,Ltd. **生产 MANUFACTURE**

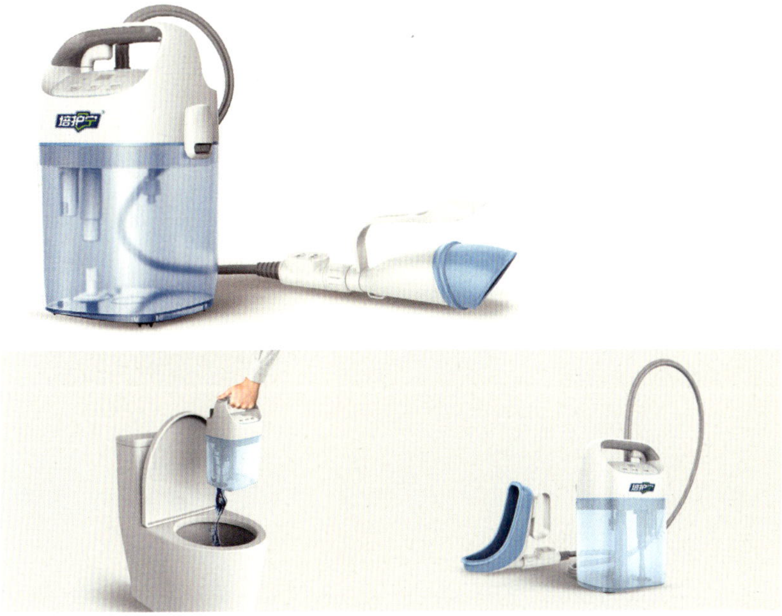

折叠二合一吸尘器
Rechargeable 2 in 1 Vacuum Cleaner

这款吸尘器可旋转旋钮折叠手柄到 180 度，减小包装体积，降低能源消耗。充电式设计，用户可清洁室内任何区域。子机配有电量显示，方便用户观察电量。整个产品零件数量最少化，降低生产成本，同时减少产品的装配步骤，使整机可以大批量生产，减少装配环节的报废率。平台化设计，可以延续产品线。整体造型设计简洁大方，使用方便灵活。

This vacuum cleaner can be switched to folded up the handle to 180 degree to not only save storage space but also cut down the energy cost. User can clean any area in the room on account of its rechargeable function. The machine is equipped with electricity display, convenient for users to observe the electricity. Reasonable design and the least part number can reduce production cost, meanwhile product steps are reduced to make the whole machine can be mass production and reduce scrap rate in assembly progress. Platform design can help continue the product lines. The product is fashion,simple and flexible and convenient to use.

设计 DESIGN 广东新宝电器股份有限公司 Guangdong Xinbao Electrical Appliances Holdings Co., Ltd.

陈龙辉、陈立明 Chen Longhui, Chen Liming **生产 MANUFACTURE**

Skyworth W9 OLED 电视
Skyworth W9 OLED TV

W9 是一件可以磁性吸附于任何墙面的显示设备。屏体采用柔性 OLED 材料，可与墙面零距离安装。主机与屏体由集成数据线连接，主机内置高保真音箱和智能语音操控中枢。用户可将智能中枢携带至客厅中的任何角落，以触摸遥控或语音的方式与 W9 进行交互。主体材质更加安全环保，产品外观更加整体，突出局部细节设计。

W9 is a display device that can be attached to any wall by magnetism. The screen adopts OLED material and can be hung on the wall seamlessly. W9 TV connects with the screen with an integrated cable. HF sound bar and intelligent voice control pivot are built in the TV. When W9 is on, users can take it anywhere, touch or speak to it to control W9. The theme material is safer and more environmentally friendly. TV is neat and tidy with partial protruding design.

设计 DESIGN 深圳创维 -RGB 电子有限公司 Shenzheng Chuangwei-RGB Electronics Co.,Ltd.

生产 MANUFACTURE 深圳创维 -RGB 电子有限公司工业设计研究院 Shenzheng Chuangwei -RGB Electronics Co.,Skyworth Design

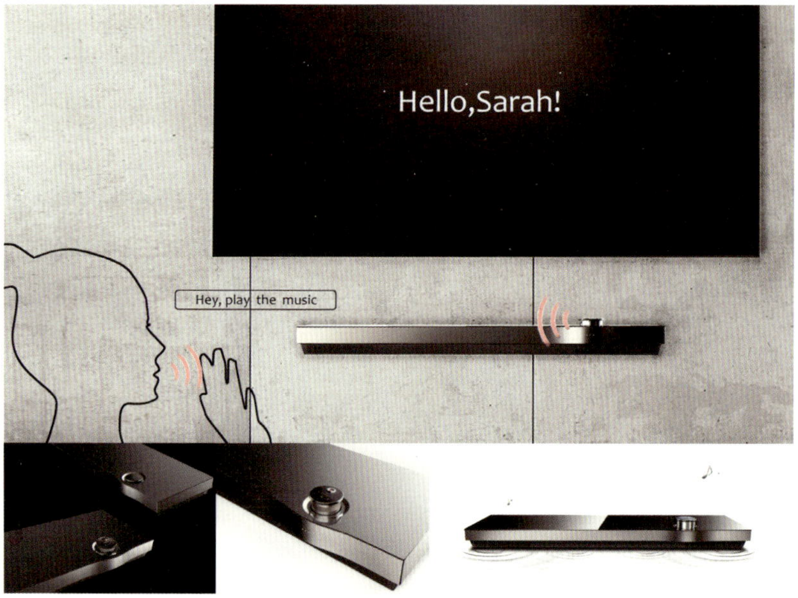

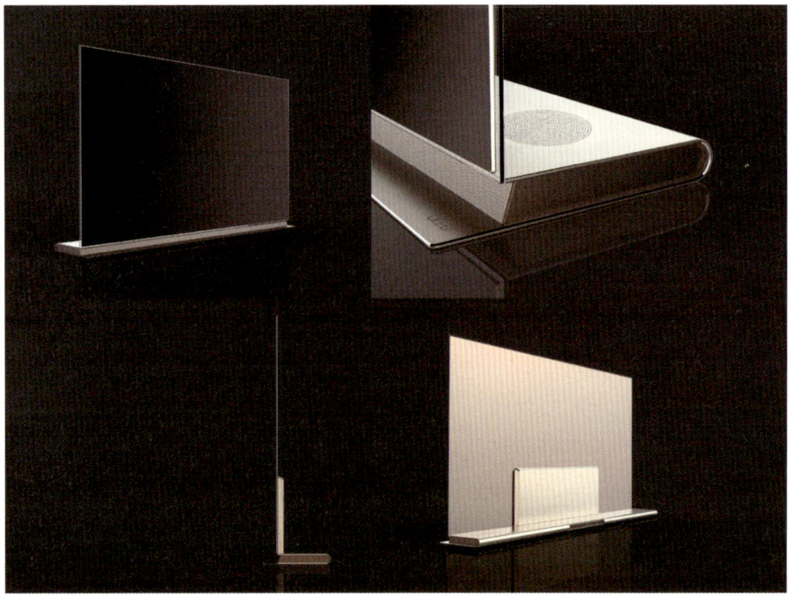

Skyworth W8 OLED 电视
Skyworth W8 OLED TV

这款电视采用全球最先进的 OLED 显示技术，屏体厚度仅为 3.9 毫米，视觉效果极佳。分体式设计，将主板、电源、音箱等集成于底座主机中；底座主机通过转轴与屏体连接，只需将底座主机向后旋转 90 度即可轻松实现挂墙。电视侧面与主机一体流线型设计，外观简洁，材质散热性能好，能耗低，并具有可回收性，更加节能环保。

The TV adopts OLED display tech with only 3.9mm slim to a great viewing experience. Split style design is adopted. The main board, power supply, sound bar, .etc. are integrated in the stand host ; the stand host connects with the screen via a spindle. Users only needs to turn it backward for 90°to hang the TV on the wall. The integrated linear design of TV side and the whole TV makes it neat and tidy with no excessive line. Metal color shows it is high level and fashionable.The materials has features of good heat dissipation, low power consumption and is recyclable.

设计 DESIGN 深圳创维 -RGB 电子有限公司 Shenzheng Chuangwei-RGB Electronics Co.,Ltd.

生产 MANUFACTURE 深圳创维 -RGB 电子有限公司工业设计研究院 Shenzheng Chuangwei -RGB Electronics Co.,Skyworth Design

JBL Bar 3.1 家庭影院条形音箱系统
JBL Bar3.1

该产品采用虚拟环绕声和杜比数字技术，配备一个专用的中置声道和一台无线低音扬声器，低音震撼，语音清亮。JBL SoundShift 技术可进一步增强用户体验，用户可以在电视声音和手机或平板电脑的声音之间迅速切换。JBL Bar 3.1 使用低功耗功放和高效的电气设计，绿色环保。产品包装使用可回收材料，可减少浪费。外观设计可确保客厅配色和谐。

The product adopts virtual surround and Dolby Digital, with a dedicated center channel and a wireless subwoofer for thrilling bass, and voice clarity. Further enhanced with JBL SoundShift, it allows you instant auto-switch between sound from your TV, and sound from your mobile phone or tablet. The JBL Bar 3.1 features eco-friendly design using low-power consumption amplifiers and a high efficiency electrical design. The product's packaging uses recycled materials and minimizes waste. Bar 3.1 is a design piece that fully blended-in with the home environment.

设计 DESIGN 哈曼国际 Harman International Industries

生产 MANUFACTURE 哈曼设计团队 Harman Design Center

JBL Boombox 便携式蓝牙音响
JBL Boombox

Boombox 是一款强大的蓝牙音响，自带把手，方便携带，声音震撼，一次充电可享长达 24 小时音乐盛宴。JBL Boombox 通过了 RoHS 和 EuP 合规测试，采用布料和橡胶保护产品本身，经久耐用。产品继承 JBL 的设计风格，独特的把手提高了其便携性，同时为 Boombox 提供了保护。采用布料、橡胶和金属材料，支持 IPX7 防水。简单便携，时尚耐用。

Boombox, made to be the most powerful Bluetooth speaker, it delivers monstrous sound along with the hardest hitting bass. Designed with a handle, it is easy to carry and can make you enjoy music for 24 hours with a single charge. The JBL Boombox passed RoHS and EuP compliance testing. Fabric and rubber is used to protext the product, making it durable. Following the JBL design guideline, the special handle is designed not only to enhance the portability of the product but also protect the Boombox itself.. Rugged with fabric, rubber and metal, the Boombox is IPX7 waterproof. Boombox is a strong, sexy, sleek and iconic speaker.

设计
DESIGN
哈曼国际
Harman International Industries

哈曼设计团队
Harman Design Center
生产
MANUFACTURE

创维 55G6D 电视
Skyworth 55G6D TV

该产品采用超高清屏体，色彩暗场层次更丰富；采用最先进的光纤传导遥控信号接收技术，体积小，灵敏度高，隐藏于喇叭网内；喇叭网结构方式创新，保护屏体省去装饰条，外观整体，结构简单更易实现。后背板采用 0.8 毫米钢板冲压，金属可回收，节省材料。至简喇叭网设计与整机搭配整机看起来整体庄重，与家庭环境契合；环抱机身的底座，有力稳重不失轻盈。

G6D uses super HD screen to achieve rich color dark field. Metal joint processing is used to the TV set. The most advanced fiber transmission remote signal reception tech is used. It is small, sensitive, hidden in the speaker mesh. Speaker mesh structure is creative and simple without decoration bar. 0.8mm steel plate is punched to make the back panel. It is recyclable, saving resources. The speaker mesh design, matching with the TV, makes the TV look decent and compatible with the household furnishing. The stand is stable and light.

设计
DESIGN
深圳创维 -RGB 电子有限公司
Shenzheng Chuangwei-RGB Electronics Co.,Ltd.

深圳创维 -RGB 电子有限公司工业设计研究院
Shenzheng Chuangwei -RGB Electronics Co.,Skyworth Design
生产
MANUFACTURE

健康高效原汁机
Healthy and Efficient Juice Machine

这款原汁机采用 DC 马达电机，黄金转速，更好切断食物纤维，减少与氧气接触，保证果汁口感及营养。研磨螺旋采用食品级 304 不锈钢，长期使用无磨损，无粉末，充分保护人体健康。产品零件数量最少化，降低生产成本，同时减少产品的装配步骤。平台化设计，可以延续产品线。采用直筒、蛋形设计，体积小巧，便于移动。外形美观，具有实用性。

The machine uses DC motor that can keep a perfect speed that turn 55 per minute. So the food fiber will be cut off more easily to Squeeze out out thick smooth delicious fruit juice. The grinding screw is made by food-grade 304 stainless steel that can be used for a long time without wear and tear to fully protect the human health. Reasonable design and the least part number can reduce production cost, reduce product assembly steps can make the whole machine can be mass production. Platform design can continue the product lines and produce new products with minimal cost. The machine is designed in straight, egg-shaped appearance that will bring small and delicate feeling in vision. The product design language is clear, good for the aesthetic and the practical.

设计
DESIGN

广东新宝电器股份有限公司
Guangdong Xinbao Electrical Appliances Holdings Co., Ltd.

陈龙辉、刘鹏
Chen Longhui, Liu Peng

生产
MANUFACTURE

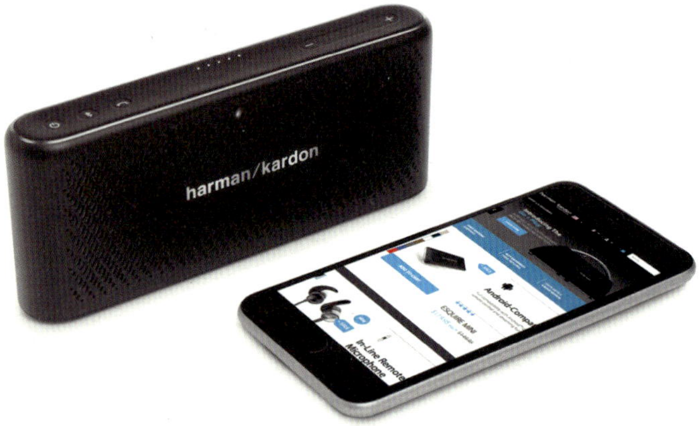

哈曼卡顿 Traveler 便携式蓝牙音响
Harman Kardon Traveler

哈曼卡顿 Traveler 是一款纤薄的蓝牙扬声器，其结合了优质声学性能的、可为移动设备充电的 USB 充电高密度电池以及高性能双麦克风通话扬声器。产品外形纤巧，性能强大，可轻松放入任何提包。一体式铝质外壳和高密度电池可提供优质声音性能。产品外观曲面美观，方便携带，造型优雅，采用织物制成，观感极佳。扬声器网罩下方配有银色反光布，巧妙地美化了外观。

The Harman Kardon Traveler is slim Bluetooth speaker, a unique combination of good acoustic performance, a high density battery with USB charge out to charge your mobile devices, a high-performance dual-mic speakerphone in a slim Bluetooth speaker. It is engineered to have great performance in a slim form factor which allows it to easily fit inside any bag or briefcase on the go. The unibody aluminum housing and high density battery allow good sound performance. The Harman Kardon Traveler' s main body is a single, premium anodized aluminum housing. The treatment of the aluminum is exceptional, with an etched design on the back panel that mirrors the front speaker grille. The fit and finish are top notch with beautiful curved surfaces, and the included carrying pouch is elegant and made of a fabric with a high quality look and feel

设计
DESIGN

哈曼国际
Harman International Industries

哈曼设计中心
Harman Design Center

生产
MANUFACTURE

智能调节变频水泵
Intelligent Adjustment Frequency Conversion Pump

产品使用 ECO 变频节能技术，立式卧式随意转换。智能调节，自由控制流量，实现多种保护与多种模式功能。应用范围广，适合水族箱、池塘造景、海鲜池畜养。节能省电，采用 ECO 变频技术，能耗更低。采用 ABS、PC 等可循环材料及新型电子变频技术，可安全用于海水生物养殖。陶瓷轴心轴套，耐磨损，不生锈。仿生外观设计，形象生动，贴合水族用品主题。

The product adopts ECO frequency conversion to be vertical and horizontal free conversion. It has intelligent regulation and free control flow, having multiple protection and function mode. The product is in wide range of applications, suitable for aquarium, pond landscaping and seafood pond. It is also energy saving, with ECO frequency conversion to achieve lower energy consumption. Using ABS, PC and other recyclable materials and new electronic frequency technology, it can be safely used for coral and other marine aquaculture. Equipped with super wear-resistant ceramic shaft sleeve, the product is wear-resistant and does no rust. With bionic design, it is vivid and fit aquarium supplies theme.

设计
DESIGN
区要光、徐训军
Oson, Xu Xunjun

生产
MANUFACTURE
森森集团股份有限公司
Sunsun Group Co.,Ltd.

Halomini 双目 AR 智能眼镜
Halomini Smart Glasses

Halomini 是一款国际领先的双目 AR 智能眼镜，视场角高达 40 度，配备 Outside-in 空间定位、3DOS 操作系统、手势操作、计算机视觉识别、全息显示技术和增强现实技术等多项高科技。用户可在任意场景中轻松使用，更直观地展示动态、立体的图像并与之交互。产品靠近皮肤部分采用 TPSIV 道康宁，细腻柔软，接触舒适。用圆环和产品结合，带给人展望未来的感受。

Halomini is a pair of internationally advanced augmented reality smart glasses with binocular displays. Its field of vision is up to 40 degree. it is equipped with outside-in orientation, 3D operation system, gesture interaction, computer visual identification, holographic display technology and augmented reality technology. Halomini can be used easily in any scene easily, enabling the users to see and intuitively interact with dynamic three-dimensional projections. The part close to the skin adopts the TPSIV of Dow Corning, which is delicate soft and comfortable to contact. The combination of rings and products brings people to the senses of the future.

设计
DESIGN
深圳市想象力产品策划有限公司
Imagination Design Co.,Ltd.

生产
MANUFACTURE
上海影创信息科技有限公司
Shadow Creator Information Technology Co.,Ltd.

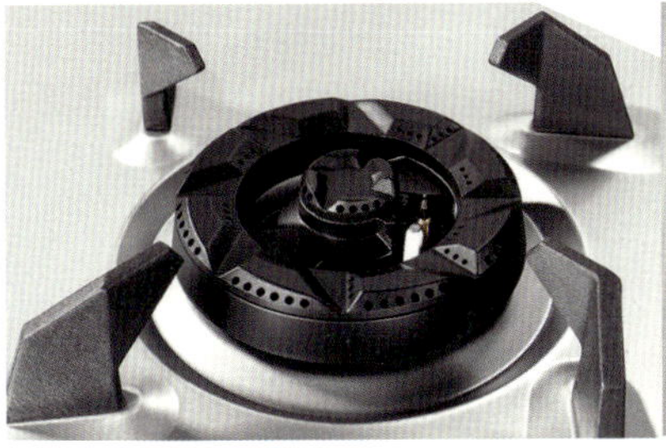

老板 58G8 燃气灶
Robam-58G8 Gas Stove

Robam-58G8 是一款全新燃气灶产品，将锅支架与面板实现一体化设计。用户在清洁灶具时，无须单独拿起锅支架，便可进行整体清洁。一体化设计方式减少了产品零部件数量，降低了产品开发的成本。一次冲压成型，经久耐用。不锈钢表面覆纳米耐指纹涂层，抗刮、耐腐蚀能力好。运用仿生的设计手法，意境如鲨鱼鳍游弋于小岛周围，从而将情趣性融入设计当中。

Robam-58G8 is the brand-new gas stove product. It adopts the integrated design of pot bracket and panel. When users clean the stove, they can clean the whole stove panel without picking up the bracket. The integrated design of pot bracket and panel reduce the number of the product components and the cost of product development. Robam-58G8 gas stove machine is shaped with once stamping, being durable. Stainless steel surface covered with nano-fingerprint coating, which has good capacity of scratch resistance and corrosion resistance. The design of Pot stent uses bionic design techniques, the mood of which is like a shark cruising around the island, so as to integrate the interest into the design.

设计
DESIGN
老板电器工业设计中心
Robam Industrial Design Dept.

生产
MANUFACTURE
杭州老板电器股份有限公司
Hangzhou Robam Applicances Co.,Ltd.

数码变频发电机（CH2000i）
CH2000i Digital Inverter Generator

超静音发电机，智能静音，双风扇双风道保证最佳散热效果，双消声器和双隔音罩保证最佳降噪效果。油耗低，冷却效果佳。专业内部风道设计，汽油燃烧更充分，电力更洁净，排放更低。全 ABS 阻燃塑料封闭式外壳，增加耐用性与安全性。软橡胶材质减震脚，有效吸收机器震动。设计形象更具视觉冲击力，符合人体工程学提手，单手操作更便携。

Ultra-quiet generator is intelligent mute. The patent which has double fan and double air flue can guarantee radiate. The double silencer and double sound-insulated cover can guarantee reduce the noise effectively. The oil consumption is low and the cooling effect is good. The design of professional internal air duct can make the gasoline burn more sufficiently, the electric power purer and the emission lower. Entire ABS plastic shell which is flame-resistant and enclosed can increase durability and security. The soft rubber material can reduce the shock and absorbs the vibration of machine effectively. The sharp side line can make the design image have visual impulse and enhance the recognition of appearance. It conforms to the human body engineering and does not hurt the hand, one-handed operation can make it more portable.

设计
DESIGN

刘渊博、 徐乐
Liu Yuanbo， Xu Le

苏州双马机电有限公司
Suzhou ERMA Machinery Co.,Ltd.

生产
MANUFACTURE

AW-S17G105 电热水壶
AW-S17G105 Electric Kettle

产品采用新型双层钢结构，内外材料都使用金属，内层使用食品级不锈钢 304 材质，外层使用彩钢材质，可根据市场需求变换颜色。壶体底部为无缝焊接，口部为广口设计，清洗、加装都非常方便快捷。产品所有零部件都使用环保无污染材料，使用过程中不产生有毒有害物质，更加安全环保。壶体采用无缝焊接技术，结构简单，端庄大气。

The product adopts new double wall structure, using metal materials SS 304 food grade inside and color coated steel sheet outside. Color can be changed according to market demand. Seamless welding at bottom of kettle and wide opening design is for easy cleaning and filling. All the parts are made from environment friendly and non-polluting materials. There no toxic or harmful substances delivered in use. Seamless welding technology is used for kettle body, making it simple structure while luxury and graceful.

设计
DESIGN

龙域设计
Loe Design

浙江爱仕达生活电器有限公司
Zhejiang Aishida Household Equipment Co.,Ltd.

生产
MANUFACTURE

老板 5610 吸油烟机
Robam-5610 Range Hood

Robam-5610 首创挥手感应控制，提升用户友好的烹饪体验；搭载 ROKI 智能模块，可通过 WIFI 连接手机，可实现烟机与手机之间的互动操作；采用双滑道式推杆机构，运行稳定高效；挡风板采用快拆装结构，方便用户清洁。Robam-5610 集成电磁感应与红外感应功能，提升操作灵敏性，降低误操作的概率 ；外观设计采用基本几何形状，表现中国文化中方和圆对比的美学韵味。

Robam-5610 is pioneering hand- induction operation, which has improved users friendly cooking experience; it is equipped with ROKI (Robam Kitchen Intelligence) intelligent module which could realize interaction operation between range hood and human hand through WIFI connected mobile phone; it adopts double slide pusher mechanism which feature stable and efficient operation; wind shield is adopted fast dismantling structure so that users could easily dismantle wind shield to clean chamber and oil screen. Robam-5610 integrates electromagnetic with infrared sensor to expand sensor area and thus promote sensitivity of operation, reduce the change of incorrect operation; the appearance design uses the most basic geometry shape, which performs contrast aesthetic charm between the circle and square in the Chinese culture.

设计 DESIGN
老板电器工业设计中心
Robam Industrial Design Dept.

生产 MANUFACTURE
杭州老板电器股份有限公司
Hangzhou Robam Applicances Co., Ltd.

Landroid 智能割草机
Landroid Robotic Mower

全球首创 AIA 技术，确保机器可以在狭窄的区域顺利行走；智能切割技术，可在狭小空间内高效工作。使用时可手机控制，通过手机远程控制割草机工作，无须编程，启动割草程序更加快速便捷；机身操作界面设计更加实用、直观、美观，使得整个操作过程便捷、简单。采用锂电池技术，安全性能好，无记忆效应，有效减少电池对环境的污染。

It patented mowing AIA cutting technology to ensure passing the narrow path easily;with intelligent cutting technology, it could effectively work in a narrow space. Mobile control – program make users able to control Landroid remotely through your smart phone without need of programming. It is more easy and fast to start mowing program. The body operation interface design is more practical, intuitive and beautiful, so that the whole operation process is convenient and simple. Using lithium battery technology, it has good safety performance, no memory effect and effectively reduce the battery to the harm of environmental pollution.

设计 DESIGN
宝时得科技（中国）有限公司
Positec Technology (China) Co., Ltd.

生产 MANUFACTURE
宝时得科技（中国）有限公司
Positec Technology (China) Co.,Ltd.

DF-EF0816V 循环扇
DF-EF0816V Air Circulation Fan

该产品采用空气动力涡轮设计，实现空气对流；能够进一步促进空气的循环，使房间温度更适宜更持久。产品在生产过程中主要部件均采用可回收利用的环保再生材料，工作功率只有 45 瓦，耗电量低，放置于暖房和空调房内能减少能源消耗。简洁时尚的外观设计，美观的进风口设计，细节处的处理及不同材质的搭配运用，增加了产品的美观性及细节感。

Aerodynamic Turbo Design offers maximum air movement，promote indoor air circulation effectively；promote indoor air circulation effectively and improve comfort in all-round way especially be used in the room with air conditioner or heater. The product uses recyclable material in the production process. Its working power is just 45W, with low power consumption. When paired with an air conditioner or heating system, it could be energy saving. Simple and chic design style, artful air intake design, the detail processing and the collocation of different material make the product more beautiful and add more details.

设计 DESIGN
联创工业设计中心
Lianchuang Industry Design Center

生产 MANUFACTURE
深圳市联创科技集团有限公司
Shenzhen Lianchuang Technology Group Co.,Ltd.

棒米耳温计
Earmo

该产品是一款以监测儿童体温为核心目标的耳温计。采用高精度红外热电堆传感器、进口抗菌塑料材料、极速热敏传感器、高亮 LED 灯和超低功耗蓝牙芯片。优化的探头使得精度提升至 0.01 摄氏度，隐藏式 LED 显示，在使用时读数更加清晰，同时外观的设计使得机身更简洁，也满足了儿童对耳温测量的需求，减轻儿童对耳温计的排斥感，方便且实用。

The product is an ear thermometer with monitoring children's body temperature as the core goal.It uses high-precision infrared thermopile sensor, imported antibacterial ABS material, high speed thermal sensor, highlight LED lights and ultra-low power Bluetooth chip. Optimized probe improves the accuracy to0.01°C, hidden LED display makes the reading more clear in the usage, while the appearance of the design makes the body more concise. The design, convenient and practical, meets the needs of children on the ear temperature measurement and reduces the sense of exclusion of children.

设计 DESIGN 杭州棒糖网络科技有限公司 Hangzhou Bangtang Network Technology Co.,Ltd.

杭州奥格工业设计有限公司 AUG Hangzhou Industrial Design Co.,Ltd. **生产 MANUFACTURE**

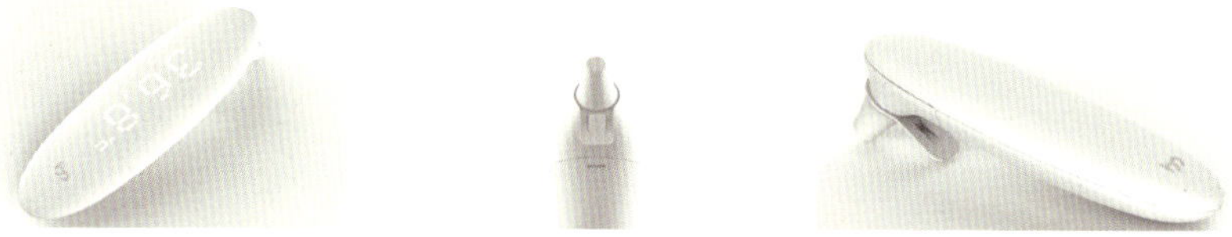

智能卧室风扇
Smart Bedroom Fan

此产品的风叶为双层风叶，由 16 片仿生双羽扇叶构成，在性能上平衡噪声、风量、柔和风三个维度。可拆卸立柱使风扇呈现落地扇和台地扇两种状态，一机两用。该风扇外观设计整体融方圆于一体，简约的一体式支撑立柱将圆形的扇头和四角圆滑过渡的方形底盘巧妙融合连接。根扇头使用双层风叶，使风扇吹出的风更柔和。

The blades of the fan-head are the double-layer blades composed of 16 bionic double feather fan blades. In the performance, it has three dimensions - balance noise, air volume and soft wind. By the removable column, the fan can have two states: stand fan and slide fan. It is a dual-use machine. The appearance design of the fan integrates "square" and "round" as a whole, and the simple one-piece support column smoothly transits "round" shaped fan head and four corners to "square" shaped base for clever fusion connection.The fan head uses double-layer blades so that the wind from the fan is softer.

设计 DESIGN 广东美的环境电器制造有限公司 GD Midea Environment Appliances MFG.Co., Ltd.

郭玉强 Guo Yuqiang **生产 MANUFACTURE**

九阳无渣豆浆机 Q7
DJ13R-Q7 Soybean Milk Maker

这款豆浆机结合了行业最新的侧面显示技术，突破性地将显示操作模块做到了机身侧面，并且增加了旋钮操控，这一设计不仅给用户带来了操作和观察上的极大便利，更是带来了一场豆浆机的外观造型革命；配合智能熬煮技术可以极大地提高豆浆的口感和营养。整机采用金属漆喷涂，提升价值感。隐藏的上提手也让产品更加简洁利落。

This soybean milk maker is combined with up-to-date technology in lateral display, which has removed display and operation module from the head to the side revolutionarily. In addition, it has added the rotary knob in operation. Not only does this design bring users great facilities in both operation and observation but also it arouses a revolution in appearance modeling of the soybean milk maker; Associated with the intelligent cooking technology, this product can greatly improve the taste and nutrition of soybean milk. The whole product uses the metallic paint spraying to increase value. The hidden upper handle makes product more concise as well.

设计 DESIGN 杭州九阳小家电有限公司 Hangzhou Joyoung Small Household Appliances Co.,Ltd.

沈健、李雁巢 Jack Shen, Jason Lee **生产 MANUFACTURE**

手机三轴稳定器 Smooth 3
3-Axis Smartphone Stabilizer Smooth 3

智云 Smooth 3 采用全新第五代蜂巢算法，电机扭矩、响应速度等均有大幅提升。在更加专业的同时，真正实现了方便地单手操作。机身配备电源输出口，可有效消除用户对于手机摄影高功耗的顾虑。独创的双向手机夹设计，让用户轻松完成手机横竖搭载切换。综合控制面板符合人机工程学，男性与女性用户均能舒适地握持。

Zhiyun Smooth 3 is empowered by the self-developed 5th Instune algorithmic system, with unparalleled motor torque and response speed. It truly realizes the one hand operation. The fuselage is equipped with power output, which can effectively eliminate the users' concerns of the high power consumption of mobile phone. With innovative dual clip design, users could easily realize the control panel switch. Both male and female users could comfortably hold with the control bard which is ergonomically.

设计 DESIGN 桂林智神信息技术有限公司 Guilin Zhishen Information Technology Co.,Ltd.

生产 MANUFACTURE 桂林智神信息技术有限公司 Guilin Zhishen Information Technology Co.,Ltd.

九阳厨下反渗透净水机
Water Purifier

智能 APP 操作，实时掌握家中水质情况。快换滤芯接头，方便滤芯更换。集成式水路板设计和水电分离技术，让产品整体更小巧。反渗透技术，达到直饮标准。环形指示灯，即时反应机器状态。超低废水率，减少浪费。简洁造型和优雅的乳白配色，让产品看起来更加整体、轻盈，可以更好地融入到厨房环境。细腻的机身磨砂纹理，让产品更加含蓄内敛。

It is equipped with smart maker App operation. Users could learn the water quality at home in real time. The Quick-change filter element's joint is convenient for changing filter element. The collection design built with completely new water and electricity circuit, it can make the product smaller and occupy less spaces; Reverse osmosis technology makes water up to the standard of direct drinking. Looped indication lamp is quick to feedback state of maker immediately. Ultra-low outlet drainage can reduce water waste. The succinct model and the elegant milky color matching in whole machine makes the product look more integrate and lighter, which can make it better to incorporate into the kitchen environment. The delicate frosted texture in the body of machine makes the product more implicative.

设计 DESIGN 杭州九阳小家电有限公司 Hangzhou Joyoung Small Household Appliances Co.,Ltd.

生产 MANUFACTURE 张岩、李雁巢 Zhang Yan,Jason Lee

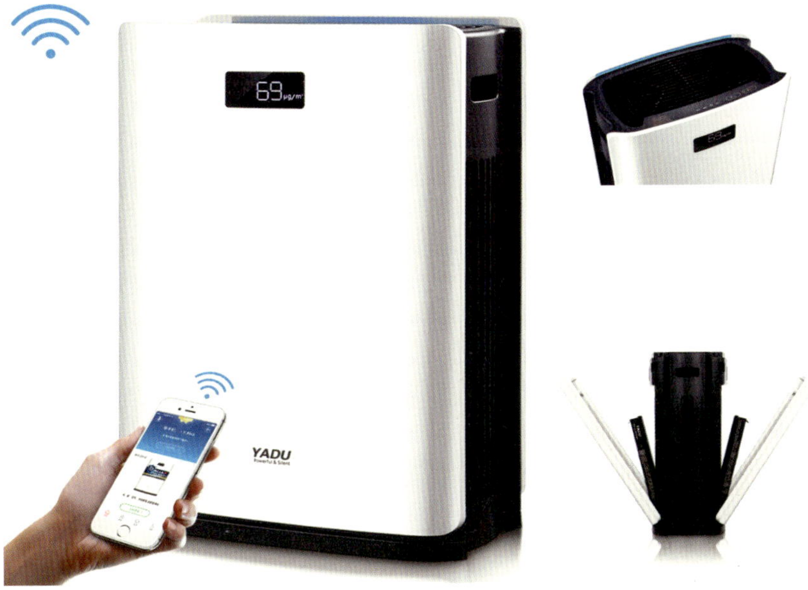

亚都 KJ455G-S4D 双面侠
YADU KJ455G-S4D Double-Faced Purifier

该产品正反两面均为左右两侧以及下侧进风，共六个进风轨道，构建大空间扰流风场，净化空气输出量翻倍，净化更彻底。智能 WIFI 链接系统，随时随地远程控制。造型模块化设计，可更换组合满足高低端需求。双面滤网加大过滤面积，提高室内净化速度和效果。正玄波无刷电机省电、静音。双面对称模组设计外观简洁大方，立体空间效果好。

The product adopts double air intake design. Air is supplied from the six air intake ducts on the left, right and bottom sides on both faces. A large turbulence field is created, and the output of purified air is doubled. The intelligent WIFI linking system ensures a remote control anytime and anywhere. The appearance design is modularized, and the removable combination can satisfy both the high-end and low-end demands. The double-face filter screen increases the filter area, and improves the speed and effect of indoor air purification. The sine-wave brushless motor saves power, and produces no noises in operation. The modules on both faces are designed to be in symmetrical distribution. With a style with layers, its appearance is simple and elegant, and shows a good stereoscopic effect.

设计 DESIGN 北京亚都环保科技有限公司 Beijing Yady Environmental Science and Technology Co.,Ltd.

生产 MANUFACTURE 北京千策良品工业设计有限公司 RCB Industrial Design

艾泡一起充电器
Ayepow Wireless Charging Station

该产品应用最新 Qi 无线充电技术，全球首创带无线充电功能的家用充电站。可同时给五部电子设备充电，极大提升家庭充电效率。充电的同时，有效美观地收纳，避免杂乱的充电桌面。产品通过欧盟 Rohs、REACH 认证，全部采用可回收材料。在生产过程中杜绝使用电镀、氧化、喷漆等工艺，避免了化学污染。外形模拟大自然，把自然景致融于家居电子产品。

Equipped with latest Qi wireless charging function, the product is the first charging station with e wireless charging function. It could charge 5 devices in same time, improving the charging efficiency greatly in family and organize your messy table. Product has passed European Rohs, REACH certification, and is made of re-cycle materials. During the production process, any craft like electroplating, oxidation, painting is prohibited to avoid chemical pollution. The appearance looks like hills and mountains, combined with a gentle color. Makes it close to nature and a nice decoration for your room.

设计
DESIGN

深圳亮明月设计有限公司
IU+ Design Co.,Ltd.

生产
MANUFACTURE

深圳市荣卓电子有限公司
Excel World International (Shenzhen) limited

暴风人工智能电视
65X5 ECHO

65X5 ECHO 是业内首款人工智能电视，采用远讲语音技术，四路阵列麦克风线性排列，实现人声远场识别。产品声音单元运用“回音壁”设计，能够有效地改善声音效果。全金属机身与主芯片可插拔设计延长了产品生命周期，降低了用户的使用成本。全新的用户体验，给用户提供全新的人工智能家庭生活方式。外观简约，精致内敛。

65X5 ECHO, is first artificial intelligence TV, using remote voice technology and 4 array array microphone linear arrangement to achieve remote recognition of human voice. Product sound unit using "echo wall" design, can effectively improve the sound effect. The main chip system can is with pluggable design to extend the product life cycle and reduce users' cost. To provide users with the latest experience, to provide users with a new artificial intelligence family lifestyle. It has simple appearance and is exquisite and restrained.

设计
DESIGN

暴风设计团队
Baofeng Design

生产
MANUFACTURE

深圳暴风统帅科技有限公司
Shenzhen Baofeng Leader Technology Co.,Ltd.

佑美 Q1 跑步机
Umay Q1

佑美 Q1 以当下的智能科技化为理念，外观抛弃操作台与主干的穿插关系，以一个简洁干练的曲线将各部件勾勒在一起，使产品更整体。将个性功能与 APP 相连进行设置，以定制符合不同人的运动计划。产品的可折叠功能符合现在“小空间高利用”的概念。 产品底部侧面融入了跑道轨道圆的特点，加强产品本身“刚中带柔，柔中带刚”的特点。

UMAY Q1 takes intelligent technologically as concept. The appearance of Q1 abandons the relation between the header and the trunk, and outlines the parts with a simple and efficient curve,so that the whole product is more integrated. This product matches personal function settings with app to make plans for different people. The folding function of the product conforms to the concept of "small space and high utilization". The bottom of the product fits into the feature of the track circle, which can strengthen the feature of the product itself " solidness in softness, and softness in solidness".

设计 DESIGN
浙江荣顺科技有限公司
Zhejiang Rongshun Techonlogy Co.,Ltd.

杭州热浪工业产品设计有限公司
Hangzhou Hotdesign Co.,Ltd.
生产 MANUFACTURE

尚酷智能保险柜
Shangku Intelligent Safe

尚酷是一款为现代家居而打造的时尚、科技型保险柜，融合了智能技术远程 APP 开启并实现远程报警功能，门板采用无把手设计方式，只需触摸表面的数字按键，通过双重密码解锁，门板便可以自动弹开，确保了保险柜安全的同时，使其操作更加方便、简易。保险柜箱体通过精良的金属加工工艺，展现了产品的高品质和现代感。

Shangku is a fashionable, technology safe which building for modern household. At the same time, it integrates intelligent technology, remote APP and remote alarm function. The door panel adopts no handle design, it can be opened by digital password and the door panel automatically open by dual password. It ensures the safety of the safe, at the same time, makes the operation more convenient and simple. The cabinet of the safe box is made of fine metal processing technology, which shows the high quality and modern feeling of the product.

设计 DESIGN
宁波永发智能安防科技有限公司
Ningbo Yongfa Intulligent Security Technology Co.,Ltd.

宁波市艺佳意工业设计有限公司
Ningbo 1and1 Industrial Design Co.,Ltd.
生产 MANUFACTURE

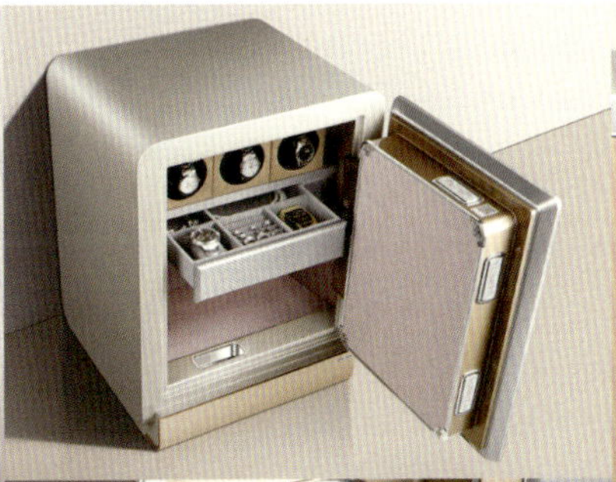

云音云锦蓝牙音箱
Cloud Sound Bluetooth Audio

产品利用传统的云锦材料作为蓝牙音箱的蒙布，是对非物质文化遗产的创新性使用。云锦采用古法编织，且用料讲究，编织紧密很好地过滤了杂音，是听觉与视觉的双重享受。云音蓝牙音箱的支架形成一个画框，创造属于自己的云音画境。采用传统非物质文化遗产云锦作为音箱蒙布是传统与现代的结合，产品采用环保材料制作。

The product uses cloud brocade as the cloth of the speaker , which is a creative use of the intangible cultural heritage. Cloud brocade is based on ancient weft-weaving techniques with dedicate materials. Because the weaving is very close, so the effect of filtering noise is very good.It is the dual enjoyment of hearing and sight. The stent of Cloud Sound Bluetooth Audio forms a frame to create their own cloud sound painting. Using cloud cloth-the traditional intangible cultural heritage as the speaker cover is the combination of traditional and modern. The product is made by the environmental protection material.

设计
DESIGN

马涛
Ma Tao

江苏汇鸿国际集团中鼎控股股份有限公司
High Hope Zhongding Corporation

生产
MANUFACTURE

PTC 暖风机系列
Series PTC Tower Haater

该产品采用新的发热出风平台，改变传统暖风机横向出风方式，竖向出风使送风距离更长。使用新结构，解决了贯流风产生的噪声问题，完成了显示屏幕由平到曲的转变 。采用系列化设计，满足了不同场所的取暖需求。可拆卸滤网，方便清洁。冷暖两用，实现冬夏两季交替使用。暖风机整体造型简洁大方，具有科技感。

The product adopts a new warm air platform to change the horizontal wind pattern of traditional fan and the vertical air makes air have a more long distance.Using the new structure, we solve the noise problem generated by the cross-flow fan. The display screen is changed from flatness to curve. By use of serial design, it meets the heating demand in different places . The filter screen is removable to facilitate the user cleaning. With cold and warm dual-use, achieve alternating use in the winter and summer season. The whole appearance is simple, having scientific and technological sense.

设计
DESIGN

孟一郎
Meng Yilang

广东美的环境电器制造有限公司
GD Midea Environment Appliances MFG. Co.,Ltd.

生产
MANUFACTURE

便携式咖啡机
Portable Coffee Machine

产品独有微电脑控制技术结合精密压力泵，标准的 15BAR 意式咖啡压力，一键操作按钮，精确萃取出咖啡油脂。用户可以随时随地享受香浓油脂的咖啡。整体保温杯大小，便于携带。分体式设计，便于拆装清洗。独特的结构设计，满足使用咖啡粉和胶囊的不同需求。产品分为内置电池版和充电宝取电版，外观设计简洁，让用户可以轻松操作，让咖啡制作变得轻而易举。

The machine adopts microcomputer control technology combined with precision pressure pump. The pressure of the machine is the standard 15BAR Italian coffee pressure. Users need only one click operation to extract coffee fat accurately. Users can easily enjoy a cup of fragrant coffee at anytime and anywhere. The overall size is similar to the thermos cup, so it is easy to carry. It is a detachable design for easy disassembly and cleaning. The inner structure is designed to satisfy the use of coffee powder and capsules. The product has built-in battery version and external mobile power version with simple appearance design for user to easily operate and coffee making easy.

设计
DESIGN
杭州九合形物工业设计有限公司
Hangzhou Johe Design Co.,Ltd.

生产
MANUFACTURE
慈溪欧能电器有限公司
Cixi Owner Electrical Appliance Co.,Ltd.

多功能电动刷
Multi-Function Electric Brush for Kitchen and Washroom

该产品是一款针对中老年使用者的无线充电卫浴清洁产品，具有可直观的透明视窗清洗液，可快速去垢；辅助照明的 LED 灯使死角无处可逃；多种刷头的更换可以应对不同的使用环境；头部的软胶材质避免磨损等实用功能。产品采用独特的安全防水材料，包胶件、透明件与 ABS 材料相结合，增加产品层次感。简洁流畅的线条使用户体验更加良好。

This product is a wireless charging bathroom cleaning product designed for middle-age and the elders. The transparent plastic parts at the handle is designed for checking leaner level. The LED light under the electric motor is designed for cleaning dark corner. The brush is able to be used for many situation because of the switchable brush head. Also, the brush head is made by soft rubber what is hard to abrasion. Rubber, transparent parts and ABS material adds level sense to the product. The comfort visual feeling is displayed by the simple and smooth outline, offering a better using experience.

设计
DESIGN
苏州轩昂工业设计有限公司
Suzhou Superdesign Industrial Design Co.,Ltd.

生产
MANUFACTURE
苏州科比电器有限公司
Suzhou kvc Electric Co.,Ltd.

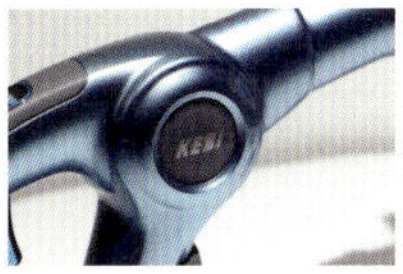

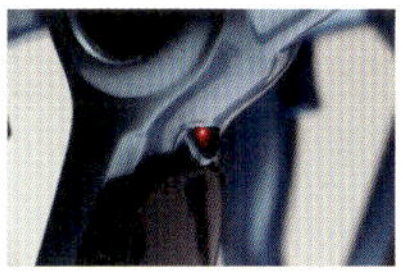
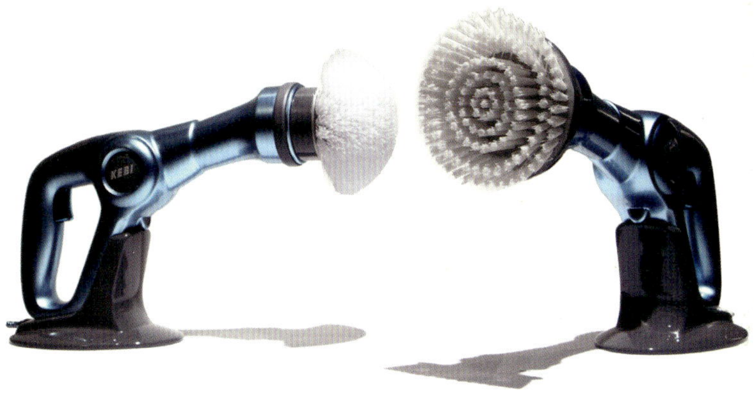

坚果 R1 遥控器
JmGo R1 Remote Control

坚果 R1 无线遥控器使用独特设计语言，机身两端以弧形收边处理，背部使用符合人体工程学的曲面后壳，加上机身表面亲肤的磨砂材质，让产品拥有良好的握感。环形五向导航键是坚果 R1 最为突出的设计符号，它使用金属作为导航键材料，在视觉效果、按键寿命、操控稳定性上，都取得了很好的平衡；搭载深度睡眠智能省电方案，延长使用时间。

JmGO R1 wireless remote control adopts unique design language. Curved edge and surface conforms with ergonomics, with the addition of dull polish, all these are for ease and comfort grip of JmGO R1 wireless remote control. The ring shaped five-dimensional navigation button is the most outstanding design symbol. It uses metal as button material and achieves a good balance in terms of visual effect, button lifespan and reliable performance. With deep sleep power-saving solution, the using time is prolonged.

设计
DESIGN
深圳市火乐科技发展有限公司
Shenzhen Holatek Co.,Ltd.

生产
MANUFACTURE
深圳市火乐科技发展有限公司
Shenzhen Holatek Co.,Ltd.

坚果 S1 激光电视
JmGo S1 Laser Television

坚果 S1 是火乐科技首款激光超短焦投影产品，为消费者提供了极佳的影音高保真体验。 S1 取材于东方文化元素，以“锦鲤成双”为意境创作，将“影”与“音”这两大部分巧妙地融合于一体，营造出剧场般的体验。产品使用符合 RoHS 标准的零部件制造，产品包装采用可回收材料。产品外观体现了“刚柔并济”的深刻哲学内涵，将对称的设计美学体现得淋漓尽致。

JmGO S1 is the first ultra-short throw projector produced by Holatek. It brings excellent visual-audio Hi-Fi experiences to users. The design inspiration of JMGO S1 comes from oriental cultural elements. The shape of "Double Fishes" means good things always come in pairs. It's a perfect combination of "visual" and "audio", which creates a cinematic-viewing experience.JmGO S1 adopts parts and accessories which are accord with ROHS standard. The product packaging is made of recyclable material. It reflects symmetrical design incisively and vividly.

设计 DESIGN
深圳市火乐科技发展有限公司
Shenzhen Holatek Co.,Ltd.

生产 MANUFACTURE
深圳市火乐科技发展有限公司
Shenzhen Holatek Co.,Ltd.

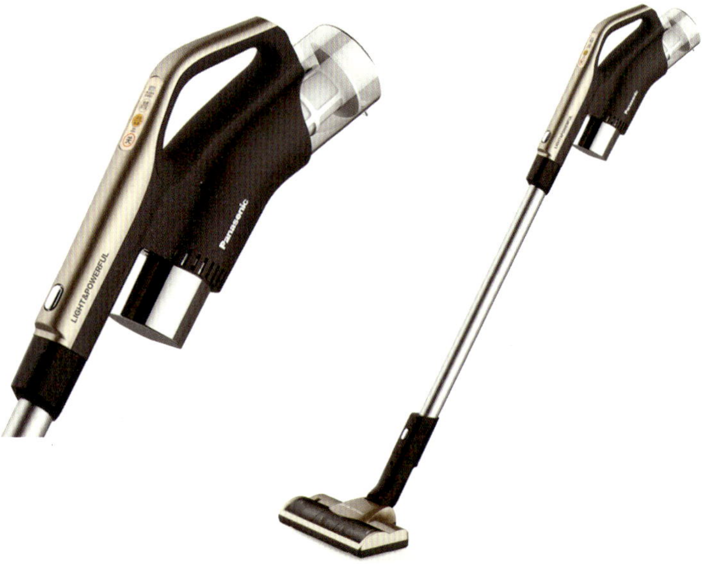

松下充电式无线手持吸尘器
Panasonic's Rechargeable Wireless Hand-Held Vacuum Cleaner

该产品为一款手持式无线吸尘器，采用科学的功能配件组合，实现家庭空间立体清扫。一台设备完成地面、墙面、沙发、桌面、床褥至墙面天花板的清扫。使用松下研发的轻型塑料以减少产品的重量，用新型表面涂装工艺替换有环境污染的电镀工艺。整体机身只有 0.99 千克，小巧精致，是当前市面上最轻的手持式无线吸尘器。

The product is a wireless hand-held vacuum cleaner. The body layout is very reasonable combination of all components to realize the three-dimensional cleaning of the family space. A device is able to complete the floor, wall, sofa, desktop, mattress and even the ceiling of the wall cleaning. Products using Panasonic developed lightweight plastic to reduce the weight of the product, with a new surface coating process to replace the more environmentally polluted plating process. The whole product is small and delicate, there is no redundant body, the overall body is only 0.99kg, is currently the lightest wireless hand-held vacuum cleaner.

设计 DESIGN
杭州汉度工业设计有限公司
Hangzhou HANDO Industrial Design Co.,Ltd.

生产 MANUFACTURE
松下电器（中国）有限公司
Panasonic Corporation of China

JBL Free 真无线入耳式耳机
JBL Free

JBL Free 是一款无线入耳式耳机。不受线缆束缚，易于使用，是通话、音乐以及积极健康生活方式的理想伴侣。产品采用省电设计，在不使用时会自动关闭设备。其防水设计能够确保在任何情况下都能正常播放音乐。充电盒的半透明盒顶不仅为耳塞提供了保护，同时支持内部 LED 指示灯闪烁光透过盒顶，为用户和产品之间创建了连接。

JBL Free is a truly wireless in-ear headphone. It is completely free from wires and easy to use. The JBL Free is your ideal companion for calls, music and an active lifestyle. It adopts the power-saving design to automatically power the unit off when not in use. Waterproof design keeps the music playing in any situation. The charging case's semi-translucent top not only offers protection to the earbuds, but it also allows the LED indicators to shine through from the inside, creating connection between the user and the product.

设计 DESIGN
哈曼设计团队
Harman Design Center

生产 MANUFACTURE
哈曼国际
Harman International Industries

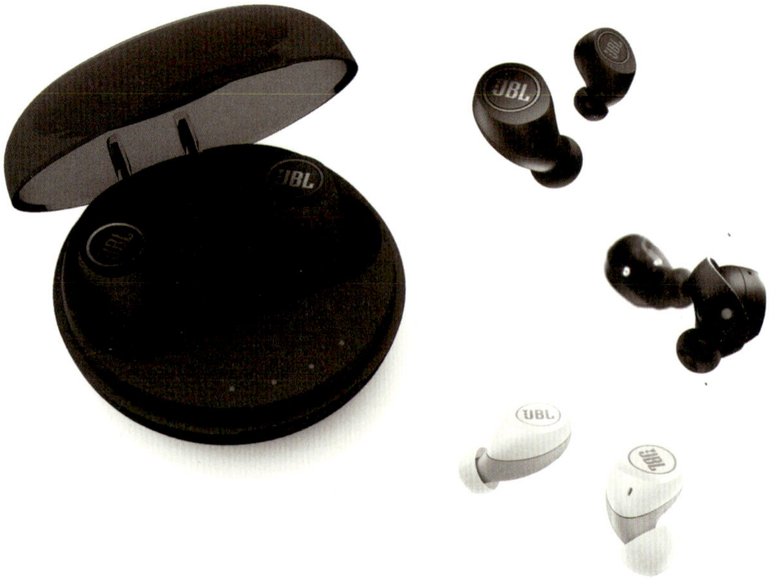

JBL Soundgear 可穿戴式微型无线音箱
JBL Soundgear

该产品为一款蓝牙耳机。通过四个喇叭单元和低音增强技术，为使用者提供长达六小时的听觉体验。一次充电仅需两小时。双麦克风会议系统和回音消除技术保障了语音通话效果。耳机采用人体工学造型，可轻轻放置在肩上，其内部弹性结构可适应各种体型，内部部件采用编制纤维制成，可为您带来舒适的听觉体验。

The product is a Bluetooth headphone. It features Quad transducers with Bass Boost for an exciting sound experience and 6 hours of playback time, with a quick recharge time of 2 hours. Thanks to its dual mic conferencing system with echo-cancelling technology it provides crystal clear phone calls . The headphone are ergonomically designed with ergonomic shape that leans gently on your shoulder, inner elastic construction that adapts to all sizes and soft-touch fabric finish of the internal parts to create an unbelievably comfortable audio experience.

设计
DESIGN
哈曼设计团队
Harman Design Center

生产
MANUFACTURE
哈曼国际
Harman International Industries

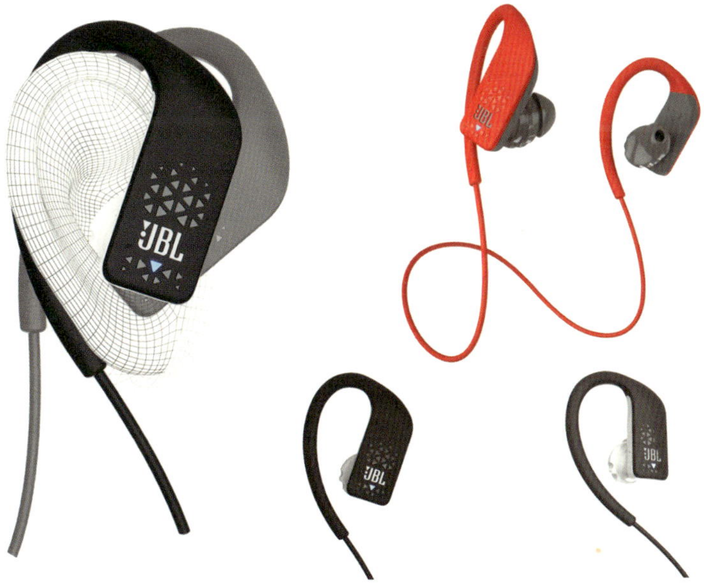

JBL Grip 500 无线入耳式运动耳机
JBL Grip 500

该款运动耳机采用触控设计，可提供长达八小时的无线蓝牙播放，通过耳机上的触控件可控制播放，是市场上技术较先进的蓝牙入耳式耳机。耳钩采用软质热塑性弹性体材料制成，耳塞采用医用硅胶制成，舒适持久。无论参加何种运动，这款耳机安全的技术和舒适贴合的材料都能令使用者感受到绝佳的声音享受和人体工学体验。

The headphones adopts innovative touch control, with a very competitive 8 hours of wireless Bluetooth playback and touch controls on the ear housing for convenient music management. They are the most technologically advanced Bluetooth in-ear headphone in the market. The ear hook is crafted using soft TPE to ensure long lasting comfort, with medical grade silicon making the ear tips that guarantee never to fall out. The JBL Grip 500 is designed for a comfortable and secure fit, using JBL's patented TwistLock technology and ergonomic ear tips that are guaranteed never to hurt or fall out. The safe technology and comfortable fitting material of the headphone provides users a great feel for sound enjoyment and ergonomic experience.

设计
DESIGN
哈曼设计团队
Harman Design Center

生产
MANUFACTURE
哈曼国际
Harman International Industries

美菱宅·酷单门冰箱
Meiling Z. Cube Refrigerator

此款单开门冰箱搭载 10.1 寸智能大屏，内置虚拟表情，在使用冰箱时通过屏幕显示的表情将产品拟人化，与用户产生情感交流。该产品除了制冷的基本属性，考虑到用户对食品温度的需求，在顶部平台区域设置热碟区间，缩短放置在冷藏内的食品温度到最佳口感温度的时间。产品内饰部分应用木质材料，减少因为化工作业对环境带来的污染。同时大量使用可回收的材料，保证资源的重复利用。

The cube refrigerator, equipped with 10.1-inch smart screen, built-in virtual expression, personates the product through the expression displayed on the screen in the usage of the refrigerator, which generates emotional communication with users. In addition to the basic properties of the cooling, the product sets the hot dish interval in the top platform area to shorten the time of the food temperature placed in the refrigerator to the optimum taste temperature. Interior part of the product uses wood materials to reduce the environ ment pollution caused by the chemical industry. While the extensive use of recyclable materials ensures the re-use of resources.

设计
DESIGN

合肥美菱股份有限公司
Hefei Meiling Co.,Ltd.

四川虹微技术有限公司、合肥美菱股份有限公司
Homwee Technology (Sichuan) Co.,Ltd., Hefei Meiling Co.,Ltd.

生产
MANUFACTURE

电脑手绘板
Computer Hand Drawing Board

该产品是一款配合电脑使用的手绘板，针对各个行业的设计目标人群进行了深度研究，经过大数据的分析，重新规划整个电子方案，全新定义按键功能及布局，同时考究不同材质的触摸手感，打破市面上同类产品长宽比例设计。全新定义后的按键功能及布局，为用户带来非凡的使用体验。极简的设计风格，最大程度兼顾了各类设计人士的要求，方便携带，彰显个性。

In order to bring a wonderful use experience to users, we conducted a deep study of hundreds of persons in target groups in each industry, carefully observed their use status, and communicated with them in-depth to tap their potential needs and dissatisfactions. We even simulated the user's feelings and moods when every finger jumps or slides on the board. With a large data analysis, we are determined to make innovation and re-plan the entire electronic program, key functions and layout, and study touches of different materials and so on. Thus, this hand drawing board was born. The minimalist design style takes utmost account of stringent aesthetic requirements of all kinds of designers. It is easy to carry and can be used to highlight the owner's personality.

设计
DESIGN

深圳市绘王动漫科技有限公司
Shenzhen Huion Animation Technology Co.,Ltd.

深圳市问鼎工业设计有限公司
Shenzhen Wing-id Co.,Ltd.

生产
MANUFACTURE

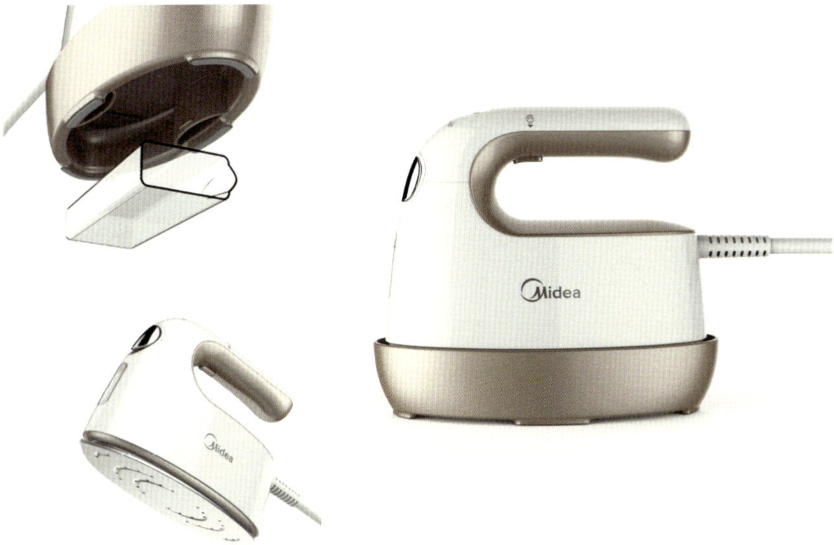

“小幸熨”迷你蒸汽挂烫电熨斗
"Little Fortune Iron" – A Mini Steam Hanging Iron

该产品为一款蒸汽挂烫电熨斗，此产品采用开放式把手设计和一体式底座设计，安全可靠。可平烫也可挂烫，平烫塑形，挂烫除皱，不同衣物都能搞定。高挡位蒸汽轻松除味。外型小巧使熨烫衣物更轻松，同时也便于携带，对于商旅人士来说，成功解决了携带衣物不能及时熨烫的烦恼。在材料上使用工艺成熟污染较少的注塑工艺，搭配防火和耐高温材料，提升安全性。

The product is a steam hanging iron. It adopts open type handle design and Integral base design, which is safe and reliable. Both flat ironing and hanging ironing can be done. The flat ironing is to form a shape and hanging ironing is to remove wrinkles. The different clothing can easily get good ironing. It can remove peculiar smell of coat or sweater smell easily. The small mini-shape iron stands out in the many iron products, so ironing clothes is easier; meanwhile, the small size is also easy to carry. For business travelers, the trouble that the clothes can not be timely ironed is solved successfully. The material of this product is made by the most mature and less pollution injection molding process, plus fireproof and high temperature materials so that the safety has greatly improved.

设计 DESIGN 广东美的环境电器制造有限公司 GD Midea Environment Appliances MFG.Co., Ltd.

孟一郎 Meng Yilang **生产 MANUFACTURE**

RO 智能净饮机
RO Smart Water Purifier

该款净饮机针对日益提高的饮水安全标准，满足增加矿物质或调节 pH 酸碱度等个性化饮水需求。集净化、加热、制冷于一体，既满足用户对健康的追求，又满足一机多用的需求，节省空间。此产品在直接接触水源的部件上采用食用级材料，防止供水的二次污染；并解决了原水耗费过多、净水效果差等问题，为用户提供了健康、安全的饮水环境，开创了直饮净水的新时代。

By aiming at increasingly high drinking water safety standards, the smart water purifier meets individualized drinking water demands, such as increase minerals or adjust pH value. It integrates with purification, heating and cooling. It not only meets users' pursuit for health, but also satisfies multiple purposes of a machine. It can save space. Parts that contact with water source directly are equipped with food-level materials to prevent from secondary pollution of water supply. It solved the problems of excessive consumption of raw water and poor water purification effect, providing users with a healthy and safe drinking water environment, and created a new era of straight drinking water purification.

设计 DESIGN 宁波轩畅电器有限公司 Ningbo Xuanchang Electric Appliance Co.,Ltd.

宁波明锐工业产品设计有限公司 Ningbo Meanew Industrial Design Co.,Ltd. **生产 MANUFACTURE**

V58 变频除湿机
V58 Frequency-Conversion Dehumidifier

该款除湿机采用变频技术，真正达到快速除湿、静音除湿、节能除湿的效果。三维立体出风将冷凝除湿后的空气快速均匀地送到房间不同角落。该产品拥有 30 升日除湿量，可以满足最大单间面积在 80 平方米左右的家庭除湿需求。高效且省电，仅 300 瓦的额定功率，运用空气动力学，保证在风力顺畅的基础上减少风阻产生的噪声。

The dehumidifier uses frequency conversion technology so that dehumidifier can achieve the effect of rapid dehumidification, quiet dehumidification and energy saving dehumidification. The three-dimensional air-out can rapidly and evenly send air which is congealed and dehumidified to different corners of the room. The product owns 30L of daily dehumidification amount and it can meet the dehumidification demands of the family with the area of 80 square meter. It is high-efficient and power saving and only needs 300W of rated power,on the basis of applying aerodynamics and ensuring smooth wind power, it can reduce noise generated by wind resistance.

设计 DESIGN 宁波德业日用电器科技有限公司 Ningbo Deye Electrical Appliance Tech.Co.,Ltd.

宁波明锐工业产品设计有限公司 Ningbo Meanew Industrial Design Co.,Ltd. **生产 MANUFACTURE**

凡帝罗法式四门冰箱 BCD-532WGPZV
Vandelo French-Style Four-door Refrigerator

该产品为一款四门冰箱，内部空间布局合理，独立多功能区，温湿度精确控制抽屉适应不同使用状态；弧形面光源配合动态杀菌状态呼吸灯，提供照明以及运行状态提示。平整的外观，U型切割的金属质感玻璃匹配家居环境；玻璃面的变温抽屉及控制面板带来良好的视觉感受，弧面光源的运用提升了内部照明的视觉体验。

The product is a four-door refrigerator with reasonable internal space layout, independent multi-functional area, sealing bin on the door and drawer whose temperature and humidity can be controlled precisely are suitable for different usage states; arc area source combined with breathing lamp that can kill germs dynamically can provide comfortable illumination and the emotionalized running status prompt.Flat appearance, U-shape cutting and metallic glasses match perfectly with living environment; heterothermic drawer with glass surface and control panel bring the simplest feeling of visual senses, the use of arched light source also greatly improves refined experience of interior decoration.

设计 DESIGN
合肥美的电冰箱有限公司
Hefei Midea Refrigerator Co.,Ltd.

美的冰箱工业设计中心
Midea Refrigerator Industrial Design Center
生产 MANUFACTURE

FOXEER BOX 运动相机
FOXEER BOX Action Camera

FOXEER BOX 运动相机，将世界先进的视频技术容于 4 厘米见方。便于人机交互的机身设计，操作简单，掌控一握之间。玻璃非球面镜头，超大广角，绝少畸变杂光，真实呈现世界之眼。金属与塑胶结合，刚柔并济，坚固耐用，足以应对复杂恶劣环境。裸机防水，镜片疏水处理，轻松应对日常防水，不让雨水成为记录的阻碍。多种配件，适应不同使用场景，无论何时何地，都可平稳流畅地拍摄 。

Foxeer Box action camera, contains the latest video technology in 4cm box. Convenient design for man-machine interface, easy to use and control. Glass Aspherical Lens,super wide FOV, rare distortion and stray light,show the real world. Combine metal with plastic, solid and durable enough to face the severe environment. Naked camera features waterproof, water repellent lens, deal with daily waterproof easily, never let rainwater block your recording. Various accessories can adapt to different usage scenario to make sure the record smooth and stunning video anytime and anywhere.

设计 DESIGN
深圳市鑫安泰视频技术有限公司
Shenzhen Xinantai Video Technology Co.,Ltd.

深圳市万有引力工业设计有限公司
SZ-Gravity Design Co.,Ltd.
生产 MANUFACTURE

游戏鼠标
Gaming Mouse

该产品是一款游戏鼠标，产品在各个环节都力求高品质，硬件配置得到全球顶级供应商支持；外部材质以耐用塑胶为主；USB 镀金、线材选型较粗且韧性适中。以高品质的用料来保障该产品的耐用性。以创新涡轮调节系统、专利的轴式按键、双滚轮支持功能及其他细节设计，提供用户优越的手感和体验。成为 2016 年初行业类的众筹明星产品。

The product is a gaming mouse, pursuing high quality in every link and hardware configuration has won the support from top suppliers in the world. The external materials are mainly consist of durable plastics ; USB is gold-plated, and wire rod is relatively rough of moderate tenacity. High-quality materials are applied to guarantee the product's durability. By virtue of the original turbine adjustment system, patented shaft-type button, D-wheel support function and other details design, it can present users with preferable handing feeling and experience. It has become a star-level product at the beginning of 2016.

设计 DESIGN
深圳富民微电子有限公司
Shenzhen Fmsemi Electronics Co.,Ltd.

深圳市问鼎工业设计有限公司
Shenzhen Wing-id Co.,Ltd.
生产 MANUFACTURE

N910 智能 POS 终端
N910 Smart POS Terminal

该产品是一款智能支付终端。该产品从内至外轻量化设计，去掉冗杂部件，优化升级内部部件，在扩大电池容量的同时保持了机身的纤细，简洁时尚的外观和强大的功能，减少了部件的开发费用。多样配件选用，满足各种不同的需求和使用场景。使用方式的多样化和功能的高集成化，满足一机多用，提升产品的使用频率。强大的硬件平台支持 APP 的开发与更新，延长机器使用寿命。

The product is lightweight designed from the outside to the inside with all unnecessary components removed. The inner parts were optimized and updated and the battery capacity was expanded, yet, at the same time, the slim body was successively maintained, resulting a thin and light device.Simple fashionable appearance and powerful function are developed with the lightweight design from the outside to the inside, reducing the development cost of components. Various accessories are selected to meet a variety of needs and usage scenarios. Diversification of usage and high integration of functions are all in one device to enhance the frequency of product use. Powerful hardware platform supports the development and update of APP, and extends the service life of the device.

设计
DESIGN

宏泰机电科技（漳州）有限公司
Kingtronics Corporation of Elec.&Mech.Techenology (Zhangzhou) Co.,Ltd.

福建新大陆支付技术有限公司
Fujian Newland Payment Techenology Co.,Ltd.

生产
MANUFACTURE

美型带线移动硬盘
Armor A62

此产品为一款移动硬盘，设计概念来自礼物盒，打破了市面上移动硬盘的带线方式，首创对角线材收纳设计，整合了硬盘和传输线，方便使用者一并携带。该产品通过美国军规防撞测试及高规格防水等级，提供全面的资料防护。采用高拉力硅胶材质，硅胶无毒无味、环保且有良好的延展性，耐热温度最高可达 220 摄氏度。

The product is a mobile hard disk and the design concept is from a gift box. It breaks the common cable-carry hard drives on the market, it is the first diagonal cable storage design with integrated hard drive and transmission lines.The convenient cable storage design makes the A62 user-friendly to carry around. In addition, A62 passed the United States MIL-STD-810G 516.7 Procedure IV (Transit drop test), a freefall test from the military, and earned a high standard IPX4 waterproof rating to provide users with a comprehensive data protection. The reason we chose to use silicone is because it is a non-toxic, environmental friendly material, which also provides good ductility with heat-resistant of temperatures up to 220°C.

设计
DESIGN

广颖电通股份有限公司
Silicon Power

蔡卉柔、许砚翔
Cai Huirou, Xu Yanxiang

生产
MANUFACTURE

看尚 iCAN 影院 P1 智能投影仪
iCAN P1 Smart Projector

该智能投影仪把书本信息概念和投影仪两个相近的概念结合，外观简约小巧，方便携带，整体金属机身，科技有质感。滑盖滑开即开机。该产品用途是手持式投影，适合小范围的画面投影。中框采用塑胶材质原色注塑，耐热耐摔，便于回收利用，可塑性高。上下金属件压铸折弯，表面喷砂阳极氧化，质感强烈。

This product combines the concept of the book information and projector, which are two similar concepts, the appearance is simple and compact, easy to carry, the overall metal body appears very high quality. Slide the slider to open the boot. The product is a hand-held projection, suitable for a small range of screen projection. Mullion uses plastic material ABS + PC, it is heat and drop resistance, easy recycling and of high plasticity. Up and down are made of metal parts, which are die-casting bending, surface sandblasting anodizing and of high quality.

设计 DESIGN
环球智达科技（北京）有限公司
Universal Wisdomtech.(Beijing) Co.,Ltd.

成都浪尖工业设计有限公司
Chengdu Artop Industrial Design Co.,Ltd.
生产 MANUFACTURE

液态金属笔
Liquid Metal Pen

此款液态金属笔可以在不同基底表面直接写出功能性电路，并实现即写即干的功能。体积小，使用便捷。该产品分成笔芯与笔杆，笔芯采用可替换方式，且笔芯内为液态金属，能保证使用者充分利用消耗材料，笔芯壳也可回收重新利用。产品使用整个过程中实现无浪费且高效。主要用于电子产品文化创意、电路设计的及时验证、教育培训等方面。电导率高，绿色环保。

The liquid metal pen can directly write functional circuit on the surface of different substrates, and it can write and dry at the same time. It is small in size and easy to use. The product is composed of penholder and cartridge. The cartridge is alternative and the inner part is liquid metal, which can guarantee the users to make full use of the material consumption, cartridge shell can also be recycled. The product is not wasteful and efficient in the whole using process. It is mainly used for cultural creativity of electronic products, timely verification of circuit design, education, training and so on. It has the feature of high electrical conductivity and environmental protection,

设计 DESIGN
云南中宣液态金属科技有限公司
Yunnan Yizhong Liquid Metal Technology Co.,Ltd.

深圳市白狐工业设计有限公司
Shenzhen Bifoxs Industrial Design Co.,Ltd.
生产 MANUFACTURE

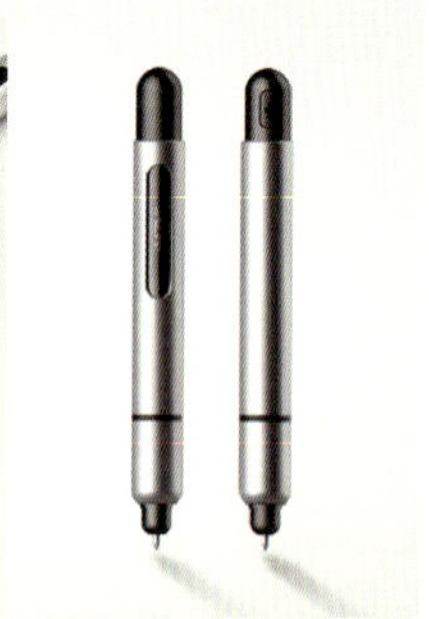

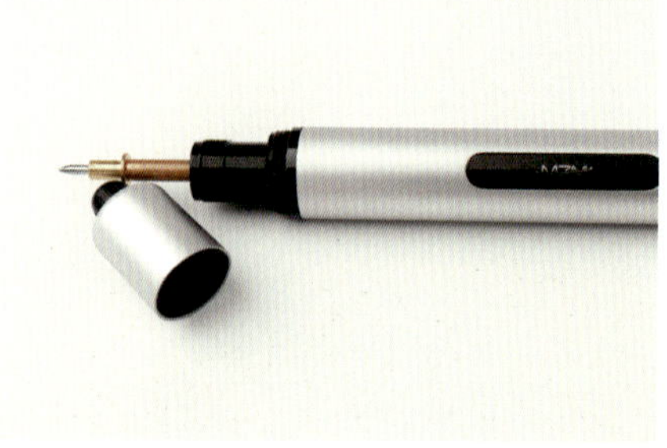

净能达空气净化机
Full Function Air Cleaner

该产品易于拆卸清洗的顶盖、方便更换滤网的双侧大开门以及磁吸式遥控器等细节解决了使用者在使用、清洗、维护、管理等诸多方面的顾虑。通过霍尼韦尔智能云平台，使用者可以手机远程连接以及维护。整机内部采用全金属框架，外壳应用高防火等级工程塑料，滤网采用独特的美国专利材料，双侧共六层大面积滤网，净化效果出众，效率高。

FFAC can clear up all the concerns users usually have during their using, cleaning, maintaining and managing of the product with thoughtful designs as detachable top cover, bilateral openning door that is easy for filter changing and magnet remote control.Through Honeywell's Intelligent Cloud Platform, users can easily connect and maintain FFAC from mobile phone everywhere remotely.The inner part of FFAC uses all-metal frame. The shell introduces high fire resistive engineering plastics. 6 layered full function filters made with specially designed US patented material make the final purification result outstanding and with high efficiency.

设计 DESIGN
张可、李海涛
Zhang Ke, Li Hailao

生产 MANUFACTURE
霍尼韦尔
Honeywell

WOW!dea 奇点 M PLUS 模块化多功能无线音响
WOW!dea M Plus Modular Wireless Speaker

该无线音响通过部件接口结构设计与特定功能组件，实现产品功能模块化。使用者可进行部件组合操作，可将该产品用作无线音响、户外照明灯具、移动电源甚至由更多可扩展模块部件所实现的多样化功能。通过共享主机所内置电池、无线连接等功能，使使用者无须携带更多类似设备，减轻旅途负担。

WOW!dea M PLUS Modular Wireless Speaker achieves modular functionality through an innovative interface and docking design and specific functional components. The user may choose and replace components freely to realize the product's versatility. With some simple combinations, the user can turn the product into a mono or stereo wireless speaker, a camp light, a mobile power pack or even a different device with more expansion modules. By integrating the functions of power pack and wireless connection, the user does not need to take other devices of similar functionalities, thus reducing the weight of luggage for trave.

设计 DESIGN
北京元隆雅图文化传播股份有限公司
Beijing Yuanlong Yato Culture Dissemination Co.,Ltd.

生产 MANUFACTURE
北京元隆雅图文化传播股份有限公司
Beijing Yuanlong Yato Culture Dissemination Co.,Ltd.

CHiQ Q5S 系列电视
CHiQ Q5S TV

该系列电视采用目前最先进的面板技术，屏幕厚度仅有 4 毫米，与家居环境相融合。主机采用超薄设计；使用简单，通过墙上两个卡扣，可将屏幕挂到墙上。主机直接摆放在桌面上，屏幕和主机只需要一根线连接。安装和拆卸都非常方便和快捷。Q5S 系列在工艺材料的选取上以金属为主，搭配可回收工程塑料。同时在设计上充分利用空间，将产品材料减到最少。

CHiQ Q5S adopts the most advanced panel technology, the thickness of the screen is only 4mm, it integrates perfectly with the home environment. The innovative slim design of the host makes the usage of TV simple. The screens can be easily added on the wall through the two thin buckle on the wall. Host directly display on the desktop, and only need a line to connect with the screen. Installation and removal are very easy and fast.Q5S series are metal-oriented and added with recycled plastic in terms of the materials. The design makes full use of space and minimize the material.

设计 DESIGN
四川虹微技术有限公司、合肥长虹实业有限公司
Homwee Technology (Sichuan) Co.,Ltd., Hefei Changhong Industry Co.,Ltd.

生产 MANUFACTURE
合肥长虹实业有限公司
Hefei Changhong Industry Co.,Ltd.

无线自组网通信设备
Wireless AD-Hoc Communication Device

自组网设备是具有自主知识产权的区域无线宽带传输系统。适用于各种复杂及恶劣环境条件下临时快速组网，远距离、大宽带无线通信应用，是专网通信、应急通讯、区域性监视监控的重要支撑条件。该自组网设备环境适应性强，覆盖范围广，组网灵活，无中心多跳网络，支持快速组网以及大规模组网能力以及多任务能力等多个特点。

Autonomous network equipment is a regional wireless broadband transmission system with independent intellectual property rights. It is suitable for temporary and fast network within complex and harsh environmental conditions. Long distance, large broadband wireless communications applications is the important supporting conditions for a private network communications, emergency communications and regional monitoring.The autonomous network equipment is of strong environmental adaptability, covering a wide range of plains, flexible in network, no center multi-hop network, supporting rapid networking and large-scale networking capabilities and has multi-task ability.

设计 DESIGN
成都奥特为通讯有限公司
Chengdu OTT for Communications Co.,Ltd.

成都浪尖工业设计有限公司
Chengdu Artop Industrial Design Co.,Ltd.
生产 MANUFACTURE

Netvue Belle 人工智能门铃
Netvue Belle

该产品是一款人工智能门铃。设备只要连接网络，用户就能随时通过终端了解家门口发生的一切。该产品采用无铅环保工艺，外壳和结构件采用可回收塑胶材料和环保烤漆表面工艺，二次电池采用锂离子电池；产品结构的固定采用螺丝连接的可拆解设计，方便废弃后的拆解回收再利用和处理。高级别防水防尘设计，外壳加喷抗 UV、抗大气腐蚀的涂层，经久耐用。

Netvue Bell is an artificial intelligent doorbell, as long as the device is connected to the network, the user can always know what happened at the gate through the terminal. The product adopts lead-free environmental protection process. The shell and structure uses recyclable plastic materials and environmentally friendly paint, uses lithium-ion battery as the secondary battery; the product fixation uses removable screw, which is convenient for dismantling, recycling, reusing and disposal of waste. It is designed with high grade waterproof and dustproof. Shell is made with ABS + PC plastic, and is coated with anti-UV, anti-atmospheric corrosion paint. It is tested under a variety of extreme environment situation and could be used durably.

设计 DESIGN
深圳市天和荣科技有限公司
Netvue Technologies Co.,Ltd.

深圳市天和荣科技有限公司
Netvue Technologies Co.,Ltd.
生产 MANUFACTURE

HQ5 电热水器
HQ5 Electric Water Heater

该产品是一款具有智能自动清洁内胆的电热水器，定期对电热水器内胆进行自动清洗，从而保证内胆清洁干净带来洁净的热水、快速加热，减少热水加热等待时间，同时大热水量能满足多个人洗浴用水需求。特有的安全技术，给使用者带来更安全的沐浴体验。该产品采用环保保温材料，减少热水器热量散失，同时整机采用可回收材料。

It is a type of electric water heater with the function of intelligent and automatic cleaning of the inner tank. The regular automatic cleaning brings clean hot water by keeping the inner tank clean. The fast heating reduces the waiting time for water heating, while the big volume satisfies multiple persons' needs for taking the shower; The exclusive safety technology brings users with a safer shower experience. The environmentally friendly thermal insulation materials reduce the heat loss of the heater, and the entire device is made of recyclable materials.

设计 DESIGN
美的集团热水器事业部
Midea Group Water Heater Appliances

美的集团热水器事业部工业设计部
Industrial Design Center of Midea Group Water Heater Appliances
生产 MANUFACTURE

智能净化系统
A-box

此产品是全球第一台光触酶空气净化器，有效地解决了室内空气的净化问题，较彻底地吸收了室内的有害物质。光触酶能吸附空气中的甲醛、苯、有机溶剂等有害物质，并将其转化为二氧化碳和水，能做到真正持续高效净化空气。内置灯光、音响、投影设备，改变环境氛围，从而做到整体优化生活空间。在 2017 上海国际消费电子展（CES）上展出，引起了广泛的关注。

This product is the world's first photocatalyst air purifier, it solves the problem of indoor air purificationan effectively and absorbs indoor harmful substances thoroughly. Light touch enzyme can absorb the harmful material in air such as formaldehyde, benzene and solvents, then transformes them into carbon dioxide and water, which can achieve sustainable and efficient purification of air . Built-in light, stereo and projection equipment change the environment atmosphere to achieve the overall optimization of living space. In 2017 Shanghai CES exhibition,it gained wide attention.

设计
DESIGN

杭州亿智智能科技有限公司
Hangzhou YSAE Design

杭州亿智智能科技有限公司
Hangzhou YSAE Design

生产
MANUFACTURE

MINI 声波洁面仪
Perfectclean MINI Sonic Facial Cleansing Device

该产品是一款便携洁面仪。以声波震动技术为基础，高频率振动技术可以更有效地清洁肌肤，达到远胜传统面部清洁方式的效果，且比旋转式洁面仪更加柔和。可深层清洁肌肤同时不伤害皮肤的天然结构，给用户带来更安全高效的清洁体验。可换刷头设计针对不同肌肤类型实现精细护理，标配刷头拥有超过 35000 根纤柔刷毛，细密柔软，触感极其柔和。

PerfectClean Mini Sonic Facial Cleansing Device is a portable design, based on the CosBeauty's patented sonic vibration technology. Soft high-frequency vibration technology is able to clean the skin more effectively, achieving far better results than the traditional facial cleansing method, and operating more gently than a simple rotating cleansing device. The product deeply cleanses the skin without irritating the skin's natural structure, thus offering the users with a safer and more efficient cleaning experience. The interchangeable brush heads have been designed for different types of skin to achieve the finest care, especially the standard brush head, which has more than 35000 soft fiber bristles, providing the softest and most gentle touch.

设计
DESIGN

深圳可思美科技有限公司
Shenzhen Cosbeauty Technology Co.,Ltd.

深圳可思美科技有限公司
Shenzhen Cosbeauty Technology Co.,Ltd.

生产
MANUFACTURE

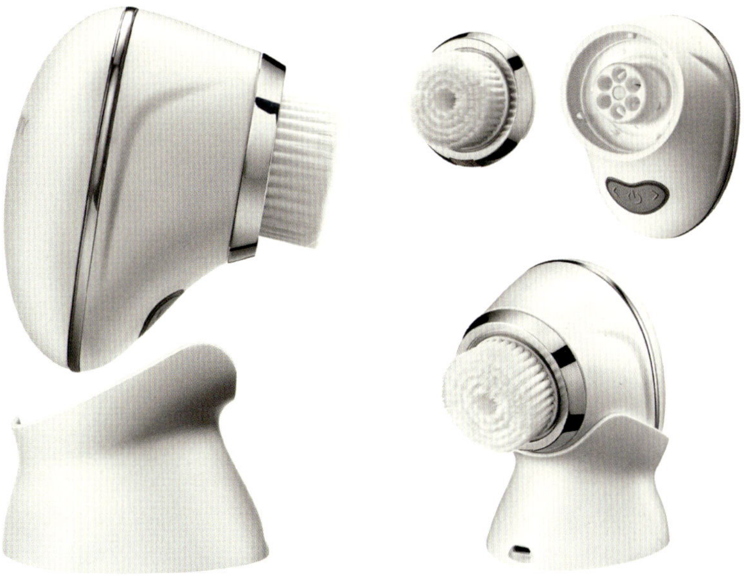

燃气热水壁挂炉 / 冷凝炉
Gas Hot Water Wall Hanging Boiler/Condensing Furnace

该产品是一款燃气热水壁挂炉，通过炉膛结构优化设计，燃烧时空气和燃气的配比更优，降低烟温热量损失，有效提高机组能效，支持自定义节能模式，用户可以自主控制采暖需求。机身采用钣金加工，一体成型，节约成本。机身采用了钣金大圆角设计，突破了工艺难点。视觉上变得圆润，更适合融入家居环境。表面质感钣金喷粉工艺，让外观更加简约，易于清洁打理。

The product is a gas hot water wall hanging boiler, the ratio of the air and gas is more optimized during combustion through the optimization design of the furnace structure, it reduces excessive flue gas emissions, reduces smoke temperature and heat loss, and effectively improves unit energy efficiency, it support custom energy saving mode, users can control heating demand independently. The body uses a sheet metal large fillet design, which breaks through the difficulties of the process.It looks mellower and smoother form the visual perspective, and more suitable for integrating the household effect.The sheet metal powder injection process makes the appearance simpler and easy to clean.

设计 DESIGN
珠海格力电器股份有限公司
Gree Electric Appliances,Inc.of Zhuhai

生产 MANUFACTURE
珠海格力电器股份有限公司
Gree Electric Appliances,Inc.of Zhuhai

万家乐 X7 家用中央热水燃气热水器
Macro X7 Domestic Center Hot Water Gas Water Heater

该产品依靠其自主研发的“东方恒热芯”系统，突破行业瓶颈，无须布管，不改装修，WiFi 控制，远程预约，全屋热水，即开即来。实现全屋所有用水点在打开水阀瞬间，带来即开即热的高品质热水生活体验。该产品面板采用珠光珍珠白覆膜板材料，相比其他的烤漆面板而言，工艺先进，效果卓越，沉稳大气。2016 年 6 月上市至今销售达到 6000 余台。

Macro X7 relies on its independent-developed oriental heatwave technology, this system breaks through the industry bottleneck, need not stringing pipe and does not change interior decoration. wherever you stay you can control your gas water heater by wifi and enjoy hot water any time you want. It brings the life experience that all water points in the house can provide instant heat water at the moment of turning on the water valve. Macro X7 center hot water gas water heater select pearl white film faced plywood, it is more advanced and outstanding compared with other baking panel. It was listed in june, 2016, Until now, Macro X7 gas water heater have already sold more than 6000.

设计 DESIGN
广东万家乐燃气具有限公司
Guangdong Macro Gas Appliance Co.,Ltd.

生产 MANUFACTURE
广东顺德东方麦田工业设计有限公司
East-Innovation Shunde GD Co.,Ltd.

万家乐“mate3 智联烟灶锅”烹饪套装
Macro mate3 Smart Cooking Appliance Suit

该款烹饪套装通过物联网技术将厨房的吸油烟机、炒锅及燃气灶具进行智能联动，利用设置于炒锅锅柄上的“智能烹饪系统”，无线控制烟机风力和灶具火力，实现各个厨具无线感应联动。该产品中的燃气灶搭载了双高火科技燃烧技术的新一代精控燃气比例阀，指尖轻划可实现多挡火力精调。其锅具采用不锈钢材质，表面不粘锅涂层，三层复合锅底，速热更耐用。

The cuisine set intelligently combines range hood, pot and gas cooker through networking technology, the wireless sensor linkage between each kitchen is achieved by wireless control of hood wind power and cooker firepower with the help of "intelligent cooking system" designed on the handle of the frying pan. The gas cooker in this product is equipped with a new generation of high burning technology, combustion technology, a new generation of precision control gas proportional valve, fingertip light stroke can achieve multi file firepower fine tune. The pot is made of stainless steel, the surface is nonstick and the pot is coated with three layers of compound bottom. The heat is faster and more durable.

设计 DESIGN
广东顺德东方麦田工业设计有限公司
East-Innovation Shunde GD Co.,Ltd.

生产 MANUFACTURE
广东万家乐燃气具有限公司
Guangdong Macro Gas Appliance Co.,Ltd.

联想 ThinkVision P27q 显示器
Lenovo ThinkVision P27q Monitor

该款显示器采用超高清显示屏，窄边框设计，全功能支架可升降、旋转和倾斜，调整更佳欣赏角度。设计理念 力求从干净简洁的几何形状创造出专业而强劲的外观。该产品支持标准 VESA 壁挂，支架上红色的束线器凸显了理线功能，提高易用性。该产品 80% 采用可回收塑料材质。显示器的制造商达到世界范围内多项严格的绿色环保和生态标准。

The monitor uses ultra-high-definition display with near borderless panel. A full function quick attach stand provides lift, swivel, pivot, and tilt capabilities, which enables us to adjust better angle to watch. The design concept radiates from clean geometric forms creating a professional and powerful appearance. The product supports standard VESA wall hangings. A red clip on the stand highlights the cable management feature and improves ease of use. The case is produced from 80% recycled plastic. The manufacturing of this monitor meets the highest green and ECO standards for multiple certifications worldwide.

设计 DESIGN
联想设计
Lenovo Design

生产 MANUFACTURE
联想集团
Lenovo Group

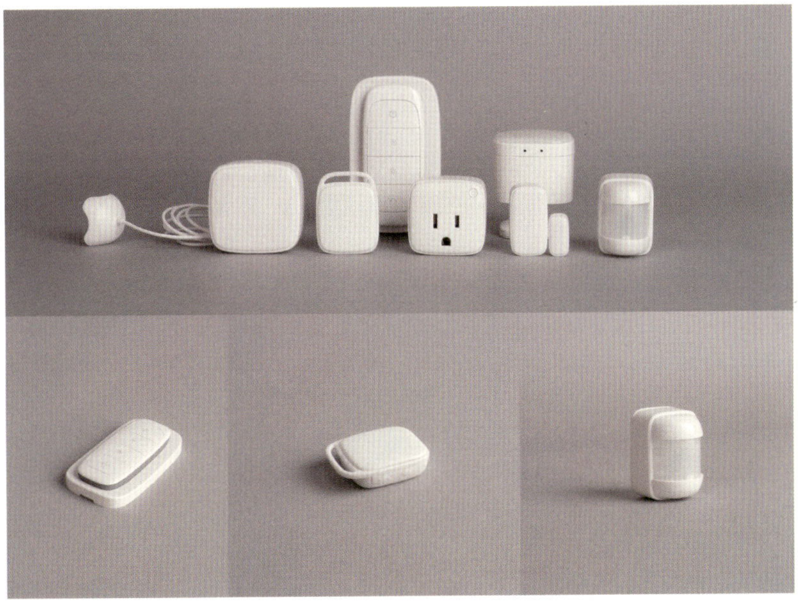

立达信智能家居系列
Leedarson Home Automation Series

该智能家居系列注重产品本身，给予使用者更可靠的感觉。从安防角度出发，寻找使用者行为与使用需求，结合新的技术提出新的安防智能家居解决方案。提供更高级别的安全保障，使用者不管何时何地，都能第一时间知道家里的状态。其系列产品包括网关、门磁等，可根据不同需求选择搭配，适用于不同安防需求的家庭。

The home automation series focus on the product itself, provides the users with a more reliable feeling; From the security point of view, they look for user behavior and the use of demand, it combines with new technology to propose a new security smart home's solution. they can provide a higher level of security so that you will know the state of the family at the first time no matter when and where you are.Its series products include gateways, door sensors etc. They can be selected and matched according to different needs, which is suitable for families of different security needs.

设计 DESIGN
立达信工业设计中心
Leedarson IDC

生产 MANUFACTURE
厦门立达信绿色照明集团有限公司
Leedarson Group

新一代多联机 sk6
New Generation of VRF sk6

该产品是新一代多联机，采用直流变频技术、优化的空调系统设计和智能控制技术，能够有效减少电费开支，实现智能化霜控制，提高换热效率，对产品运行进行智能控制，此外，该产品智能控制噪音，营造良好的生活品质。该产品的设计亮点为正面采用钻石切割纹理，具有较强的视觉冲击力，符合该产品的使用属性，在同类产品中极具创新性和辨识度。

As the new generation of VRF, the product uses DC inverter technology, optimized air conditioning system design and intelligent control technology, which will effectively reduce electricity costs, realize intelligent defrosting control, improve the heat transfer efficiency and conduct intelligent control on the product; in addition, the product will control the noise in an intelligent manner to create life of good quality. The design highlights of the product is using the diamond cutting texture for the front panel,which has a strong visual impact; it is consistent with the use attributes of the product and makes it have a highly innovation and identification among the similar products

设计 DESIGN
珠海格力电器股份有限公司
Gree Electric Appliances,Inc.of Zhuhai

珠海格力电器股份有限公司
Gree Electric Appliances,Inc.of Zhuhai
生产 MANUFACTURE

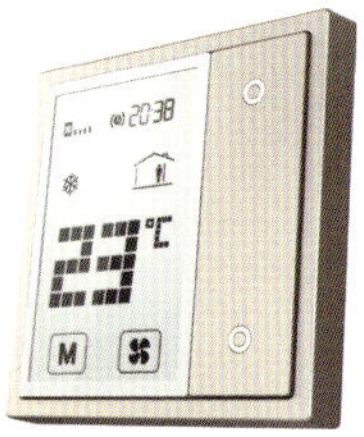

西蒙 i7 智能温控器
Simon i7 Thermostat

该产品是一款一体化边框设计的智能温控器，实现对家庭空调、地暖、新风等设备的控制，安装后，提高了墙面开关和温控器的一致性。使用传统开关的控制方法，通过上、下两个物理按键，快速实现对家庭环境温度和空气质量的设定和操作。产品壳体采用德国拜耳 PC 塑料。产品结构和模具设计采用卡扣结构，减少螺丝，使生产环节更为高效和环保。

This product is an intelligent temperature controller with an integrated frame design, realizing the control of the air condition, floor heating and fresh air ventilator. There is the huge improvement of the consistency and uniformity between the wall switches and thermostats. The traditional method of the control of the switch is the major feature of this product. There are two physically button (Up and down) for the setup and control of the environment of the house and the quality of air. We selected the PC material from Bayer (Germany) for the enclosure of our product. In order to keep the high production efficiency and environment protection, we adopted the buckle structure in product structure design and mold design which can minimize the usage of screw in our product.

设计 DESIGN
西蒙电气（中国）有限公司
Spain Simon （China） Ltd.

上海犀科环境科技有限公司
Shanghai Seekco Environmental Tech Co.,Ltd.
生产 MANUFACTURE

海信 Ta 空间冰箱
Hisense Ta Sapce Refrigerator

该款冰箱将冷藏部分空间分为上下两个部分，双循环系统，独立控温，减少了冷藏门打开时的耗电和串味，设计更加人性化。90 度开门的设计完美解决一边靠墙，一边紧挨橱柜尴尬位置。外观玻璃面板采用 KMI 印刷工艺，暗拉手装饰件采用铝合金表面抛光工艺，亮度达到电镀效果，制作工艺领先同类产品。

The space of the refrigerator is divided into two parts, the upper part and the lower part, the double circulation system and the independent temperature control greatly reduce the power consumption and odor when the refrigerator door is open, the design is more humanized. The design of 90 degrees opening of the door solves the awkward position that is adjacent to the wall at one side and next to ambry at another side. The exterior glass panel adopts KMI printing process, and the decorative of the dark handle adopts aluminum alloy surface polishing technology, the brightness reaches the plating effect, and the production process leads other similar products.

设计 DESIGN
海信（山东）冰箱有限公司
Hisense (Shandong) Refrigerator Co.,Ltd.

海信集团工业设计中心
Hisense Industrial Design Center
生产 MANUFACTURE

比佛利高端燃热系列
Beverly High-End Gas Water Heater Series

该产品是一款燃气热水器。一体注塑成型底壳，减少产品装配件数和开模成本，提升产品产能和工人劳动量 。标准化设计和精益制造，共用模具和零部件，通过配置的差异化实现产品线的扩展，减少模具投入，实现绿色环保。该产品顶部无螺钉设计，强调每一个细节完美处理；经典面包底设计一体成型让产品外观更加整体，减少分型线对外观的破坏，同时保证产品的整体感。

The product is a gas water heater. One injection molding bottom shell reduces the number of assembly and mold opening costs, improves product capacity and labor capacity. It is with the standardized design and the lean manufacturing, the shared molds and parts, the differentiated configuration expands the product lines and decreases the mold costs and realize green environmental protection.The classic bread-shaped design and the integrated molding at the bottom present a more integrated look, which diminishes the disturbance of the parting line to the appearance while ensuring the integrated look of the product.

设计 DESIGN
美的集团热水器事业部
Midea Group Water Heater Appliances

生产 MANUFACTURE
美的集团热水器事业部工业设计部
Industrial Design Center of Midea Group Water Heater Appliancesv

海尔 U5 净水器
Haier U5 Water Purifier

这款净水器相比传统的净水器，设计小巧漂亮，没有了硕大的储水罐，从净化龙头到滤芯都采用快装设计，五分钟即可完成安装，仅需一张 A4 纸大小的地方就可以放下净水器，节省了厨房有限的台面空间。将新的草莓造型引入家用净水机设计中，张扬的红色草莓，透出令人愉快的美，改观了设备的外形造型，很容易融入厨房的整体家居氛围中。

Unlike the traditional water purifier, the purifier is small and pretty without any huge water container, which save the kitchen space for you. It can be put in a place not larger than a A4 paper. The whole water purifier could be assembled in 5 minutes from tap to filter core. By using the cheerful shape and red color of strawberry, this water purifier brings a bright color to kitchen and gives user a happy mode everyday, which makes it easy to fit into the kitchen as a whole.

设计 DESIGN
海尔施特劳斯水设备有限公司
Haier Strauss Water Equipment Co.,Ltd.

生产 MANUFACTURE
广州大业产品设计有限公司
Guangzhou Daye Industrial Design Co.,Ltd.

爱米优系列双向快充移动电源
OUHUO Two-Way Fast Charging Mobile Power Series

该系列产品用大字体印花设计标示电量，使电量信息高效传达，塑造产品设计风格的同时有效缩短安检时间。产品的细节设计均围绕使用方便，以自然亲和力为中心。通过多维曲面的运用，巧妙的安置电芯，降低厚度。快充技术的应用及电芯位置的合理搭配，在体型大小方面更加符合现代审美，更容易被消费者接受。

The series of products design charge electricity with large font printing so that the power information can be communicated efficiently and shorten the security time while shaping the product design style. The design details of the product focus on the convenience of use and highlighting the natural affinity. The thickness of the product was reduced with the use of Multi-dimensional surface design and the appropriate placement of batteries. The application of fast charging technology and the reasonable match of batteries' location make the body size more in line with modern aesthetic and more easily be accepted by consumers.

设计 DESIGN
北京隆通科技有限公司
OUHUO

生产 MANUFACTURE
北京华新意创工业设计有限公司
Beijing Ideas Design Co.,Ltd.

婴儿用品消毒器
Baby Accessory Sterilizer

该款婴儿用品消毒器改变传统以蒸汽消毒的方式，采用顶部 UV 灯加热灯结合的方式，对婴儿用的物品进行加热消毒，同时内置风道系统，使物品在消毒的同时也能得到干燥，不需要用户进行二次取出与存放。以注塑工艺为主要工艺，不使用喷涂工艺。容器内部以大圆形钣金折弯工艺，与塑料顶盖的良好工艺配合，富有良好的亲和感。

Compared with the traditional steaming sterilizer, this baby accessory sterilizer uses UV lighting and heating light for sterilizing accessory, the build-in fan flow system make sure the sterilized accessory dry, the user does not need to maintain the accessory with the other box. It uses injection molding as the main process, no spraying process is used. The inside of the container is made of big round sheet metal bending process, and it matches well with the plastic top cover. It has a good sense of affinity.

设计
DESIGN

合肥方块工业设计有限公司
Square Industrial Design Co.,Ltd.

生产
MANUFACTURE

安徽匠造物科技有限公司
An Hui Artisan Creator Technology Co., Ltd.

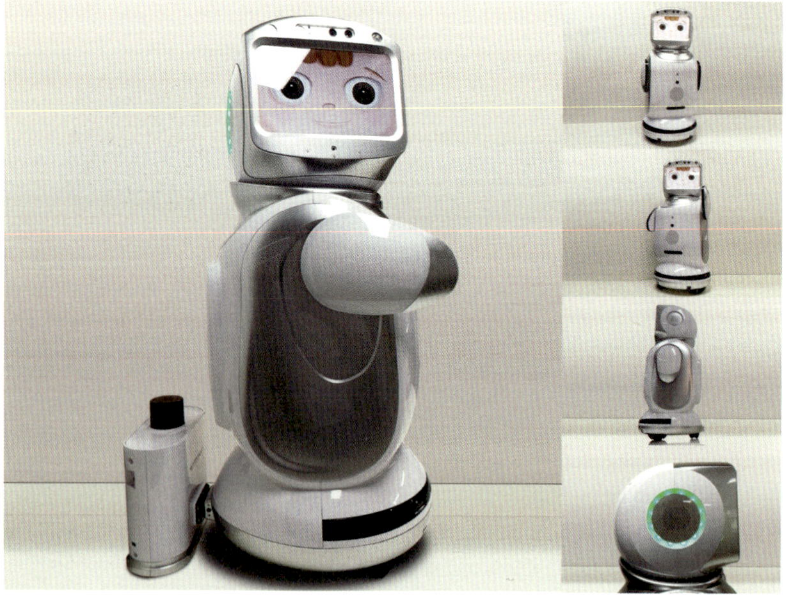

三宝家庭机器人
Sanbot Family Robot

三宝家庭服务机器人基于互联网，成为身处异地的家庭成员交流平台，使得家庭可以跨越地理交流无障碍。 三宝机器人可以帮助使用者解决各种问题，如天气 、交通等；拥有音乐、新闻、故事等各类精彩的娱乐内容。该产品具有远程操控、360 度旋转、智能循声、人脸跟随、自动捕捉拍摄录像等功能，使家人可以随时随地知晓家中情况。

Base on Internet, Sunbo is a communicating platform for family members in different places. It can help family overcome the distance and share every sweet moment. It helps users solve all kinds of problems such as those of weather and transportation; Sunbo can provide the information and entertainment you need in the daily life including music, news and story. The functions of Sunbo include remote control, 360 degrees swivel, voice and face identify and automatic motion capture and filming. So you can know the situation of your house,

设计
DESIGN

广州大业产品设计有限公司
Guangzhou Daye Industrial Design Co.,Ltd.

生产
MANUFACTURE

旗瀚科技有限公司
Qihan Technology Co., Ltd.

气泡智能音箱
Bubble Smart Speaker

该产品与同类音箱比具有良好的手感和柔韧性，一体成型的工艺使其高度防水，不惧怕磕碰；产品独特的形态结合挂绳设计，使用者可以任意放置，提供了更多的使用方式，让用户可以在更多的场景中享受音乐带来的乐趣；拥有为户外场景考虑的独立音腔设计，辅以简洁明确的语音提示及多种连接方式以提高它的适用性；采用 3800 毫安电池设计，保证将近 9 小时的续航时间。

Compared with other similar speakers, Bubble is better in its hand feeling and flexibility. With integral forming process, it is waterproof and anti-shock.The unique form of the product combines the lanyard designq allows user to put or keep it at anywhere, which provids various ways of using and brings joy of music in different scenarios. The applicability of Bubble can be improved with independent acoustic chamber designed for outdoor scenarios, concise voice prompt and various ways of connecting. 3800 mAh battery capacity ensures nine-hour battery life.

设计
DESIGN

北京智能管家科技有限公司
Intelligent Steward Co.,Ltd.

叶菲梓、陈焕鹏
Ye Feizi, Chen Huanpeng

生产
MANUFACTURE

储能式电暖器
Thermal Energy Storage

该款储能式电暖器采用绿色蓄能形式达到节电的作用，充分利用大量废弃的夜间电力，晚上利用电蓄能 8 小时，白天停止用电释放热量 16 小时，即将大量夜间的电力，转化为热能的形式储存起来，第二天使用时释放出所需的热量，缓解对环境的污染。采用圆润的造型，在美观的同时更安全放心，减少碰撞带来的伤害；通风口侧面出风设计减少灰尘，便于清理。

The thermal energy storage uses the green “peak-valley” electrical energy storage method to realize electricity saving.It makes full use of a lot of wasted night power, storing electricity for 8 hours at night by using electricity and releasing thermal energy at daytime for 16 hours without using electricity,that is to say, a large amount of nighttime electricity will be stored in the form of heat energy, releasing the required heat for second days and alleviating the pollution to the environment. It adopts a round shape, and is safer and more comfortable at the same time. It can reduce the harm caused by the collision. The ventilation on the side of the vent is designed to reduce dust and make it easy to clean.

设计
DESIGN

北京凯昆广胜新能源电器有限公司
Beijing Kaikunguangsheng New Energy Electric Appliance Co.,Ltd.

武汉市本源造物设计咨询有限公司
Source Design

生产
MANUFACTURE

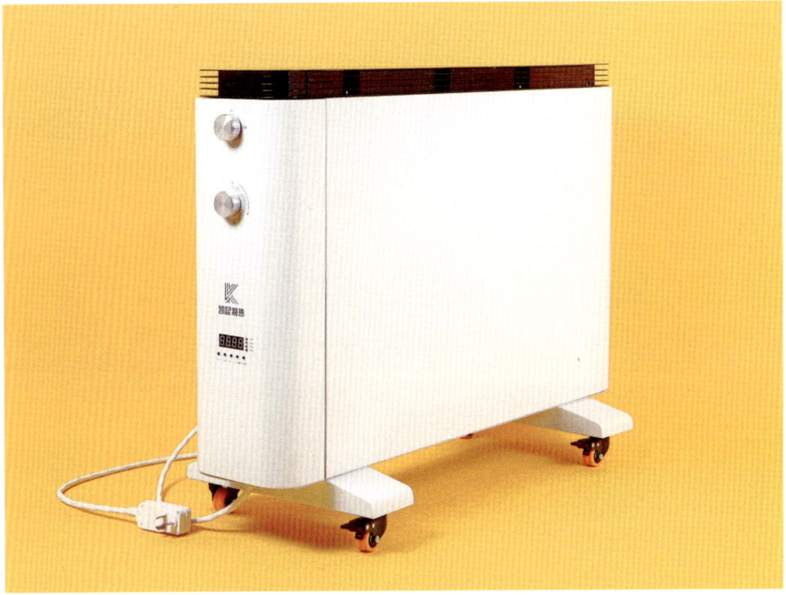

ASNAP 手机夜拍补光灯
ASNAP Fill-in Light for Smartphones

该款手机补光灯首次将专业“棚拍级”摄影灯光放到手机配件中。重新设计了双层盖光板，定制 36 颗显色力 95+ 并满足高散热效能的医用级 LED 白光灯珠，形成明亮、高显色且均匀不伤眼的光源。灯源透光亚克力遮光罩使用双色注塑的方式，实现表面晶莹剔透、内部散射光线的目的。表面哑光 UV 漆在保证手感顺滑的同时，也顾全了表面喷漆的持久耐用性。

For the first time，professional “studio level” photography lighting is put in a small and portable phone accessories. We redesign the double cover plate, and customize 36 medical grade LED lamp bead with 95+ color force and high cooling efficiency. The light source isbright, high color, even and doesn't hure eyes. Light source through the acrylic hood uses two-color injection molding method to achieve the the purpose of surface crystal clear and scattered light inside.The surface matte UV varnish ensures the smooth hand feeling and also considers the durability of surface painting.

设计
DESIGN

深圳宗匠科技有限公司
Accompany Tech. Co.,Ltd.

杭州正负极工业设计有限公司
Hangzhou Pmuse Industrial Design Co.,Ltd.

生产
MANUFACTURE

I90-TWS 对吸蓝牙耳机
TWS-H2

此款蓝牙耳机实现双边无线，可同时或单独连接两部手机，左右耳由 CRS63120 芯片提供技术支持，精准无延迟地实现双边音乐的输出，无线材限制，自在倾听双耳立体声。创新式充电座加存储功能设计，充电一次可畅听 5 小时。同时配 250 毫安充电胶囊可给单耳续电 4 次，可延长听歌时间 16 小时。对吸式的收藏方式小巧携带方便，吸住后自动待机，操作人性化。

The bilateral wireless bluetooth headphone can connect with two mobile phones at the same time or individually. The left and right earsets are provided with technical support by CRS63120 chips and can achieve bilateral music output accurately without delay, and it will also have a wire-free limit that can let you enjoy more free Binaural Stereo. Innovative charger plus storage design enable users to listen up to 5 hours of music per charge. While it is also equipped with 250mAh charge capsules, which can charge single-ear 4 times and extend listening time by 16 hours. Impose-manner of collection is compact and easy to carry. When absorb the earsets, it will go to automatic standby, and operation is humanized.

设计
DESIGN

广州海蔚特科技有限公司
Guangzhou Havit Technology Co.,Ltd.

深圳市恩佳产品策划有限公司
Shenzhen N Plus Product Planning Co.,Ltd.

生产
MANUFACTURE

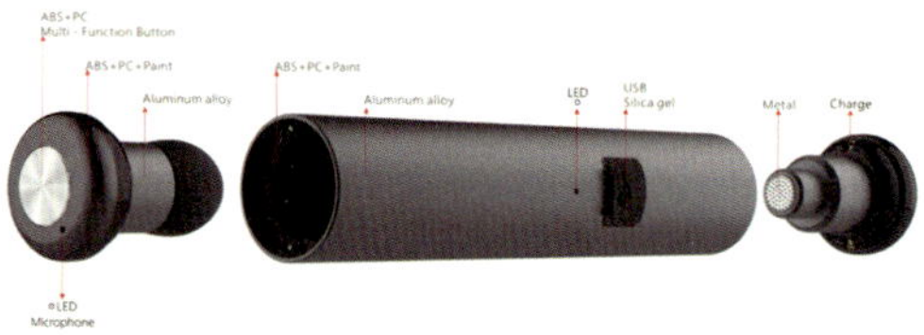

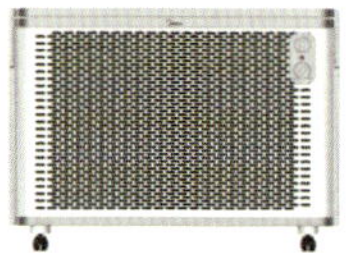

热辐射电暖器
Heat Radiator

该款电暖器采用铝板发热体，表面有特殊辐射涂层，对比传统的对流式散热更快，辐射范围更广，无异味，不发光，没有光污染，能快速提高房间内温度。环绕跑道型的简约设计，更符合现代生活家居的风格。为了追求产品整体感和功能性需求，结合了辐射式的双面发热原理，采取了贴合外形的形态设计了双面衣架，使得产品的原始形态统一而简洁。

This heat radiator uses aluminum heating element and the surface has a special radiation coating. Compared with the traditional convection heat dissipation, it is faster, the radiation range is wider, and it has no peculiar smell, no light, and no light pollution. It can quickly warm up the room. The simple design of the surround runway is more in line with the style of modern home life. In order to pursue the overall sense of product and functions, combined with radiation type double side heating principle, we adapt the shape fitting to the appearance and design the double-sided clothes hanger, making the original form of the product uniform and simple.

设计
DESIGN

广东美的环境电器制造有限公司
GD Midea Environment Appliances MFG.Co., Ltd.

郭玉强
Guo Yuqiang

生产
MANUFACTURE

巧克力电视
Chocolate TV

该电视是一款有着全新屏占比的落地艺术电视，拥有全新的声学设计。直接在喇叭上覆盖特制透音棉，声音的阻挡几乎为零，使声音表现高度通透清晰。通身铝合金采用玻璃砂处理出表面细腻质感，再氧化出深色金属光泽。塑料后壳采用亮面与哑面对比设计。横竖两根几何金属支撑，巧妙搭接使机身悬浮，脱离地面，视觉上端庄优雅。

The chocolate TV is console art model with a new screen-to-body ratio and a new acoustic design. A special sound transmitting cotton is directly covered on the loudspeaker and the sound barrier is almost zero, so that the sound performance is highly transparent and clear. The Aluminum Alloy body adopts glass sand to make the surface has delicate texture and oxide dark metallic luster. The plastic back shell poses the comparison of bright and mute. The horizontal and perpendicular geometry metal stands make the body suspended, giving users elegant visual view.

设计
DESIGN

微鲸科技有限公司
Whaley Technology Co., Ltd.

微鲸工业设计部
Whaley Technology ID Team

生产
MANUFACTURE

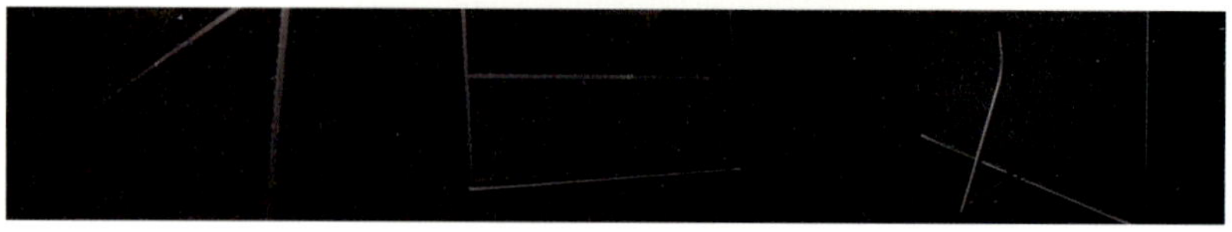

布丁豆豆智能机器人
Pudding BeanQ Smart Robot

该产品是一款面向中国市场的儿童（3—6 岁）智能机器人。拥有视频通话、双语教学、实时翻译、益智游戏及第三方的内容资源。自然语言交互、人脸跟随技术配合身体的转动斜轴进行人性化交互；头部和身体两侧触摸区可以进行触摸交互；为儿童定制的交互界面，辅以拟人化的情绪系统；为了保护孩子的健康和安全，特别设计了近距离提示、防蓝光护眼模式等。

Pudding BeanQ is an intelligent robot for children from 3 to 6 in China. It has rich functionality such as video call, bilingual education, real-time translation, puzzle game, third-party resources and so on. It carries natural language interaction and human interaction in which face recognition technology fits to body's rotating tilting axis.You can interact with it by touching multiple touch areas on the head or sides of its body. Customized interactive interface ia assisted by anthropomorphic emotional system. For children's health and safety, we specially design close-up tips, anti-blue eye protection mode and so on.

设计 DESIGN
叶菲梓、郑斌
Ye Feizi, Zheng Bin

生产 MANUFACTURE
北京智能管家科技有限公司
Intelligent Steward Co.,Ltd.

“X7PRO 家用中央热水”燃气热水器
“X7PRO Domestic Centr Hot Water” Gas Water Heater

传统燃气热水器开机后，先会排出冷水，后出热水，等待恒温热水时间长，先排出来的冷水被直接排弃。该产品实现 0.7 秒出恒温热水，开机不再出冷水，提升用户使用体验。按国标出水量每分钟 9 升保守计算，三口之家，一年节约水资源 13 吨。操作面板采用 ITO 技术，实现点滑控温，简化操作。大屏设计符合消费趋势，弧面设计，厚实饱满，工艺成熟稳定。

When the traditional gas water heater is switched on, the cold water will be discharged first, then the hot water will come out, it takes a long period of time to wait for the constant temperature hot water, the cold water discharged first will be directly drained. X7PRO water heater discharges constant hot water after 0.7 seconds of turning on and without any cold water, which improves user experience. Calculate conservatively according to the water outlet of 9L/Min (national standard), a family of three members will save 13 tons water resources a year. The operation panel uses ITO technology to achieve point slip temperature control and simplify the operation. Large-screen design in is line with consumer trends, combined with arc design, the whole is full of solid with mature and stable process.

设计 DESIGN
广东顺德东方麦田工业设计有限公司
East-Innovation Shunde GD Co.,Ltd.

生产 MANUFACTURE
广东万家乐燃气具有限公司
Guangdong Macro Gas Appliance Co.,Ltd.

摇滚之星蓝牙音箱
Rockstar Bluetooth Speaker

该产品专为音乐发烧友、专业音乐人、户外表演狂热者以及唱片爱好者等群体定制，集成了立体声多接口以及数字功放系统，保证了独特的高保真音质表现以及发烧友级别的品质。产品支持蓝牙链接以及多路链接。配有特色的吉他功放以及转调器效果，均衡器功能，麦克风以及音频输入级。26000 毫安大容量锂电池支持 12 小时重放，支持交流电适配器充电，约 4—5 个小时充满。

With extreme HiFi performance and audiophile quality, this all-in-one, multi-input portable stereo and digital PA system is designed for aspiring professional musicians, outdoors enthusiasts and audiophiles. It supports Bluetooth connection and multi-pairing, featuring Guitar amplifier and modulation effects, effects and equalizer for microphone and Aux level adjustment. 26,000mAh built-in lithium battery supports 12 hours audio play back and AC adapter charging, it takes just 4~5 hours to fully recharge the RockStar.

设计
DESIGN
君伍科技（北京）有限公司
Dreamwvae Audio USA,LLC

深圳市麦锡工业产品策划有限公司
Maxypro Industrial Product Scheme Co.,Ltd.
生产
MANUFACTURE

中兴蓝牙麦克风
ZTE Bluetooth Microphone

该款麦克风支持蓝牙及 USB 连接，覆盖多种接入场景需求，灵活匹配主设备接口能力。全向灵敏的咪头组件，匹配精密的3A 音频处理算法，在复杂场景下保障超优质的音频水平，解决了回声、增益和降噪的三大问题 。强力锂离子电池实现长续航功能，充电半小时，续航 8 小时，USB 可供电和为电池充电。整体操作以触摸按键为主，给人高科技的操作感。

ZTE Bluetooth microphone supports Bluetooth / USB connection, covering the needs of a variety of access scenarios, it is flexible in matching the main device interface capabilities. Omnidirectional ultra-sensitive microphone components matches with the sophisticated 3A audio processing algorithms to ensure the ultra-high quality audio level in complex scenes, solving the three major problems of echo, gain and noise reduction. Powerful lithium-ion battery has long battery life, it can charge 30 minutes and life for 8 hours, USB can supply power and charge the battery. The overall operation is touch-key based, giving high-tech operation sense.

设计
DESIGN
中兴通讯股份有限公司
ZTE Corporation.Shenzhen,China

中兴通讯股份有限公司
ZTE Corporation.Shenzhen,China
生产
MANUFACTURE

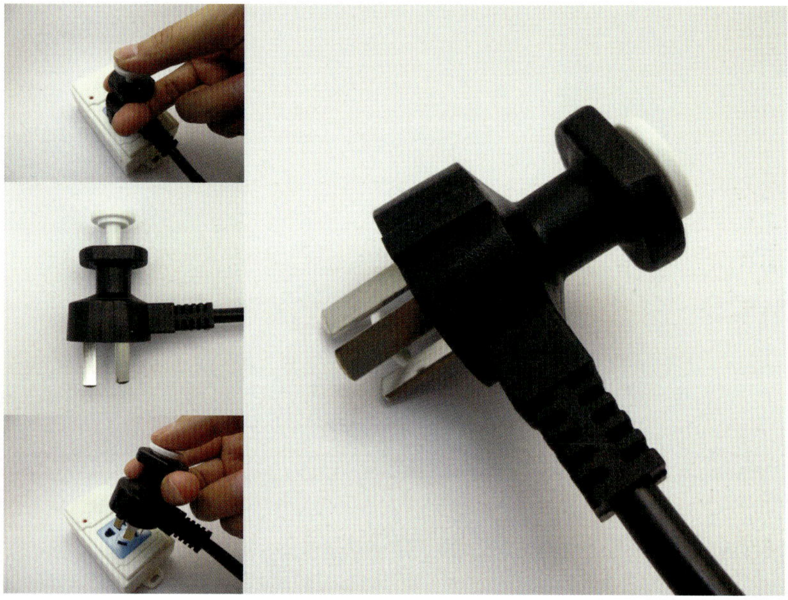

单手快拔电源插头
Single Hand's Power Plug

单手快拔电源插头通过增加顶杆机构设计，创新性地实现了单手即可安全轻松拔出插头的目的。无论墙上插座或移动插排上的插头，均可任意角度单手快速拔出。顶杆及手柄自然融合到一起，使得食指和中指可以从任意角度伸进，在拇指的按压配合下，轻松弹出。该产品插头金属插片为纯铜镀镍，内部支架使用坚固阻燃材料，电源线导线使用纯铜材料。

Single hand's Power Plug is added the new design of one plunger structure and can be unplugged safely from socket with one hand. it can be pulled out with one hand quickly at any angle Whether from the wall socket or mobile socket plug. The top bar and the handle naturally fuse together so that the index finger and middle finger can put in from any angle and it can easily eject under the thumb press. The plug metal insert of the product is made of pure copper nickel plated, the inner bracket is made of strong flame retardant material, and the power line and lead wire are made of pure copper material. The operation panel adopts ITO technology to realize point sliding temperature control and to simplify the operation.

设计
DESIGN

苗亮
Miao Liang

绍兴市锦涛电子有限公司
Shaoxing Jintao Electron Co.,Ltd.

生产
MANUFACTURE

踢踢桶
Kick Bin

踢踢桶创造了全新的垃圾桶使用方式——轻碰开盖，自动关盖。集成震动感应器，使用者可用更自由随意的方式打开垃圾桶。该产品以 ABS、PP 和不锈钢材料为主，符合环保要求，可回收利用。其能源由四节五号电池驱动，低功耗芯片与智能程序控制让产品待机时间长达三年，开关盖次数超过 10000 次。该产品上市后，就得到了中高端消费者和经销商的认可。

TT (touch tin) has created a brand-new way in the usage of trash bin—touch to open and close automatically. Built-in vibration sensor allows user to open the lid of TT more casually and freely. The materials of TT mainly include ABS, PP and stainless steel, all are in compliance with environmental protection norm and recyclable. TT is driven by 4 AA batteries, the low-energy-consumption chipset and smart program control software extend its standby time to as long as 3 years and the batteries may support over 10,000 times of open-close-action, which is also far more than other competitive products. After listing, the product has been recognized by middle and high-end consumers and distributors.

设计
DESIGN

许坤南、吴康松
Xu Kunnan, Wu Kangsong

米巢（厦门）信息技术有限公司
Micasa (Xiamen) Info Technology Co.,Ltd.

生产
MANUFACTURE

Hello 焖烧罐
Hello

该款焖烧罐将设计融于生活，在满足焖烧罐功能的同时，在造型上进行了创新。硅胶提手，方便携带。碗状上盖，方便使用；使用焖烧罐焖粥带饭，节约燃料，更加健康环保；食品级 PP，健康安全，食物接触用 304 不锈钢，耐腐蚀，不生锈。整体造型圆润可爱，碗状的盖子与硅胶提手相结合，既方便又美观。上线半年热卖 222950 只 。

The stew pot integrate design into life, while satisfying the function of stewing pot, it is innovative in shape. Silicone handle makes it easy to carry and the bowl shaped upper cover makes it convenient for eating; use stewing pot to stew gruel and rice saves fuel, which is more healthy and environmental protection; food grade PP is health and safe and 304 stainless steel is corrosion resistance and no rust. The whole shape is round and lovely and the bowl shaped lid is combined with the silica gel handle, which is convenient and beautiful. On-line six months, it sales 222950.

设计
DESIGN
合肥颂智商贸有限公司
J&V (Hongkong) Industrial Limited

合肥行言产品设计有限公司
Hefei Xingyan
生产
MANUFACTURE

天使与恶魔保温杯
Angel and Devil Cup

该款产品是以天使和恶魔为元素设计的情侣保温水杯，此产品外观的主要设计点为一个盖子，在特殊造型的情况下直接采用一体出模（恶魔款上多了硅胶安全配件部分），根据产品元素特点在头部做成一个能够稳定站立结构，在正放的时候是一个小恶魔或小天使的形态，反放为一个类似咖啡杯的造型。两种状态都能呈现出很好的外观形态。

The product is a couple insulation Cup with angels and demons as design elements, the main design points of this product appearance is the cover, in the case of special molding, the whole mold is adopted directly, (there are silicone safety accessories part for the demon one), a stable stand structure is made in the head according to the characteristics of the elements, when put it in a right place, it is on a small devil or angel form while the oppoaite side is a similar coffee cup shape. Both the two states can have a good appearance.

设计
DESIGN
广州市可莓日用品有限公司
Guangzhou Kemei Daily Necessities Co., Ltd.

广州市可莓日用品有限公司
Guangzhou Kemei Daily Necessities Co.,Ltd.
生产
MANUFACTURE

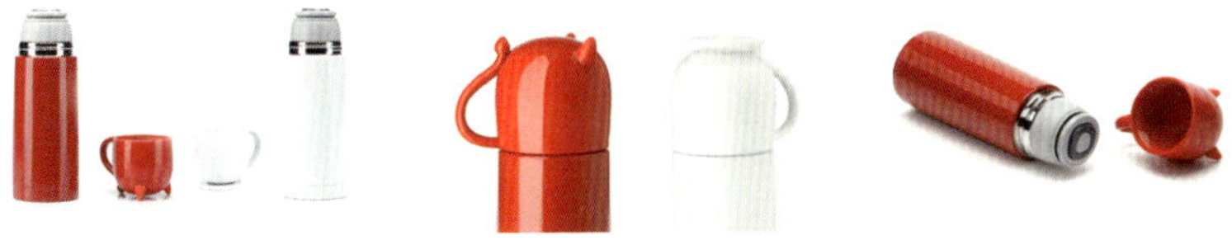

无畏旅行商务背包
Backpack for Business Trips Wuwei Co

该款商务背包首次将 EVA 材料和面料一体成型技术运用到了背包正面，并形成流畅的外观表面。采用的背部材料具有超强减震性能，将重力分散到身体各个部位，同时让空气进入背部循环，使背负时轻松凉爽。在背包的打开方式上打破常规，更方便整理背包内的物品。背包内部分隔为两个独立空间，将旅行功能和商务功能完美融合，使收纳整齐有序。

For the first time the EVA materials as well as the fabric integration technique are applied to the front of backpack to form a smooth look on the surface.The back material used has super shock absorption performance and disperses the weight to the whole body. Meanwhile the air can circulate at your back to make it lighter and cooler while carrying your backpack. Another reform which overturns the convention is how we open the backpack. The design makes it more convenient to pack things in backpacks. The interior space is divided into 2 independent ones, which combines the trip function and business function perfectly, keeping it neat and organized.

设计
DESIGN
重庆传梵服装设计工作室
Chongqing Creative Fashion Design Studio

胡庆峰
Hu Qingfeng
生产
MANUFACTURE

早先生组合式枕头
Mr.Z Modular Pillow

该款组合式枕头为满足使用者对睡枕的个性要求，推出自由组合式枕头，实现新的睡眠体验。解决了传统枕头的单一睡感问题，利用不同单体包的高度材质及软硬度来组合出符合每个人不同睡眠状态下的睡感需求。根据产品的连接布、纽扣、弹力带以及绳扣等结构部件，使产品的不同模块可以通过连接结构进行拼接，减缓缝隙感，提升枕头舒适度。

In order to meet the user's personality requirements of the pillow, the modular pillow introduces free combination pillow to achieve a new sleep experience. To solve the single sleeping problem of the traditional pillow, the modular pillow use the height and softness of different monomer package to meet the different sleep conditions in accordance with everyone's sleep needs. According to connection cloth, buttons, elastic band and rope buckle and other structural components of the product, different modules of the product can be stitching through the connection structure to slow down the sense of gap and enhance the comfort.

设计
DESIGN

广州市欧亚床垫家具有限公司
Guangzhou Eurasia Mattress & Furniture Co., Ltd.

广州早尚创意文化有限公司
Guangzhou Mrz Creative Culture Co.,Ltd.

生产
MANUFACTURE

贝壳餐椅
Lord Chair

贝壳椅灵感来源于大海深处的贝壳，产品使用范围广，适用于办公、家居环境，其优雅的造型，在环境中显得沉稳冷静，易于配合其他的家具共同使用。软包胶合板内框架附海绵软包，铝合金一次成型脚架，产品使用寿命周期长。软包内部木纹清晰美观，采用环保型松木木材，健康安全耐用。贝壳餐椅有铝合金脚架和木脚两款可供用户选择。

The inspiration of Lord chairs comes from pad in the sea, Lord chair has a wide range of applications, it not only can be used in working environment, but also can be put in the living environment. The chair is easy to be matched with other furniture and surroundings, Its elegant shape makes it look calm in the whole environment. Soft package within the plywood frame attached to the soft bag and aluminum alloy molding feet at a time help the product has a long life cycle. Lord chaira provides two options to users, including luminum alloy tripods and wooden feet.

设计
DESIGN

杭州科沃工业设计有限公司
Gradodesign

柴晓东
Alex Chai

生产
MANUFACTURE

嗒嗒桌
Dada Table

嗒嗒桌的灵感来源于女人的高跟鞋，取名嗒嗒是女人踩着高跟鞋从远处走来的声音。整体线条干净轻盈，流线型细节衬托出功能与轻盈的完美结合。桌脚通过铝合金一体成型，如此大的投入是我们的产品兼顾产品美学和结构稳定度的保证。产品为最大的灵活使用而设计，分别有餐桌、茶几、工作位、办公桌，可用于家里、办公室、会议室等。

Dada table is inspired by women's high heels,and Dada refers to the voice of a woman stepping from the distance on high heels. The overall line of it is clean and light with streamlined details to bring out the perfect combination of the function and lightness. Table feet adopt aluminum alloy unibody, and such a large investment is the guarantee of product aesthetics and structural stability of our products. Dada designed for the greatest flexible use, has table, coffee table, work position, desk, and can be used for home, office, conference room and so on.

设计
DESIGN

杭州科沃工业设计有限公司
Gradodesign

柴晓东
Alex Chai

生产
MANUFACTURE

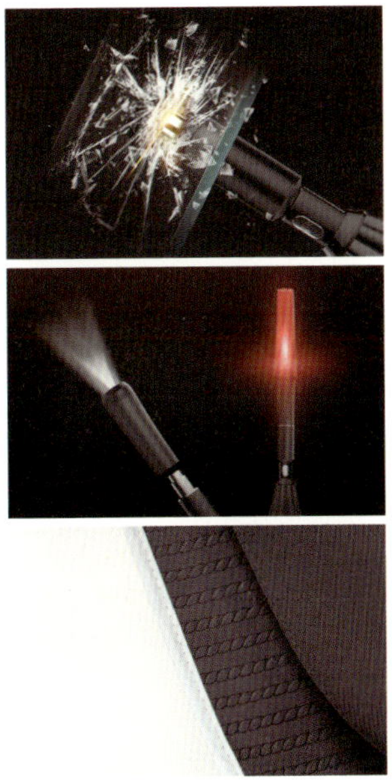

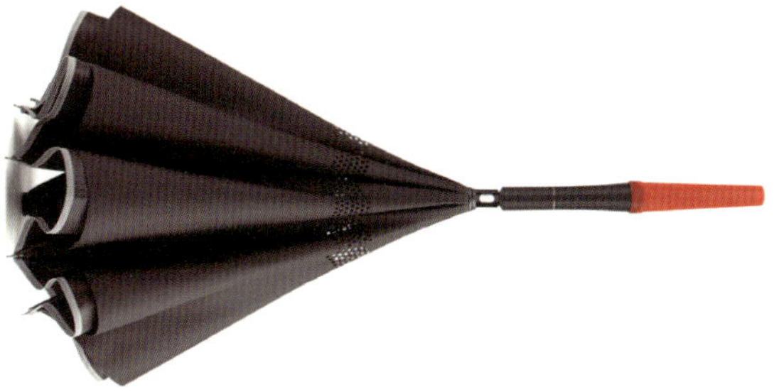

反向汽车安全伞
Reverse Safety Umbrella

反向汽车安全伞将汽车破窗器、反光警示条、照明、警示灯、反向开收伞融入平时使用的晴雨伞，在不影响晴雨伞正常使用的情况下，实现了一伞多功能。破窗器隐藏于伞柄内，伞柄电筒带有三档可调式 LED 灯，可以用来照明、警示灯、求救等。反向开收的方式，解决了传统雨伞滴水和开收的问题。产品采用可直立设计，遇到紧急情况时可将伞立于车后起到警示作用。

Reverse safety umbrella includes integrated car broken window, reflective warning strip, lighting, warning lights and reverse open umbrella into the usual use of sunny umbrella to achieve a multi-functional umbrella without affecting the normal use of sunny umbrella. Broken window is hidden in the umbrella handle on which umbrella flashlight with three adjustable LED lights can be used to lighting, warning lights, SOS and so on.The way of reverse opening up solves the problem of dripping and opening of the traditional umbrella. The umbrella is designed to be upright and can be placed behind the car for warning in case of emergency.

设计
DESIGN

李若权
Li Ruoquan

惠州市鑫和丰雨伞制品有限公司
Huizhou Xinhefeng Umbrella Products Co.,Ltd.

生产
MANUFACTURE

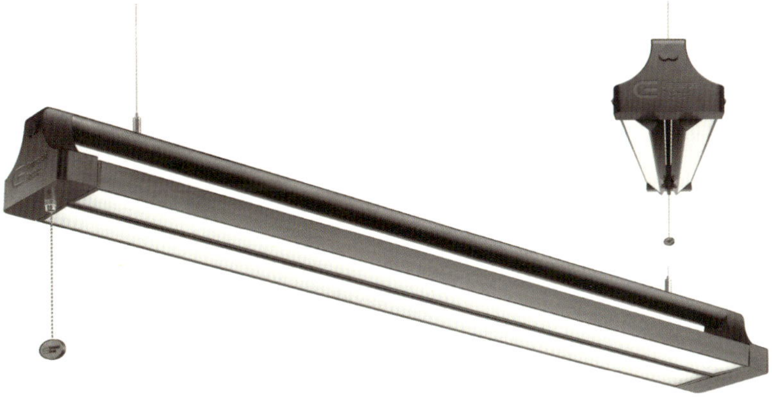
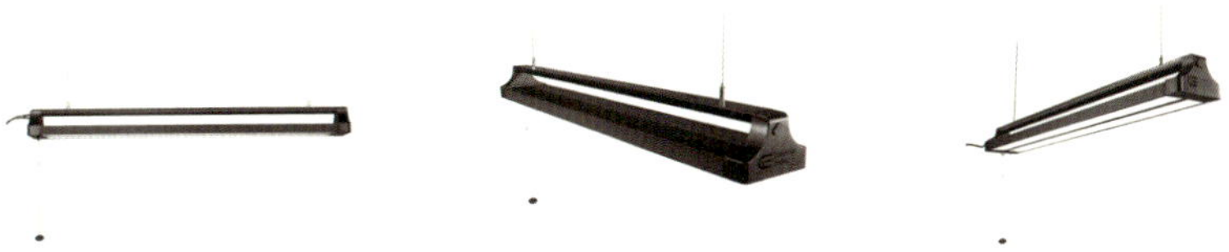

LED 条形灯
LED Shop Light

本产品应用于北美家居市场或者办公场所，光效可达每瓦 100 流明，有吸顶和悬挂两种安装方式。与同类 LED 灯具相比具有重量轻、散热好、安装方便等优势。产品的外观设计采用了展翼的概念，两侧的光源部分可以像翅膀一样展开，根据不同的照明环境需求，用户可以自己调整光照的角度，同时支持多根灯具并联的使用，可应用在超市货架照明以及办公室照明等环境当中。年销售量在 10—20 万只左右。

This product is used in North American home furnishing market or office with light efficiency up to 100lm/ w, and ceiling and suspension installation are available. Compared with similar Led lamps, it possesses light weight, good heat dissipation, easy installation and other advantages.The appearance of the product design using— uses the concept of wings and both sides can light like wings. According to the different needs of the lighting environment, the user can adjust the illumination angle, and the fixtures can be linkable for each other. It can be used in the supermarket shelves, office lighting and other lighting environment. Annual sales of the products is 100-200 thousand or so.

设计
DESIGN

季剑辉、白云飞
Winston Ji, Charly Bai

上海顿格电子贸易有限公司
Dangoo Electronics

生产
MANUFACTURE

曲智系列
Quzzi

曲智班台的台面造型源于三星曲面屏的设计，将当代流行的手机外观融入家具产品的设计当中。班台弧面的边型较为圆润，在使用时，手臂靠在台面的边缘可以加大人体手臂与台面的接触面积，提升使用舒适度，防止有棱角的边缘给人带来不舒适的使用感，同时也降低偶然的磕碰带来的伤害。该产品的双曲面造型工艺较为复杂，是行业内的首次尝试。

Quzzi office table takes shape from the Samsung curved screen design, blending the contemporary popular mobile phone appearance into the furniture product design. The edge of the curve surface of the office table is more rounded, so the contact area of arm and table surface will be increased when arm is against the edge of the table in use to—which enhances the comfort of use, prevents the edges and corners of the edge to bring uncomfortable use and reduces the damage caused by accidental bumps. The hyperboloid modeling process the product is more complex and is the first attempt of the industry.

设计 DESIGN
浙江科尔卡诺办公家具有限公司
Kano.Cn

生产 MANUFACTURE
浙江科尔卡诺办公家具有限公司
Kano.Cn

梦旅人
Picnic

自主研发 APP 录入指纹，将指纹解锁应用到箱包中，了解箱包开锁记录。在加强私人物品安全性的同时，使开锁的过程变得更为方便，避免忘记密码的状况。蓝牙距离警报可提醒用户了解行李远离或靠近的状态，避免行李丢失。产品外壳采用德国拜耳进口的聚碳酸酯材料，符合国际环保标准，材料可回收成颗粒二次利用，使产品在轻体量的同时确保抗冲击的强度。

This product is our own research and development app of inputting fingerprint. The fingerprint will be applied to unlock the luggage to understand— know about the luggage unlock record. It can strengthen the satefy of personal items, at the same time make the process of unlocking more conventient and avoid forgetting the password. The Bluetooth distance alert alerts the user of the condition that the bag is far from or near and prevents the baggage from being lost. Product shell adopts polycarbonate materials imported from German Bayer which is in line with international environmental standards and can be recycled into the secondary use in particles and also make the product in the light weight and ensures impact of strength.

设计 DESIGN
李快
Li Kuai

生产 MANUFACTURE
越甲科技（北京）有限公司
Yuejia Technology (Beijing) Co., Ltd.

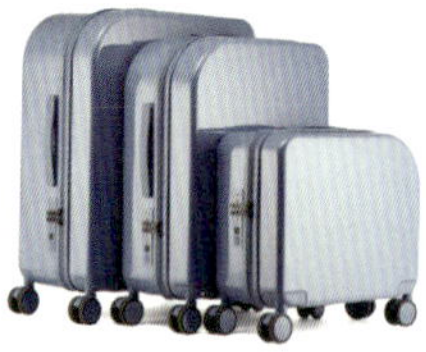

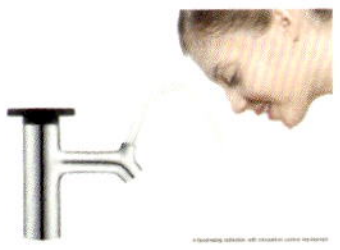

珂莱浴室龙头
Kola Basin Mixer

珂莱浴室龙头为用户漱口、卸妆等多种需求提供了解决方案。新颖的造型集实用与舒适于一体，通过简单的左右机械旋转实现上下出水方式的随意转换，有效调节水流和温度，圆盘状把手带来人机互动的愉悦体验，体现舒适性、安全性及趣味性。通过功能集成节省了空间和能耗，满足用户不同的使用需求。产品设计简约，搭配花纹雕刻，呈现灵动高雅气质。

Kola basin mixer provides a solution to meet the demands of mouthwash, makeup and other needs for the user. It combines novel style and practicability and comfort in one, achieves free conversion of spray styles from the upper and lower through the simple mechanical rotation to left and right, effectively adjusts the water flow and temperature, and disc-shaped handle brings human-machine interaction experience, reflecting the comfort, safety and Interestingness. Through functional integration, space and energy consumption is saved to meet the different needs of users. Product design is simple with pattern carving, showing smart and elegant temperament.

设计
DESIGN
广州海鸥卫浴用品股份有限公司
Guangzhou Seagull Kitchen and Bath Products Co.,Ltd.

黄彩云
Huang Caiyun
生产
MANUFACTURE

智能足球鞋
Smart Football Shoes

这是一款专门为足球运动者研发的智能穿戴设备，将智能芯片植入鞋体中，记录球员的运动数据并上传至云端存储，速度、冲刺次数、移动距离等关键性指标都可被量化呈现在体验者眼前，为球员训练提供了真实可靠的数据，从而指导球员发现自身的训练短板，综合分析，以便提高整体水平。相较于传统的运动手环，产品在提高运动数据专业性的同时提升了穿戴舒适性，也规避了运动中可能产生的危害。

This is a intelligent wear equipment specially designed for football players. The smart chip implanted in the shoe body can record the player's movement data and upload to the cloud storage including speed, sprint times, moving distance and other key indicators which can all be quantified and presented in front of the experimenters so as to provide a reliable and reliable data for the player's training, thus guiding the players to find their own training short board for comprehensive analysis and finally improve the overall level. Compared to the traditional sports bracelet, this product not only improve the professionalism of the movement data but also enhance the wear comfort and avoid the possible harm in the movement.

设计
DESIGN
双驰实业股份有限公司
Shuangchi Industrial Co.,Ltd.

福建省莆田市双驰智能信息技术有限公司
Fujian Putian Semsx Information Technology Co.,Ltd.
生产
MANUFACTURE

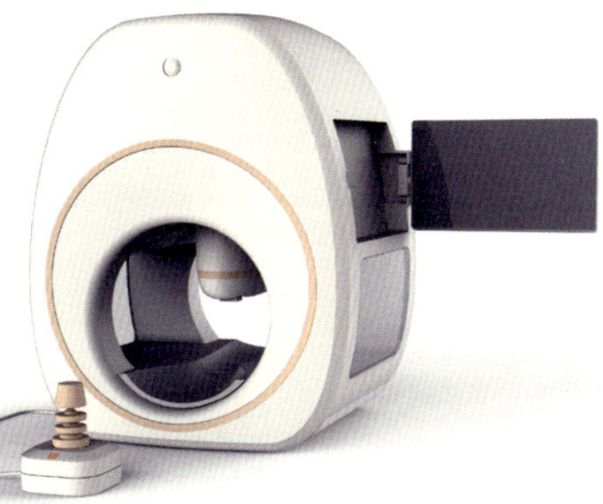

脉诊仪
Instrument of Pulse

本款产品融合中医理论及大数据的信息采集，通过编程系统进入波形分析，从而更加精准地确定病因，使患者在家中或小型医疗会所即可进行诊断。利用中医手法，进行药方的选用，具有较高的经济价值。触控可翻转屏幕能够同时将脉象结果与患者分享，可外接电脑进行数据采集及归档等工作。操作简便，性能稳定，拆卸方便，便于维护。

This product combines traditional Chinese medicine theory and large data collection and enters the waveform analysis through the programming system thus it can determine the cause more accurately and patients can be diagnosed at home or small medical clubs. It owns high economic value to select prescription by the use of traditional Chinese medicine. Touch can flip the screen can share the results of the pulse with the patient and can be connected to computer for data collection and archiving work. It is easy to operate and disassemble, convinient for maintenance and it has stable performance.

设计
DESIGN
辽宁瓦基机器人科技有限公司
Liaoning Wakirobot

沈阳创新设计服务有限公司
Shenyang Innovation
生产
MANUFACTURE

李宁超轻 13 跑鞋
Li-Ning Superlight 13 Running Shoes

单只仅重 185 克，可满足马拉松比赛级的功能需求。鞋面利用中国传统织锦外观及缂丝工艺的原理改良一体织造技术，实现柔软织物和高强度 MONO 织物之间的转换，以满足功能需求。一体化织造鞋面减少了材料拼接和车缝，降低脚部受热起泡的概率。足弓处鸟类胸骨形态 TPU 支架，轻量化同时保证强度，对足弓有效支撑并抗扭转。外观上追求统一，从不透明到透明的转换带来更轻盈的观感。售价控制在人民币 469 元。

A single one weighs only 185 grams and can meet the functional requirements of the marathon level. The upper improves one-piece kntitting technique design to achieve the conversion between the soft fabric and high-strength MONO fabric through the use of traditional Chinese tapestry appearance and the principle of the tapestry to meet the functional requirements. One-piece knitting upper reduces material stitching and sewing in order to reduce the chances of blisters at the feet caused by heat. TPU in foot arch has a lightweight while ensuring strength that has a effective support for the arch and anti-twist. The appearance realizes the conversion from opaque to transparent to bring more light perception. The price is about RMB 469 yuan.

设计 DESIGN
孙京颐
Sun Jingyi

生产 MANUFACTURE
李宁（中国）体育用品有限公司
Li- Ning (China) Sports Goods Co., Ltd.

蒙斯书盒
Mons

蒙斯书盒可实现分类收纳，有效存放书籍，同类书籍存放在同个书盒中，更加清晰地管理书籍。同时具有阅读提醒功能，书盒最前方可正面存储一本书籍，将书籍封面展示出来，方便找寻，也能够提醒、鼓励用户更好地执行阅读计划；半开放设计，书盒上方不完全封闭，可以轻易将需要的书籍抽取出来。为了满足不同开本的书籍，设计大小两种规格。

Mons book box can realize classification of storage and store books effectively, and similar books are stored in the same book box for more clearly managing the books. At the same time, it has a read reminder function: the front of book box can store a book of which the cover displays for easy to be found and to remind and encourage users to better conduct a reading program; it adopts a semi-open design, and the book box is not completely closed which allow the user to easily extract the required books. In order to meet the different specifications of the books, we have two designs in the size of specifications.

设计 DESIGN
厦门松霖家居有限公司
Solux Home Lifestyle Co.,Ltd.

生产 MANUFACTURE
厦门松霖家居有限公司
Solux Home Lifestyle Co.,Ltd.

施陶芬实木软垫扶手椅
Fantasy

范特西椅采用无缝榫接结构，靠背与坐垫角度设定合理，使两根圆杆分担受力。一体化设计展现出柔和的曲线美，底座圆弧曲面设计保证实木结构稳定性又增添了轻盈的时尚感。椅子整体均采用柔和的曲线设计，通过曲线之间的穿插支撑起座面，降低受伤风险。黑胡桃木内敛的黑褐色柔和光泽，搭配黑色舒适的皮革坐垫，低调有内涵。

Fantasy chairs adopt seamless mortise structure with a reasonable angle in backrest and cushion that the two round rod to share the stress. The integrated design of chair shows a soft beauty of the curve, and the design of circle arc surface base ensures the stability of solid wood structure and adds a sense of light fashion. The overall chair adopts a soft curve design with the interspersed lod between the curve to support the seat surface so as to reduce the risk of injury. With black comfortable leather cushions,the dark brown color of black walnut reveals a sense of low key and emits soft luster.

设计 DESIGN
厦门松霖家居有限公司
Solux Home Lifestyle Co.,Ltd.

生产 MANUFACTURE
厦门松霖家居有限公司
Solux Home Lifestyle Co.,Ltd.

折纸椅
Bend Chair

作品灵感来源于童年时期的折纸飞机，再现手工折纸的概念，并将这种思路用到最适用这种手工艺的钣金行业内。钻石般切割的造型设计，环保健康的静电粉末喷涂降低了生产成本。炫酷的颜色打破沉静，对于公共场所无疑是个时尚的选择。由于材质的特性，这个产品可以运用于室内室外。

Bend chair inspired by paper airplanes in childhood is a process of re-realizing the concept of hand-made paper folding, and it made this idea be used in the sheet metal industry which is most suitable for this handicraft. The design of diamond-like cutting and environmental friendly and healthy electrostatic powder coating also reduces the cost of production. Cool colors to breaking the quiet in public places is undoubtedly a fashionable choice. Due to the characteristics of the material, this product can be applied to indoor and outdoor.

设计
DESIGN

柴晓东
Alex Chai

杭州格度家具设计有限公司
Gradodesign

生产
MANUFACTURE

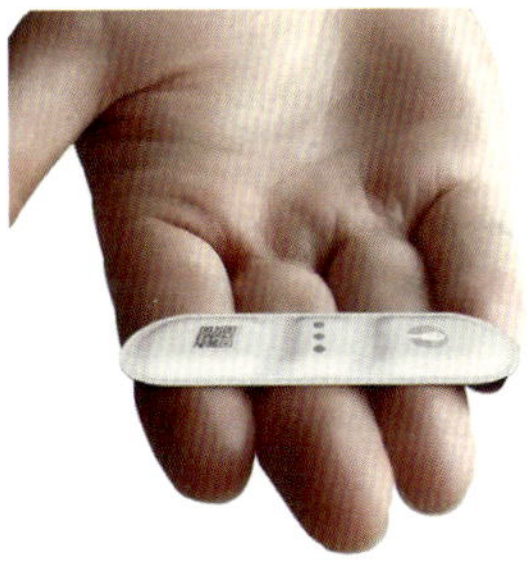

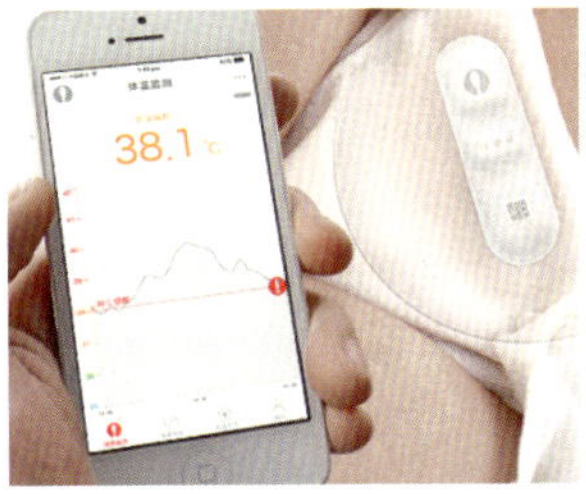

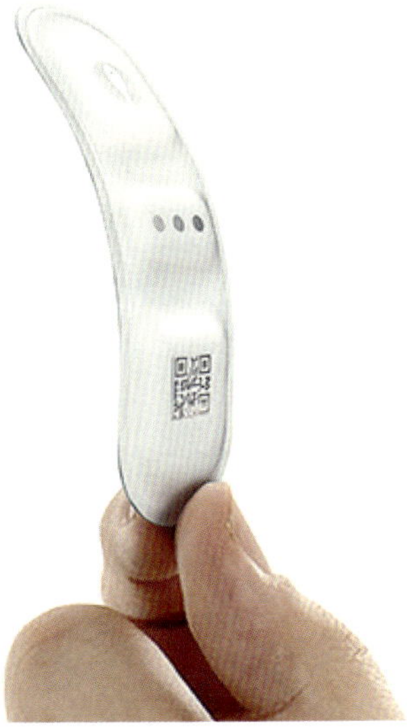

宝护片智能婴幼儿体温监护仪
BHP Intelligent Infant Body Tempesrature Monitor

“宝护片”独创婴幼儿腹部持续体温监测技术，通过采用独创的微量热感应技术和研发的纳米仿生材料把冰冷生硬的体温计变得轻薄柔软，让婴幼儿佩戴时感觉不到产品的存在。产品可实时监测并记录宝宝体温变化信息，并在体温出现异常变化时及时提醒用户，提升医护人员的工作效率以及减轻父母夜间照顾的难度和焦虑情绪。目前销量已突破百万。

“BHP” original infant abdominal continuous body temperature monitoring technology, through the use of the original micro-thermal induction technology and nano-biomimetic materials, turns the cold stiff thermometer light and soft so that infants and young children do not feel wearing monitoring products. The Products can real-time monitor and record information changes in body temperature of babies, and remind users when body temperature changes abnormally so as to improve the efficiency of health care workers and reduce the difficulty of night care and anxiety of parents. The current sales have exceeded one million level.

设计
DESIGN

北京宝护科技有限公司
Beijing Baohu Technology Co.,Ltd.

富士康精密组件（北京）有限公司
Foxconn International Holdings Co.,Ltd.

生产
MANUFACTURE

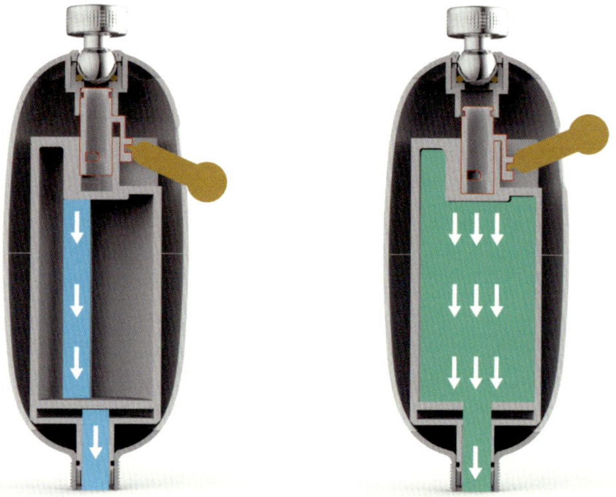

节能过滤器
Green Filter

节能过滤器增加了原水和净水的切换功能，让用户在使用花洒的不同用途时可以随心切换过滤器，这种创新让滤芯的寿命得到了延长，减少了用户更换滤芯的次数。花洒过滤器能去除水中杂质、余氯等，可以保护敏感肌肤；当用花洒清洗浴室时，可以把花洒过滤器的开关关掉，让原水不经过滤芯直接流出来，从而延长了滤芯的寿命，减少更换滤芯的次数。

Green filter adds the switching function of raw water and pure water, allowing users to use the shower to switch the filter in free for different purposes, and this innovation extends the service life of filter core and reduces the times to replace the filter for users. Sprinkler filter can remove impurities, chlorine in water and protect sensitive skin; when cleaning the bathroom with a shower, you can turn off the shower filter switch so that the raw water can directly flow out without through the filter, thus extending the serive life of the filter core and reducing the times to replace the filter.

设计 DESIGN
张桃燕
Zhang Taoyan

生产 MANUFACTURE
厦门建霖工业有限公司
Xiamen Runner Industrial Corporation

滑背椅
Imove

该款椅子采用的同步倾仰、波纤曲面技术可自动贴合腰部，将人的腰点与椅子的腰点紧密贴合，满足日常工作的需求，解决了人在办公中腰部出现的一些不适症状。产品选择环保舒适性材料，部件选用金属件抛光工艺。金属件的价值感、自动滑背的贴合让滑背椅更加满足现代办公的需求。本产品年销量达几百万，参展德国科隆家具展，得到国内外业内人士的好评。

The simultaneous tilting, wavefront technology the chair adopted can make the waist of the user automatically fit to the waist of the chair close to solve the troubles of daily work and to remit some discomfort symptom of people in the office. The product uses environmentally friendly materials and the parts use metal parts polishing technique. The sense of value of metal parts and conformability of automatic sliding back make the chair more meet the needs of modern office. Annual sales reach several million. It wins praise in the industry at home and abroad in Germany Cologne Furniture Fair.

设计 DESIGN
佛山市米朗工业设计有限公司
Foshan Milon Industrial Product Design Co.,Ltd.

生产 MANUFACTURE
佛山市谷腾家具有限公司
Goodtone Furniture Co.,Ltd.

手绘椅
Sketch Chair

本产品的灵感来源于设计师的手绘，整齐而有灵性、交接却不凌乱的排线。产品将线条的美感从二维的平面置入三维的空间，将平面的趣味以家具的方式呈现出来。本产品通体用圆形铁线表达线条。采用全线条的元素，在空间中显得轻盈明快，以折弯的线条将柔和寓于素静，兼容于家里、办公室、会议室等多种环境。

Sketch chair is inspired by the designer's hand sketching in which has neat and spiritual, but not messy lines. The product takes the beauty of the lines from the two-dimensional plane into the three-dimensional space and brings the fun of the plane to more people in the way of furniture. Sketch chair expressed lines by the round wire of the whole body. The element of lines reveals a sense of light and bright in the space and the bended lines contains the softness in the quiet which make the product compatible with the home, office, conference room and other environments.

设计 DESIGN
柴晓东
Alex Chai

生产 MANUFACTURE
杭州科沃工业设计有限公司
Gradodesign

国人迷你打蛋器
Mini Egg Whisk

这是一个基于东方人使用习惯的物美价廉的迷你打蛋器。借鉴竹编的结构原理，采用竹编弹性结构设计，通过经纬线上下交替用材料本身的弹性固定在筷子上，并可以兼容不同的筷子，可帮助筷子提高打蛋效率 2—3 倍。产品采用食品级 PP 为原料，模具简单，只有一个零件直接注塑而成。打蛋器体积小巧，方便收纳和清洗，且拆装方便。产品的成本只有不到一毛钱，远远低于同类产品。
This is an inexpensive and convenient mini whisk based on the using habit of oriental people. Drawing on the structural principles of bamboo weaving and the bamboo elastic structure design, the product fixes the material in the chopsticks with the elasticity of the material itself through the alternating latitude and longitude principle, and it can be compatible with different chopsticks to help improve the efficiency by 2-3 times. The Product uses food-grade polypropylene (PP) as raw material, and the mold is simple that is made of only one part through the direct injection. The whisk is small, easy to store and clean, and easy to disassemble. The cost of the product is less than a dime, far lower than similar products.

设计 DESIGN
宁波江东矩成创意产品设计有限公司
Ningbo Galachy Creative Product Design Co.,Ltd.

生产 MANUFACTURE
宁波市鄞州立翔塑胶有限公司
Ningbo Yinzhou Lixiang Plastic Co., Ltd.

乐摇筛筛盆
Leyao Sieve Basin

该产品通过结构的巧妙设计来完成铲屎官给猫轻松快速铲屎过程，三个同样的猫砂盆的叠加，无方向限位的设计，令用户的使用更加方便。正常过长的铲屎时间，被缩短到 6 秒，且可使用户在使用过程中远离宠物的排泄物。产品表面有纳米涂层，方便产品的清洗。京东众筹一天时间完成 10.2 万元的销售额，产品与美国、新西兰等国家外贸企业达成采购协议。

The product helps to clean cat feces easily and quickly through the clever structure design. The stack of the same three cat litters and no-limit direction design bring more convenience to the users. It shortens the normal clean time to 6 seconds, and keeps users away from the pet excrement when using it. The product wears a nano-coating to facilitate the cleaning of the product. It completed the sale of 102,000 yuan in Jingdong crowdfunding, and we have reached a procurement agreement with foreign trade enterprises in the United States, New Zealand and other countries.

设计 DESIGN
陈涛
Chen Tao

生产 MANUFACTURE
宁波海嘉塑料有限公司
Ningbo Haijia Plastic Co.,Ltd.

极致净水龙头
Slim Drinking-Water Faucet

该净水龙头设计遵循少即是多的设计理念，融合经典的点线面设计，功能专一明确，只留有必要的管、座与手柄，达到极简设计，设计更注重用户的使用体验感。产品出厂前完成装配，用户只需拧紧螺套连接水管便完成安装，操作简单。材料使用 SUS304 不锈钢，经久耐用，设计简洁易生产，工艺流程简便快速，可提高批量生产的效率，节省生产资源。

Slim drinking-water faucet follows the design concept of minimalism— less is more combined with the classic point line design, with a specific and clear function, leaving only the necessary tube, seat and handle to reach a minimal design and paid more attention to user experience. Products complete assembly before out of factory, the user simply tightens the screw to connect the water pipe to complete the installation. The material of products uses durable SUS304 stainless steel. A simple and easy design and a simple and fast technological process improve the efficiency of mass production and save production resources.

设计 DESIGN
珠海普乐美厨卫有限公司
Primy Corporation Limited.

生产 MANUFACTURE
珠海普乐美厨卫有限公司
Primy Corporation Limited

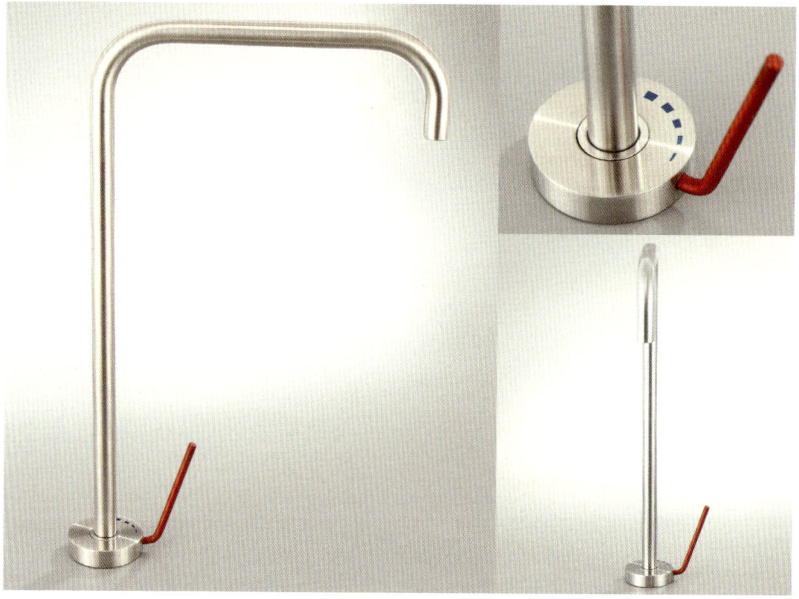

20V 高压清洗机
20V High Pressure Washer

该单柱塞水泵的创新设计，利用气泵自吸原理，使产品具备自吸功能，实现随时随地，在任何水源下都能实现吸水清洗。采用防回流电液联动技术，多级开关同时工作同时停止。外露电池包防水技术有效避免漏电等问题。产品的多功能喷头、多档调速可实现清洗、浇灌功能集成，扩展了产品的应用场景。长短枪自动切换高低压，实现用户轻松使用。

The product adopts a creative design of single plunger pump to equip the product with self-absorption function by the air pump self-priming principle for to achieve water absorption and cleaning in anytime and anywhere. It uses anti-return electro-hydraulic linkage technology to achieve multi-level switch working and stopping at the same time. Exposed battery pack waterproof technology effectively avoids leakage and other issues. The multi-function nozzle and multi-speed control can achieve cleaning and watering function integration, expanding the application scene of the product. Long and short guns automatically switch high and low voltage and bring users more convenience.

设计 DESIGN
宝时得科技（中国）有限公司
Positec Technology (China) Co., Ltd.

生产 MANUFACTURE
宝时得科技（中国）有限公司
Positec Technology (China) Co.,Ltd.

20V 智能枪钻
20V AI Drill

该产品采用的自动夹头技术可以实现单手更安全地安装工作头，解决工作头安装不直的问题。自动扭力识别技术可解决工具破坏表面、不好控制的问题。脉冲技术解决在光滑的表面定位问题，也更容易拆除坏头螺钉。采用锂电池技术，循环寿命长，安全性能好，无公害，无记忆效应，有效减少电池对环境污染的危害。手柄上黑色软胶与橙色软胶采用三次注塑工艺。

The automatic chuck technology adopted by the product can achieve more security to install the working head in—with one hand and solve the problem of distortion in the installation of working head. Automatic torque recognition technology can solve the problem of damage to the surface of the tool and bad control. The pulse technique solves the problem of smooth surface positioning and makes the removing of bad head screws easier. It uses lithium battery technology which has many advantages such as a long cycle life, good safety performance, free of pollution, no memory effect and it effectively reduces the battery harm to environmental pollution. The black soft and orange soft plastic on the handle uses the three-times injection molding process.

设计 DESIGN
宝时得科技（中国）有限公司
Positec Technology (China) Co.,Ltd.

生产 MANUFACTURE
宝时得科技（中国）有限公司
Positec Technology (China) Co., Ltd.

儿童趣味手工皂——极地系列
Children Handmade Soap - Polar Series

兜宝儿童趣味手工皂——极地系列，就像两块淡蓝色的“冰块”，里面有两只连着挂环的硅胶动物玩具（北极熊和企鹅），洗手的时候“冰块”（手工皂）逐渐变小，手工皂使用完剩下的是一只小动物，增加了利用率的同时让儿童体验不一样的洗手过程，培养孩子爱护动物、保护环境的意识。使用时和使用后可以将皂体挂起来，防止皂体滑落和保持干爽卫生。

The product children handmade soap - polar series look like two pieces of light blue ice in which there are two silica gel animal toys (polar bears and penguins) linked by a loop. It becomes smaller when you wash your hands till leaving a small animal toy. The interesting using process not only increases the utilization but allowing children to experience different washing process and develop a consciousness to love animals, protect the environment. You can hang up the soap body in use or after use to prevent slipping off and keep it dry and clean.

设计
DESIGN
唐雅、徐霍成
Tang Ya，Xu Huocheng

生产
MANUFACTURE
兜宝（上海）教育衍生品科技发展有限公司
Doubao (Shanghai) Technology Development Co.,Ltd.

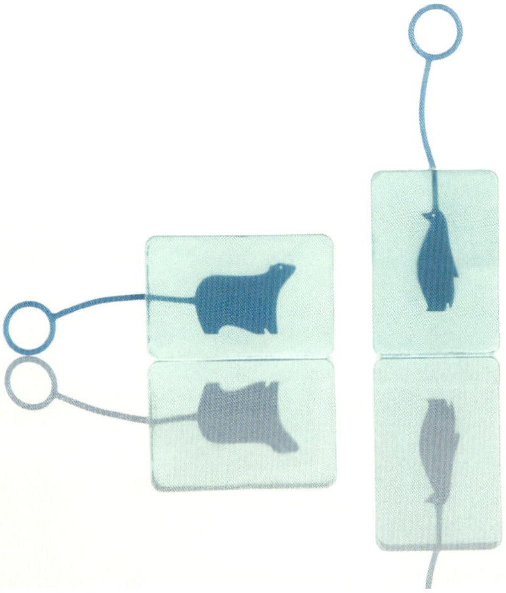

卷挑桌
Roll Picking Table

本产品采用弯曲木工艺一次性模压成型，采用桦木和橡木结合使用，浸油工艺（油为天然环保蓖麻油）制成。边缘纯手工打磨，触感细腻，精工制作的弯曲木工艺，让人坐上去舒适凉爽。且造型比例优美，材料规格用材考究且利用率高，符合工业化生产需求。整体模具压制，无接缝，结构稳固耐用，使用寿命长。

This product is a one-time molding of curved wood technology which is made of birch veneers and oaks and impinged in natural castor oil which is environmentally friendly. The edge is pure hand-polished and it has a delicate touch. It is cool and comfortable to sit due to the work-intensive curved wood technology . And the beautiful shape and the sophisticated use of materials are in line with industrial production needs. An integer mould is used for pressing. The chair has no joints and adurable structuren with long service life.

设计
DESIGN
张永和
Zhang Yonghe

生产
MANUFACTURE
曲美家居集团股份有限公司
Qumei Home Furnishings Group Co.,Ltd.

黛尔花洒
Slight Nod Shower

手持花洒面板中间的钢片采用了高镜面冲压工艺和激光打孔技术，并运用了按压面板切换功能技术，通过按压面板这一简单操作来实现切换淋浴水花功能的目的，给使用者带来舒适、便捷、趣味的操作体验。同时这种操作方式不仅仅局限于双手操作，也可以单手操作：将面板的接触点放在任何一个地方，通过单手用力轻轻一压就能达到切换的目的。

The steel plate in the middle of Slight Nod shower adopts a panel stamping process and laser drilling technology, and the press panel switching technology, through the simple operation of pressing panel to achieve the purpose of switching shower function, and brings the users comfortable, convenient and fun operation experience. At the same time this mode of operation is not limited to both hands, but also one-handed operation: the contact point can be on any one place of the panel, through a gentle pressure by single hand can achieve the purpose of switching shower.

设计 DESIGN
张桃燕
Zhang Taoyan

生产 MANUFACTURE
厦门建霖工业有限公司
Xiamen Runner Industrial Corporation

小巨蛋 T6
Mini Tea Set T6

该产品在外观上打破传统茶具有圈足和边脚等特征设计，采用更为简洁的一体成型设计。采用创新的扣烧工艺，原木防烫结构，拥有出色的手感和很强的防烫效果。无圈足正圆壶身结构与合理尺寸设计，不受左右手限制。环保 ABS 耐高温茶盘，组合式收纳结构，拥有 520 毫升储水空间，还可将整套茶具收纳进茶盘。淘宝众筹获得 1046% 的支持率，单月 52 万销售额。

The product uses a more simple one molding design, giving up the design of a circle foot and side feet characterized by the traditonal tea set in the way of appearance. Due to innovative deduction burning process and log scald-proof structure, mini tea set T6 owns an excellent feel and a strong scald-proof effect. A round body structure without a circle foot and a reasonable size design are easy to both left and right hand. The tea tray made of scald-proof environmentally friendly ABS material has a modular storage structure, with 520 ml of water storage space, and a capacity to hold the entire set of tea set. It gains a support rate of 1046% in Taobao crowd funding. A single monthly sale is 520 thousand.

设计 DESIGN
百伦设计
Balance Design

生产 MANUFACTURE
厦门泊喜科技有限公司
Xiamen Pertouch Co.,Ltd.

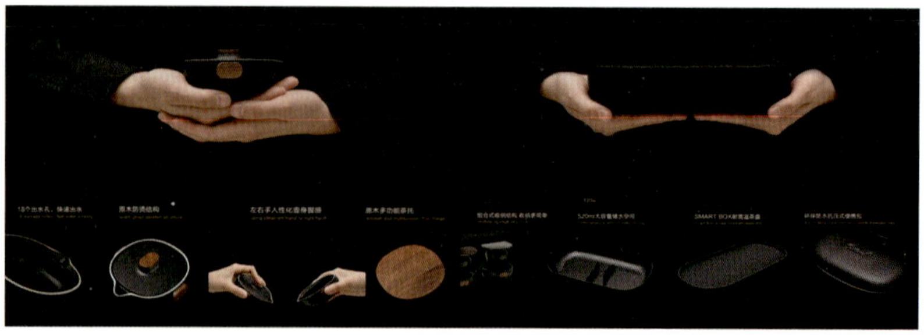

格调
Style

该款沙发具有强大的组合性，对不同的空间都有不俗的表现力。纯布艺的坐垫和靠背，贴合身体曲线，流线型的外展扶手更加实用美观。造型独特，使用了薄而坚韧的弯曲木单板，结构稳固耐用，配合超纤皮革搭配，清理方便，利用率高，符合工业批量化生产，且整体没有使用任何污染材料。内部框架使用了曲美专门的多层单板高频模压工艺，外面包覆皮革和布艺。

The sofa has a strong combination ability and a good expression in different space. Pure fabric cushion and backrest fit the body curve and the streamlined outreach armrests are more practical and beautiful. The unique shape, thin and tough curved wood veneer, durable structure, and ultra-fine leather, without using any pollution materials, all these elements make it easy to clean up with high utilization and in line with industrial mass production. The internal frame uses a special multi-layer veneer high-frequency molding process, and the outside is covered with leather and cloth.

设计
DESIGN

曲美设计中心
QM Design Center

曲美家居集团股份有限公司
Qumei Home Furnishings Group Co.,Ltd.

生产
MANUFACTURE

23 平方米 LOFT 变身七居室 停车库也能搬回家
Transformable Smart Home

该设计通过两个楼板的在不同高度的控制，满足不同的空间需求。靠里的红色楼板可在三个标高变化，靠窗的蓝色楼板可在五个标高变化。不同模式下，房间的布局各有不同。 在起居室、餐厅、健身房、家庭影院、书房、多人居之间来回变化与切换。智能系统主要包括了三大模块：大数据查看、安全系统、智能控制家电。

The design of the product can meet different space requirements through controling two floors at different heights. The red floor can be changed in three scales, the blue floor of the window can be changed in five scales. In different models, the layout of the room are different, which can change and switch among the living room, restaurant, gym, home theater, study, multi-human residence. The intelligent system mainly includes three major modules: large data view, security system, intelligent control of home appliances.

设计
DESIGN

张海翱
Zhang Haiao

上海华都建筑规划设计有限公司
Shanghai Huadu Architectural Design Limited

生产
MANUFACTURE

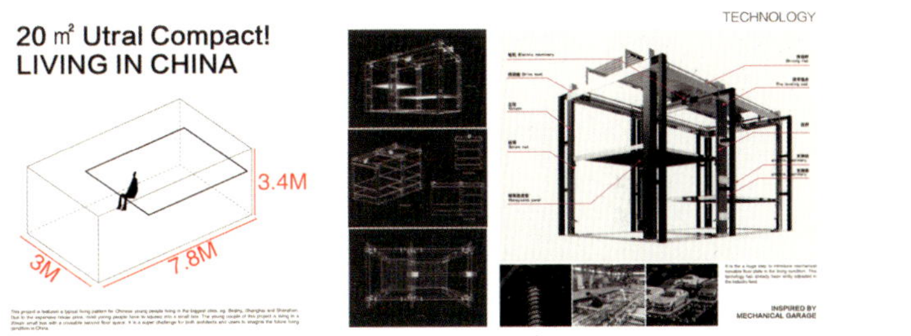

微烹宝 2
Microwave Cooking Pot

微烹宝采用超薄高硼硅玻璃为内胆，保障食品安全，可以放入微波炉进行加热烹饪，外层聚氨酯发泡工艺，长时间保温，对食材进行焖烧。玻璃与 PU 保温层的完美结合，比玻璃保鲜盒重量更轻，还可以达到 6 个小时的保温。用户带饭再也不用吃隔夜菜，只需将新鲜食材放入微烹宝中，微波加热 5 分钟，即可带走上班。目前订单数量已达 10 万只。

Microwave cooking pot uses ultra-thin borosilicate glass for the liner to ensure food safety and it allows to use in the microwave oven. The outer adopts polyurethane foam process for a long time insulation, allowing stewing the ingredients. Compared with the glass crisper, the perfect combination of glass and PU insulation layer has a lighter weight and a longer time of insulation for 6 hours. Users do not have to eat food cooked last night again, they just need to put the fresh ingredients into the microwave cooking pot and wait for 5 minutes of heating, they can take it away to work. The current number of orders has reached 100,000.

设计
DESIGN

王晓作、吴涛
Wang Xiaozuo, Wu Tao

台州优家塑业有限公司
Uka Home Production Co.,Ltd.

生产
MANUFACTURE

智能主动降噪助听器
Intelligent Active Noise Reduction Hearing Aid

智能主动降噪助听器，是由中国航天降噪研发团队针对老年人等听障人士所研发的带有主动降噪性能的助听耳塞。该产品有别于传统的助听器，它运用了航天 A.N.C 主动降噪技术及 D.S.R 数字信号修复技术，将独特的声音识别算法应用在识别有效声音、反馈抑制技术、噪声抑制技术以及降低功耗等方面。能有效过滤环境噪声，最大限度还原佩戴者听到的声音信号。

Intelligent active noise reduction hearing aid is a listening button with active noise reduction performance for the elderly and the hearing impaired developed by the Chinese aerospace noise reduction R & D team. Differing from the traditional hearing aids, it uses the aerospace ANC active noise reduction technology and DSR digital signal repair technology to apply the unique voice recognition algorithm to effective sound identidication, suppression technology feedback, noise suppression technology and power consumption reduction. It can effectively filter the environment noise and restore the sound signal the wearer heard to maximum extent.

设计 DESIGN
深圳航天金悦通科技有限公司
Shenzhen Aerospace Golden Shine Technology Co., Ltd.

深圳市知行创新工业设计有限公司
Shenzhen Thinkdo Design Co.,Ltd.
生产 MANUFACTURE

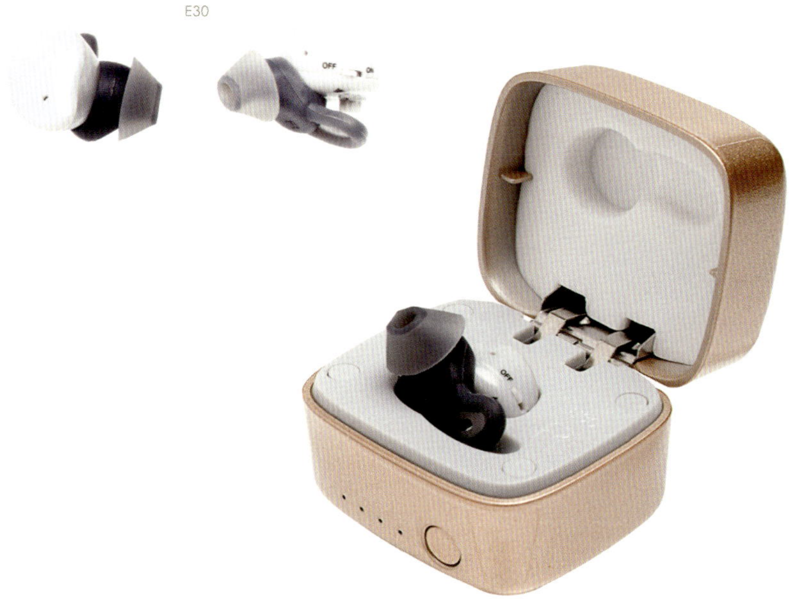

“视界”签字笔
Wide Vision Signature Pen

该产品是一支新概念的时尚签字笔，笔尖采用偏置结构，突破了中性笔笔芯中置的常规结构，书写时不易遮挡视线，并且类似钢笔的造型给人仪式感；尾部嵌入缓冲弹簧，提供舒适的书写弹性。偏芯结构和缓冲弹簧提供了新的书写体验，且可更换笔芯。产品完成了特殊的笔芯偏置结构工艺，偏置的笔颈、渐变效果的转印膜，尾部露出的缓冲弹簧都突出了整支笔的科技感与时尚感。

The product is a fashional signature pen with a new concept. The nib with offset structure broke through the conventional structure of the neutral refill, and it is not easy to block sight when writing, and the similar appearance to a pen gives the user a sense of formality; also the buffer spring embedded in the tail provides proper flexibility in writing. The offset-core structure and the buffer spring provide a new writing experience. It is avaliable for repalcement of refills. The offset pen neck, the gradual effect of the transfer film and the buffer spring appeared in the tail all highlight the sense of science and technology and fashion sense of the whole pen.

设计 DESIGN
上海晨光文具股份有限公司
Shanghai M.G Stationery Inc.

晨光文具大众品牌中心工业设计部
M&G R&D Center
生产 MANUFACTURE

种植栓
Seed Capsule

植物栓采用秸秆等自然回收材料制作而成。秸秆经过粉碎加工再混合环保胶与生态肥利用模具成型，通过高温处理并植入活性酵母菌制成栓体。植物栓产品使用现代生物和工业设计技术确保种子育苗和移栽过程的种植深度、温度和湿度控制。利用植物栓进行种子播种和幼苗移栽可以使作物提高成活率 100%，作物增产 20%—40%。

Seed Capsule is made of natural recycled materials such as straw. After crushing and processing straw, then the straw is mixed in with green plastic and ecological fertilizer and mold forming then it is molded with mould, finally it is dealt with it with high temperature and implanted active yeast to form capsule. Seed Capsule uses modern biological and industrial design techniques to ensure seeding depth, temperature and humidity control during seedling and transplanting processes. The adoption of Seed Capsule can increase crop survival by 100% and crop yield by 20%—40%in seedling and transplanting processes.

设计 DESIGN
马鞍山三卅工业设计有限公司
Ma'anshan Sansa Industrial Design Co., Ltd.

马鞍山三卅工业设计有限公司
Ma'anshan Sansa Industrial Design Co.,Ltd.
生产 MANUFACTURE

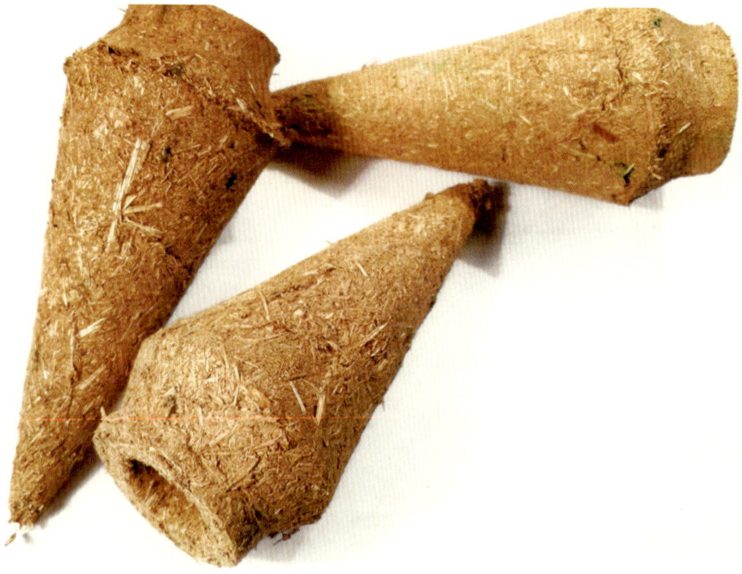

天元智能宠物喂食机
Tianyuan Intelligent Pet Feeder

该喂食机可通过智能手机软件，根据不同宠物品种与体重、年龄制定科学的喂养计划，内部设有高精度称重模块定时定量出粮。创新的高清摄像头与双向通话功能（高配版），可通过手机远程控制投食及喊话吸引宠物靠近，随时随地掌握宠物状态。不仅解决主人没时间喂养的烦恼，又解决不科学喂养导致宠物过于肥胖的问题。依靠自身电池可工作半年，整机使用寿命长达五年。

Tianyuan intelligent pet feeder can develop a scientific feeding plan according to different pet species, weight and age through the smart phone software, and in the internal set high-precision weighing module with regular quantitative food. The innovative high-definition camera and two-way call function (high version) allow users feeding and calling for pets to attract them near through mobile phone remote control and grasp the pet state in anytime and anywhere. This product not only solves the trouble that the owner has no time to feed pets, but also solves the obese problem of pets caused by unscientific feeding. The product can work for six months relying on their own battery, the life of the machine is up to 5 years.

设计
DESIGN
杭州天元宠物用品股份有限公司
Hangzhou Tianyuan Pet Products Co.,Ltd.

杭州热浪工业产品设计有限公司
Hangzhou Hotdesign Co.,Ltd.
生产
MANUFACTURE

智能电子锁设计
Intelligent Electronic Lock Design

该款智能电子锁打破传统电子锁的傻瓜模式，添加智能硬件设施，具有蓝牙开锁、刷卡开锁、远程开锁、钥匙管理、手机绑定、手机登录控制等功能。产品结合了云技术、信息安全技术和物联网技术，实现便捷、高安全性的开锁方式。主体铝合金和部分亚克力件的搭配使用，使其具有更好的环保性、品质感、散热好等特性。

The intelligent electronic lock broke through the fool mode of traditional electronic lock, adds intelligent hardware facilities, it has bluetooth unlock, swipe unlock, remote unlock, key management, cell phone binding, mobile phone login control and other functions. The product combines cloud technology, information security technology and Internet of things technology to achieve a convenient and high-security unlock mode. The combination of aluminum main body and some acrylic parts makes it has a better environmental protection, sense of quality, good heat radiationand other characteristics.

设计
DESIGN
安钥（北京）科技股份有限公司
An Key (Beijing) Technology Co., Ltd.

北京赛佳图工业设计有限公司
Beijing Saga FIG Industrial Design Co.,Ltd.
生产
MANUFACTURE

蜂巢插座
Comb Socket

蜂巢插座用模块化的思路重新定义了插座。该产品是一款方便模块化延展的六边形插座，进行阵列使用时，带来自然界蜂巢的视觉感受。底部设计有磁铁，方便吸附于任何铁质的桌腿和底部，也便于线的收纳。产品体积小、容量大，不占空间，顶部 USB 方便直接使用。灵活多样的组合方式，减少耗料，节省制造成本。每个棱面设计有圆角，手感舒适。

The comb socket redefines the concept of socket with a modular approach. The product is a hexagonal socket which is convenient for modular extension, and it brings the natural honeycomb visual experience when used in the array. The bottom has a magnet, which is easy to adsorb on any irony table legs or bottom and manage wires. The product has a small size, large capacity, occupies little space, and USB on the top is convenient for direct use. The flexible combination reduces the consumption of materials and saves manufacturing costs. Each prism designs with rounded corners making it feel comfortable.

设计 DESIGN
成都白云互动科技有限公司
Magicwe Technologies (Chengdu) Limited

成都意町工业产品设计有限公司
Chengdu Iding Industrial Design Co.,Ltd.
生产 MANUFACTURE

双层沥水篮
Double Drain Basket

双层沥水篮采用食品级可降解小麦秸秆原材料制成，自带小麦清香，健康环保可降解。坚固耐用，双层设计可一边洗物品，一边盛放物品，从而方便清洗、盛放瓜果蔬菜等。花型镂空设计，可快速沥水，上下套装一起使用，可防止台面积水。不用时，可直接叠加放置，节省存储空间。产品上线当日销量破万，半年破百万，并持续增长。

Double Drain Basket is made of food-grade wheat straw-biodegradable raw material, with wheat fragrance and a feature of health-friendly and environmental degradation. It is sturdy and durable, and the double-decker design can allow users to wash items while put items so as to facilitate the cleaning and the placement of fruits and vegetables. Flower-type hollow design can quickly drain, and the use of upper and lower packages together can prevent logged water in the table area. It can be directly stacked and placed when not in use to save storage space. The on-line sales of the first day on the market exceeded ten thousand, sales of six months surpassed one million and it continued to grow.

设计 DESIGN
义乌市品沐电子商务有限公司
Yiwu Pinmoo Electronic Commerce Co.,Ltd.

杭州热浪工业产品设计有限公司
Hangzhou Hotdesign Co.,Ltd.
生产 MANUFACTURE

H1 多功能拉杆箱
H1-Hybrid Luggage

该产品是一款多功能拉杆箱。独立式凹陷腔体设计，能够分离旅行中常用物品与不常用物品。外袋的形式可根据用户需要自由搭配选择材质和颜色，并可加装移动设备接口、夜行灯等功能配件，并划分不同的功能分区，适合不同职业人群的旅行储物需求。框架设计保证了边缘的挺括和外观的坚硬，防止撞击。外观设计大气，结构规整统一，外观时尚简约。

H1-Hybrid Luggage is a multi-function suitcase. The design of an independent sunken cavity can separate common items from other common items in travel. Users can have a choice of free collocation of material, color on the form of the outer bag according to their need, they also can even assemble some functional accessories such as USB, night lights and divide different functional partitions to meet the travel storage needs of different occupations. The frame design ensures firm of the edge and hard of the appearance to prevent impact. The appearance design is handsome, simple and fashionable, and the structure is uniformed.

设计 DESIGN
江苏汇鸿国际集团中鼎控股股份有限公司
High Hope Zhongding Corporation

马涛
Ma Tao
生产 MANUFACTURE

易用定时器
Easy Timer

该产品是一款可编程的电子定时插座，用来控制用电设备的定时通断电或者周期性工作。产品应用广泛，适用于电动车、电子产品等充电以及周期性照明等，节省电力资源，避免浪费。产品重新设计了用户界面和操作逻辑，精简了按键数量，不同于现有电子定时插座复杂的操作体验，更易使用，无需说明书便可完成设置。整体采用极简设计，表面质感亲肤细腻。

The product is a programmable electronic timed socket which can be used to timed break-make control of power equipment or power cycle work. Products are widely used for electric vehicles, electronic products such as charging and periodic lighting to save power resources and avoid waste. The product has redesigned the user interface and operational logic, simplified the number of keys, unlike the existing electronic timed sockets, which is easier to use and easier to set up without instructions. The overall product uses minimalist design, and the texture of surface is delicate.

设计 DESIGN
公牛集团工业设计团队
Gongniu Design Team

生产 MANUFACTURE
公牛集团有限公司
Gongniu Group Ltd.

沁宝 650
Atmobot 650

该产品是一款智能空气净化器，通过 LDS 激光定位扫描系统建立家庭平面图，实行巡航净化。内置颗粒、亮度多重智能感应，主动感知生活环境变化。超声波传感器和红外传感器使机器在移动过程中灵活躲避障碍物，操控界面实时显示数据，结合灯效变化，使用户对空气质量一目了然。造型为简洁的几何圆柱形，顶部采用镜面效果，搭配灯效彰显产品科技感。

The product is an intelligent air purifier, it uses the LDS laser positioning scanning system to establish a family plan and put house the purification on cruise. Multiple built-in particle and luminance smart sensors automatically perceives changes in the environment. Ultrasonic transducers and infrared sensors help the machine avoid obstacles flexibly when in motion. The operation and control interface displays PM2.5 data on a real-time basis. Color of lighting changes in accordance with the real-time pollution level, which is easy and direct for the users to read. The simple geometric cylindrical molding style and the mirror effect on the top, together with the effect of light, make the product a technological sense.

设计 DESIGN
科沃斯机器人股份有限公司
Ecovacs Robotics Co.,Ltd.

生产 MANUFACTURE
科沃斯机器人股份有限公司
Ecovacs Robotics Co.,Ltd.

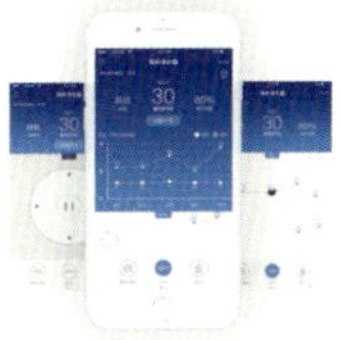

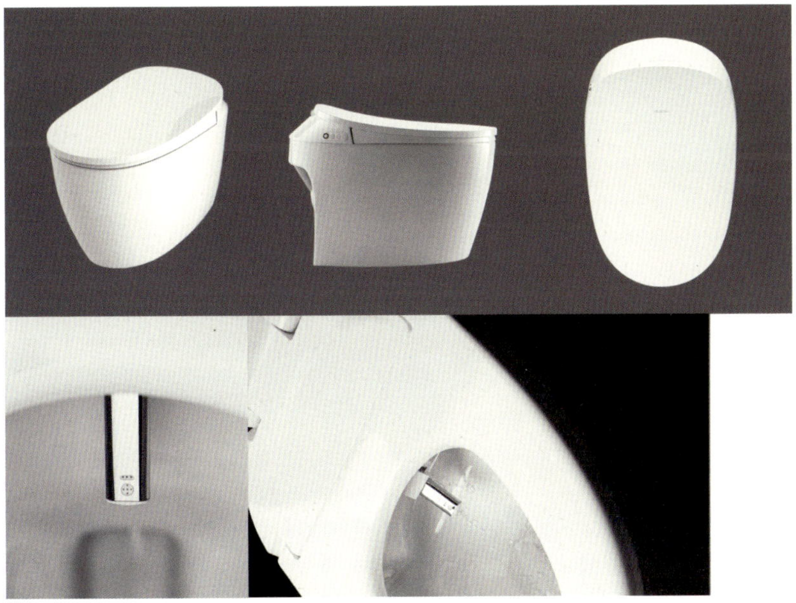

HDE5001T 智能连体坐便器
HDE5001T Smart Toilet

该产品是一款智能坐便器，引入医用级紫外线喷头杀菌技术，能高效杀灭细菌污物，并增加停电冲水功能。提出座圈 30 点加热标准，确保圈温分布均匀。采用变频即热，缩短水温加热时长，比储热式节能 70%。按键周围采用微凸设计，引导盲操作，防止磕碰和误操作。产品具有漏电保护、泄压保护、气泡保护、低压保护、水温保护、防火保护等功能。

The product is a smart toilet. The introduction of medical grade UV nozzle sterilization technology can effectively kill bacteria and dirt and increase the flushing function when power-off. The toilet seat 30 point heating standard of the product ensures uniform distribution of seat temperature. The adoption of variable frequency heating and shortened water temperature heating time is 70% of energy saving than that of thermal storage. The surrounding area of button applies a micro-convex design to guide the blind operation and prevent bump and misoperation. Products have leakage protection, venting protection, bubble protection, low voltage protection, water temperature protection, fire protection and other functions.

设计 DESIGN
惠达卫浴研发中心
Huida R

生产 MANUFACTURE
惠达卫浴股份卫浴有限公司
Huida Sanitary Ware Co.,Ltd.

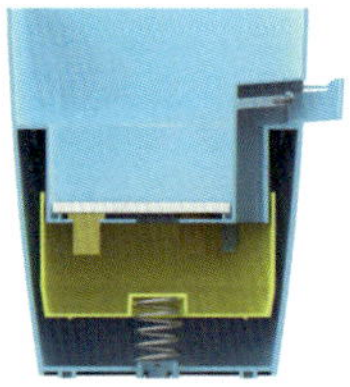

旱博士养花器
Hydro-Box Flower Pot

旱博士养花器解决了传统盆栽浇水量和浇水时机不易控制的难题，利用弹簧支撑储水盆，使水面位置不变，保证为植物持续供水。自动升降供水装置，确保泥土湿度恒定，营造稳定健康的生长环境，提高成活率。花盆外侧设置弹出式加水口，一键开关，方便操作，避免花泥冲刷流失和板结退化。盆底多孔吸水陶瓷板利于根系吸收水分和空气交换，避免烂根。

Hydro-box flower pot solves the problem of difficult control to watering quantity and watering time of traditional potting, it uses the spring support reservoir to keep the same water surface position so as to ensure continuous water supply for the plant. Automatic lifting water supply devic ensures the constant soil moisture, creates a stable and healthy growth environment and improves the survival rate. Outside the flower pot set pop-up nozzle, a key switch, is easy to operate, which can avoid mud erosion and board degradation. The porous water absorbing ceramic plate bottom is conducive to absorption of water and air exchange for root and can avoid rot.

设计 DESIGN
刘豪、胡越强
Liu Hao, Hu Yueqiang

生产 MANUFACTURE
浙江泰索科技有限公司
Zhejiang Taisuo Technology Co.,Ltd.

微波烧烤锅
Microwave Grill Pot

微波烧烤锅将内胆把手设计为外露并可独立拿出，每次使用只需要清洗内胆，不需要清洗整个产品。外露的把手包裹橡胶材质，防烫伤，手感好。产品将微波与食物隔离，减少食物营养的流失。使用程序简单，易掌握，热效率高、节约时间和能源。产品采用大圆弧的设计手法，具有亲和力，整体造型简约，符合现代年轻人审美，能够很好地融入家居中。

The liner handle of microwave grill pot is designed to be exposed outside and can be independently taken out, so after use you only need to clean the liner and do not need to clean the entire product. Exposed handle was wrapped rubber material which is anti-scald and it is easy to hold. Products isolates microwave from food to reduce the loss of food nutrition. The use procedure is simple and it is easy to use. It has a high thermal efficiency in favour of saving time and energy. The large arc shaped design makes the produuct a sense of affinity, and the simple overall shape is in line with the modern young people aesthetic so as to be compatible to the home furniture.

设计 DESIGN
苏州奔马厨具有限公司
Suzhou Benm Kitchen Appliance Co.,Ltd.

生产 MANUFACTURE
苏州奔马厨具有限公司
Suzhou BenM Kitchen Appliance Co.,Ltd.

智能多功能电动执行器
Intelligent Mutual Function Circuit Actuator

智能多功能电动执行器采用硅胶与金属融合的设计风格，并创新了指针形式。产品结构设计合理，流线型的设计起到完美的导流作用，有效防水。产品使用先进的设备和优秀的喷漆技术处理铸铁表面，表面质感优越。整体设计摒弃以往方正的风格，外观采用流线型设计，黄黑配色提升产品气质，提高产品档次。

Intelligent mutual function circuit actuator uses a unique style with a combination of silicon and metal and innovates pointer form. Product structure design is reasonable, and streamlined design plays a perfect diversion role and it is effective waterproof. The product uses advanced equipment and excellent painting technology to deal with cast iron surface and the surface texture is superior. The overall design abandons the past square style, and the appearance adopts streamlined design, and yellow and black color enhances product temperament and improves product level.

设计 DESIGN
浙江澳翔自控科技有限公司
Zhejiang Aoxiang Auto-Control Technology Co.,Ltd.

温州先临左岸工业设计有限公司
Wenzhou Shining Left Bank Industrial Design Co.,Ltd.
生产 MANUFACTURE

G28 连框开关
G28 Grid-Type Switches

该连框开关通过连框、通框设计，让单体产品可先接线后拼装，避免漏装外框导致重装，连框的卡扣定位设计使产品排布更均匀，解决开关上墙高低差、漏装、重装等痛点，满足不同使用场景的需求。产品使用倒拔模工艺，减小缝隙，提升精致度。外观简洁大方，采用大面板造型，增强整体感。表面采用幻影纹理，体现产品的差异化，微弧面更显居家感。

Grid-type and component-type design of G28 grid-type switches allowing connecting wire before assembly in case of neglected installation. The button positioning design makes the product more uniform arrangement to solve problems sucn as height difference of the wall above the switch, neglected installation, heavy equipment and other pain points to meet the needs of different use of the scene. Products use inverted draft process to reduce the gap and improve the degree of sophistication. Simple and generous appearance and the use of large panel shape enhance the overall sense. The surface uses phantom texture to reflect the product differentiation, and the micro-arc surface reveal more home feeling.

设计 DESIGN
宁波公牛电器有限公司
Ningbo Gongniu Electric Co.,Ltd.

严熙银、田发文
Yan Xiyin, Tian Fawen
生产 MANUFACTURE

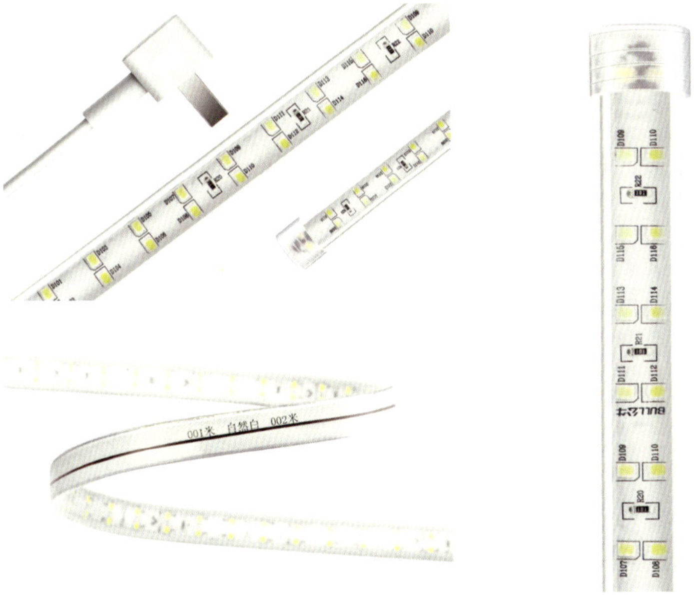

LED 灯带
The LED Lights Bring

LED 灯带采用弧形设计，营造大发光角度，使空间通透明亮，洗顶效果优秀。穹顶折射技术使光色均匀无暗角，光线质感好，装饰效果强。搭配开合式卡扣的良好人机体验设计，快速牢固连接，方便使用。弧面设计便于正面朝上安装，防止灯带扭转，保证光线正常。背面米数标记，方便快速选择所需。采用环保铜箔基板、环保 PVC 和优质灯珠，节约电力资源。

The LED lights bring adopts curved design, creates a large luminous angle, makes the space transparent and bright and an excellent effect of lighting up the smallpox. Dome refraction technology makes light color uniform without dark corners, and good light texture builds a strong decorative effect. With a combination of good experience of retractable button design, the fast and secure connection makes it is easy to use. The curved design makes it is easy to install toward upside and prevent the light belt from twisting to ensure normal light. The meter mark on the back side is easy to quickly select the required. The use of environmentally friendly copper foil substrate, environmentally friendly PVC and high-quality lamp beads save power resources.

设计 DESIGN
宁波公牛光电科技有限公司
Ningbo Gongniu Optoelectronic Technology Co.,Ltd.

宁波公牛光电科技有限公司
Ningbo Gongniu Optoelectronic Technology Co.,Ltd.
生产 MANUFACTURE

智立方插座（F1330/F1331）
PowerDock

本产品不仅是插座，也是一个小型电源管理平台，可结合手机应用程序管理用电设备，远程控制设备通断电。插座与理线盒一体设计，解决插头多、乱、脏的现象。拥有电量统计、过载预警、防雷失效等提示功能，保障安全。具有稳定性好、阻燃性强、耐冲击、防开裂的优点，使用寿命长。采用北欧极简设计风格，精炼造型、色彩、光效，完美融入家居环境。

This product is not only a socket, but also a small power management platform, which can be combined with mobile phone applications to manage electrical equipment and remote control on and off power of equipment. Socket and management box integrated design solves the problem of sundry and messy plugs. The function of electricity statistics, overload warning, lightning protection failure ensure safety. It has advantages of good stability, strong flame retardant, impact resistance and anti-cracking, long service life. It uses the Nordic minimalist design style and refined modeling, color and light efficiency to be perfectly compatible with home environment.

设计 DESIGN
公牛集团工业设计团队
Gongniu Design Team

生产 MANUFACTURE
公牛集团有限公司
Gongniu Group Ltd.

米格 S LED 台灯
Mi-Ge S LED Desk Lamp

米格 LED 台灯是一款保护视力的台灯。发光面呈蜂窝造型，专业光学设计有效防止眩光。特别设计的背后补光，在昏暗环境下降低环境照度的落差，提高视觉舒适度，有助于视力保护。光源采用 LED，有效降低照明能耗。整体选用高质量导热塑料，注塑而成。为防止灯头变形扭曲，采用模内塑包铝的制作工艺。整体设计简约精致，给用户带来朴素实用的体验。

Mi-GeS LED Desk Lamp is a lamp of protecting eyesight. The luminous surface is honeycomb shape and the professional optical design effectively prevents glare. Specially designed fill-in light behind can reduce the difference of environmental illumination in the dark environment, improve visual comfort and contribute to vision protection. Light source uses LED and effectively reduces lighting energy consumption. The overall product is made of injection of high-quality thermal plastic. In order to prevent distortion of the lamp cap, it uses in-mold plastic aluminum production process. The overall design is simple and elegant and bring the user a simple and practical experience.

设计 DESIGN
欧普照明全球研发中心
Opple Lighting Global R&D Center

生产 MANUFACTURE
欧普照明股份有限公司
Opple Lighting Co.,Ltd.

free lady 哑铃杯
Free Lady Dumbbell Cup

该产品将办公室轻运动概念植入日常饮水杯中，帮助女性用户利用碎片时间锻炼，有效缓解久坐产生的颈椎、腰椎等部位的积劳，提高身体素质，摆脱亚健康，形成积极向上的生活方式。产品容量合理，重量变化科学。水杯方便携带，便于随时随地锻炼。杯身采用精致的不锈钢材质，具有良好的保温性能。收腰造型打造线条美感，也提供舒适的手握位置。

The product is a daily drinking cup desinged with the concept of office light sport. It helps female users to use small moments to exercise and effectively alleviates exhaustion of cervical and lumber vertebra and other parts of the body caused by sedentariness, improves physical fitness, gets rid of sub-health and forms a positive lifestyle The Product has a proper capacity and a scientific weight. The cup is easy to carry and be used as a dumbbell for users to exercise in anytime and anywhere. Cup body is made of exquisite stainless steel and it has a good insulation properties. Waist shape not only reveals beauty of lines, but also provides a comfortable position to hold by hand.

设计 DESIGN
杭州领跑者工业设计有限公司
Hangzhou LPZ Industrial Design Co.,Ltd.

生产 MANUFACTURE
杭州领跑者工业设计有限公司
Hangzhou LPZ Industrial Design Co.,Ltd.

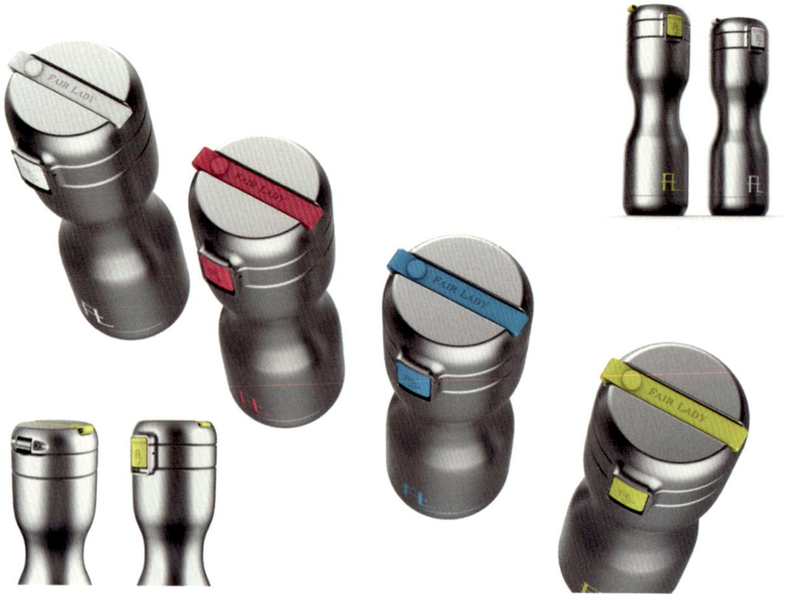

必迈全程马拉松跑鞋
MILE 42K

必迈全程马拉松跑鞋注重长距离奔跑后程由疲劳引起的伤病防护，鞋底材料做了四重密度，引导正确步伐姿态。产品利用参数化理念和工具设计了精确对位的排湿透气网孔，机器编程的方式改进网孔的透气和支撑强度。采用参数化形式满足运动功能，参照东方瓷器落款方式放置品牌 LOGO，实现理性科学与传统美学结合。注重建立长久的品牌识别。

BMAI marathon running shoes pay attention to injury prevention caused by fatigue after long-distance running, and sole material designs with a four-density to guide correct gesture of pace. The product uses parametric concepts and tools to design a ventilating mesh of precise alignment, and machine programming improves the permeability and supporting strength of the mesh. The adoption of parametric forms meets the motor function, and the reference to the way of oriental porcelain inscription to place brand LOGO achieves a combination of rational science and traditional aesthetics. It focuses on building long-term brand recognition.

设计
DESIGN
刘铮
Axis Liu

北京必迈体育用品有限公司
Bmai Sports
生产
MANUFACTURE

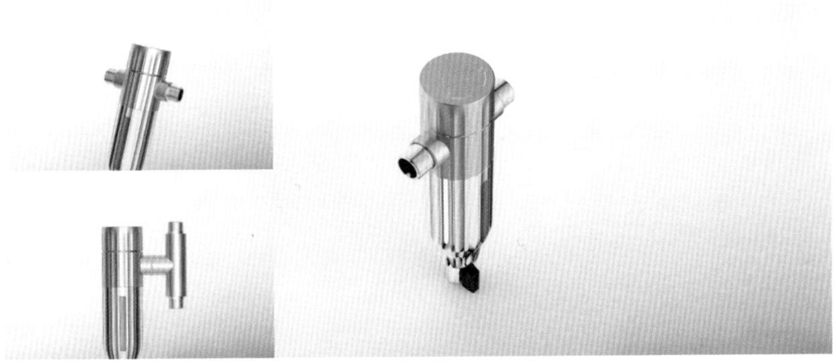

畅流 反冲洗前置过滤器
Flow Backwash Pre-Filter

该产品是一款反冲洗前置过滤器，比基本过滤增加了“反冲洗技术”，利用水流对滤芯进行由内向外的反向冲洗，深度清洗附着在滤网上的泥沙、杂质，净化全家用水。产品无须更换滤芯，只需定期清洗。万向进出水口设计，增强了产品安装的空间灵活性。独特的纹路造型设计，保证了产品的操控便利性。杯体外壳上设计透明窗，过滤清洗效果清晰明了。

The product is a flow backwash pre-filter. Compared to the basic filter, it increases the "backwashing technology" and uses water to backwash the filter from the inside, deep cleans the sediment, impurities attached to the filter and clean family Water. Products do not need to replace the filter but just regular cleaning. The design of universal inlets and outlets enhances the spatial flexibility of the product installation. Unique pattern design ensures the convenience of the operation of product. Cup body designs with a transparent window and filter cleaning effect is clear.

设计
DESIGN
彭江明、林细勇
Peng Jiangming, Lin Xiyong

日丰企业集团有限公司
Rifeng Enterprise Group Co.,Ltd.
生产
MANUFACTURE

家居两用刷
Dual-use Brush

家居两用刷将硅胶与塑料相结合，有效利用不同材料，针对材质不同的衣物可分别使用毛刷和硅胶刷进行清洁，高效解决不同材质衣物的清洁问题，开启一种新的家居生活体验。简洁的造型、别致的设计提高了产品的实用性，工艺简单，结构紧凑，减少了原材料使用，降低了生产成本，具有高性价比。盆栽造型为卫浴空间进行了装饰点缀。

Dual-use brush combines silica gel with plastic. It effectively uses different materials, can be used for different clothing cleaning with hairbrush and silicone brush, and provides an efficient solution to different-material clothing cleaning problems and brings a new home life experience. Simple shape and unique design improve the practicality of product, and the simple proess and compact structure reduce the use of raw materials and production cost, so the product owns a cost performance. Potting-like appearance decorates the bathroom.

设计
DESIGN

义乌市浪尖工业设计有限公司
Yiwu Artop Design Co.,Ltd.

生产
MANUFACTURE

义乌市良舍家居用品有限公司
Yiwu Liangshe Household Articles Co.,Ltd.

折叠收纳盒
Folding Storage Box

该产品是一款可以进行合理分类的收纳盒。其构造方式运用了折纸的原理，仅需要一个步骤即可打开使用，免去复杂的组装过程，解决桌面物品摆放杂乱的问题。利用等比例的单元结构的特点，每个收纳盒均可提供不同大小的区域，方便收纳各种不同类型的物品，满足多种收纳需求。产品采用扁平包装，减少了包装与运输体积，方便实用。

The product is a storage box with a reasonable classification. The construction of the product applies the principle of paper folding, and only one step can open it, which eliminate the complex assembly process and solve the problem of messy items on the desktop. Due to application of the characteristics of isometric unit structure, each storage box can provide area with different sizes to facilitate the storage of different types of items to meet a variety of storage needs. The product adopts flat packaging and reduces the packaging and transport volume, and it is convenient and practical.

设计
DESIGN

叶晋豪、麦结恩
Ye Jinhao, Mai Jie'en

生产
MANUFACTURE

阳江市爱立德实业有限公司
Yangjiang Ailide Industries Limited

安全瓜刨
Peeler S

该产品是一款解决了日常烹饪中安全问题的瓜刨，简洁实用。产品通过移动把手将刀片藏在塑料壳内部，避免用户被割伤，并可进行合理收纳或挂在墙上。瓜刨以钢丝作为把手的骨架，刀片焊接在钢丝上，既降低了材料成本又减少了瓜刨的重量。产品整体由简单的胶囊形状塑料外壳和钢丝组成，几何造型简洁极致。产品部件可拆解分离，便于回收再利用。

The product is a simple and practical peeler to solve the security problems in daily cooking. The product can hide the blade inside of the plastic shell by moving the handle to keep the user from being cut and can be properly stored or hung on the wall. The peeler uses wire as the skeleton of the handle, and the blade is welded to the wire to reduce the cost of materials and the weight of the peeler. The product consists of a simple capsule-shaped plastic shell and steel wire, and the geometric modeling is concise and extreme. Product components can be disassembled and is easy to recycling.

设计 DESIGN
叶晋豪
Ye Jinhao

生产 MANUFACTURE
阳江市爱立德实业有限公司
Yangjiang Ailide Industries Co.,Ltd.

提篮几
Tii Table

该产品是一款仿照提篮设计的茶几，提手可上下活动，兼顾移动与收纳两种功能，放下提手可阻挡物体掉落，将使用功能与设计趣味相结合。产品巧妙设计了提手与桌面圆盘连接的转折处，通过简单半圆形的铣形处理，使提手与圆盘完美契合，实现开合模式自由切换。产品组装简单，只需六颗螺丝即可轻松完成。材料采用北美白蜡木与 E0 级多层板，实用美观。

The product is a tea table based on basket design. The handle can move up and down and has functions of movement and storage. Put Laying down the handle can prevent the object to fall, and it combines using function and interesting design. The handle is cleverly designed to connected to the round desktop to form a perfect conjunction through a simple semi-circular milling processing so as to achieve the free switching of opening and closing mode. Product assembly is simple, just six screws is enough. Tii table is made of north America ash wood and E0 grade multilayer board, which is very handsome and practical.

设计 DESIGN
周安彬
Zhou Anbin

生产 MANUFACTURE
广州一起住家具有限公司
Guangzhou Living Together Furnither Co.,Ltd.

随心控厨房龙头
Free Control Kitchen Faucet

随心控厨房龙头可以通过遥控器控制水流开关，避免无法及时关闭龙头造成水资源浪费。通过把手设置水温和流量，用户可用手背、手肘、膝盖操作遥控器，控制水流开关。遥控器符合人体工学设计，采用自发电技术，无需连接电源线，操作简单。遥控按键无须打孔安装，方便放置。利落干脆的线条，诠释现代简约之美。

Free control kitchen faucet can control the switch of flow through the remote control to avoid waste caused by forgetting closing flow. The user can set the water temperature and flow through the handle, also can use the back of the hand, elbow and knee to operate remote control to control the water switch. Remote control accords with ergonomic design, adopts self-power technology, has a simple operation without need to connect the power line. Remote control buttons do not need perforation for installation and is easy for placement. The neat lines is the interpretation of the modern simple beauty.

设计 DESIGN
林纪巧、卢玲
Lin Jiqiao, Lu Ling

生产 MANUFACTURE
九牧厨卫股份有限公司
Jomoo Kitchen&Bathroom Appliances Co.,Ltd.

分装奶粉盒
Formula Container

分装奶粉盒设计灵感来源于亲子制作陶器情景，视觉纹理结合细腻的磨砂质感，让产品拥有独特的手感设计，操作更加贴合和方便，提供良好体验。产品改进了旋转结构，外形更加简练，盒身紧凑，方便携带。外观设计拓展了产品的使用范围，不仅可以装儿童奶粉，也可以装蛋白粉、代餐粉等。盖子采用鲜亮的设计，并配合球形，既简洁现代，又具有童趣。

The design of formula container is inspired from the scene of parent-child pottery, visual texture combined with delicate matte texture to make the product have a unique touch feeling and make the operation more proper and convenient so as to provide a good experience. The product improves the rotation structure to make the shape more concise, compact and easy to carry. The appearance design expands the range of use of the product, not only can be used for storing children's milk powder, but also protein powder, meal meal and so on. The ball-shaped cover with bright color reveals senses of simple, modern and childlike.

设计 DESIGN 德珂（上海）母婴用品有限公司 Decobebe (Shanghai) Co.,Ltd.

李曼、向华 Li Man，Shine Xiang **生产** MANUFACTURE

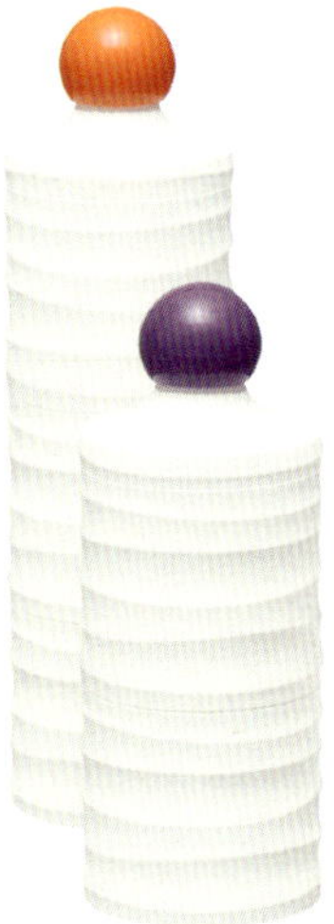

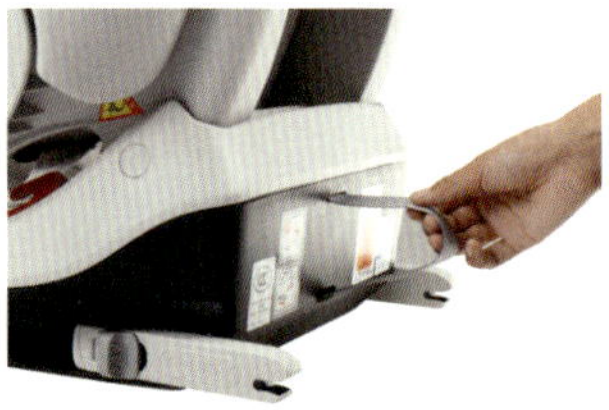

铠甲舰队 V505A PLUS
V505A PLUS

本产品是一款儿童安全座椅，新型安全带安装方式拥有国家发明专利，比传统方式具有更高的稳定性和可靠性。产品具有强大的弹出式侧面防撞系统，安全可靠。头枕肩带可联动无级调节，简单方便。椅背角度设置三档调节，舒适实用。本产品造型优雅，线条流畅，而且符合人机工程学，使不同年龄段的儿童都有舒适的乘坐体验。

This product is a children safety seat. The new type seat belt installation method has a national invention patent and a higher stability and reliability than the traditional way. The product has a strong pop-up side collision avoidance system, which is safe and reliable. Headrest shoulder strap can be linked to stepless adjustment, simple and convenient. Back angle sets third gear adjustment, which is comfortable and practical. This product is elegant and ergonomic, has smooth lines, and brings children of different ages a comfortable ride experience.

设计 DESIGN 麦克英孚（宁波）婴童用品有限公司 Max-inf (Ningbo) Baby Product Co., Ltd.

麦克英孚（宁波）婴童用品有限公司，研发部 Max-inf (Ningbo) Baby Product Co.,Ltd. R **生产** MANUFACTURE

物理防烫吸管
Anti-Scald Straw

物理防烫吸管创新应用了记忆金属材料智能识别水温，防止使用者饮水时由于误喝等因素烫伤。巧妙的防烫伤设计可以适用诸多领域的应用，如热饮、热茶等。适用于真空杯等隔热效果好的水杯，解决壶装热水喷溅现象。外观采用了“海星”语义，使解构后的形态简化的同时不失趣味性，微笑波浪纹理设计给使用者带来愉悦舒适的心情。

Anti-scald straw innovatively apply the memory metal material to identify the water temperature in case of being burned when drinking water. Clever anti-burn design can be applied to many areas, such as hot drinks, hot tea and so on, thus is suitable for vacuum cups and other cups with good insulation effect to solve the problem of pot hot water splashing. The appearance adopts semantics of "starfish" to simplify the shape after the deconstruction without losing interest and smile wave texture design brings the user pleasure and comfort.

设计 DESIGN 合肥为先产品设计有限公司 Hefei Weixian Product Design Co., Ltd.

合肥为先产品设计有限公司 Hefei Weixian Product Design Co.,Ltd. **生产** MANUFACTURE

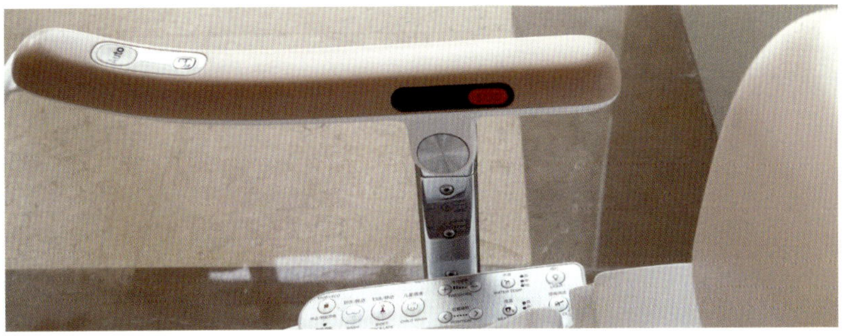

老人马桶升降辅助器
Protected-Toilet Seat Lifting Equipment

老人马桶升降辅助器针对老人、病人、孕妇等腿脚不便的特殊群体而设计，方便他们的坐下与起立，恢复其半自理能力。产品应用场景广泛，可安装于浴室、卫生间、医院、疗养院等空间。产品采用不锈钢材质，经久耐用，并且具有很强的抗腐蚀性。扶手表面进行抗菌处理，材料可回收利用。整体造型圆润，配色温馨。

Protected-Toilet seat lifting equipment is designed for the elderly, patients, pregnant women and other special groups with legs and feet inconvenient for convenience of their sit and stand up to restore their semi-self-care ability. Application of the product has a wide range of scenes including bathroom, hospitals, nursing homes and other palces. Products are made of stainless steel, durable, and has a strong corrosion resistance. Armrest surface is dealt with antibacterial treatment and the materials can be recycled. The overall shape is round and the color is warm.

设计
DESIGN

董平莉、吴冬
Dong Pingli, Wu Dong

九牧厨卫股份有限公司
Jomoo Kitchen&Bathroom Appliances Co.,Ltd.

生产
MANUFACTURE

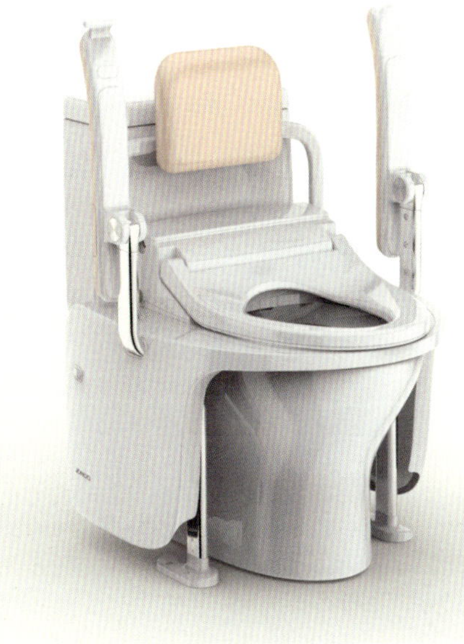

暖言一人食器
For One

暖言一人食器是针对吃饭时间不规律的人群所设计，通过蜡烛加热的方式将食物温度长时间保存，将餐具的功能从单一的放置食物扩展到保温，无须二次加热，让饮食更加健康，开启新的生活模式。产品采用原木把手进行点缀，不仅能够起到防烫作用，也让整套产品更显活力。造型采用简单线条，形态圆润，清新秀气。

For one is designed for people with irregular eating time. It can preserve the food temperature for a long time through candle heating, and extend the function of the tableware from single food store to the insulation without secondary heating to make the diet more healthy and open a new lifestyle. The product uses log handle for embellishment, which not only can play the role of scald prevention, but also make the whole product more dynamic. The modeling with simple lines and round shape is fresh and delicate.

设计
DESIGN

刘培清、陈文
Liu Peiqing, Chen Wen

杭州膳佳家居用品有限公司
Hangzhou Shanjia Lifestyles Co.,Ltd.

生产
MANUFACTURE

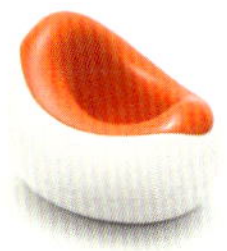

儿童坐便器
Baby Potty

儿童坐便器通过外形及功能的设计，为儿童带来安全舒适的使用体验。产品使用进口抗菌技术和材料，有效抑制细菌增长。部分区域表面光滑，容易清洗。便槽可以活动清洗，使用方便。把手设计在背后方，减少弯腰幅度。接触皮肤部分经磨砂处理，可以减少出汗后与坐便器粘连。整体造型圆润流畅，上下壳之间分割线采用立体曲线。

Baby potty brings children a safe and comfortable experience through the design of shape and function. The products uses imported antimicrobial technology and materials to effectively inhibit bacterial growth. Part of the surface is smooth and easy to clean. The tank can be mobile to clean and use. Handle is designed in the back to reduce the bending range. The part of surface contact the skin has a matte treatment to reduce the adhesion to toilet after sweating. The overall shape looks round and smooth, and between the upper and lower shell three-dimensional curve is designed in segmentation line.

设计
DESIGN

李曼、向华
Li Man，Shine Xiang

生产
MANUFACTURE

德珂（上海）母婴用品有限公司
Decobebe (Shanghai) Co.,Ltd.

全景天窗锅具
Panorama Pan

全景天窗锅具从操作体验的角度出发，突破了传统的烹饪方式，以全景的视野更好地观察烹饪过程，防止食物烧糊。该款锅具拥有良好的不粘性能，实现烹饪零油烟。通过延长锅盖的手柄，减少油渍喷溅，并可实现悬挂和单手滤水的功能。产品采用绿色环保陶瓷涂层，保证食品安全，提升耐磨性。锅盖采用硅胶与钢化玻璃结合的工艺，防滑设计提高安全性。

Panorama pan breaks the traditional way of cooking from the point of view of operating experience, and users can observe the cooking process better from panoramic view to prevent food burning to paste. The pan has a good non-stick performance to achieve zero-smoke cooking. By extending the handle of the lid to reduce the oil splash, it can achieve the function of hanging and one-hand water filter. The product uses green ceramic coating to ensure food safety and improve wear resistance. The lid is made of silica gel and tempered glass, and the anti-skid design improves safety.

设计
DESIGN

梁佳、李华民
Liang Jia，Li Huamin

生产
MANUFACTURE

上海嘉通电子科技有限公司
GreenTec Enterprise Limited

Mini 艾灸器
Mini Moxibustion

该产品是仅由有三个独立的模块所组成的迷你艾灸器，最大限度地减少人组装的步骤，节约时间，适应现代人的生活节奏。迷你艾灸器在保证药效好的前提下精简了每一个操作步骤，让用户更好体验产品。在燃烧温度、燃烧时间做了深入的思考，让用户使用产品时更加享受。素雅圆润的造型，磨砂质感，视觉上柔和温馨。

This product is a mini moxibustion which is only made of three 3 independent parts. It reduced the assembling steps to the maximum extent, saved time and fit the modern pace of life. On the promise of good result, the moxibustion simplified every steps and the user can have a better experience of the product. The burning temperature and time was adjusted to make the user feel more comfortable while using it. With round shape and matte texture, it looks soft and warm.

设计
DESIGN
广州绿源堂健康科技有限公司
Guangzhou Green Yuan Hall Health Technology Co., Ltd.

深圳市融一凤巢设计发展有限公司
Shenzhen Rone Phoenix Nest Design Development Co.,Ltd.
生产
MANUFACTURE

红壹佰厂矿灯
Red100 Factory Lamp

该产品是一款新型的散热系统，采用大的中空来加大温度的散发，不仅节省了材料，延长了产品的使用寿命，并且节省了能源。在对灯罩角度多次测量和分析后，使同样灯泡可以照射到更大的范围。产品主体采用铝板冲压，一次成型。上部的微笑线条使得产品生动了起来，让使用者感受到了温度和安全感。

The product is a new type of radiator system. It uses large hollow to increase the heat radiator, and not only saves material and extend the product life, but save energy. After multiple measurements and analysis of the lampshade angle, the same bulb can be irradiated to a larger range. The main body of the product uses integrated aluminum plate stamping molding. The upper part of the smile lines makes the product vivid up so as to make users feel the temperature and security.

设计
DESIGN
红壹佰照明有限公司
Red100 Lighting Co.,Ltd.

马鞍山金马工业设计有限公司
Ma'anshan Jinma Industrial Design Co.,Ltd.
生产
MANUFACTURE

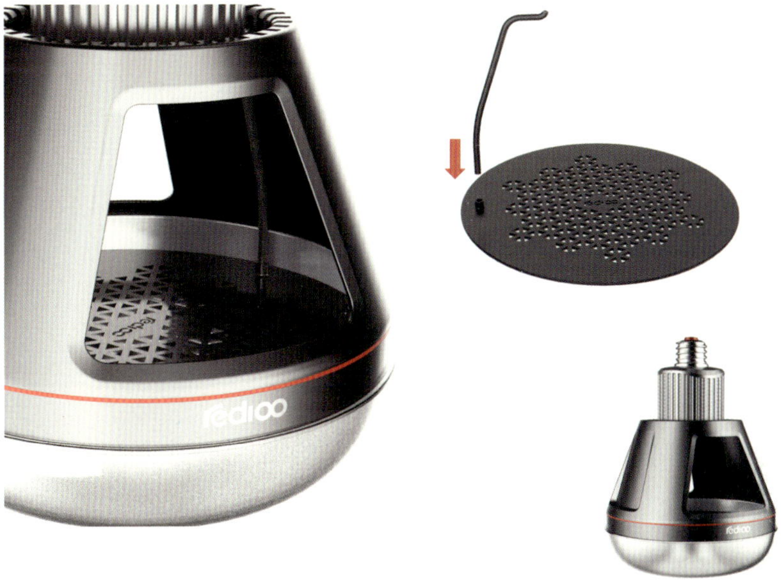

艺术椅
Artchair

该产品装饰画可以任意制作替换，巧妙地运用磁胶作为载体，吸附到铁制椅子面板，形成一个装饰画面。利用磁性材料的可吸附性来打造一种新型张贴方式，非常简易的附着安装方式，操作简单快捷，可创意性地反复、重叠使用，节省成本。具有空间环保的理念，材料可回收利用。产品造型简约，最大的功能特点就是装饰画的作用。

This decorative picture can be switched randomly by yourself. It uses magnetic sticker as supporter to adsorb to the faceplate of the iron chair thus a decorative picture is done. It is a simple attached installation way to take the absorbability of magnetic material to create a new posting method. The operation is easy and fast that it can be reused and overlapped innovatively and the cost can be saved as well due to the idea of space environmental protecting and material recyclable. The style of the product is simple and the biggest feature is decoration.

设计
DESIGN
广州艾彻艺术品有限公司
Guangzhou Artchair Artwork Co.,Ltd.

深圳卓瑞文化礼品有限公司
Shenzhen Greensong Design Consultant Co.,Ltd.
生产
MANUFACTURE

小鹿按摩棒
Baby Deer Massage Stick

该产品提取小鹿的元素，流线型的设计使产品既时尚又美观，外观全新的流线型，更具有动感和美感。充电方式采用针孔式全防水设计，无须担心产品进水。抽象可爱的造型使产品增加了使用者的好感度，极大地开发了隐性消费群体；一键模式多功能操作，可加热可 APP 控制，满足客户的多种需求，其性价比不言而喻。

The product uses the elements of deer, and streamlined design makes the product both stylish and beautiful . A new streamlined appearance is more dynamic and aesthetic. Charging method uses pinhole full waterproof design without worrying about product into water. The abstract and lovely shape of the product increases the user's favorability and greatly develops the hidden consumer groups. A key mode of multi-functional operation and heatable APP control meet the various needs of customers, so the cost performance is self-evident.

设计 DESIGN
山东丽波电子科技有限公司
Shandong Wave Electronic Technology Co., Ltd.

杭州木马商务咨询有限公司
Hangzhou Moma Business Consulting Co.,Ltd.
生产 MANUFACTURE

超薄一体智能坐便器 AKB1197
Ultra - Thin One Intelligent Toilet AKB1197

本产品是一款具有红外遥控、入座感感应、座圈保温、温水冲洗、离子交换净水、智能节电、妇洗、夜灯、蓝牙预留、停电冲水等功能的超薄一体智能坐便器，并设有过热保护和漏电保护等多重安全设置，使用方便舒适更安全。“超薄”成为产品的设计语言，恰到好处的“薄”使产品整体更加简约精致，突破以往一体智能坐便器的厚重。

This product is an ultra-thin intelligent toilet with infrared remote control, seat sensor, seat ring insulation, warm water rinse, ion exchange water, intelligent energy saving, women wash, night light, Bluetooth reservation, flushing when power-off and other functions, and with overheating protection and leakage protection and other multiple security settings, which makes it easy to use and more comfortable and more secure. "Ultra-thin" has become the product design language, and just right "thin" makes the whole product more simple and elegant, breaking through the shortcoming of heavy of intelligent toilet in the past.

设计 DESIGN
佛山市乐华恒业卫浴有限公司
Foshan Lehua Hengye Sanitar Co.,Ltd.

箭牌卫浴
ARROW
生产 MANUFACTURE

竹质落地灯
Bamboo Floor Lamp

该产品是以落地灯与功能为切入点，打造多方位的家居生活。在照明的同时也可以放置物品和悬挂衣物，方便实用。满足了房间局部照明和点缀装饰家庭环境的需求。木质落地灯采用竹木工艺，天然环保。可拆卸结构设计，拼装方便。一物多用，美观大方。

The product based on floor lamps and functions creates a multi-faceted home life. It not only can be used for lighting but also for placing items and hanging clothes, convenient and practical. It meets the needs of the room local lighting and ornament in the home environment. Wood floor lamp adopts bamboo technology, natural and environmental. Removable structural design is easy for assembly. It is multi-purpose, beautiful and generous.

设计 DESIGN
马鞍山江东工业设计发展有限公司
Ma'anshan Jiangdong Industrial Design Development Co., Ltd.

马鞍山江东工业设计发展有限公司
Ma'anshan Jiangdong Industrial Design Development Co.,Ltd.
生产 MANUFACTURE

Code 桌
Code

Code 系列以多样的规格与配置适用于多种空间。模块化设计，使产品连接结构全部隐藏，外观看不到一颗螺丝的同时，实现产品稳固。从培训、会议、办公、餐厅，Code 满足所有空间的配置需求。塑料件及合金件可拆卸循环利用，使产品在整个生命周期中对环境更加友善。纵、横梁端口采用激光切割断面工艺，确保产品品质，视觉上使产品更加精致美观。

Code series with a variety of specifications and configuration is applicable to a variety of space. Modular design hides all the joint structure of the product, even a screw can not be seen from the appearance, and it realized solidness of product at the same time. From the training, conference, office to restaurant, Code meet configuration requirementsthe of all space. Plastic parts and alloy pieces can be dismantled for recycling, so that the product is more friendly to the environment throughout the life cycle. Vertical and horizontal beams uses laser cutting section technology to ensure product quality, and make it more refined and beautiful in visual.

设计
DESIGN

震旦（中国）有限公司
Aurora（China）Co.,Ltd.

震旦创新中心
Aurora Innovation Center

生产
MANUFACTURE

手抓片
Hand Grip

该产品是一款健身器材手抓片外观设计，解决了目前市场上健身器材外观同质化的诟病。手抓片造型时尚而简洁，诠释了“运动释放＋时尚个性”的产品语义，外观新颖而大方干练，为企业品牌国际化而建立统一的视觉形象。区别于传统的健身器材给使用者“健身房机械”的印象，将健身运动逐渐向家庭化转变。让全民健身变得更加可能。

The product is a fitness equipment-hand grip, which solves the problem of the homogeneous appearance of fitness equipment in the current market. Hand grip has a fashionable and simple form, which is the interpretation of the product induction that "release by movement + fashion and personality", and the novel and generous product appearance establishes a unified visual image for the internationalization of corporate brand. Different from the traditional fitness equipments which provide users "gym machinery", the product gradually changes the fitness movement to a "family turn", making it a possibility of "national fitness".

设计
DESIGN

苏州嘉友运动休闲用品有限公司
Suzhou Jiayou Sports Leisure Products Co., Ltd.

苏州上品极致产品设计有限公司
Suzhou Top Industrial Design Co.,Ltd.

生产
MANUFACTURE

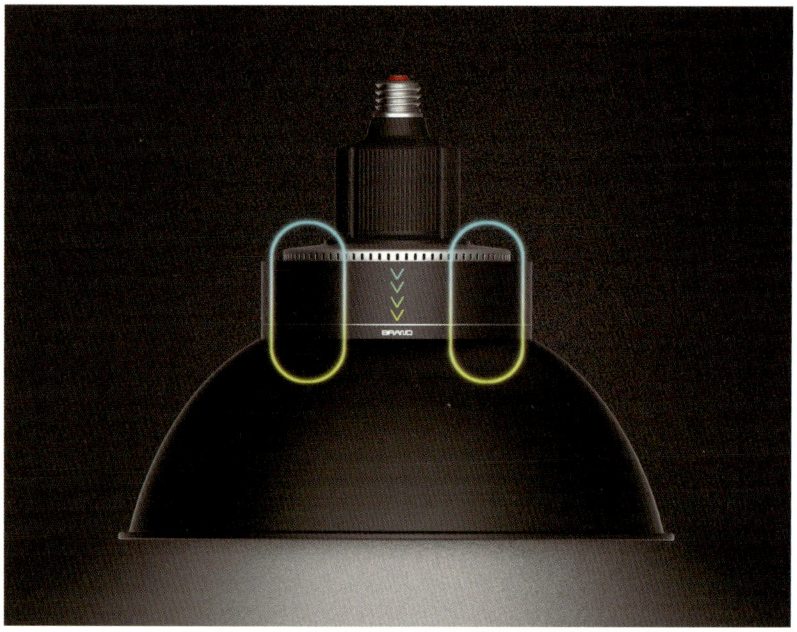

红壹佰厂高棚灯
Hongyibai Lamp Factory

该产品采用了中空对流的散热方式，极大程度上满足了设计与使用的要求。新型的散热方式降低了红壹佰此款厂矿灯的成本，并延长了产品使用寿命，为今后的发展带来了极大的帮助。在外观设计上整体走极简风，改变工矿灯传统的工业感造型，与现代艺术审美相结合。

The product uses a hollow convection thermal method to meet the design and use requirements to a large extent. The new thermal method reduces the cost of the lamp, and extends the life of the product, which will bring great help to the future development. The appearance design of the whole is simple style, it changes the shape of traditional industrial lamp and combines with modern art aesthetic.

设计
DESIGN

合肥木马工业设计有限公司
Hefei Moma Industrial Design Co.,Ltd.

红壹佰照明有限公司
Red100

生产
MANUFACTURE

仓鼠之家
The Home of A Hamster

仓鼠之家通过模拟鼠类在自然界中的生存状态，创造出与现存仓鼠笼迥然不同的仓鼠生存空间。设计利用混凝土和透明亚克力，将地上和地下分区处理，运用混凝土自身特点，模仿黄土层的颜色和表面机理，营造出野外观察仓鼠生活的效果。在仓鼠感觉自然、安全、放松生活的同时，让其具有更强的景观性，提升观赏效果和饲养乐趣。

The hamster's home created the living space of hamsters that are different from existing hamster cage by simulating their existence in nature. The design use concrete and transparent acrylic to realize the partition processing of both ground and underground. It also takes the advantage of the concrete itself to simulate the color and surface mechanism of the loess layer in order to create an effect of observing hamster's life in the field. Thus the hamster feels natural, safe and relaxed and the ornamental value is stronger while visual effect and feeding interest will be improved.

设计
DESIGN

曹晓昕、卢精蕾
Cao Xiaoxin, Lu Jinglei

北京品那创意设计有限公司
Beijing Pinar Creative

生产
MANUFACTURE

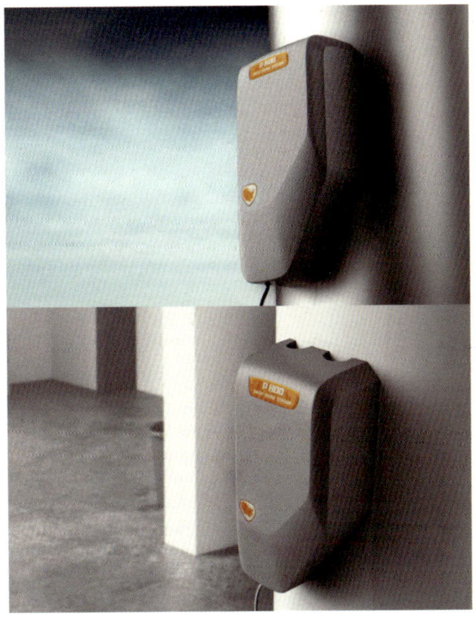

犀科泵站一体式热交换水箱
Seekco Solar Tank with Pump Station

该产品最大的特色是将目前的现场装配式的太阳能热水器产品，进行功能整合，将循环和控制器一体化设计，从而简化现场的安装，使得产品具有整体的外观效果，便于用户的操作。整体的外观设计，并采用定制规格的连接铜件，减少安装的连接点，确保产品更长期稳定、经济地运行。

The most attractive feature of this product is that it integrated the functions of the field assembled solar water heater, making the circulation and controller as an integrated design. Therefore the field installation will be simplified and the product has a holistic visual effect which is convenient to users. As for the holistic visual design, it adopts standardized connection copper parts, decreased connection parts during the installation to ensure the product has a long-term stable and economic running.

设计 DESIGN 上海犀科环境科技有限公司 Shanghai Seekco Environmental Tech Co.,Ltd.

生产 MANUFACTURE 上海犀科环境科技有限公司 Shanghai Seekco Environmental Tech Co.,Ltd.

舒福德 MIO 智能床
Intelligent Bed of MIO Softide

该产品是一张可以调节各种角度的智能床，能够满足用户各种姿态下的不同需求。MIO 智能床使用大功率微电机，让床体变得更轻更薄；机电设备整体采用非接触式力学传感器，这是智能睡眠系统在同类目中第一次使用。另外使用者可以通过手机APP实时检测身体状况，通过对心率、呼吸率等数据的检测，一旦出现健康异常，可及时通知到家人。

This product is an intelligent bed which can adjust various angles to meet the different needs of users under various postures. Mio intelligent bed uses high-power micro-motor to make the bed lighter and thinner; mechanical and electrical equipment as a whole uses non-contact mechanical sensors. It is also the first trying in the field of intelligent bed. Besides, users can track their physical conditions through the handset app in real-time. By detecting the data of people's heartbeat, the respiration rate and other information, it will notify the family members promptly if there appears any health abnormality with the user.

设计 DESIGN 麒盛科技股份有限公司 Keeson Technology Co.,Ltd.

生产 MANUFACTURE 北京洛可可科技有限公司 LKK Design Beijing Co.,Ltd.

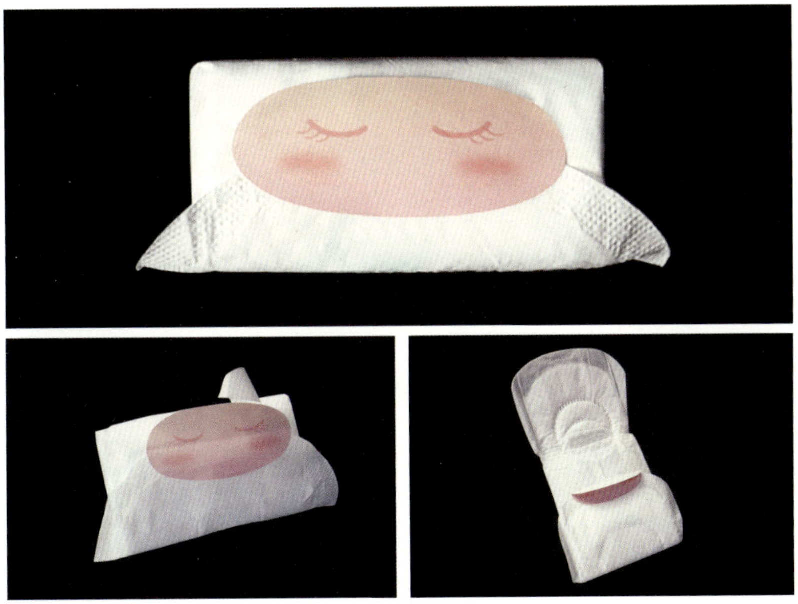

秘密卫生巾
Secret-Sanitary Napkin

该产品的设计为解决女性在生理期的隐私被暴露的尴尬。运用纳米技术，减少卫生巾厚度，使用更贴身。卫生巾将采取单品包装模式，方便使用者携带和拿取。可爱的双层折叠式便利贴设计使产品在使用后方便将卫生巾包裹，避免其暴露在垃圾桶里并且散发异味并且有效减少垃圾桶内占用空间。

This design is designed to solve the embarrassment of women's privacy exposure during the female physical period. The nanotechnology is taken to make the sanitary napkin thinner and more personal. The sanitary napkin will be individually wrapped which would be convenient for the user to take and carry with. The design of lovely double folding sticker provides convenience for the after-using packing, which avoid the exposure in the dustbin, the off-flavor and effectively reduce space in the dustbin.

设计 DESIGN 杭州斯帕克工业设计有限公司 Hangzhou Spark Industrial Design Co., Ltd.

生产 MANUFACTURE 杭州斯帕克工业设计有限公司 Hangzhou Spark Industrial Design Co.,Ltd.

康铭魔法灯泡
KMS-Magic Bulb

该产品是一款魔法球泡灯，用户使用三手指接触，可连通灯光系统，使灯泡发亮。在灯泡离开基座时仍会发亮，创新了传统灯泡需要与基座相连才能发亮的使用方法。可以独立使用，方便携带，也可用作装饰灯。另外具有声光感应设置，用户操作方便。

This product is a magic bulb. Users can connect the light system and light the bulb through three fingers. The bulb will continue to be lit after leaving its base which innovates the traditional way that the bulb can only be lit with the connection to the base. It can be used independently which is easy to carry and be used as ornamental light. Besides, the sound and light sensor make it easier for users to use.

设计 DESIGN 深圳市康铭盛科技实业股份有限公司 Shenzhen Kangmingsheng Science and Technology Industrial Co., Ltd.

广州大业产品设计有限公司 Guangzhou Daye Industrial Design Co.,Ltd. **生产 MANUFACTURE**

机械咖啡机
Mechanical Coffee Machine

该产品是一款不带电的机械式咖啡冲泡机。产品主体基本采用塑料原色注塑，内部通过发条计时器时序精准控制出水时间及速度，实现不插电自动化，低碳环保。外观独特的设计，突破了传统的咖啡机外观束缚，利用“斜杠”来连接底座和盛水容器，具有极强的空间感；通过机身拨动开关发出的滴答计时声，传递出产品“点滴之美”。

This is a kind of mechanical coffee machine without electricity. The main part of the product basically injected with primary colors of plastic. The internal part takes timer timing precision to precisely control the spring water time and speed in order to achieve unplugged automation which is low-carbon and environmentally-friendly. The unique appearance breaks the limitation of traditional coffee machine. It takes a "slash" to connect base and water container which are full of sense of space. And the sound of ticktack made by sliding switch transmits the "beauty of ticktack".

设计 DESIGN 北京爱滴咖啡有限公司 Beijing Love Drip Coffee Co.,Ltd.

北京乐品乐道科技有限公司 Beijing Ledao Thenaropin Technology Co.,Ltd. **生产 MANUFACTURE**

可调奶粉勺
Adjustable Milk Spoon

该产品是一个可调奶粉勺。利用推拉卡扣的设计，设计出不同的档位，可以满足使用者不同的需求。解决了不同品牌的奶粉配水量不同导致不能调出宝宝想要的任意数量这一问题。产品生产成本低，外观独特新颖。配合的产品改变按钮的颜色，有多种颜色方案可以供用户选择。

This product is an adjustable milk spoon. It uses the push button design for different length to meet various needs for users. It mainly solves the problems that due to different water distribution of mild powder brands, we cannot get any quantity for baby. The product is of low cost, unique in appearance. Matching different colors of the brands, it provides multiple colors for users.

设计 DESIGN 安徽康得安工业设计有限公司 Anhui Kang Dean Industrial Design Co.,Ltd.

曹晶 Cao Jing **生产 MANUFACTURE**

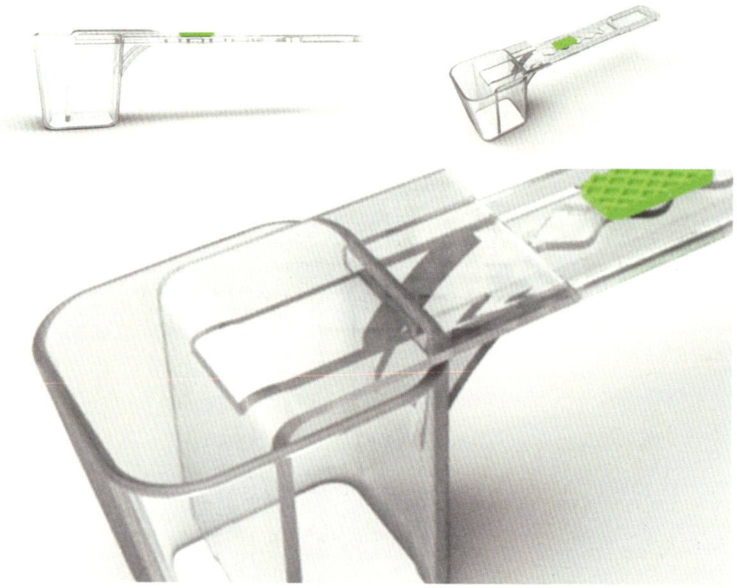

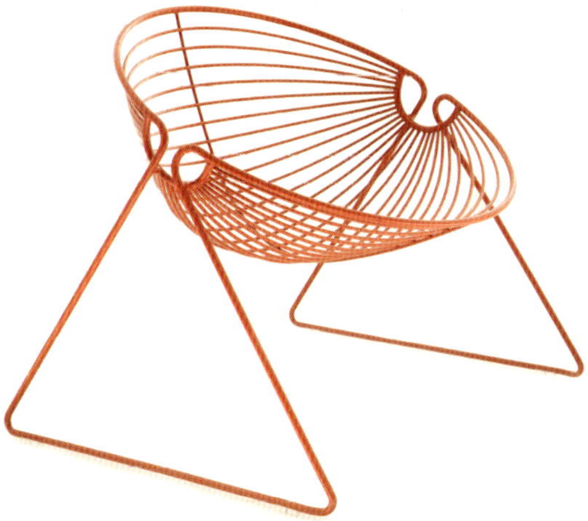

壳椅
Shell Chair

该座椅可作为休闲椅，椅身简约大气，牢固耐用，细节精致耐看。壳椅的设计灵感来于贝壳。材质采用金属，给人一种舒适的归属感与安全感。壳身由金属框架、弧形坐面以及靠背组成。前后腿弯曲的结构亦是座椅本身的一大亮点。硬朗造型与极简流畅的线条保证了它的稳定性。坐面弧度完美符合人体工程学，让用户在上悠然享受一份专属的安宁与放松。

The chair can be used as a leisure chair, whose body part is simple, solid and durable and delicate in detail. The shell chair was inspired by shell. The material of metal gives us a sense of belonging and safety. The body part consists of metal frame, arc seat and back part. Bending chair legs is also another feature. The powerful modeling and the fluent line make the shell chair more stable. The arc seat perfectly meets the ergonomics which ensure an exclusive sense of peace and relaxation for the user.

设计
DESIGN

王树茂
Femo Wang

北京市第五季家具有限公司
The Fifth Season Furniture (Beijing) Co.,Ltd.

生产
MANUFACTURE

便携加热封口机
Mini Bag Sealer

该产品是一款便携加热封口机，封袋十分便捷，旋钮转向加号，夹住包装袋均匀侧拉即可密封；旋钮转向减号，开袋快捷、平整。整机为可回收材料，特别采用磷铜材料，提供了高能效的发热回路。标签铭牌材质为可回收超纤维，无油墨印刷，不仅保护环境，也不会在生产时带来危害健康的污染。

This product is a portable heating sealing machine which is very convenient to seal. You can seal it when turning to the plus sign, clamping the packing bag and evenly pulling. While turning to the minus sign, you can open it easily and smoothly. The machine adopts recyclable material; especially the use of phosphor copper provides a high effective heating circuit. The tally is made of recyclable super fiber with no-ink printing which is both environmental protecting and won't bring pollution which is harmful to health during production.

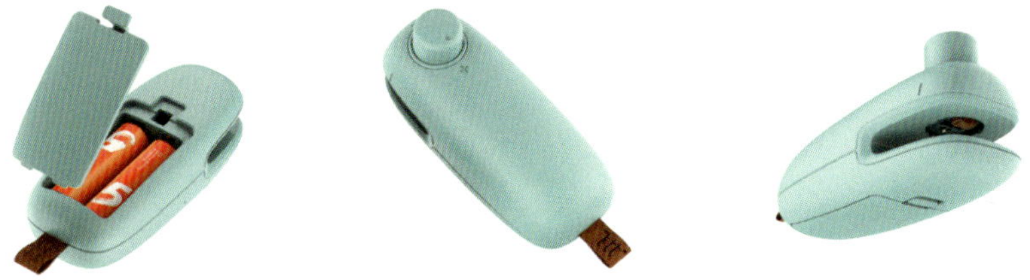

设计
DESIGN

广东顺德可可麦科技产业孵化有限公司
Kekemai Technology Industry Incubation Shunde GD Co., Ltd.

广东顺德可可麦科技产业孵化有限公司
Kekemai Technology Industry Incubation Shunde GD Co.,Ltd.

生产
MANUFACTURE

宝命甲北斗防弹防刺背包
BMJ Bedou Bulletproof&Stab Resistant Backpack

本产品具备符合国际 NIJ standard-0101.06 和国内公安部防弹防刺 GA141-2010 标准的防护性能，且前胸和后背均能在最短时间能实现同时防护。在正常收纳功能的基础上还具有卫星定位功能，紧急情况下发出求救信号。背包的正面分割为中国的“中”字图案造型，制作上将手工缝制与机械制造相结合，一百零七道严谨工序，无处不体现中国制造。

The product conforms to the international bulletproof standard-NIJ 0101.06 and the stab resistant standard-GA141-2010. The chest and back can be effectively protected at the same time in a short time. Besides the basic incorporate function and the satellite positioning system allow users to send a distress signal to the monitoring platform for emergency situation. The front of the backpack is divided into word pattern of Chinese character ." 中 ", and the production combined hand-sewn and machinery manufacturing. The 107 strict processes embody the Chinese manufacturing.

设计 DESIGN 北京中艺创联文化传播有限责任公司
Beijing Zhongyichuanglian Cultural Communication Co., Ltd.

朱利峰、杨戈
Zhu Lifeng, Yang Ge **生产 MANUFACTURE**

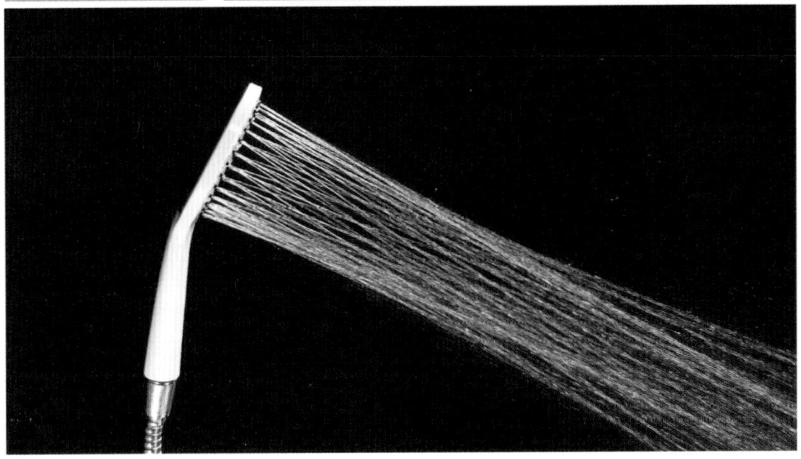

“时空隧道”花洒
Space Time Tunnel Shower

该款花洒是首款采用“时空网”水花设计，出水独特新颖。首款“变色龙”无电路温显技术的突破，使产品感温既准确又敏捷，颠覆了行业传统水力发电和电池显示的耗能污染，为使用者提供了舒适的水温参数，同时也提高了洗浴安全性。自洁点具有出水记忆功能，可用手通过顺时针或逆时针触摸自洁点，来变幻出水面积大小，又可以起到防堵塞作用。

The shower is the first to use the “space time network ” spray design and the spray is unique and novel. It is also the first to use the “chameleon technology” which is the water temperature display technology without electronics to make it induce temperature accurately and agile, which overturns the pollution of energy consumption caused by traditional hydropower industry and battery, provides the user with a comfortable temperature parameters, but also improves the safety of bathing. The self-cleaning nozzle has the function of the water memory, and the user can touch the nozzle clockwise or anticlockwise to change the size of the area of the spray and to prevent the nozzle from plugging.

设计
DESIGN

刘建南
Liu Jiannan

厦门艾贝斯卫浴科技有限公司
Ibath

生产
MANUFACTURE

卷曲系列 UHPC（超高性能混凝土）家具
Series "Curve" UHPC (Ultra-High Performance Concrete) Furniture

该产品采用混凝土材料，耐高温、耐潮湿、牢固、坚硬，适用于室内外任何场所，经久耐用。卷曲的曲线拉伸，形成了数个隧道状空间，是宠物娱乐休息的绝佳场所；产品原材均不含放射性元素，正面及背面机理和颜色一致，表观及触感滑润，保留清水混凝土表面，追求混凝土本原的归宿，亦是设计者及使用者追求质朴的生活哲学的体现。

This product is made of concrete which is heat resistance, humidity resistance, fixed and hard. It is suitable for all the places whether inside or outside. The curved stretching lines forming several tunnel-like spaces provide an ideal place for recreation of pets. The raw material is without any radioactive elements. The back and face have same color and texture which are smooth both in appearance and tactility. The product maintains bare concrete which is the trace to its source and also the philosophy of life for pursuing simple to both the designer and user.

设计
DESIGN

兰征
Lan Zheng

成都金圣实业有限公司
Chengdu Kingsun Industrial Co.,Ltd.

生产
MANUFACTURE

色空音舌鼓
Sekong Drum

该产品集艺术品、身心灵疗愈、打击乐器三合一的综合体，色空设计有八个发音舌片，经艺术家人工专业调音，能准确发音且演奏音乐作品，其声空灵通透不乏细腻，音起之时，转瞬若入奇妙乐音之境。在保证浑厚饱满低音的同时发挥了金属乐器特有的空灵悠远的中高音，且手或鼓槌敲打力度的不同，能呈现出不同的质感，娴熟演奏者亦能运用其呈现电子音乐的质感。

"Reality Phantom" drum integrates artwork, physical, mental curing and percussion instrument. The sekong has eight articulation tongues which can sound precisely and perform musical piece after professional tone turning. Its sound is ethereal, transparent and fine, immediately letting you enjoy its wonderful sound. it can give vigorous and solid bass, and also the unique ethereal and distant mediate and high pitch, and different strength knocking at the drum with hands or drumstick can send out different sounds, the skillful player can utilize it to send out electronic music feeling.

设计 DESIGN
张迪
Zhang Di

生产 MANUFACTURE
艺海心常态（北京）文化传播有限公司
Yihaixinchangtai Beijing Culture Communication Co.,Ltd.

酷神笔 E1
Cool Smart Pen E1

该产品与日常用的笔一样，具有笔的基本属性，广泛应用于各类书写场景，解决了日常手写文字等数据难以采集、分析，难以转化为有价值的数据并高效利用的问题。酷神笔使用可充电锂电池，让产品耐用性更强。笔杆采用铝合金挤出工艺一体成型，表面阳极氧化处理，使用寿命长。优雅出众的三角造型和独特切面，造就纯粹的功能性和炫酷的科技美感。

Cool smart pen has the basic functions as the daily pens which is widely used in every kind of writing setting, solving the day-to-day handwriting problems such as data is difficult to collect, analysis, it is difficult to translate into valuable data and efficient use. Cool smart pen use rechargeable lithium battery to strengthen the durability. The penholder adopts aluminum alloy extrusion process integrated molding and its surface adopts anodic oxidation treatment to ensure long service life. The elegant triangular style and unique section make the pure functionality and cool scientific beauty.

设计 DESIGN
泰吉新业科技（北京）有限公司
TAZIK Solution（Beijing）Ltd.

生产 MANUFACTURE
北京新国人智慧科技股份有限公司
Beijing New Chinese Wisdom Technology Co.,Ltd.

六合竹丝扣瓷茶具
Liuhe - Bamboo Buckles Porcelain Tea Set

该茶具壶体的设计更好地解决壶身出水的问题。这套茶具在沿用了极简设计风格壶的材料，采用景德镇白瓷。竹丝扣采用环保有机的绿色竹子材料，材料的选择上更加环保与健康。整体设计工艺方面采用了传统陶瓷制作工艺、竹丝工艺制作、铜艺工艺，三者的结合更好把中国传统工艺加以融合，更好地继承中国传统工艺和发扬中国优秀文化。

The design of this pot body perfectly solved the problem of pot body watering. It follows the simple style, using Jingdezhen white porcelain as pot material and environmental organic bamboo as buckles which are more environmental protecting and healthy. The overall design skills take traditional porcelain craft, bamboo craft and cooper art craft. The combination of the three did a better fusion of traditional Chinese craft, which inherits the traditional Chinese craft and carries forward the Chinese fine cultures.

设计
DESIGN

黄志辉
Huang Zhihui

生产
MANUFACTURE

华南师范大学
South China Normal University

木屋香器
Roof Incense Burner

该香器采用了原木作为主材，木是一种环保且再生的可持续材料，经过精细的打磨，使得木屋的表面有着天然的木纹及手感，在视觉与触觉上达到统一。烟囱部分采用了铜管制作，简单又方便。这次的设计用最简单的方式表达意境，用一个带烟囱的小木屋非常简单的方式表现出了一幅袅袅炊烟的景象。设计简化使得生产过程中也具备方便性及经济性。

The Roof incense burner uses log as the main material, the wood is an environmentally friendly and renewable sustainable material. After fine grinding, the surface of it has a natural grain and hand feeling which reaches a unity in visual and tactile. The chimney part uses copper production which is simple and convenient. The design use the simplest way to express feeling, a hut with a chimney shows the scenery of curling smokes. The simple design makes the production process also has the convenience and economy.

设计
DESIGN

杭州本来工业设计有限公司
Beladesign

生产
MANUFACTURE

杭州提格科技有限公司
Hangzhou Teague Technology Co.,Ltd.

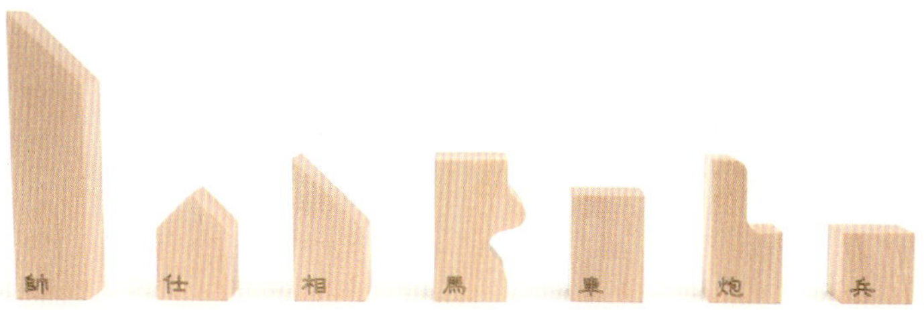

中国象棋
Chinese Chess

该产品将中国象棋进行抽象简化立体化的设计。棋子、棋盘分别用了枫木、黑胡桃木、榉木制作而成，整体设计尽量简化，便于生产与打磨，打磨后的棋子，棋盘视觉和触觉细腻，使得整副棋高档而精致。枫木与黑胡桃木自身的木色差异可以区分了玩家双方。下棋时，棋子的高低错落在棋盘上布局，就像一个立体的战场画面，生动而有趣。

This product makes an abstraction, simplification and three-dimensional design of Chinese chess. Pieces and chessboard are made of maple, black walnut and beech. The overall design is as simple as possible to provide convenience for production and gridding. After polishing, the pieces and chessboard is exquisite in visual and tactile, making the whole chess with high level and delicacy. The color difference between maple and black walnut can distinguish the two players. While playing, the size of the pieces scattered on the board layout, like a three-dimensional battlefield picture, vivid and interesting

设计
DESIGN

杭州本来工业设计有限公司
Beladesign

生产
MANUFACTURE

杭州提格科技有限公司
Hangzhou Teague Technology Co.,Ltd.

大碗茶情怀
Big Bowl Tea

该产品为老舍茶馆“老二分”礼盒，是企业文化的代表性产品。装帧质朴、色调雅致，内装独具老北京风情特色的茉莉花茶，品质上乘、茶香四溢，于不经意间，默默传承着前门情思大碗茶的别样情怀。运用了纸张和画面的结合，体现年代特质，运用旧时同材质竹木桌条，作为整个产品中心点贴片表现，呈现着当年创业历程大碗茶给历史留下的印迹。

This product is “Old Two Cents” tea gift in Lao She teahouse, a represent product for enterprise culture. The package is simple and delicate in color with special old Beijing style's nice jasmine tea, silently inheriting the affection for big bowl tea in Qian Men. The combination of paper and picture shows the sense of time and the use of old style bamboo table as the center sticker of the whole product represents the influence of big bowl tea during the entrepreneurial process at that age.

设计 DESIGN
焦哲
Kurt Jiao

生产 MANUFACTURE
老舍茶馆
Laoshe Teahouse

寻见自然 超有机亚麻籽油
Xunjianziran

该款亚麻籽油精选自晋蒙交界、无可复制的高寒亚麻籽油核心产地，采用现代物理低温冷榨工艺，九道工序，滴滴萃取，凝结成了一滴赋有诚意、孕育希望的纯净好油。玻璃瓶采用特别用纸打造出复古纯手工感觉，瓶口处采用麻绳捆绑，加强手工打造感。包装外盒采用取油原产地插图包裹，将自然美好的事物原原本本地呈现出来。

This kind of linseed oil is selected from the border between the Jin and Inner Mongolia, no duplication of Alpine flax seed oil core production. The use of modern physics, cold pressing process, nine-process drip extraction, condensates into a drop of sincerity, nurture the hope of pure good oil. The glass bottle with special paper to create retro hand feeling, the mouth of the bottle uses rope to strengthen the sense of handmade. The package uses the pictures of the source area, showing the natural and beautiful things exactly.

设计 DESIGN
青岛知行天下品牌策划有限公司
China Kdc Brand Design Co.,Ltd.

生产 MANUFACTURE
青岛知行天下品牌策划有限公司
China Kdc Brand Design Co.,Ltd.

铝合金触感签字笔
Aluminium Alloy Sensual Pen

该产品是一款可持续耐用的笔。手持部分，做了两个相同曲率的切面，曲面的切面大小由厚到薄，最终贴合笔身的造型，更加贴合手指握笔书写时候的习惯，降低了长时间握笔书写所产生的疲劳感。由于握笔出曲面的特殊造型，使笔不容易滚落。为保持美观性，笔身顺着曲面的形状做了美观线，但是因为表面经过酸洗，所以美观线并不会残留污垢。

This pen is sustainable and durable. The holding part has two sections with the same curvature. The shape of section is gradually from thin to thick which better meets the behavior of writing and lowers the fatigue due to long-time writing. The special shape of the surface prevents the pen from rolling down. In order to make it more artistic, there is an artistic line in the pen body along the surface. Nevertheless, residual stains won't be found inside these lines because they were processed with acid leaching procedure.

设计 DESIGN
南京可可青工业设计有限公司
Co-Green Design Consultants

生产 MANUFACTURE
南京坦途机械制造有限公司
Nanjing Tantu Machinery Manufacturing Co.,Ltd.

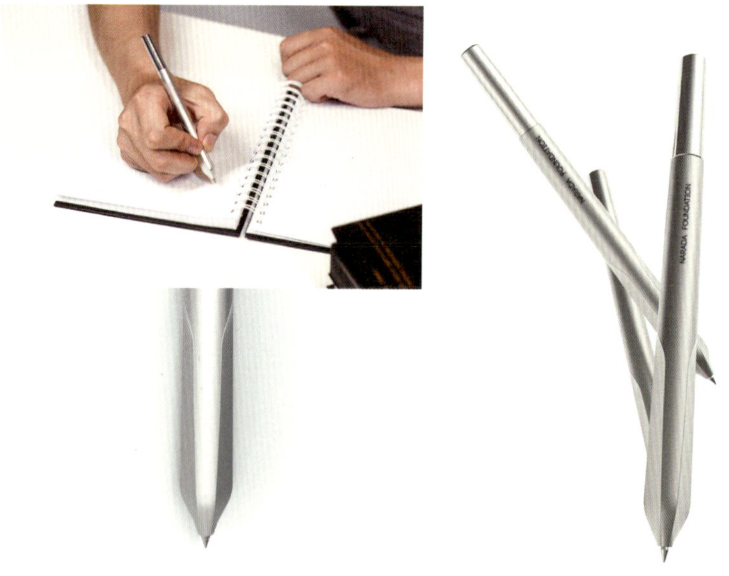

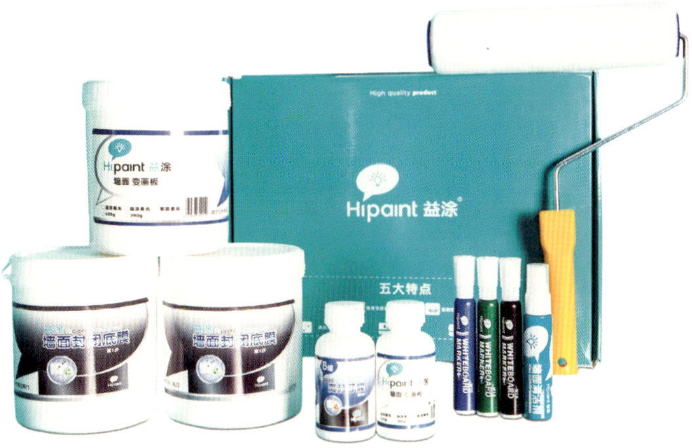

益涂纳米书写膜
Hipaint Nano-Tech Writing Shield

该产品为纳米书写膜。墙面可以擦写、投影，能够轻松书写、擦洗次数 10 万次以上，同时具备耐污、耐水、防霉、防菌等性能，延长墙面使用寿命。 产品配合设计师定制各种颜色、大小和形状的书写墙面，打造兼具互动性和创意性的环境氛围。开辟了涂料行业的蓝海模式，具备环保、创新、实用等优势，成为全球书写墙领导品牌。

This product is hipaint nano-tech writing shield. The wall can be used to write and project. It can write and ease more than 100 thousand times, with stain resistance, water resistance, dust resistance and antibacterial properties to extend the life of wall. Cooperated with designer, the product has different color, size and shape, creating an interactive and creative environment. It opened up the paint industry in blue ocean model, with environmental protection, innovation, practical and other advantages, thus has become a global writing wall leading brand.

设计
DESIGN
程思祺
Cheng Siqi

生产
MANUFACTURE
境洁环保科技（上海）有限公司
Jingjie Environment Technology (Shanghai) Co.,Ltd.

岛城头条
Daochengtoutiao

该产品是鱼食品的包装设计。甜晒鲅鱼，青岛最具代表的干海货之一，包装主体采用超写实的鲅鱼插画表现形式，用独特的顶视图视角，营造出鲅鱼正在纸面上游动的场景，视觉表现力极强，吸引消费者目光。内盒直接沿用岛城头条的新闻感觉，将相关信息直接用报纸的形式表现出来增加趣味性，强化青岛特色及品牌主题。

This product is a package design for fish food. Sweet sun Qingdao Spanish mackerel is one of the most representative dry goods in Qingdao. The packaging body with surreal illustrations of Spanish mackerel form, with a top view of the unique angle of view, to create a paper swimming scene is Spanish, visual expressive, the first time to attract the attention of consumers. The inner box directly follows the Daocheng headlines feeling, relevant information will be directly with the form of the newspaper to increase the fun, but also fit the brand theme.

设计
DESIGN
青岛知行天下品牌策划有限公司
China Kdc Brand Design Co.,Ltd.

生产
MANUFACTURE
青岛即东鳌山湾食品有限公司
Qingdao Jidong Food Co., Ltd.

时光隧道辉光管时钟
Time Pipeline Clock

该产品是一台辉光管显示的时钟，具有 12/24 小时计时功能，30 天断电保留记忆功能。将库存的辉光管被重新启用，外壳使用避风干老榆木，低碳环保。时钟使用数控车床对榆木进行精确的整块雕刻、镂空处理。显示管从木块的一侧穿出，看起来像能显示时间的管道悬浮。电路板藏在木块的内部，用雕刻的非常有质感的铜板做盖板，最后用 60 年代的机床螺丝封装。

Time Pipeline Clock is a glow tube clock display clock, with 12/24 hour chronograph function, 30 days off to retain the memory function. The glow tube is reused from the stock and the shell adopts old elm which is of low carbon and environmental protecting. The clock uses a CNC lathe to make an accurate engraving of the elm and to hollow out. The circuit is hided in the wood block. The covering plate was made of a carved bronze plate that had an excellent texture and sealed with machine screws manufactured in the 1960s.

设计
DESIGN
杨帆
Yang Fan

北京腾达万喜科技有限公司
Beijing Tengdawanxi Technology Corporation
生产
MANUFACTURE

"伏笔"书写工具
Full-Pen

该款笔满足了用户提升生活品质、追求优质产品的心理需求，同时丰富了高端书写工具的产品市场。产品使用环保无毒的本色纸进行包装，最大程度地降低包装的用料，颠覆了传统礼品包装。运用"挖空芯思"的设计语言，在完整的金属笔杆上精铣出纤细的开口，露出施耐德金属笔芯，纤细的开口巧妙规避了手指与笔体握持时的接触区域，在美感与人体工程学之间找到了最佳平衡。

The pen meets the psychological needs of users to improve the quality of life. At the same time, it enriches the product market of high-end tools. Environmentally non-toxic color paper has been used as packaging, decreasing the cost of packaging and change the traditional way of packing. The design language is "hollow out". A slender hollow has been milled on the complete body, to show the Schneider metal Refill inside. The slender hollow is cleverly avoided the finger contact area to hold the pen, which find the balance between beauty and human engineering.

设计
DESIGN
刘松
Liu Song

嵘器（北京）创意设计有限公司
Rongqi(Beijing) Creative Design Co., Ltd.
生产
MANUFACTURE

可平置的酒瓶
X-Sir

该产品是专门为年轻人做的红酒，更加适合年轻人出行或聚会时享用，无论是在室内或外出携带都不需要额外配置。红酒瓶的外侧壁面上一个酷似 X 型的领结，让瓶身和 X 型的领结形成一个十字形的支撑面，这样红酒瓶就可以稳定地平躺在桌面上。是一个具有功能性的红酒瓶创新设计，它颠覆性的装饰也具有实用功能。

X-Sir is designed especially for young people, fitting in their travelling and party circumstances. They don't need to carry wine bottle bracket anymore, neither indoors or outdoors. The design of tie form bulge on the red wine bottle so that the bottle could be laid down and put away safely. The X-shape bulge forms a stable bearing surface for the bottle to be laid low on a desk. It is a functionally innovative of bottles which subversively gives the decoration a function.

设计 DESIGN
张剑
Zhang Jian

生产 MANUFACTURE
北京最红科技有限公司
Beijing Zuihong Technology Co.,Ltd.

龙先生强化维生素饮料
Mr.Long Fortified Vitamin Drinks

该产品是一款强化维生素饮料，黑色与黄色的搭配给人强烈的视觉冲击，包装插画使用功夫巨星李小龙剪影作为形象元素，体现“龙先生强化维生素”主题，从包装上消费者就能感受到力量。瓶子造型圆润给人亲近的感觉。瓶盖的环状设计符合人体工程学，便于用户携带。目前产品分为罐装和听装两种，满足不同消费人群需求。

This product is a fortified vitamin drink. The collocation of black and yellow gives people a strong visual shock. The illustration takes Kungfu star Li Xiaolong's sketch as image icon, showing the theme of "Mr.Long fortified vitamin drinks", so people can feel strength from the package. The round shape of bottle cap gives a sense of close. The bottle cap's ring shape meets ergonomics and provides convenience to carry. So far, there are canned type and tinned type to satisfy different needs of customers.

设计 DESIGN
上海奎燕广告有限公司
Shanghai Key Advertising Co.,Ltd.

生产 MANUFACTURE
佛山市三水区隐雪食品有限公司
Foshan Sanshui District Hidden Snow Food Co.,Ltd.

十六岁石榴水
Pomegranate Fruit Drinks

该产品是一款石榴水饮料包装设计。将普通的饮料推向具有功能联想的饮品，外形小巧瓶身以白色为底色，包装插画颜色多选用橘粉色和绿色，整体色调清新色彩纯粹，传达出十六岁的美好。包装插画以石榴为主体并配有其他元素，明确传达出饮品元素，使消费者一看便知。包装整体清新富有灵气，洋溢着花季青春的美好气息。

This product is a package design for pomegranate fruit drinks. It develops a normal drink to an associated one. The bottle is small in size with white as the background, the color of packaging illustrations are of orange pink and green and the overall color is fresh and pure, conveying the 16-year-old beautiful. Packaging illustrations to pomegranate as the main body and with other elements clearly convey the beverage elements, so that consumers know at a glance. Packaging is fresh and full of aura, filled with the beauty of the beautiful youth season.

设计 DESIGN
上海奎燕广告有限公司
Shanghai Key Advertising Co.,Ltd.

生产 MANUFACTURE
武汉天喔茶庄饮料有限公司
Wuhan Tenwow Tea Company Beverage Co., Ltd.

药梨膏
Yao Li Gao

该产品是一款药梨膏的包装设计。内包装为罐装，透明的材质让使用者方便看到梨膏的使用情况。外包装为方形，端庄稳重，药梨膏的字体让人对产品信息一目了然。包装插画运用了豫园的吉祥兽元素和梨膏的历史文化故事，增加趣味性的同时也传达出品牌故事，新颖时尚，颠覆传统老字号的形象，实现老字号品牌的创新。

This product is a package design for Yao Li Gao. The inner package is canned with transparent material to let the user know how much he has used. The out package is of square shape, dignified and stable, the character of Yao Li Gao letting people know the information of the product clearly. The package illustration uses the auspicious beast in Yu garden and the historical story of Yao Li Gao to increase interest and carry out brand stories which are new and fashionable. It changes the image of traditional old brand and realizes the innovation of old brand.

设计 DESIGN
上海梨膏糖食品厂
Shanghai Pear Sugar Food Factory

上海奎燕广告有限公司
Shanghai Key Advertising Co.,Ltd.
生产 MANUFACTURE

演艺系列纪念腕表
A Souvenir Watch of Acting Collection

该表款在表盘高难度油压以及表壳和圈口采用夸张缩放摄像头结构组合设计，使整个手表展现清晰细腻多层次多角度多变化的棱线美，同时表壳与底盖采用仿真高压锅组合结构，让使用者简易极速拆装变换手表模式，配合装置老式电影放映机精美的底盖铜片。打破了原来固有传统模式的缺陷，开创手表工艺化和艺术化以及多元化（活动变换拆装）相结合的先河。

The style uses exaggerated zoom camera structure design of case and bezel combine with deep press pattern dial so that the watch shows clear and delicate multi level and multi angle as well as diversified beauty change; at the same time case and the back cover using simulation pressure cooker combination, allowing user to disassembly and change watch mode in simple and fast, with the back cover sheet by exquisite old film projectors. It breaks original traditional defects, creating a watch for the craft, art and diversification combination (Flexible and changeable disassembly).

设计 DESIGN
深圳市雷诺表业有限公司
Shenzhen Rarone Watch Industry Co.,Ltd.

深圳市雷诺表业有限公司
Shenzhen Rarone Watch Industry Co.,Ltd.
生产 MANUFACTURE

缩变的立方体
Shrinking Cube

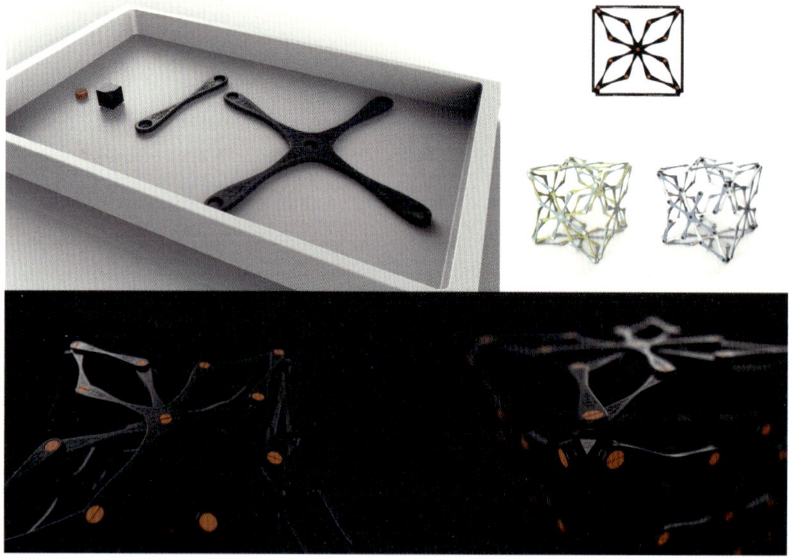

该产品主要应用于教学中，可重复多次利用。产品表面纹理模仿细胞、星系、几何等元素符号。整体采用铝合金加工制成，轻便，不易损坏。当小朋友拿到玩具开始拼接时，每个条每个连接件每颗螺丝都需要合理的安装搭配，增强小朋友的协作能力及自身的动手能力。让小朋友加深对科学的印象和理解，让学习和玩耍达到完美统一。

The utility model is mainly used in teaching and can be used repeatedly. Product surface texture mimics cellular, galaxy, geometric, and other elemental symbols. The whole aluminum alloy processing is lightweight and not easy to damage. When teenagers get toys, start stitching, each strip, each connector, each screw needs a reasonable installation and collocation, therefore, their cooperation ability and manipulative ability can be enhanced. Through this, children can deepen the impression and understanding of science, so that learning and play to achieve a perfect unity.

设计 DESIGN
北京交通大学
Beijing Jiaotong University

北京上品极致产品设计有限公司
Beijing Top Industrial Design Co.,Ltd.
生产 MANUFACTURE

月时陶瓷月相灯
Moonii

该产品既是时钟和日历，也是气氛装饰灯。“月相时间”模式下灯带的亮暗变化显示出时间，“时钟”模式将光斑变成为传统时钟的时针、分针、秒针，更能精准表示时间。材质为中国宝贵的传统工艺陶瓷，通过将陶瓷工艺与电子技术结合的产品创新，使中国的传统工艺符合发展趋势，在保留传统制陶工艺的同时，也弘扬中国的工匠精神。

Moonii is not only clock and calendar but also mood light which can be the decoration on the wall. In Moon Time Mode the light belt displays for showing time by the changing of light and shade. In the Clock Mode the bright dot will be replaced by clock hands, which makes time more accurate. The material of the product is ceramics which is the treasure of traditional Chinese craft. The innovation by combining ceramics craft and electronic skill makes traditional Chinese craft in accordance with the trend. It inherits traditional ceramic craft while also promotes Chinese craftsman's spirit.

设计
DESIGN

上海墨睿工业设计有限公司
Shanghai Moori Design Co.,Ltd.

庞鸣、郑鑫鑫
Pang Ming，Zheng Xinxin

生产
MANUFACTURE

海宴品牌全案策划设计
The Design of The Whole Package of Sea Feast Brand

该设计打破传统餐饮行业形象古板，把海晏的品牌形象赋予海鲜盛宴的趣味性和中国传统的品牌文化。将鱼型结合中国传统节日，通过桌面立牌、店面异形合影墙、抱枕礼品等对品牌形象进行线上线下和谐衔接，打造充满品牌认知和具有独特识别性的半岛餐饮品牌。该设计一经应用，就得到顾客和同行的高度好评，海宴品牌也被消费者和大众广泛关注和喜爱。

This design broke the old-fashioned image of traditional catering industry and put the interests and traditional Chinese brand culture to the brand image of sea feast. It combined the shape of fish and traditional Chinese festivals. By setting cards on the table, setting special-shaped photo wall in the store and sending souvenirs to make harmonious cohesion of online and offline for the brand image, creating a peninsula catering brand which is full of brand cognition and unique recognition. The design was highly appraised by customers and peers once applied to the market. Accordingly, the sea feast brand is widely concerned and favored by customers and the public.

设计
DESIGN

青岛十三月餐饮管理有限公司
Qingdao March Food Management Co.,Ltd.

青岛悟本正奇广告有限公司
Qingdao is now the odd advertising Limited

生产
MANUFACTURE

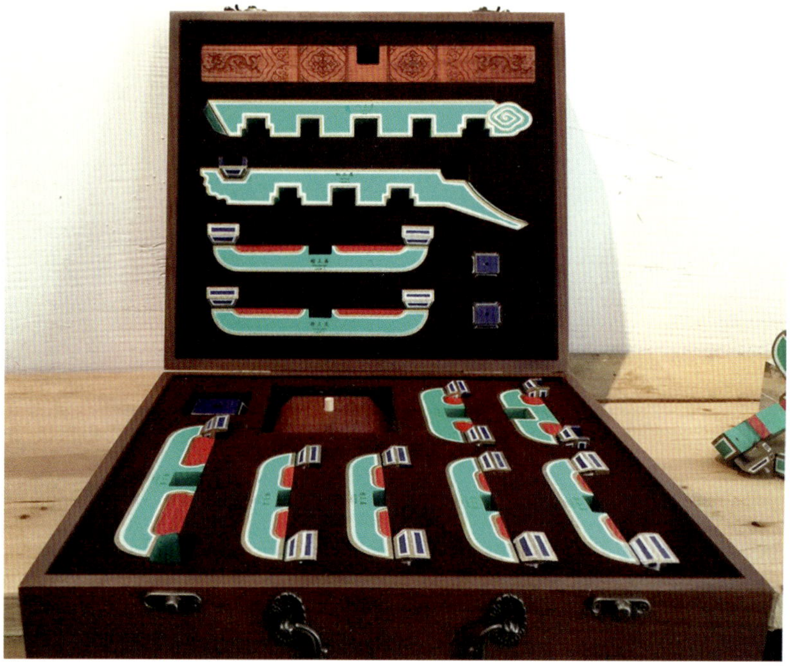

斗拱探秘
Dou Gong Confidential

该产品选取故宫建筑中明式斗拱的基本元素，具有知识性、趣味性、艺术性、观赏性。从平面零散部件组成立体造型，组装成功后成为一件美丽的立体装饰品，增加游客对中国文化的兴趣和了解。人们通过亲自组装了解中国建筑的精美玄妙同时体验安装、彩绘等工作，对诠释工匠精神，对传播中国文化具有一定作用。

This product is a selected work of the basic elements of bright type stone in imperial palace of Ming Dynasty which is full of knowledge, interest, artistry and ornament. From the plane scattered parts stereo modeling, to the success of the assembly a beautiful stereo adornment, it increase the tourists' interests in Chinese culture and their understanding. By assembling and understanding Chinese construction and experience the installing and painting work, the product plays an important role in expressing craftsman's spirit and transmitting Chinese culture.

设计
DESIGN

马珺
Ma Jun

北京菁草堂文化艺术中心
Beijing Jingcaotang Art&Design Center

生产
MANUFACTURE

剑脊·直尺
Jianji-Ruler

本产品形态取自剑身的元素，采用铝合金型材制作，尺身直挺刚毅。尺面氧化电镀，刻度为激光雕刻，精致准确，耐磨耐用。尺子的截面为菱形，方便尺子拿取的同时也解决了普通尺在使用中拖墨的问题。尺面斜向刻度，在使用时可以轻松读取指尖按压区的数值。体现了“方圆有矩，执尺天涯，剑的脊梁，去刃化为尺”的精髓。

The shape of the product is from the elements of sword, taking aluminum alloy material. The ruler is straight and fortitude. The ruler is oxidized, plated and marked with laser engraving. It is not only exquisite and accurate, but also wearable and durable. The cross section of the ruler is a diamond, which is convenient for taking the ruler and solves the problem that the common ruler can pull the ink during use. The scale of the foot face is inclined, and the finger press area can be easily read when used. This shows the spirit of sword and ruler

设计
DESIGN

乔安琪、汤懿
Qiao Anqi, Tang Yi

什物计画文化创意有限公司
Shiwujihua Cultural Creative Company Limited

生产
MANUFACTURE

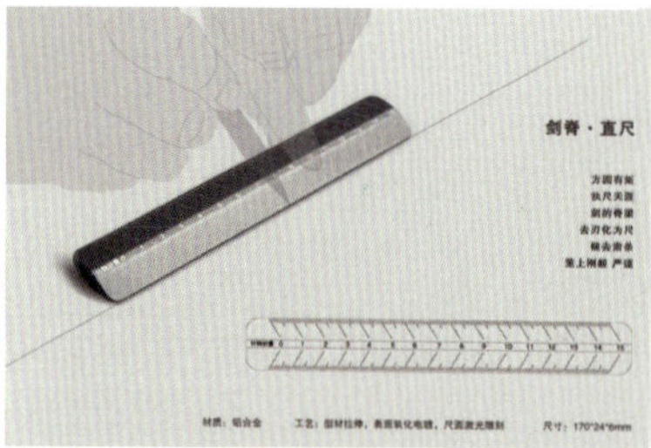

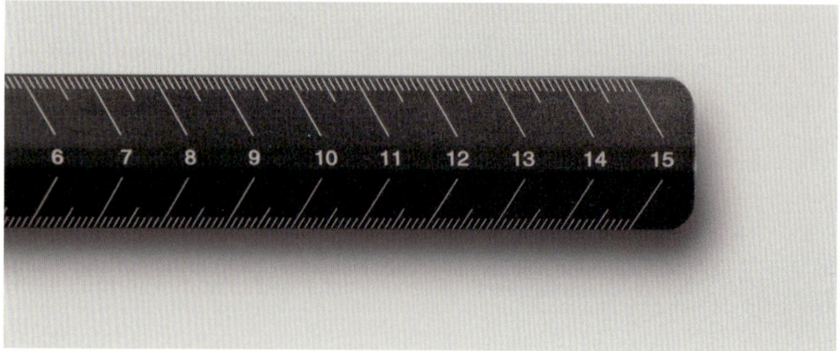

智存
Cyber

本产品是一支集书写和存储于一体的笔，解决了传统的书写记录与电脑时代的数码存储两个需求。产品材质主要使用了铝合金与塑料，铝合金的表面进行了阳极氧化处理，使产品表面光滑，线条也更加流畅。在外观设计上将数码储存巧妙地隐藏在笔帽夹出，使整体造型更加简洁，全黑的笔身简洁稳重，保持了 KACO 品牌的产品语言。

Cyber Pen combines the USB flash and traditional writing pen, solving the traditional writing records and digital records two needs. Main material is aluminum and PC plastic. The appearance of aluminum alloy uses anodic oxidation treatment to make the product more smooth and fluent. On the exterior design, the USB is hidden skillfully in the cap of the pen and the whole black design is simple and stable. It keeps the product language of KACO brand.

设计
DESIGN

谢磊、林帆
Xie Lei, Lin Fan

上海文采实业有限公司
Shanghai KACO Industrial Co.,Ltd.

生产
MANUFACTURE

品致
Square

本产品采用紧密的数控机床加工技术，严格控制正方形四个面的尺寸，所以笔帽对准任意一个面都可以严丝合缝地盖上。独特的方形造型，硬朗中兼顾流畅的线条，采用铝合金阳极氧化处理，使笔身光滑流畅，带出一种现代的高端金属笔气质。四种可选配色满足不同消费者需求，色彩轻快，从视觉上可以调节使用者心情。

This product adopts CNC manufacturing technology to strictly control the size of the square shapes of each face, so the cap of the pen can be covered at each face precisely. The unique square shape, hard but fluent line and the anodic oxidation treatment of aluminum alloy make the pen smooth with modern metal luxury image. There are four colors to satisfy the need of customers, the colors are bright which can moderate user's mood visually.

设计
DESIGN

林帆
Lin Fan

上海文采实业有限公司
Shanghai KACO Industrial Co.,Ltd.

生产
MANUFACTURE

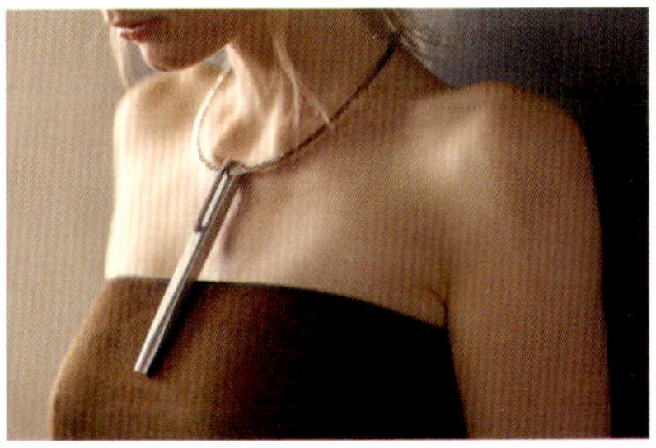

大内咪探 AR 画册
AR Picture Album of The Imperial Palace Cat

本产品首创了文化产业和增强现实技术相结合，以故宫全景地图为向导，通过视觉、听觉、触觉让孩子们深刻感受中华传统文化的乐趣，深入浅出地介绍宫廷建筑知识，并融合宫廷音乐和历史对白生动活泼地将历史活化，配合彩色铅笔等手工绘图让儿童有更多的想象空间和共享能力，使儿童轻松了解中国文化，让中国文化的精髓可以薪火相传。

This product initiates the combination of culture IP and AR technology. Guided by the panoramic map of the Imperial Palace, children can learn traditional Chinese culture with fun through visual, sound and feeling methods. The history is vitalized by royal music and vivid dialogues, and paintings can enlarge children's imagination space and sharing ability. Therefore, children can know Chinese culture easily and the essence of Chinese culture can be transmitted.

设计
DESIGN

北京洛可可科技有限公司
LKK Design Beijing Co.,Ltd.

北京洛可可科技有限公司
LKK Design Beijing Co.,Ltd.

生产
MANUFACTURE

知竹快客杯
Zhizhu Quick Cup

本产品是国内唯一具有360度双层紫砂结构的紫砂快客杯，隔热防烫效果均超过业内同类产品。在制作过程中以纯手工或模具辅助成型，不施釉，不掺杂其他化学物质与矿料，烧制的窑炉为电窑或天然气窑，零污染，低排放，符合安全环保的标准。多种颜色的紫砂泥，增添了产品的时尚感。双层中空结构，一壶一杯，随身便携，独乐自在。

"Zhizhu" is the only red-stoneware quick cup with a 360° double-deck structure, and the thermal insulation effect is better than that of the similar products in the industry. It is formed by pure handwork or molds during the manufacturing operation, which doesn' t apply a glaze and has no chemical substances or mineral aggregates in the whole process. The raw materials are only prepared through ferrous soil and water, and the fired furnace is an electrical kiln or a natural-gas kiln, with zero pollution and low emissions, fully complying with the standards for security and environmental protection. Various colors add a sense of fashion to the product. The double-deck structure and one pot one cup is easy to carry with and is of lots of fun.

设计 DESIGN
崔建赟
Cui Jianyun

生产 MANUFACTURE
北京新绎爱特艺术发展有限公司
Beijing Ovation Art Development Co.,Ltd.

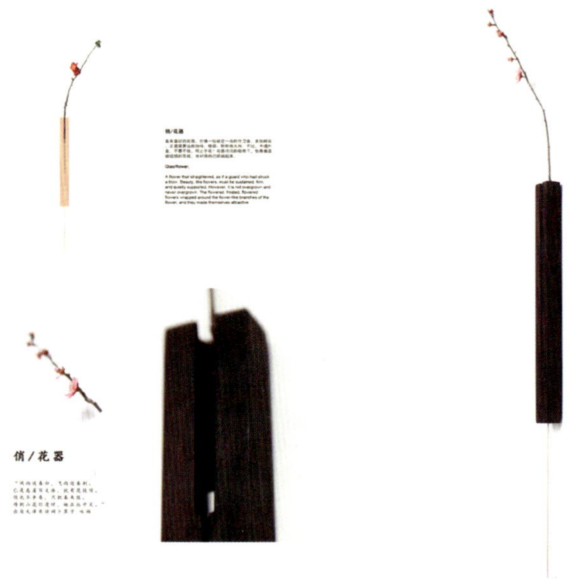

俏 / 花器
Qiao/Flower

该花器以金属为材质，环保性比较强，工艺性结合机械与人工，简练的造型，一实一虚，美观大方。直来直往的花器，仿佛一位破空一击的守卫者。美如鲜花，正是需要这般持续、稳固、默默地支持。中通外直，不蔓不枝，何止于花。花器冷淡的躯壳下，包裹着温婉绽放的花枝，优雅大方，也衬得自己娇俏起来。

This product is made of metal and is environmental protecting. It combines mechanical and manual process which is simple, virtual-real synthesis and of elegant appearance. It is a flower that straightened, as if a guard who had struck a blow. Beauty, like flowers, must be sustained, firm, and quietly supported. However, it is not overgrown and never overgrown. The flowered, frosted, flowered flowers wrapped around the flower-like branches of the flower, and they made themselves attractive.

设计 DESIGN
彭钟
Peng Zhong

生产 MANUFACTURE
北京汉今国际文化发展有限公司
Beijing China Today International Culture Co., Ltd.

人看花 花看人
People See Flowers and Flowers See People

本产品以文雅的特种纸印刷，采用裸装、护封、腰封的形式处理装帧结构，版式开阔，字形精致，信息清晰，阅读节奏明确，封面上采用了丝印荧光蓝色书名加手车红线的装帧特点，强调出浓烈的手工味道，呈现设计创作中人看花花看人的忘我与投入的状态。是为设计专业学生和从业新人写就的一本关于设计和就业的参考书。

People See Flowers and Flowers See People uses the tasteful special paper to print. The structure of binding handled with the naked binding, book jacket and the paper taps. There was a widen format, perfect typeface, clear information and the reader will have a great reading. The cover of this book, emphasizing the strong artificial work, was used the screen printing the title with fluorescent pigment blue and sewing machine to binding the red line, which shows the condition, a man to the flowers and the flowers from a man, of selflessness when a man in the creation of design. The book, as a reference book written about learning design, doing some work in design, looking for a job or establishing a company for the students who were major in the graphic design and the flesh people in the graphic design job.

设计 DESIGN
彦辰设计
Iseead Design

生产 MANUFACTURE
彦辰设计（深圳）有限公司
Iseead Design Co.

月老红绳戒
Goddess

本款情侣对戒的设计灵感来源于中国传统的经典服饰——旗袍和中山装。提取这两款衣服的领口与纽扣为设计元素。在戒指一处设计了一个像领口的开口，然后用红绳将戒指开口的两端连接在一起，形成纽扣的形状。就像是两个相爱的人，用一条绳子将他们的心紧紧地连在一起一样。整体造型简约、时尚，优雅的舒适感，同时也有爱情的象征。

The sources of design inspiration: Chinese costumes - cheongsam and Chinese tunic suit. We use collar and button as the modeling elements. The ring's shape is a simple circle and there is a neckline-like opening at one side of the ring which is connected by a tiny red string, like a button in the wedding dress and representing that the lovers are closely connected by the string. The unusual design of these couple rings gives them the new identity of simplicity, fashion and elegance, besides they are also the symbol of love.

设计
DESIGN

杨朝生
Yang Chaosheng

上海品漫网络科技有限公司
Shanghai Pinman Network Technology Co.,Ltd.

生产
MANUFACTURE

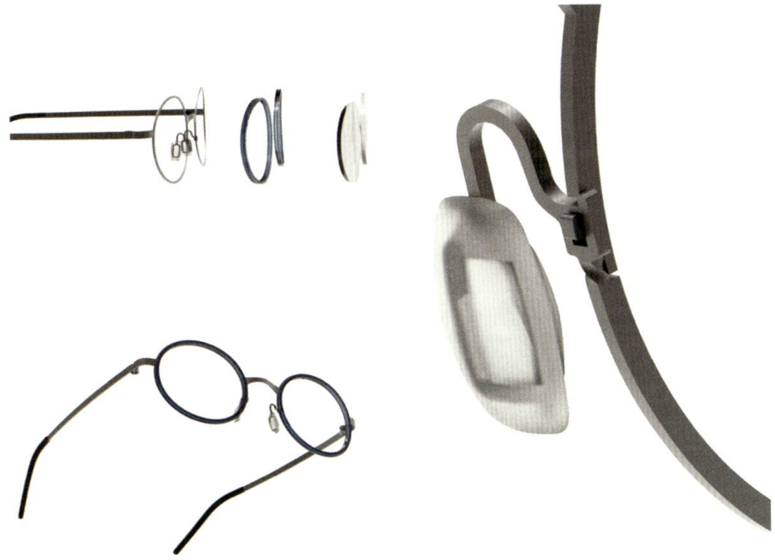

Tapole T 系列
Tapole Series T

该系列眼镜利用钛合金材料的特性，提供了极好的可调节性和弹性的镜腿，重量不足 5.8 克。眼镜在结构技术上有所改进，钛合金薄片经过激光切割后打弯而形成的铰链结构，新设计铰链结构由激光切割后的钛合金薄片弯曲形成，而不使用螺钉焊接。可调式鼻垫结构有助于提供舒适持久的佩戴，在运动中不容易脱落。

This series eyewear takes the advantages of titanium alloy to provide an extremely good flexibility and elasticity of glasses' legs. The whole weight is less than 5.8g. The glasses have made improvements in structural technology, the titanium alloy sheet after laser cutting and bending to form a hinge structure. The new design hinge structure is formed by bending the titanium alloy sheet after laser cutting without using screw welding. The specially developed adjustable nose pad structure helps to provide comfortable, long-lasting wear, Even in the movement is not easy to fall off.

设计
DESIGN

丁栋
Ding Dong

深圳图谱人文科技有限公司
Tapole Co.,Ltd.

生产
MANUFACTURE

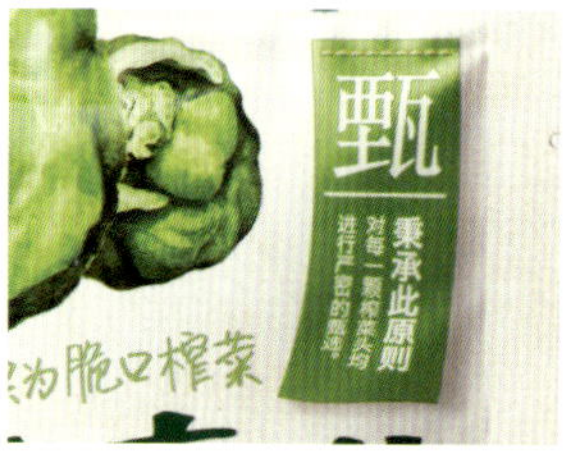

吉香居榨菜真芯
True Heart

该榨菜包装打破了消费者心中固有的陈旧、简易的、低廉的印象。用水彩风格的插画和手写字体，表现了对于产品原料的自信。以整体新鲜榨菜的绿色为主色调，配以新鲜、美味、脆口的菜品图，扑面而来的清新感加上食欲感，让人产生强烈购买欲。手写字体“60% 的榨菜芯部分”直接给消费者传达出产品的特点。

This package of pickle broke the fixed, outmoded, simple and cheap impression of customers. It takes the watercolor style illustrations and hand writing character to show the confidence of the materials of the product. The main color background is green accompanied by fresh, delicious and crispy food picture, all this fresh feeling and appetite give a strong sense of purchasing. The hand writing "60% is of the heart of pickle "straightly conveys the features of the product to customers.

设计
DESIGN
四川省吉香居食品有限公司
Jixiangju Food Co.,Ltd.

希杰（青岛）食品有限公司
CJ(Qingdao) Foods Co.,Ltd.
生产
MANUFACTURE

nubia Z17 智能手机包装
nubia Z17 Smartphone Packaging

该产品为努比亚新一代高端旗舰级智能手机的包装礼盒。盒面外观采用模具镜面抛光技术，LOGO 烫红金的制作红圈作为视觉元素，简约精致，突出品牌名称，让人印象深刻，从而更好地区别于其他品牌。整套设计风格简约，设计理念明晰，颜色的搭配沉稳大气，配上产品外观流畅的曲线让人感受到精致之美。

This product is a package box for nubia's new generation of high-end flagship smart phone. The surface of package box takes the mould mirror polishing technology. The designed red circle in hot red gold of the logo is the visual element, which is delicate and simplicity, impressing so as to better distinguish from other brands. The whole design is simple in style with clear design concept and the collocation of color is of good taste letting people feel the beauty of delicacy with flowing smooth curves.

设计
DESIGN
努比亚技术有限公司
Nubia Technology Co., Ltd.

努比亚技术有限公司
Nubia Technology Co.,Ltd.
生产
MANUFACTURE

竹叶青
Bamboo Liquor

该产品包装运用仿生学，巧妙地将竹子的自然纹理和结构、造型、质感在包装上再现，清晰传达出产品的特点。包装材质上，循着道法自然、崇尚自然的法则，运用自然环保包装材质，带来的不仅是视觉上冲击，更是一种关怀，一份对大自然的敬畏与尊重，让设计回归自然。体现了产品“源于自然，归于自然”的低调内敛气质以及真实朴素之美。

The package uses bionics and tacitly applies bamboo's natural texture and structure to reappear the shape and texture of bamboo on packaging, clearly expressing the features of the product. The packaging material follow the laws of Tao follows nature, respect for nature, using eco-friendly packaging material to bring not only the visual impact, but also a care, a reverence and respect for nature, make design returns to nature. It's also reflects the product's low-key and reserved temperament as well as true and simple beauty, "what comes from nature returns to nature."

设计
DESIGN
深圳市柏星龙创意包装股份有限公司
Shenzhen Baixinglong Creative Packaging Co.,Ltd.

水星组
Mercury Team
生产
MANUFACTURE

文化茶
Wenhua Tea

本产品命名为“文化”，其表达意义为文字在融化。产品从汉字中提炼了 28 个笔画，用黑茶压制出来，包装为原色秸秆浆材料，形成“白纸黑字”的效果，营造极富现代感的视觉冲击力，美不可言。通过意向形态 + 体验的设计手法表现汉字魅力，呼吁大家重视汉字文化，意在汉字是中国传统文化的根基和载体，不能被“融化”。

The name of product is “culture”, meaning the word is melting. The product extracted 28 strokes from the Chinese character. The dark tea is pressed by special method. The packaging uses the original straw pulp material. The strong contrast of "black words in white paper" brings the splendid feelings of modern visual impact and the beauty is out of words. Through the design, it expresses the charm of Chinese characters, and call attention to the culture of Chinese character. Chinese characters are the foundation and carrier of traditional Chinese culture and cannot be "melted".

设计
DESIGN
深圳市字在文化传播有限公司
Zizai Culture Communication Co., Ltd.

深圳市麦锡工业产品策划有限公司
Maxypro Industrial Product Scheme Co.,Ltd.
生产
MANUFACTURE

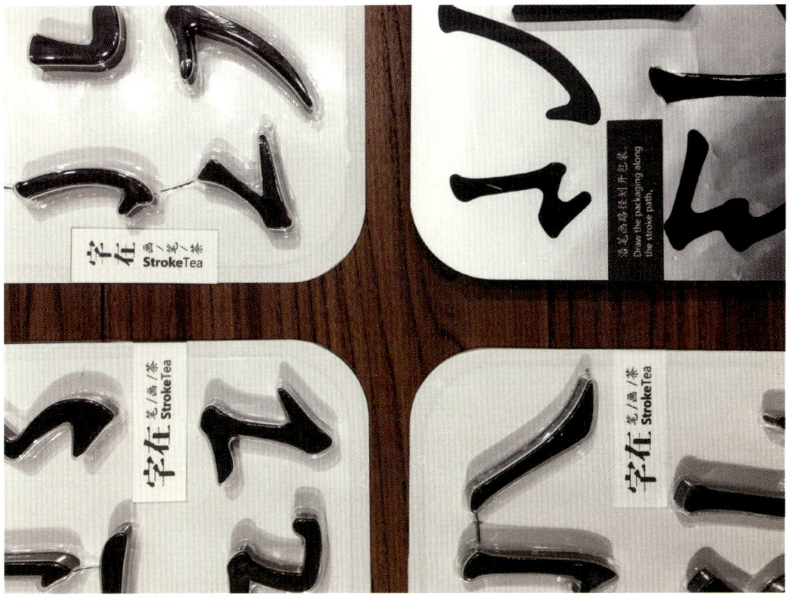

五色本草
Tie-Dye Teaching Kit

本产品为扎染教学套装，以天然植物染料为依托，操作简便，用户利用这个套装可以完成纯植物扎染作品。套装的外观呈手提包样式，展开后是一条包含扎染所用的织物和扎染材料工具的围裙；套装配有详细操作步骤的纸质扎染教程和视频教程，可以让用户快速掌握扎染技艺，这使得扎染技艺能够不断传承，发扬光大。

The tie-dye teaching kit is based on natural plant dyes which is easy to operate. The user can complete pure plant tie-dye works by using this kit. It looks like a handbag in appearance, and turns into an apron with the fabric, materials and tools for tie-dye after being unfolded; the kit attached with the paper tie-dye instruction and guiding video in detailed operating procedures. With high availability and accessibility, the tie-dye technique will be constantly passed down and carried forward.

设计
DESIGN
北京泓羽文化艺术有限公司
Beijing Hongyu Culture and Arts Co., Ltd.

林泓魁、李岩
Lin Hongkui, Li Yan
生产
MANUFACTURE

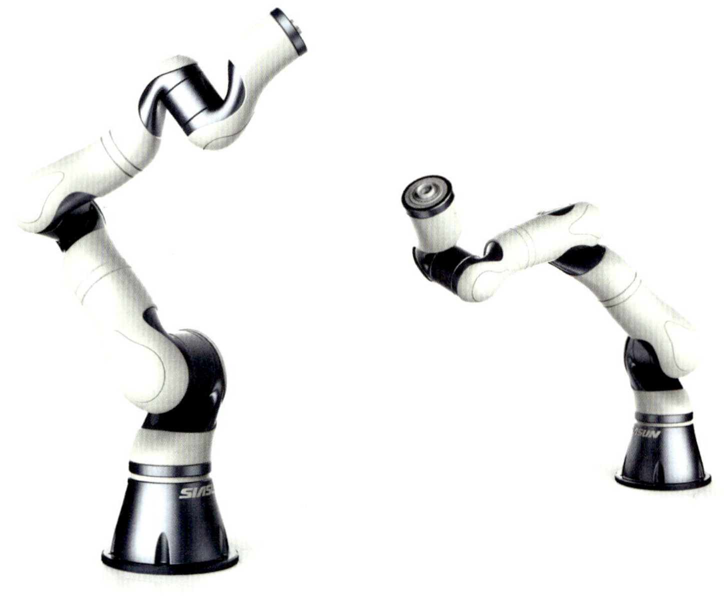

七轴协作机器人
Seven Cooperative Robot

七轴协作机器人对推动社会节约能源，促进可持续性发展起到了积极的引领作用。产品外观采用轻量化和流线型设计，提高自身的灵活性，使其适合安装在狭小的空间内，产品可以在障碍物较多的狭小空间帮助人们避开障碍从而顺利搬运物件。圆润饱满的曲面与富有弹性张力的线条使机器人看起来更具生命力、亲和力。

The seven axis cooperative robot is playing a positive leading role in saving energy and promotes sustainable development of the society. Due to the lightweight and sleek design of seven axis robot coordination, flexibility of itself, make it very suitable for installation in narrow space, small space products can be found in many obstacles to help people avoid obstacles to the smooth handling of objects. The rounded and full surface and elastic stretch line make the robot look more vigorous and friendly.

设计
DESIGN
沈阳创新设计服务有限公司
Shenyang Innovation

生产
MANUFACTURE
新松机器人自动化股份有限公司
SIASUN

蜂鸟
Hummingbird

该产品是一款便携式车应急启动电源，解决人们当汽车电瓶出现馈电或因为其他原因无法启动这一问题。产品上壳、下壳、开关按键都是采用塑壳 ABS，此塑料比较环保，无毒、无味，兼有韧、硬、刚的特性，且防火安全等级符合行业安全标准。 外观采用格子纹理设计，局部凹凸对比，黄黑两色搭配，整机的工具感更强 。

This product is a portable emergency starting battery aiming to solve problems like people are unable to start the electronic car due to power off or some other reasons. Products on the shell, under the shell, switch keys are made plastic shell ABS, this plastic is more environmentally friendly, non-toxic, tasteless, both tough, hard, just the characteristics of fire safety level in line with industry safety standards. The design brings in quadrille pattern, ups and downs with perfect proportion, black above yellow, which endows the product strong sense of tools.

设计
DESIGN
胡益丹、王 群
Hu Yidan，Charlie Wang

生产
MANUFACTURE
惠州市卡儿酷科技有限公司
Huizhou Carku Technology Co.,Ltd.

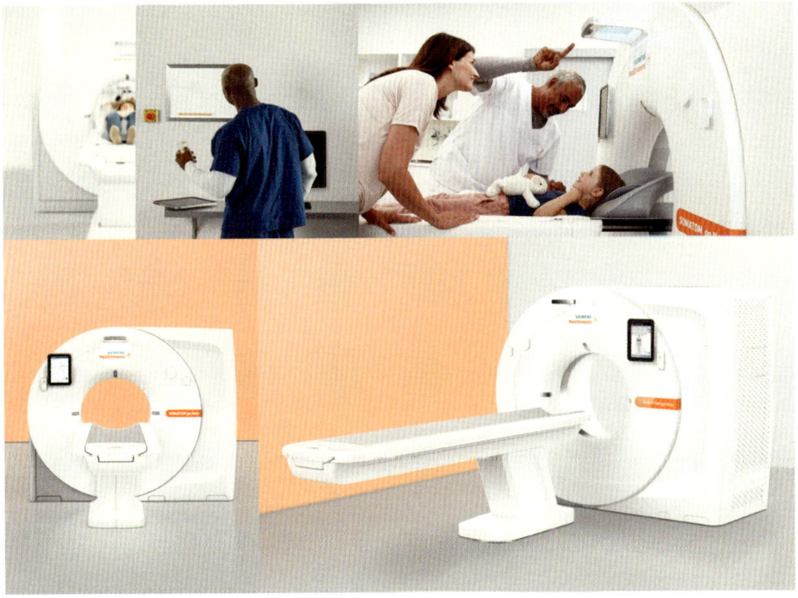

西门子 SOMATOM go. CT 扫描平台
Somatom go.

该产品强化且平衡了技术和人因两个要素，通过技术部件的精确性呈现出硬朗和可靠感来加强病人的舒适度。轻便的平板赋予操作员更多自由，患者等候时便可提前准备，图像无线传输至平板，可与放射医生及时交流。桶台内置的摄影机便于时刻观察用户，90 度摄制角可清晰记录通道。桶台一体的计算机和移动工作让使用者可操作灵活。

This product fortified and balanced the two elements of technique and human operation. The patient's comfort level is strengthened by solid and reliability delivered by the precision of technical parts. The portable pad gives more freedom to operators, they can prepare in advance while the patient is waiting and the picture can be sent to pad via wireless so as to communicate with radioactive doctor in time. The gantry-integrated camera makes it easy to provide better care and its 90° viewing angle gives you a superb view of the tunnel on the stationary monitor. The gantry-integrated computer and mobile work make the operator do more flexible.

设计
DESIGN
西门子医疗
Siemens Healthcare GmbH

Designaffairs 设计公司
Designaffairs
生产
MANUFACTURE

物证勘查仪
Material Evidence Exploration Instrument

本产品在专属领域使用，提高了警察办案效率和证据可靠程度。产品本身采用紧凑式结构设计，在体量上控制空间的占用和材料的消耗，材料上采用优质合金，提高产品使用寿命的同时还能达到材料回收再利用的目的。圆润而丰满的外形寓意着任何案件的隐情总有浮出水面的时候，打破警用产品常规的直线条，体现饱满而有力量的美。

The product is used in specific industry, with which it is available to improve the case handling efficiency, save the case handling time, enhance the reliability level of evidence and case handling accuracy. Compact structure design is adopted, it controls the space occupation and material consumption as well as adopts high-quality alloy, thus the service life is improved and material can be recycled. Round and plump appearance is based on the image of submarine, which means that the hidden facts of any cases will emerge from the water someday. The round modeling breaks the normal straight line of police product, reflecting full and powerful beauty.

设计
DESIGN
艺可意工业设计（北京）有限公司
Ecoe Industrial Design （Beijing）Co.,Ltd.

艺可意工业设计（北京）有限公司
Ecoe Industrial Design （Beijing）Co.,Ltd.
生产
MANUFACTURE

掘进机
TBM

该产品是一辆运输能力突破每小时 1500 吨的掘进机，解决了煤矿面临采掘失衡的问题。采用全断面连续截割、巷道一次成型技术，双刀盘加横滚筒的独特设计实现矩形断面一次成型，掘进断面 25 平方米，掘进速度每分钟 0.3 米。外观设计采用不锈钢装饰条，打破传统掘进机外观冰冷的固有形象，赋予节奏和韵律新的产品形象。

This product is a tunnel boring machine whose transportation ability is over 1500tons per hour, solving the imbalanced problem in mining. Using whole section continuous cutting molding technology of roadway, double plate realize rectangular cross section is a unique design of horizontal roller forming, excavating section 25sqiare meters, the driving speed is 0.3meters per minute. The application of stainless steel decorative strip, breaks the cold natural influence of traditional excavator's appearance, gives rhythm of new product image.

设计
DESIGN
北方重工集团
NHI

沈阳创新设计服务有限公司
Shenyang Innovation
生产
MANUFACTURE

超声药物导入治疗仪
Ultrasonic Medicine Import Therapeutic Apparatus

该产品利用超声改变细胞通透性，使药物可以在不打针的情况下，直接通过皮肤表层渗入病灶治疗疾病。解决传统静脉注射导致对非病灶部位造成不良影响，同时解决怕打针的问题。较国外产品相比，产品渗透性强，可以深入到皮肤下 60-80 毫米，任何病灶基本都可以直达；药物适用性强，可以适应更多药物，用药少，浓度高，让超声导入治疗成为更主流的治疗方式。

The product uses ultrasonic cell permeability, so that drugs can directly go through the skin surface infiltration of lesions without injection, so as to avoid the traditional meridians injection which will lead to adverse effects on the other lesion and bring benefits to those who are afraid of needle injection. Compared with counterparts at home and abroad, this product has stronger permeability can go deep into the skin below 60-80 - mm, and can reach basically any lesions in human body. The product also has strong applicability can accommodate more drugs, so that the ultrasonic import after treatment can be a more mainstream treatment.

设计 DESIGN
上简设计（武汉）有限公司
Up Design(Wuhan)

生产 MANUFACTURE
安徽省玉林医药有限公司
Anhui Yulin Pharmaceutical Co.,Ltd.

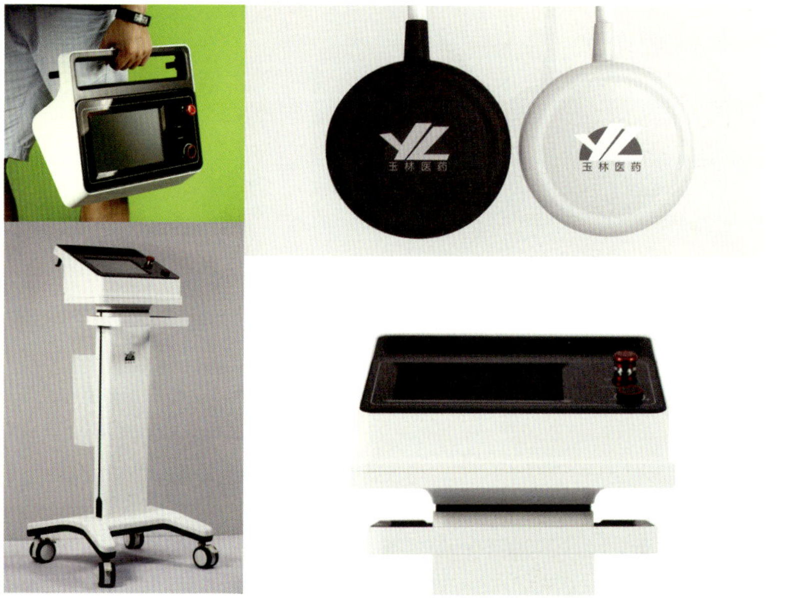

DZ931 系列塑壳断路器
DZ931 Series Moulded Case Circuit Breaker

该产品采用双断点结构辅助磁吹和能量脱扣功能，达到分断能力高，体积小，零飞弧。产品结合大电流电压精密采集技术，可实现电量监测。产品有遥调、遥信、遥测、遥控四遥功能，使产品可对电网的数据参数、自身健康状态进行分析，将参数输给客户端，同时在通讯状态下接受远程控制和调节。产品的数据采集和处理性能，在智能电网中有很大的市场前景。

DZ931 series Moulded case circuit breaker have rotary double contacts, electromagnetic blowing and energy press trip structure which can make the MCCB with high short-circuit breaking capacity, small volume and zero arc distance. It can measure lots of parameters of power grid with the electronic trip unit combines advanced current sensors. The product can be remotely adjusted, communicated, measured and controlled, allowing it to measure the parameters of power line and health status of itself and transfer these data to data-center. At the same time, the breaks can be adjusted and controlled with communication with long distance.Its data collecting and handling performance own wide market prospect in smart power grids.

设计 DESIGN
杭州木马商务咨询有限公司
Hangzhou Moma Business Consulting Co.,Ltd.

生产 MANUFACTURE
常熟瑞特电气股份有限公司
Changshu Ruite Electric Co.,Ltd.

压裂车
Fracturing Truck

该压裂车适合我国特殊路况、地质条件和压裂施工工艺要求，达到国际先进水平的页岩气压裂成套系列产品，并具备批量生产制造能力。压裂车配备本地控制、远程控制、便携式控制多种操作方式，经济性高。采用国际一流品牌的柱塞泵，排量大、效率高、压力波动小、可靠性高。具有超高压力、大功率、大排量和长时间连续作业的特点。

This fracturing truck is suitable for China's special conditions, geological conditions and meets the fracturing construction technological requirements. Series products of complete sets of shale gas fracturing have reached the international advanced level, and have the batch production manufacturing capacity. Fracturing truck series products is equipped with local control , remote control, portable control of various operation mode and high economy. Adopt the first-level brand plunger pump, higher efficiency, smaller fluctuations of pressure, higher reliability. It has the characteristics of ultra high pressure, high-power, large displacement and long time continuous operation.

设计 DESIGN
沈阳创新设计服务有限公司
Shenyang Innovation

生产 MANUFACTURE
北方重工集团
NHI

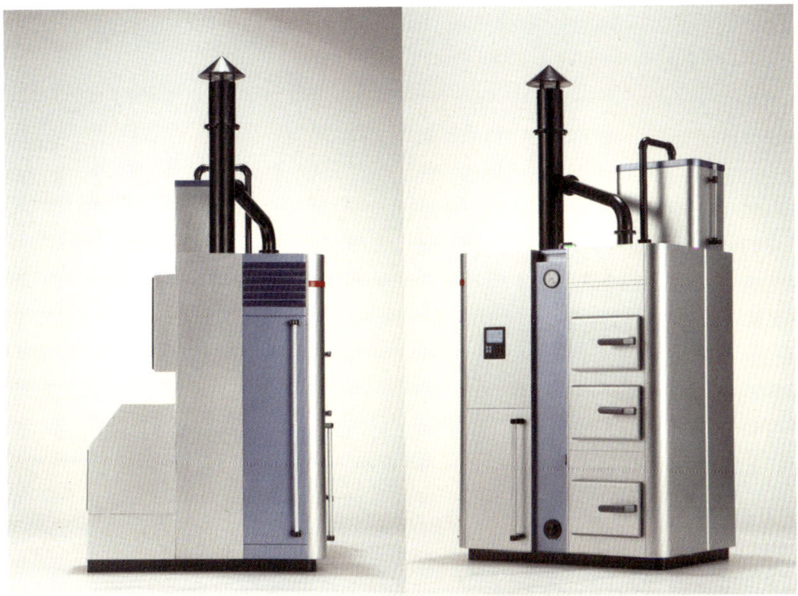

易操作省空间生物质自动化锅炉
Easy to Use and Saving Space Automatic Biomass Boiler

该产品全新研发模式化一键操作，通过内部结构优化使体积缩减，设计出易操作省空间生物质自动化锅炉。技术上，攻克方形炉门密封性难点，替换圆形炉门，加料口扩大。设计上，底部的反射式观火口解决弯腰看火情况，降低劳动强度。储煤仓增加炉膛受热面，多点配风装置，内设水冷炉排，产品功能区域划分合理，结构排布规整。

The product newly develops one-button modular operation and designs easy to use and saving space automatic biomass through internal optimization in order to contract volume. Technological bottleneck of sealing is overcome by replacing square furnace door for rounded furnace door, with stuffing port expanded. In design, reflective-type fire sightglass at bottom can perfectly remove inconvenience of bending down for observing fire in a cost-effective way, reducing labor strength. Coal storage warehouse broadens combustion reaction area, multi-point air distribution device was equipped,and water-cool fire grates was designed. The product function area is divided reasonably and its structure and layout are tidy.

设计 DESIGN 河北鑫华新环保科技有限公司 Hebei Xinhua New Environmental Technology Co., Ltd.

广东顺德东方麦田工业设计有限公司 East-Innovation Shunde GD Co.,Ltd. **生产 MANUFACTURE**

ST858 破拆机器人
ST858 Broken Robot

该产品采用电动机驱动，无有害气体排放或低污染尾气排放；负载式反馈式变量泵系统，系统的输出功率随着负载的需求而自动调整，无能源损失。外观是通过模块化的钣金件组合而成，易于拼装，主旨是利用简洁的造型赋予产品科技感，并将钢铁侠的脸部造型元素提炼融入机器人造型中，让生硬的机械造型有灵动性。

This product is driven by motor, with no emissions of harmful gas emissions or low pollution emissions. It uses the load feedback type variable pump system and the output power of the system is adjusted automatically with the load demand so there is no energy loss. The appearance of this product is made up of modular sheet metal parts which are easy to assemble. The aim is to give a sense of technique to the product through simple shape and make the solid iron shape more flexible by inverting ironman's facial shape into the robot.

设计 DESIGN 惊天智能装备股份有限公司 Giant I-Equipment Co.,Ltd.

马鞍山飞渡工业设计有限公司 Ma'anshan Feel Do Industrial Design Co.,Ltd. **生产 MANUFACTURE**

GT20-S 工程机器人
GT20-S Machine Robot

此款产品是室内及室外清拆与小型施挖掘作业的理想选择，也适合大多数材料类型的建筑清拆，也可在地震等救援工作中起到重要的作用。外观设计通过模块化的钣金件组合而成，易于拼装；拥有动感时尚的线条，清新氧气感的配色，简洁大方；旋转流畅的机械臂，双炮筒式卤素大灯，让生硬笨重的机械造型多了生命力与灵动性。

This product is the ideal choice for indoor and outdoor cleaning and removes small application of mining operations, but also for most types of building demolition materials, can also play an important role in earthquake relief work. The appearance of this product is made up of modular sheet metal parts which are easy to assemble. As a robot, it has dynamic fashion lines and fresh oxygen color which is simple and elegant. The smooth rotation arm and double barrel type halogen lamp let the blunt heavy machinery be more vital and flexible.

设计 DESIGN 惊天智能装备股份有限公司 Giant I-Equipment Co.,Ltd.

马鞍山市安工大工业技术研究院有限公司 Ma'anshan, Anhui University of Technology Industrial Technology Research Institute Co.,Ltd. **生产 MANUFACTURE**

生物质链条热水锅炉
Biomass Chain Hot Water Boiler

该产品综合应用了反烧法、煤制气法、悬浮燃烧等多种洁净燃烧技术，使生物质燃料燃烧完全，解决了冒黑烟的本质问题。产品使用的燃料是将农作物的秸秆、木屑、玉米芯、稻壳等通过压缩成型直接利用的生物质颗粒燃料。生物质锅炉因其清洁性和经济性的特点，受到国家能源局的重点推广。它的使用将代替煤炭等不可再生资源的使用，节能环保。

The product integrated application of the burning, coal gas, suspension combustion, and other clean combustion technology, the biomass fuel combustion, completely solving the problem of the nature of the smoke. It takes the crops straw, wood chips, corn cobs, and rice husks as biomass granular fuel which are compressed and used directly. Biomass chain hot water boiler is greatly promoted by National Energy Administration because of its cleanability and economy. Its use will replace non-renewable sources such as coal so it is energy saving and environmental protecting.

设计
DESIGN
郑州一诺工业产品设计有限公司
Zhengzhou Enor Industrial Product Design Co.,Ltd.

生产
MANUFACTURE
河南绿探集团
Henan Green Agent Group

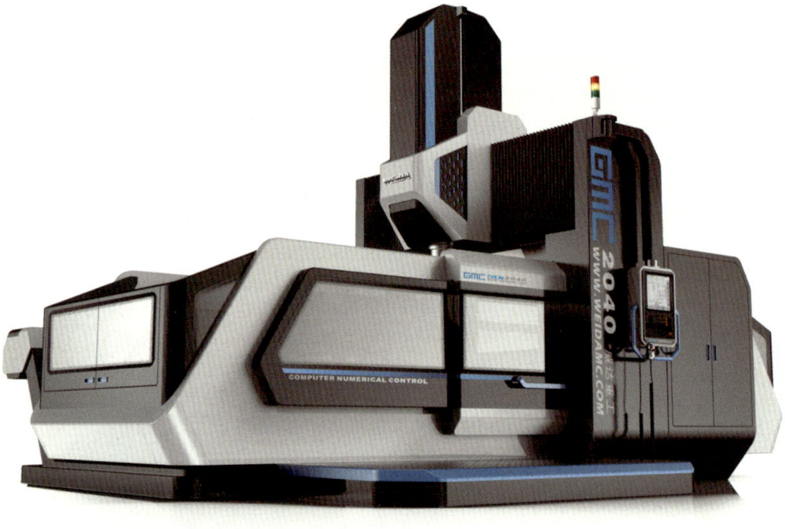

GMC2040 定梁龙门式加工中心
GMC2040 Fixed Beam Gantry Machining Center

本机床由床身、工作台、立柱、横梁、溜板、滑枕、润滑系统、刀库系统、冷却系统、气动系统等组成。床身以箱型结构体设计与周密肋骨支撑。且床身、立柱、横梁、工作台采用优质铸铁件并经过时效处理消除应力，具有良好的刚度；床身底座采用铸造工艺，床身外壳采用钣金加工，坚固耐用，能通过再制造技术修复循环使用，有效降低成本、能耗和排放。

The machine consists of bed, table, column, beam, slide plate, ram, lubrication system, knife system, cooling system, pneumatic system and other components. The bed is designed with a box-like structure and a tight rib support. The bed, column, beam and table use high-quality cast iron pieces and after aging treatment to eliminate stress, with good stiffness. The bed shell uses sheet metal processing, which is durable and can be recycled through remanufacturing technology to effectively reduce costs, energy consumption and emissions.

设计
DESIGN
区耀光、吕慧彬
Oson, Lv Huibin

生产
MANUFACTURE
山东威达重工股份有限公司
Shandong Weida Heavy Industry Co.,Ltd.

YSF 全身健康扫描系统
YSF Full-Body Health Scanning System

该产品通过生物点传感器采集测量组织细胞的电阻，点传导性、电压及动作电位，通过数据库对比进行数学模型 3D 重建，一次节省病人常规体检所花费的费用的 60%。从而得出科学完整的人体健康报告。针对全身各个器官生物活性和生理功能的检测，预测潜在的危险因素和疾病发展方向，并给予合理的饮食指导和运动建议。

This product measures the resistance of cells and conductivity, voltage and action potentials through biological point sensors. By comparison with the database mathematical model for 3D reconstruction, it save 60% of the cost fees for patient at a time and draws a scientific and complete human health report. It focuses on the prediction of the whole body organ, tissue and the function of the system changes, reveals early disease and the health of the body have risks, to evaluate the body existing health risk grading tips, and avoid random given dietary appropriate guidance.

设计
DESIGN
郑州一诺工业产品设计有限公司
Zhengzhou Enor Industrial Product Design Co.,Ltd.

生产
MANUFACTURE
河南恒东医疗器械有限公司
Henan Hengdong Medical Instrument Co.,Ltd.

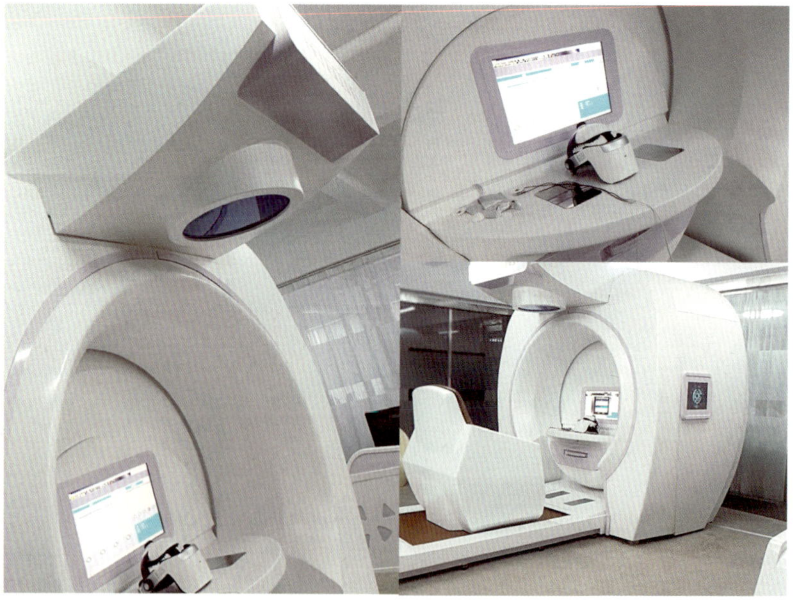

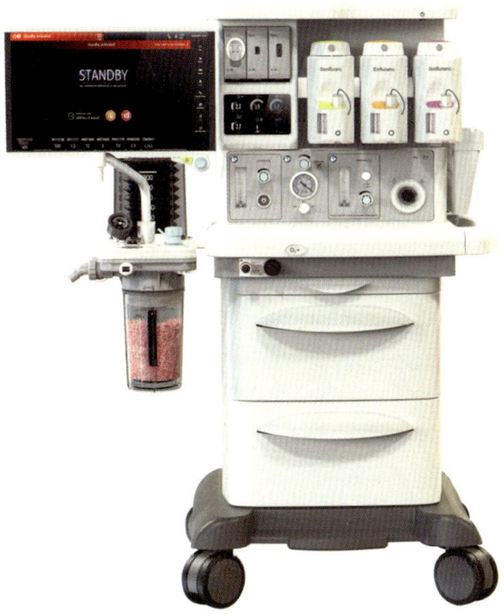

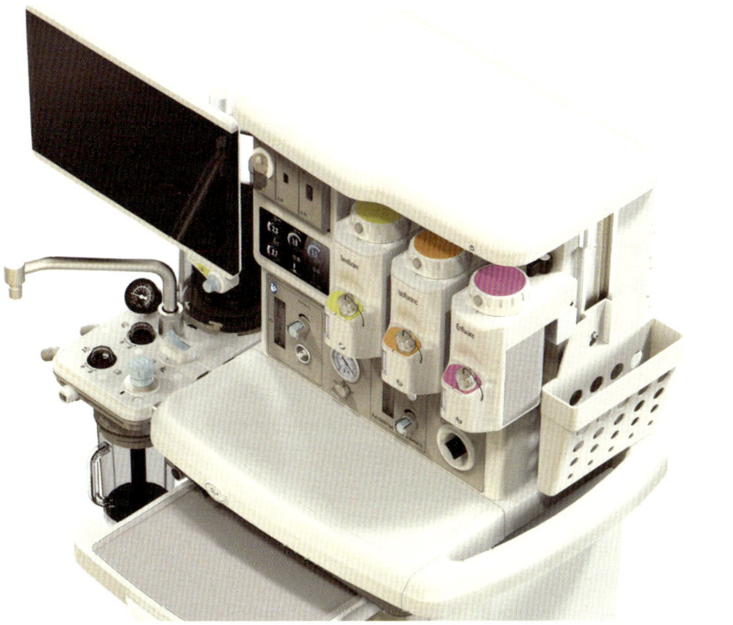

Gray Sculpture 麻醉工作站
Gray Sculpture Anaesthetic Workstation

"Gray Sculpture" 整体灵感来自于砖雕石雕木雕融合在一起的徽派建筑。匠人的精神在产品中体现得淋漓尽致。功能模块化设计让医院随时选择想选配的功能，方便快捷的满足院方的各种新的需求，所有的功能操作区都采用了浅灰进行区分，突出操作重点。整机在各种系统集成的情况下，充分考虑人机工程和黄金分割的美学理念，增强人机交互体验。

"Gray Sculpture" inspired by the brick carved stone carvings together Huizhou architecture. The spirit of the craftsmen in the product embodies the most vividly. The modular design allows the hospital to choose functions at its will, thus can meet all kinds of needs of the hospital. All the functional areas are used light gray to distinguish, highlight the operational focus. In a variety of systems integration circumstances, the machine takes full account of ergonomic and golden aesthetics of the concept of functional division of the region to increase the interaction between human and machine.

设计
DESIGN

李俊杰
Leo Li

北京思瑞德医疗器械有限公司
Beijing Siriusmed Medical Device Co.,Ltd.

生产
MANUFACTURE

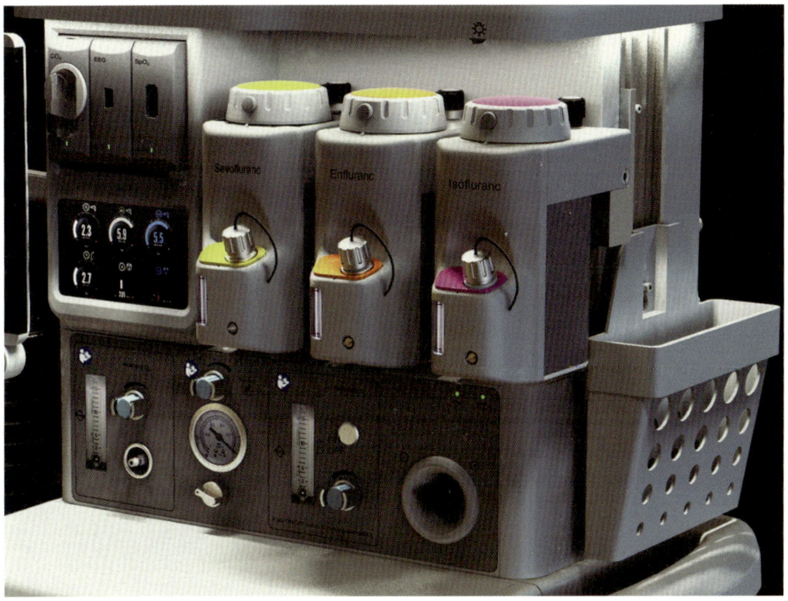

PUE0810 履带式破碎机
Tracked Mobile Plants

该产品是一台履带式破碎机。整机运用颚式咬合的机械原理，采用智能控制安全保护、负载自适应控制技术，能将大体积的建筑垃圾进行破碎，并通过多级筛分输出为尺寸相对均匀的物料。有效解决越来越短缺的天然砂石资源和日益严重的建筑垃圾堆放处理等问题，减少开山取石，并能将建筑垃圾资源化，实现循环再生，节约有限的地球天然资源。

This product is a tracked mobile plant. The whole machine take the jaw crush mechanism assisted with intelligent control safety system and self-adapt work load control system which enables the machine to crush large piece construction waste and divides them through multiple degree sieving system into even parts. The machine tries to solve the problem of shortage of natural gravel resource and the construction wastes, it also turns the construction wastes in to resource to recycle and save the limited natural resource in the world.

设计
DESIGN

徐州工程机械集团有限公司
Xuzhou Construction Machinery Group Co., Ltd.

江苏徐州工程机械研究院工业设计中心
ID Center of Xuzhou Construction Machinery Group Co.,Ltd.

生产
MANUFACTURE

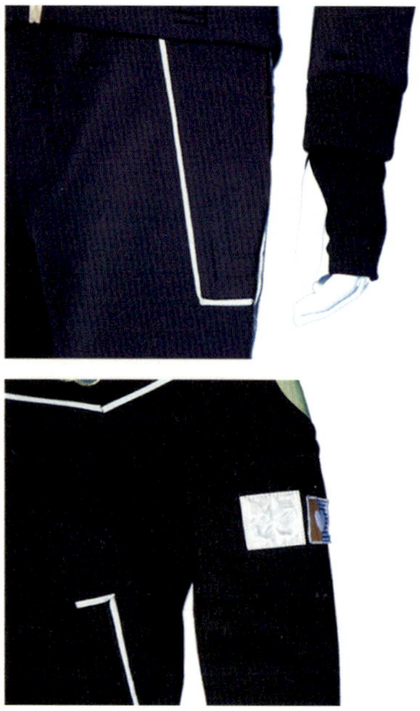

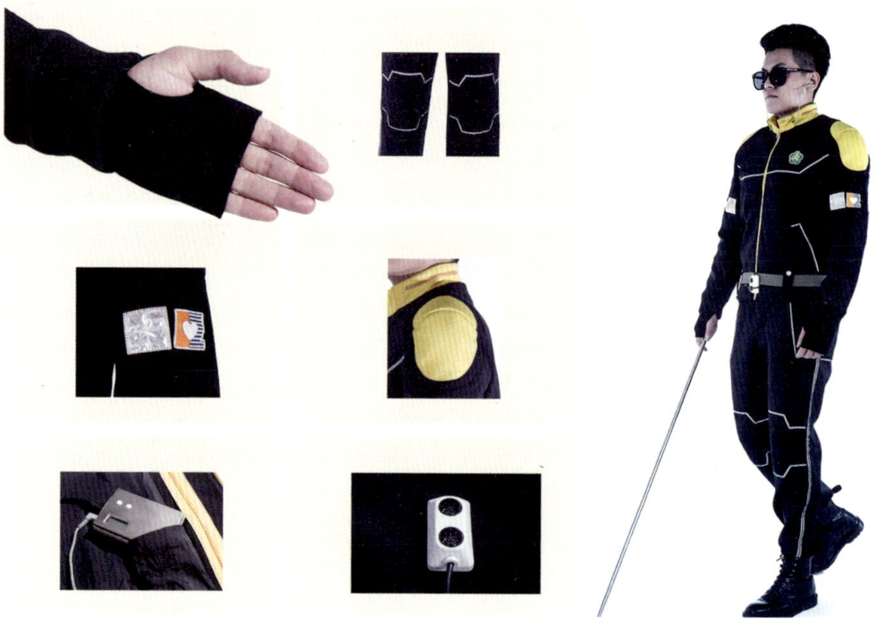

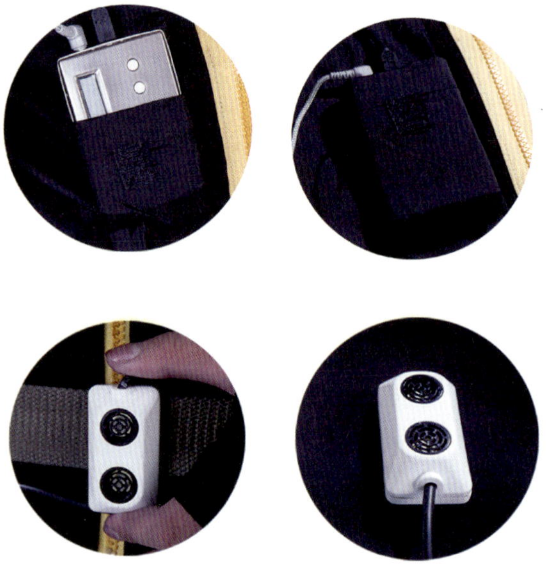

QT-216 型智能语音导盲服
QT-216 Intelligent Voice Guide Clothing

智能语音导盲服“光明使者”，增强盲人出行的安全性，以“步”代替“米”为单位，为盲人提供更加人性化的语音导航。设计研发的新型智能语音导盲仪，使这款产品能够在视力障碍者出行时做到对前方障碍物的提前预警，为他们的安全出行和生活提供了帮助。此服装已通过中国中文信息处理产品质量监督检验中心检测，被纳入北京市残联作为辅助装备。

Intelligent voice director "light messenger" strengthens the safety for the blind while going out. It takes step rather than meter as a unit to provide more humanized voice guide for the blind. The new designed intelligent voice guide instrument can make advanced alert of the in front obstacles for the blind during their going out, providing help for their safety in going out and in life. This costume has passed Chinese Information Processing Product Quality Supervision and Inspection Center in China and involved in Disabled Persons Federation in Beijing as assistance.

设计 DESIGN
北京绮彤子姗服装有限责任公司
Beijing Qitong Children's Clothing Co., Ltd.

周萍
Zhou Ping
生产 MANUFACTURE

GMC-2015 数控龙门加工中心
GMC-2015 CNC Gantry Machining Center

该机床在材料工艺上打破了传统铸造工艺。机床的钣金采用模块化设计，通用性强，方便更换与维修，在国内龙门加工中心领域开创了先河。机床的整体防护设计，使加工时所产生的铁屑、切削液与废油能够得到很好的收集、回收与再利用，保证了生产加工时的卫生问题，减少废油废屑对加工件精度与光洁度的影响。

The machine broke the traditional casting process in material skill. Machine sheet metal design uses modular design which is versatile, easy to replace and maintain. This kind of design did a pioneering work in the field of domestic gantry processing center. The machine tool take the overall protection so that the iron filings, cutting fluid and waste oil can be a good collection, recycling and re-use during the processing, ensuring the health problems in production and processing and reducing the impact of waste oil on the work piece precision and cleanability.

设计 DESIGN
南通聚田机电科技有限公司
Nantong Jutian Electrical and Mechanical Technology Co., Ltd.

重庆道合工业设计有限公司
Chongqing Daohe Industrial Design Co., Ltd
生产 MANUFACTURE

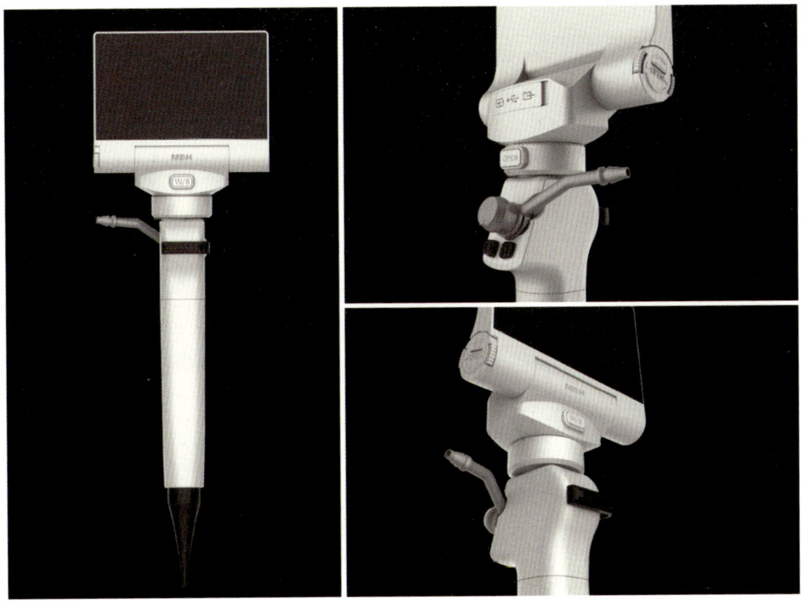

可视插管软镜
Video Flexible Intubationscope

该产品代替了部分大型医用内窥镜系统的使用。带摄录功能；用于气管插管，ID6.0 以上气管导管和气管内注药、分泌物吸引、气管检查等；自带可充电锂电池，使用时间长。消毒以后可多次循环利用，从产品角度做到降低病人的医疗费用负担。产品重心一致性、立体多角度旋转的屏幕、按压式电池盖、吸附式插电接口、方便的可拆卸机构，把人机工学运用到了极致。

This product replaces the use of some large medical endoscope systems with a video recording function. It is used for tracheal intubation (through the mouth or nose), ID6.0 above endotracheal tube and endotracheal injection, secretion suction, tracheal examination, biopsy, treatment. It has rechargeable lithium batteries with long service life. After disinfection, the product can be recycled many times, and the medical expense burden of the patient can be reduced from the product point of view. The consistency of the product center, the three-dimensional multi angle rotating screen, the press type battery cover, the adsorption plug-in interface, the convenient removable mechanism, the man-machine engineering has been applied to the acme.

设计
DESIGN

李兰华
Lory Li

珠海迈德豪医用科技有限公司
Zhuhai Mindhao Medical Technology Co., Ltd.

生产
MANUFACTURE

医用压缩雾化器 - FC08-W（启泰）
Medical Compression Atomizer

本医用压缩雾化器采用医用高分子材料制成，一次性使用耗材用医疗 PP 制成，采用环氧乙烷灭菌技术，为无菌产品。采用的高品质压缩机内芯，雾化量可调功能适用于不同种类呼吸道疾病的病患。主体设计运用“跑道型”的线条为构成方式的现代主义设计方法，以简约和富有亲和力作为核心设计理念贯穿整个产品，打破整体几何形状的冰冷感。

This medical compressed atomizer uses medical polymer materials, disposable medical consumables using PP, the ethylene oxide sterilization technology, so it is a sterile product. Product uses the high quality compressor, the inner core through the structure to achieve adjustable amount of atomization, atomized particles adjustable function which is suitable for different kinds of respiratory disease patients. It takes the modern design style of "track" line as formation way, and the design concept of simple and friendly runs through the product, breaking the coldness of geometrical shape.

设计
DESIGN

张俊生
Johnson Zhang

英华融泰医疗科技股份有限公司
ENTIE Medical PLC

生产
MANUFACTURE

“辽”矢量多旋翼无人机
Woozoom Tandem Wing Tilt Rotor UAV

该产品为第一款 X 型倾转多旋翼无人机平台，结合黑科技级别的 THEONE-I 型飞控技术加成，成为一款时速高达 100 千米的多旋翼无人机。还具备自主起飞，自主巡航，自主返航，绕点飞行，变姿态飞行等多种控制功能。在外观设计上体现了产品的流线型与肌肉感，半包围的设计更能为产品减轻重量，独特的外观设计解决了常规多旋翼在飞行时不能分清前后的问题。

This product is the first X type tilt multi-rotor UVA at speed of up to 100km, combining with flight control technique of THEONE-I type at black tech level. It has control functions as independent off, autonomous cruise, self return, around the point of flight, the flight attitude variable and other control function. The appearance design shows the streamlined and muscular style of the product. The half-surrounded design reduced the weight and unique design solved the problem of can not distinguish front and back in normal multi rotors while flying.

设计
DESIGN

沈阳无距科技有限公司
Woozoom

沈阳无距科技有限公司
Woozoom

生产
MANUFACTURE

军用四旋翼（折叠翼）无人机
Military Four-Rotor UAV

该四旋翼无人机主要是为特种部队提供，用于寒冷地带的军事侦察。折叠结构以及紧凑的内部布局实现了其体积小便于携带的特点，电池仓的保温设计以及云台透明罩的增加为在恶劣环境下飞行提供了保障。机身顶盖的整体造型通过棱线切割与高低错落的层次对比使其更为硬朗。结构的紧凑性增强了产品的精致感，更好地体现军工类产品的独有气质。

The four rotor unmanned aerial vehicle (UVA) is mainly to provide Special Forces for military investigation in cold strip area. Folding structure and compact internal layout shows the feature of small size and portable. The insulation design of the battery and the increase of the transparent cover have provided the safeguard for flying in harsh environments. The holistic type in the cap of UVA is more tough by the transected curves and strewn at random of the level. The compactness of the structure enhances the refinedness of the product and reflects the unique temperament of military industry product.

设计 DESIGN 山东蜂巢航空科技有限公司 Honeycomb Aerospace Tecnologies (Shandong) Co., Ltd.

北京赛佳图工业设计有限公司 Beijing Saga FIG Industrial Design Co.,Ltd. **生产 MANUFACTURE**

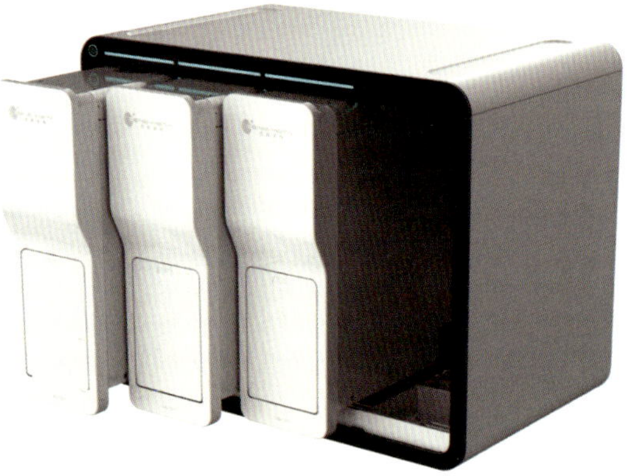

全自动核酸检测仪
Automatic Nucleic Acid Detector

该产品运用高通量基因测序，相比传统检测手段，基因测序效率是前者的 6 倍，准确率可以达到 99.97%，准确度更高。它更加准确，效率更高。机器之间能够进行联机堆叠，可以满足孕前检测。整机外观设计简洁。采用黑白配色，突出医疗检测类产品科技感的视觉效果，前面板为无边框设计的玻璃钢面板，手部按压自动弹出卡盒操作平台，增强人机交互体验。

This instrument is used in pregnancy examination of department of gynecology. Comparing with the existing down syndrome screening, its gene sequence efficiency is 6 times higher and the accuracy can reach 99.97%, which is more accurate and effective. The machines can stack online to satisfy the pre-pregnancy inspection. The whole machine design is simple. The black and white are used to highlight the medical testing products science and technology the visual perception of feeling. The front board is FRP with no frame. The operation platform which can automatically pop card case by hand pressing intensifies interaction experience between human and machine.

设计 DESIGN 杭州杰毅麦特医疗器械有限公司 Hangzhou Gene-Meta Medical Device Co., Ltd.

杭州汉度工业设计有限公司 Hangzhou Hando Industrial Design Co.,Ltd. **生产 MANUFACTURE**

红外温热治疗仪
Optical Instrument

本治疗仪灯头通过液压轴升降调节垂直高度，可适用于病人坐卧等不同使用情景。实现可照射范围广、节省支撑臂占用空间；车身采用环绕型手柄设计，方便医护人员在不同使用场景多个角度移动推车位置；车身后盖下部为快拆门设计方便治疗仪的维护工作。整体造型将饱满的弧线与富有节奏感的折线相结合，圆弧和柔和的质感使产品富有亲和感。

The cap of this treatment instrument's vertical height is adjusted by a hydraulic lift shaft and it can be applied to different situations such as the sit and lying for patients. It has a wide range of exposure and save the space of supporting arm. The body adopts a surround type handle designed to facilitate the movement of the cart position at different angles in different situations for the medical staff. The lower part of the back cover of the car body is designed for quick disassembly door, so as to facilitate the maintenance of the therapeutic instrument. The overall design combined the plump arc and the popping broken line, the softness of the arc makes the product full of rapport.

设计 DESIGN 北京斯丹姆赛尔技术有限公司 Beijing Adams Damm Purcell Technology Co.,Ltd.

北京上品极致产品设计有限公司 Beijing Top Industrial Design Co.,Ltd. **生产 MANUFACTURE**

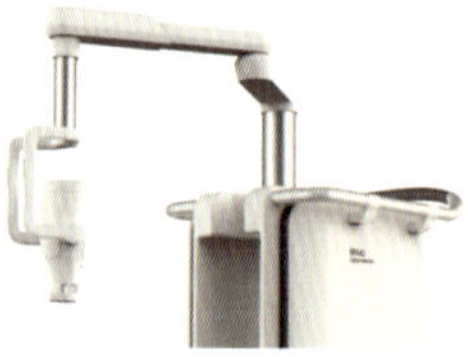

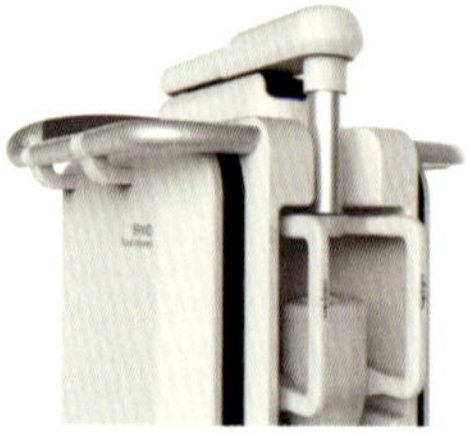

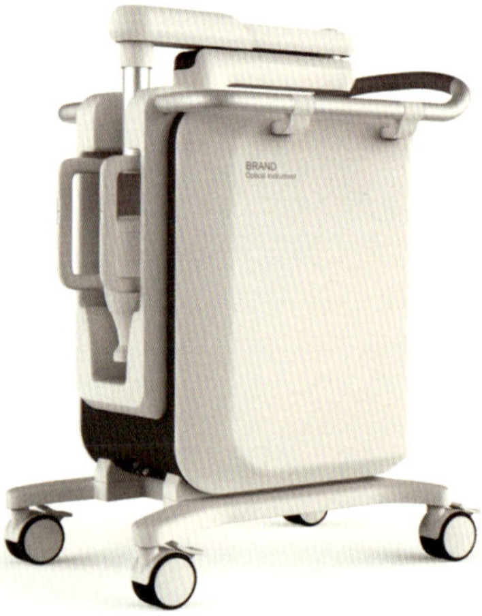

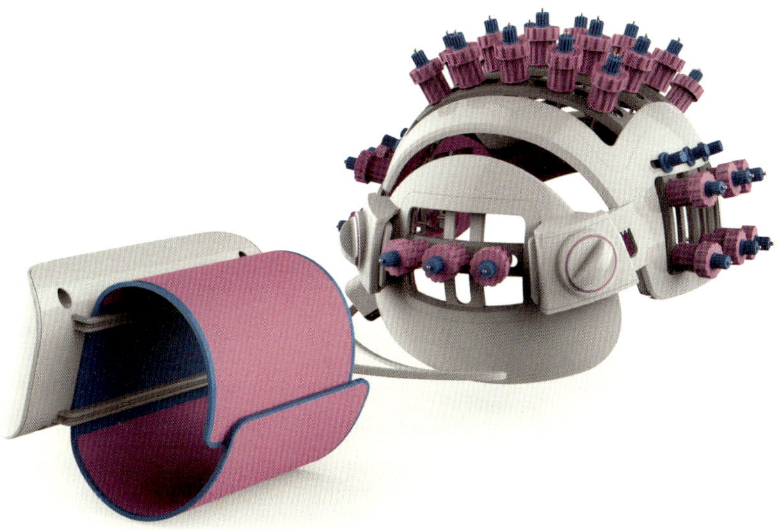

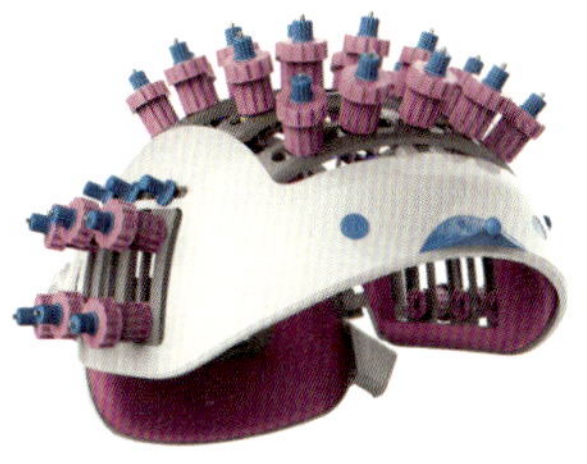

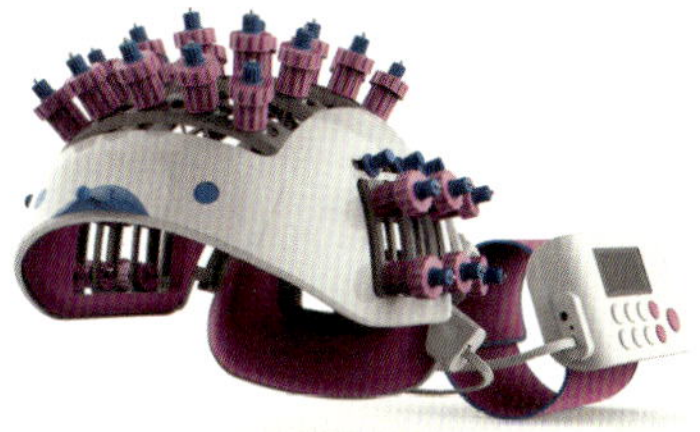

儿童脑瘫治疗仪
Pediatric Cerebral Palsy Treatment Apparatus

该产品利用新型脉冲电流治疗方法设计出更容易被儿童患者接受和亲近的治疗仪。设计上通过头盔前后部分调节来适应不同的头型，盔体上四个区域的滑条和电极针能上下左右的调节，使每个治疗穴位都能得到准确定位，保证治疗的有效性。控制盒佩戴在手臂上，使用更加便捷舒适，内置的锂电能提供半个月的续航治疗需求，使复杂的治疗操作变得简单稳定。

The new pulse current treatment method is used to produce a therapeutic device that can be easily accepted and used by children patients. The before and after part of the helmet can be adjusted to adapt to the different head type. Helmets on the four areas of the slider and electrode needle can be adjusted up and down, so that each treatment points can be accurately positioned to ensure the accuracy of treatment and Effectiveness. The control box is worn on the arm, making the whole instrument wear and use more convenient and comfortable. Control box built-in lithium power can provide half a month of life treatment requirement. All these turns an originally complicated treatment operation into a simple and stable one.

设计 DESIGN
杭州汉度工业设计有限公司
Hangzhou Hando Industrial Design Co.,Ltd.

生产 MANUFACTURE
浙江新丰医疗器械有限公司
Zhejiang Xinfeng Medical Instrument Co.,Ltd.

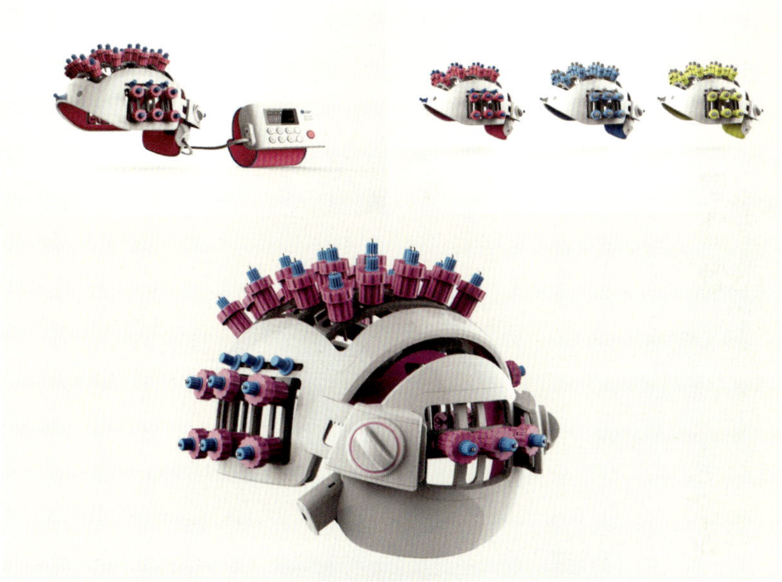

XYGC800 手持式动力切割机
XYGC800 Cutting Machine

该产品可以广泛应用于消防抢险救灾、破拆、路桥建设、道路养护、房屋拆迁、电力抢修等野外作业。在设计上，发动机和启动器可确保迅速、轻松启动机器；低量冲水湿切割套件，可以有效地进行除尘处理。产品上，两级空气清洁可延长机器的使用寿命和保养间隔；安装有可倒置切割头，在使用过程中达到最佳的人机舒适感和操作体验。

The product can be widely used in accident rescue and relief, forcible entry,road and bridge construction,road maintenance, housing demolition and electricity repair. The motor and starter can ensure a quick and easy start of the machine. Low volume water wet cutting kits can be effectively dedusted as for the product,and two-stage air cleaning can extend machine's operation life and maintenance interval. Inverted cutting head is equipped to achieve the best man-machine comfort and operating experience.

设计 DESIGN
杭州源骏工业产品设计有限公司
Hangzhou Runite Industry Design Co.,Ltd.

生产 MANUFACTURE
星月集团有限公司
Xingyue Group Co.,Ltd.

DOBOT Magician 智能机械臂
DOBOT Magician

该产品是高精度 4 轴消费级桌面智能机械臂，可以实现一机多能，是很好的创作发明工具。产品采用一体化设计，创新走线方式，使运动部分和控制部分结合。自主研发高精度步进电机和减速机，实现高精度和高稳定性。产品控制软件横跨多种终端，丰富的扩展接口，集成图形化编程开发环境，还可以二次开发，成为机器人学习平台。

Dobot Magician is the high precision 4-axis robotic arm for desktops with multi functions with only one machine. It is a great tool to create and invent. The unibody design can combine the movement part and controlling part together through the innovation of alignment way. Stepper motor and reducer with high precision are all independently researched and developed to achieve the repeated positioning accuracy and high stability. Product control software covers various terminals, and with its multiple extension ports and visualized programming environment, it can be redeveloped and becomes a robot learning platform.

设计 DESIGN
吴志文
Wu Zhiwen

生产 MANUFACTURE
深圳市越疆科技有限公司
Shenzhen Yuejiang Technology Co.,Ltd.

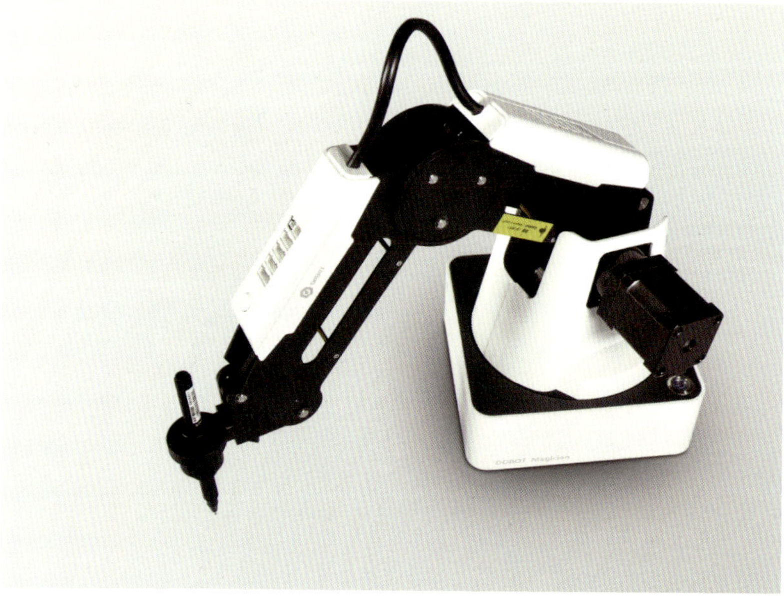

双子塔智能加油机
Twin Towers Intelligent Oiling Machine

该产品拥有“双子塔”式的独特外观设计。支持多种电子支付，提升加油支付体验；全新触摸屏式操作，全程语音提示播报，实时打印每笔加油记录，同时可以直接按下加油机对讲按钮呼叫总机进行一对一对讲。多种智能化控制，减少加油站的人力成本和操作时间。产品一机多枪，降低加油站布局成本。加油机局部模块化通用，生产安装更便捷。

The product has the unique appearance design just like "Twin Towers". It supports various electronic payment and improves oiling payment experience. It also has the new touch screen operation, the whole process of voice prompt. You can print each refueling record in real time. Meanwhile, pressing the intercom button directly on the tanker, you can call the switchboard for inquiry. A variety of intelligent operations shorten the manual costs and operation time. One machine will control several oil guns,thus the gas station reduces layout costs. The oiling machine has the advantages of local modularization, which is more convenient for production and installation.

设计 DESIGN
广州易用设计有限公司
Ease Design Guangzhou Co.,Ltd.

生产 MANUFACTURE
珠海市贝林加油设备有限公司
Zhuhai Beilin Fueling Equipent Co.,Ltd.

汽油数码变频发电机组（GS950i）
Gasoline Inverter Generator

该产品是一款汽车数码变频发电机组。产品 0.7 千瓦功率可满足用户普遍需求，避免输出过剩。同时又搭载更小排量引擎，结合优化的核心部件，以及通风散热系统，使产品更具价格优势。产品装备轻巧中频永磁发电机，实现减重 25%。设计启动减压装置，操作更轻松。产品引入电子油门转速控制技术，精确控制发动机转速，提高工作效率，降低油耗。

The product is a car digital inverter generator unit.0.7kw power can meet the general output power demand of the target users and avoid output excess. It also carries a smaller displacement engine, which is combined with the optimization of all core components and the ventilation cooling system, making the product more price competitive. Small, light, more efficient IFPMG (Intermediate Frequency permanent magnet generator)achieved 25% weight less on the products. We have designed a start-up decompressor to make it easier to operate. We also introduced the electronic throttle speed control technology to control the engine throttle actuator precisely. This not only improves the work efficiency, but also reduces the fuel consumption.

设计 DESIGN
天津爱谷工业设计有限公司
Tianjin I.Co Industrial Design Co.,Ltd.

生产 MANUFACTURE
浙江星月实业有限公司
Zhejiang Xingyue Industry Co., Ltd.

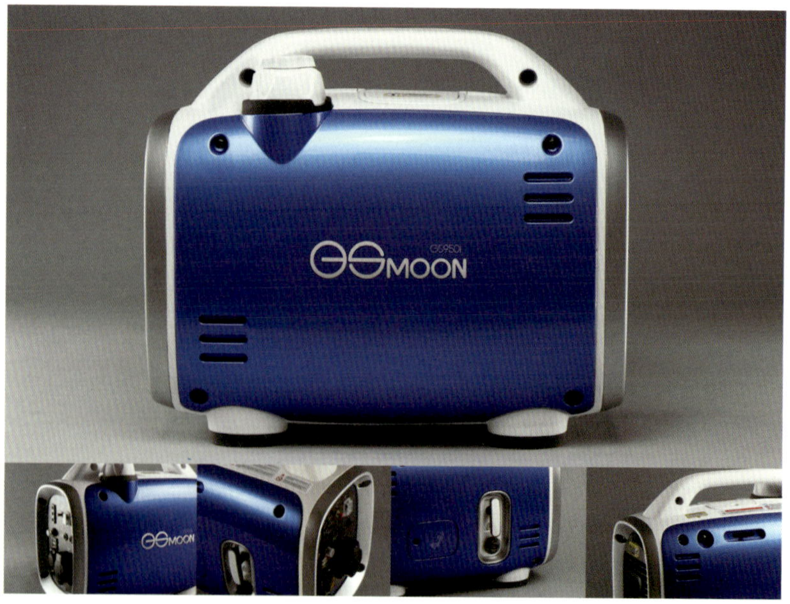

LERA S1 62V 锂电吹风机
LERA S1 Series 62V Lithium Electric Blower

该产品是以锂电电芯为能源的一款吹风机。这款无绳便携式充电式吹风机的开发，旨在解决吹风机在手提使用时的轻便性和功能性。并联锂电电池包拥有行业领先电芯控制技术，更高功率、更高续航。独创上下进风道，尺寸短小，元器件散热更高效。在操作上，设计符合人机工学，握持部分采用软胶二次注塑工艺，减轻操作疲劳感，给用户带来舒适的使用体验。

The development of the portable cordless rechargeable blower aims to solve the portability and functionality at portable pruning time. The machine is lighter, of higher efficiency and of longer life time. Dual parallel connection of lithium battery pack, with “high endurance, and high power” as well as industrial leading battery cell control technique; Exclusive upper and lower air inlet ducts, shorter size, more efficient heat dissipation of components; In operation, the design is in line with ergonomic principle The over injection molding process with soft grip is used in the holding part, and it has a good feel and reduces the operational fatigue; from the user's actual needs,

设计 DESIGN 宁波动一电器有限公司 Ningbo Lera Electric Appliance Co.,Ltd.

生产 MANUFACTURE 杭州源骏工业产品设计有限公司 Hangzhou Runite Industry Design Co.,Ltd.

LERA S1 62V 锂电链锯
LERA S1 Series 62V Lithium Electric Chain Saw

该产品旨在满足长时间高强度树木绿化需求。产品选用清洁环保的锂电电芯作为动力来源，对保护环境具有重要的意义，也可作为 LED 应急灯和数码产品充电宝。该产品拥有无刷电机、保护控制集成器，采用数字变频控制，可控性强，动力强劲，操作方便。比市场上的同类产品节能，在欧美绿化面积较广泛的国家，深受好评。

The product aims at satisfying long-term and high-strength trees greening demand. It selected clean and environmentally friendly lithium battery cells as its source of dynamics, which is of great implication to the environment. The product can also be used as LED emergency lamp and power bank for digital products. The motor is brushless, the integrated device is protection control and digital frequency conversion control is used with strong controllability, driving force and convenient operation. It is more energy-saving compared with the similar products in the market. In particular, in European and American countries of wider green area, it is well received.

设计 DESIGN 宁波动一电器有限公司 Ningbo Lera Electric Appliance Co.,Ltd.

生产 MANUFACTURE 杭州源骏工业产品设计有限公司 Hangzhou Runite Industry Design Co.,Ltd.

“无距”串列翼倾转旋翼无人机
Woozoom Series of Wings Tilting The Rotor

该产品是一架可应用于各种领域的无人机。在国内首发，由中科院出身的无人机团队打造，拥有 11 项技术专利，主要在飞控、气动、结构等方面有所创新和突破。将固定翼、直升机和多旋翼无人机的优势融合在一起，具备多种飞行模态。产品采用工业级标准的复合材料，无污染。在高速巡航过程中，能耗小、省电，是远距离多点作业最佳选择。

The product is an unmanned aerial vehicle (UAV) which can be applied in various fields. It is first launched in domestic environment by the Chinese Academy of Sciences origin unmanned set-top team, having 11 key technical patents, mainly in flight control, pneumatic, structural and other aspects of innovation and breakthroughs. The product combines the advantages of fixed wing, helicopter and multi rotor UAVs with a variety of flight modes.The product uses industrial grade standard composite material,which is free from pollution. During the high-speed cruise, the energy consumption is small and the electricity is saved. It is the best choice of multi point remote operation.

设计 DESIGN 沈阳无距科技有限公司 Woozoom

生产 MANUFACTURE 沈阳无距科技有限公司 Woozoom

40V 高压清洗机
40V High Pressure Washer

该产品是基于全球汽车占有量扩大，家庭生活品质提升，饮用水短缺、环境污染加剧等问题，设计出的节水、锂电环保、户外便携的高压清洗机。产品运用先进的锂电科技，做到电池可更换、无线户外使用。无刷调速，一键启动等技术，实现其 360 度旋转移动，还增加了多功能水箱，收纳便携节约空间等功能。整体设计简约饱满，富有活力。

Nowadays,automobiles become more and more popular all over the world, and the quality of people's life become better. In the meantime, drinking water become less and environment pollution become more and more serious. Therefore the needs of high pressure washer, which is water-saving, lithium-ion environment friendly and outdoor easily carried, go higher and higher.This product uses advanced lithium-ion technology and the changeable battery. It can be used in outdoor with WIFI. Brushless speed adjust technology and one-button start technology can help realize the functions of 360 degree spinning and moving, It's also designed with a multi-function water tank to make storage portable and save water.The design is succinct, vivid and fashionable.

设计
DESIGN

浙江亚特电器有限公司
YAT Electrical Appliance Co., Ltd.

蒋祥军、孙山虎
Sky Jiang，Tiger Sun

生产
MANUFACTURE

无人机干扰器
UAV Scrambler 300

该产品采用三根天线的设计，能够对消费级无人机的工作频率进行定向干扰。拥有三个不同频率可通过选择按钮控制，实现单独或同时干扰，有效迫使无人机返航和降落，保护相关空域安全。产品设备符合人机工程学，解决操作时的疲劳。整体设计采用模块化的方式，使生产装配更简单，降低成本。壳体材料可回收和再生循环利用，减少对环境的污染。

The three antenna design enables directional interference to all operating frequencies of the UAV. Three different frequencies can be controlled by the frequency selection button to achieve separate or simultaneous interference.The UAV Scramber can effectively force the UAV to return and landing, to protect the relevant airspace security. The product is designed according to ergonomics, which can solve the fatigue during the operation. The modular design makes the production assembly easy and be helpful to keep the cost.Shell materials are recyclable and recycling, which will reduce the pollution of the environment.

设计
DESIGN

四川益丰电子科技有限公司
Sichuan Yifeng Electronics Science & Technology Co.,Ltd.

成都意町工业产品设计有限公司
Chengdu Iding Industrial Design Co.,Ltd.

生产
MANUFACTURE

NUX 折叠电子鼓
NUX Foldable Digital Drum

NUX 折叠电子鼓折叠方便，重量和占地空间都是目前市面上最小的电子鼓产品之一。配置标准的五鼓三嚓，独有的效果、教练功能、录音功能可记录你的每一次的进步。产品内部关节经过优化设计，实现了结构稳定和可折叠两种完全相反的机械特性，鼓面、鼓架都使用可以回收循环利用的环保材料，节约能源消耗，减少排放。

NUX Foldable Digital Drum is easy to fold and is one of the tiniest electronic drum sets (both in weight and size) available on the market. It has a standard drum set in an impressively compact size.A build-in One Knob effect control and coach and recording will record every progress you make.All the joints of the drum are made of special PC+ABS material, which makes it have two opposite mechanical characters, so stable and foldable. Drum head and stand are all recyclable environmentally friendly materials, which will reduce resource consumption and emission.

设计
DESIGN

深圳市蔚科电子科技开发有限公司
Cherub Technology Co.,Ltd.

邱剑锋、王琳
Kevin Qiu, Wang Lin

生产
MANUFACTURE

多功能扫路机
Multi-Function Sweeper

该产品适用于狭小区域的保洁作业，具有基础功能的同时，配备手持高压水枪，并可以拓展剪草、除雪等功能模块。解决了大型清扫车的保洁问题，改善了环卫工人艰苦的工作环境。采用前后铰接式车架设计，使其能在狭小区域保持机动灵活。具备自动化控制系统，驾驶室配备智能触摸屏、扶手控制器等，高效工作的同时，带给用户舒适的使用体验。

The product is perfectly suited for cleaning of confined areas. It has the basic functions of road sweeping, high pressure cleaning and sewage recycling. Useful extras such as high pressure squirt gun can be used as lawn mowing system and snow clearing system. It solved the cleaning problem of large cleaning vehicles and improves the hard working environment of sanitation workers. The product uses front and rear articulated carriage, making it really easy to maneuvre even in narrow areas. The product possesses automatic control system, and there are smart touch screen and handle controller in the driving room. High efficiency work and comfortable using experience can both be gained by using it.

设计
DESIGN

邓扬、吕志涛
Deng Yang, Lv Zhitao

长沙中联重科环境产业有限公司
Zoomlion

生产
MANUFACTURE

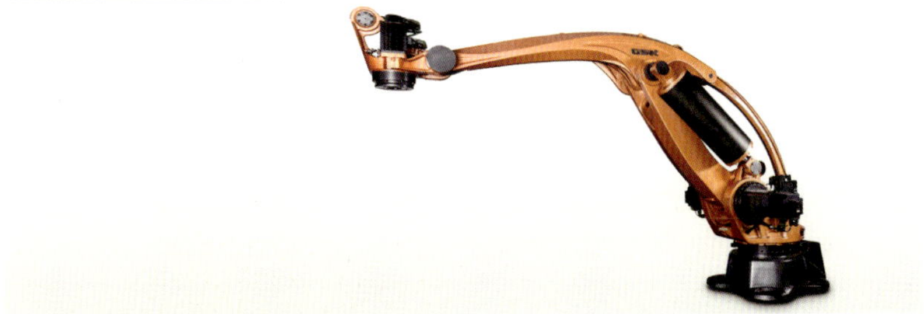

四轴码垛机器人
Four-Axis Palletizing Robot

该产品是主要用于工厂生产线进行高质量大频率活动的码垛机器人。产品采用弹簧缸上置的布局，使其体积小，占地面积小，重量轻，适合在各种环境下布置。设计上，优化机械臂结构和重心位置，降低机械臂重量和力矩，有利于节省能耗，是我国国内同类机型运行效率最高的机型之一，提升了生产的自动化、智能化。产品靠电力驱动，节能环保。

This product is a palletizing robot mainly used for the factory production line for high-weight, large-frequency activities. The product puts the spring cylinder on the layout, making the whole product smaller, small footprint, light weight, suitable for a variety of environments. In the design process, the product optimizes the mechanical arm structure design and the position of center of gravity, effectively reducing the weight of robotic arm and shortening the torque, and is beneficial to save energy consumption. It is one of the highest efficiency models in Chinese domestic market, greatly enhancing production of automatic and intelligent.Since this product is powered by electricity, it is energy saving and environmentally friendly.

设计
DESIGN

广东顺德潜龙工业设计有限公司
Chinno Design Co.,Ltd.

广州数控设备有限公司
Guangzhou CNC Equipment Co., Ltd.

生产
MANUFACTURE

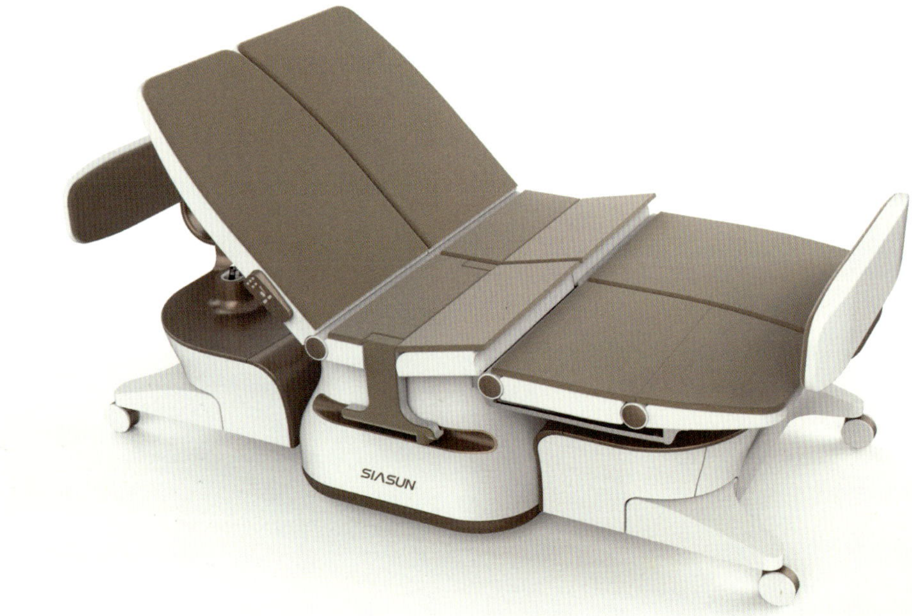

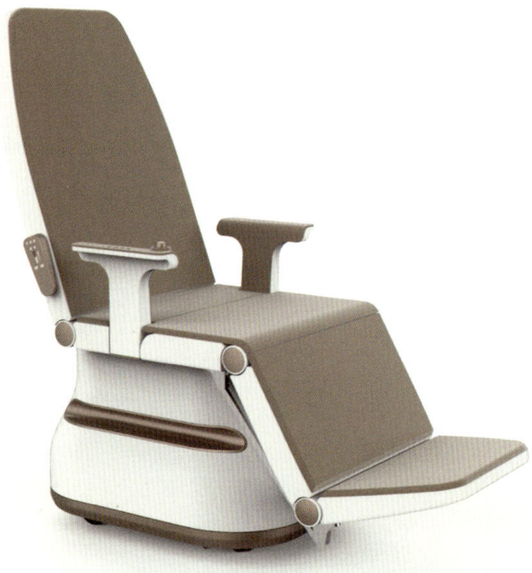

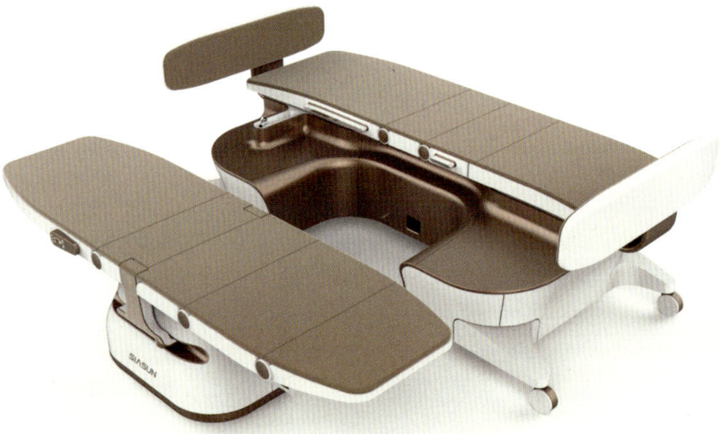

新松床椅一体化机器人
Siasun Bed-Chair Integrated Robot

该产品将医疗床和电动轮椅有机结合，帮助社会弱势群体和病患在医院和日常生活中可以更加方便的治疗和生活。产品采用模块化设计思想，适用于用户在睡眠和行走不同的场景。设计上采用多自由度设计，可以实现更高灵活度。同时，采用直驱控制技术，大幅提高产品精度和定位准确度。注重体验创新，产品使用更家居化的颜色，给病人更舒适的感觉。

The product automatically combines medical bed with electric wheelchair, helping vulnerable groups and patients to accept treatment and live their lives more conveniently. The idea of modular design is used to achieve different scenarios for users such as sleeping and walking. It is designed with multi degrees, which makes it possible to achieve higher flexibility. At the same time, it adopts direct drive control technology to greatly increased precision and positioning accuracy. The product focuses on experience innovation and uses more household colors to create a comfortable environment for patients like their home.

设计 DESIGN
沈阳新松机器人自动化股份有限公司
Shenyang Siasun Robot&Automation Co., Ltd.

生产 MANUFACTURE
杭州领跑者工业设计有限公司
Hangzhou LPZ Industrial Design Co.,Ltd.

无溶剂凹版印刷机
Solvent Free Intaglio Press

该产品相比传统印刷设备使用无污染的无溶剂墨水，同时将传统横向排布的印刷模块纵向布局，产品线长度横向缩短了三分之二，在维持原有生产效率和生产品质的前提下节省空间和人力。创新升降式的操作，使作业更高效、舒适。设计采用标准化和模块化的理念，部件通用性更强，突出智能、高效的产品属性。产品功能区域划分明显，减少误操作。

The printing equipment matches solvent-free, safe and pollution-free ink better compared to traditional equipment. Meanwhile, it contracts the production line to 2/3 of pre-width by changing traditional horizontal layout of printing module to the vertical.The product also saves space and workforce under the premise of keeping the original production efficiency and production quality. Innovative operation of lifting and dropping make the work more efficient and more comfortable. By adopting the standardized and modularization conception, it gives the product a better commonality and highlights the intelligent and efficient product attributes. Product functional area is divided obviously to reduce maloperation.

设计 DESIGN
中山松德印刷机械有限公司
Zhongshan Sotech Printing Machinery Co.,Ltd.

生产 MANUFACTURE
广东顺德潜龙工业设计有限公司
Chinno Design Co.,Ltd.

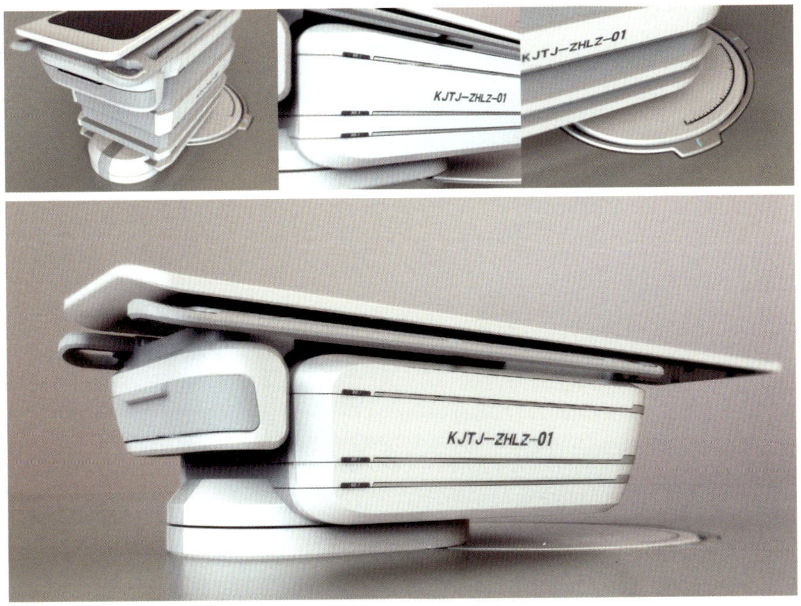

重离子治疗床
KJTJ Heavy Ion Medical Bed

该产品是基于改善用户在进行重离子治疗时体验的一款设计。为解决患者在治疗中会产生过度紧张的问题，将医护床套筒升降结构改进为分段式，保持外观整体性；增加辅助把手设计，方便调整床位；地面转盘刻度线设计，位置更直观。床头箱式设计，便于收纳。产品给患者提供更好的治疗体验，而且硬件排布严谨，节省空间，一经上市，就获得了业内好评。

The product is designed to improve patients' experience in the process of accepting heavy ion treatment. In order to solve patients' problem of over-nervousness in the process of treatment,the lifting structure was improved from traditional sleeve lifting to sectional sleeve. This design maintains the integrity of the appearance on the edge of the bed and make the bed convenient to adjust by adding auxiliary handle at the same time.The scale of the rotary disc of ground makes the location memory easier. The headstock-type design is for convenient keeping of manual operator. The product provides patients better treatment experience and its internal hardware of the product is compact and without wasting any space. As soon as it went introduced, it received positive reviews from the industry.

设计 DESIGN
兰州科沂泰基新技术有限责任公司
Lanzhou Kejintaiji Co.,Ltd.

杭州领跑者工业设计有限公司
Hangzhou LPZ Industrial Design Co.,Ltd.
生产 MANUFACTURE

智能物流机器人
Intelligent Logistic Robot

本产品通过机器人产品和人工智能技术实现柔性和智能的物流自动化解决方案，为物流领域提供一站式企业级服务。该产品融合了机器人、嵌入式软/硬件、软件工程、人工智能等技术，并全部自主研发、拥有核心专利，产品性能达到国际一流水平。产品部署于仓储运作各个环节，打破了对照订单去货位找货的模式，提升效率、减少人工成本、降低了投资风险。

The product aims at achieving high flexibility and intelligent logistics automation solutions through advanced robot products and AIT (artificial intelligence technology), offering advanced and reliable one step enterprise service. The product merges technologies in such aspects: robot, embedded hardware/software, software engineering and artificial intelligence. All products were independently researched and developed and has core patent. The product performance has achieved the international first-class standard.The product is deployed in every link of warehouse operations,breaking the models of "people to goods" looking for goods in goods lot according to the order, therefore tremendously increase the selecting efficiency of storage and reduce labor cost and effectively reduce the investment risk.

设计 DESIGN
北京极智嘉科技有限公司
Beijing Zhijia Science and Technology Co.,Ltd.

北京乐品乐道科技有限公司
Beijing Ledao Thenaropin Technology Co.,Ltd.
生产 MANUFACTURE

近红外荧光成像系统
Near-Infrared Fluorescence Imaging System

该产品是基于近红外荧光成像方法用于微创肿瘤手术中的一体式医疗设备。产品通过提供白光和荧光双模态图像，来实时识别肿瘤位置和诊断边界，提高手术成功率，降低术后复发率。产品在功能、形式、人机以及设计心理的层面实现了高度的均衡。未来光学分子影像手术导航系统设备将应用于更多种类型的癌症治疗中，推动临床医学的进步。

The product is an integrated medical equipment for minimally invasive surgery. It is based on near-infrared fluorescence imaging method which provided simultaneously white-light and fluorescent imaging to detect real time tumor position and identification boundaries, increasing survival rates and reducing the recurrence rates of patients. The product is highly balanced in function, form, man-machine and design psychology. In the future, the product will be used in more types of cancer for promoting the progress of clinical medicine.

设计 DESIGN
北京数字精准医疗科技有限公司
Beijing Digital Precision Medical Technology Co.,Ltd.

迟崇巍、毛亚敏
Chi Chongwei, Mao Yamin
生产 MANUFACTURE

体感假肢机器人
The Upper Limb Exoskeleton Rehabilitation Robot

该产品通过运动神经功能障碍患者的眼球凝视点和人机交互力等信息，来识别患者的运动意图，实时提供反馈与评估构建人机交互接口，按照临床需求下达命令后，机器人会完全按照指令行事，不会有一点偏差，改善患者治疗效果并缩短治疗时间。产品加工制造全程都采用数控自动化设备进行，展示出作为高科技产品独特的气质。

The product uses eye movement nerve dysfunction in patients with gaze point and interactive force and other information to identify patients with exercise intention and builds a human-computer interaction interface to provide feedback and evaluation in real time. Once the order is issued, the robot will act in accordance with the instructions, and there will be no deviation, thus improving the therapeutic effect and shortening the treatment time. In order to fully fit the robot's high-tech label, the whole process of manufacture is controlled by numerical control automation equipment.

设计 DESIGN
武汉与木造物工业设计有限公司
Wuhan and Wooden Industrial Design

上简设计（武汉）有限公司
Up Design(Wuhan)
生产 MANUFACTURE

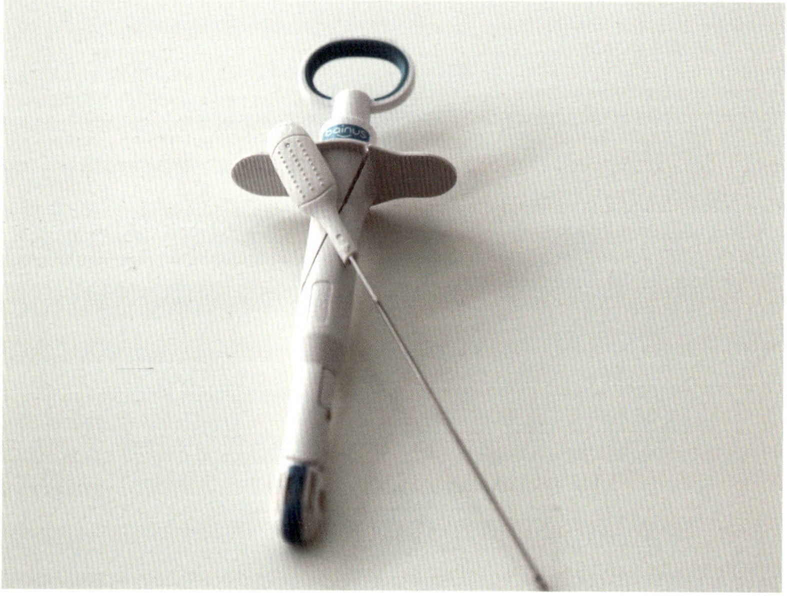

手术缝线推结器
Surgical Suture Pusher

该产品是一款用于微创手术创口内层缝合的手术缝线推结器。通过设计安全限位和针头挡片，避免医生误操作在底部挡板未打开时插入导向针刺伤患者内脏器官，同时减少医生的操作步骤和手术时间，降低医生劳动负荷。该产品减少了患者手术后恢复时间，同时弥补了市场空白，为企业带来巨大效益。产品全部使用环保可回收材料，减少对环境的破坏。

The product is a surgical suture pusher used in wound suture of minimally invasive surgery. The design of safety limit and needle cover will avoid the doctors' misuse of the bottom of the baffle when it's not open and guide needle insert in patients' internal organs, causing injuries. At the same time, the product will reduce doctors' operating procedure and operation time, lowering doctors' working load. It shortens patients' postoperative recovering time and closes market gap, while brings huge benefit to enterprises. The product uses recyclable and environmentally friendly materials to reduce damage to the environment.

设计 DESIGN
山东贝诺斯医疗器械有限公司
Shandong Bainus Medical Instrument Co.,Ltd.

日照工业设计中心有限公司
Rizhao Industrial Design Center Co.,Ltd.
生产 MANUFACTURE

新松 柔性手臂机器人
Siasun Flexible Arm Robots

该产品基于智能移动和柔性多关节机器人、视觉识别等技术综合应用，可在仓储物流领域，实现自动搬运、分拣等作业。通过灵活的机械手，解决物品形状、大小不同的搬运工作。多样化导航配置，满足工作现场高效布置。产品采取模块化更换或升级，避免在损坏后连带性不必要的成本。该产品功能多样，解决了仓库作业的人力资源投入大、资金占用多等问题。

The product is based on the comprehensive application of intelligent mobile robot, flexible multi-joint robot and visual identification technologies. It can realize automatic material handling, goods loading and material sorting in storage and logistic fields. The flexible manipulator can move goods of all sizes and shapes. A variety of navigation configuration can satisfy your efficient navigation field layout. The product adopts a modular robot replaces or upgrades to avoid collateral unnecessary costs. With its various functions, the product solves many problems in warehouse such as huge input of human resources and occupation of large amount of money.

设计 DESIGN
沈阳新松机器人自动化股份有限公司
Shenyang Siasun Robot&Automation Co.,Ltd.

杭州领跑者工业设计有限公司
Hangzhou LPZ Industrial Design Co.,Ltd.
生产 MANUFACTURE

银河（GALAXY）系列高清显示租赁屏
(GALAXY) Series HD Display Rental Screen

本产品是一款适应各种场所的高清显示租赁屏。全高清点对点精细化显示，色彩细腻逼真色域广，亮度色温自由调整。产品模块化设计，可以拼接成多种规格的屏幕大小，灵活拆装方便。丰富的多媒体接口，使用方便快捷。整体材料运用铝合金，散热性好，重量较轻。在搬运的位置上用软胶材质，有效保护现场施工人员的安全。

The product is a HD display rental screen suitable for various situations. It has full HD point fine display, 16bit color lifelike wide color gamut and brightness temperature to adjust to various places. Designed in modular type, the screen can be spliced into a variety of specifications of the screen size, flexible to assemble and disassemble. The screen owns rich multimedia interface, which will be quick and convenient to use. The overall use of Aluminum Alloy materials makes it easy to do heat dissipation its light in weight. In the moving position, soft texture was used to protect the site construction personnel efficiently.

设计 **DESIGN**
深圳市威尔科视光电有限公司
Shenzhen Weier Christie Photoelectric Co.,Ltd.

深圳市木马整合设计有限公司
Shenzhen Moma Integrated Design Co.,Ltd.
生产 **MANUFACTURE**

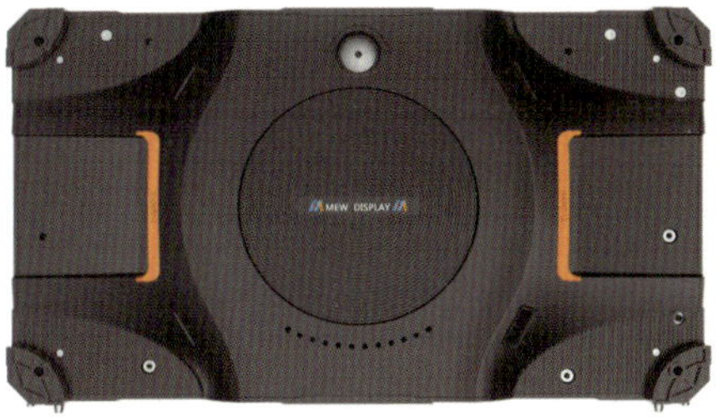

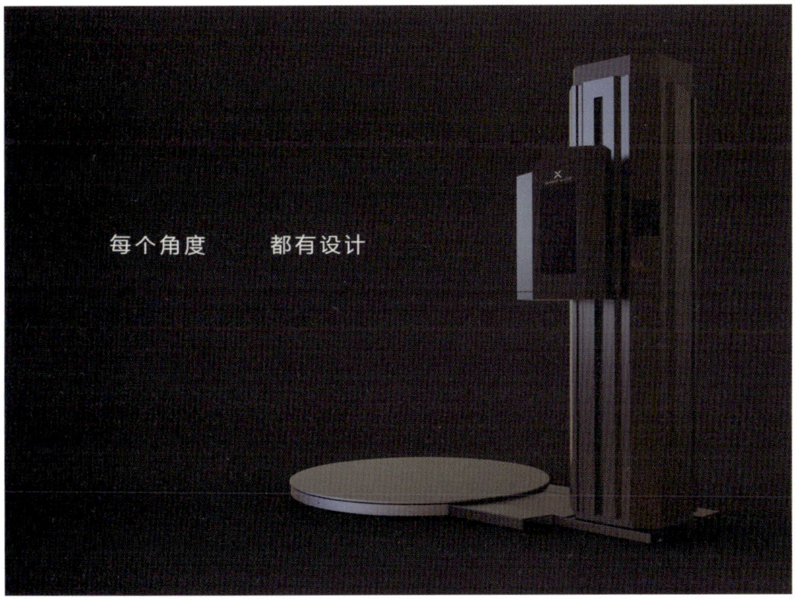

自动缠绕机
Automatic Winding Machine

该产品可对各种尺寸的产品进行自动化包装。设计上，将设备划分功能区域，载物平台自动进行尺寸识别、定位、旋转、切割工序，使出膜、切膜自动检测完成。配备一体触摸屏，操作便捷，提高效率。产品采用高强度的膜，抗拉伸力强，同时电脑自动控制出膜量，实现包装上真正的智能自动化。节约时间、人工成本，使产品本身和工作流程利润率提高。

With the help of this product, various sizes of products can be automated packaging. In design, the machine is divided into several function areas, and cargo platform can be automatically used to identify the size, location, rotation, cutting process, in order to automatically complete film and film cutting. Equipped with a touch screen, the operation efficiency was greatly improved. The product adopts high strength film with strong tensile strength. At the same time, the computer automatically controls the amount of film, realizing actual intelligent automation in packing. It saves time, reduces time and labor costs,and improves profit margins for both the product itself and the work flow.

设计 **DESIGN**
江苏小黄蜂智能科技有限公司
Smart Wasp Intelligent Technology(Suzhou) Co.,Ltd.

苏州上品极致产品设计有限公司
Suzhou Top Industrial Design Co.,Ltd.
生产 **MANUFACTURE**

工业用防护口罩
Industrial Protective Respirator

该产品是应用于工厂环境的内置风扇防护口罩。产品在内部新增风扇，通过呼吸带动风扇使空气进入，随着运动量增加，可以改变带入空气量多少，更注重产品使用体验。能随时更换滤芯，保证安全卫生。创新增加耳机模式，在嘈杂作业环境中，可以通过耳机相互沟通。产品贴合面部，佩戴方便；使用环保材料，低碳成本低，满足用户针对不同作业需求的选择。

The product is a built-in fan protective respirator used in industrial environment. The design of this product has the new fan inside. Through their own breathing to drive the fan, The air will be inlet. With the increase of physical exercise, air volume amount inhaled will also change. The product pays attention to the experience of product when users use it.Replacing filter at any time can guarantee the safety and sanitation. Adding headphone mode in the work environment where voice is not convenient, people can communicate with each other through the headset.Products mainly use recyclable materials with lower carbon cost, meeting the different choices users made according to different work requirement.

设计 DESIGN
北京华创矿安科技有限公司
Beijing Huachuangkuangan Technology Co.,Ltd.

北京智加问道科技有限公司
Beijing ZCO Design Co.,Ltd..
生产 MANUFACTURE

阿帕奇 VR 直升机模拟器
Apache VR Helicopter Simulator

该产品是模拟直升机飞行体验的虚拟现实体验舱。产品在视觉虚拟现实技术上，增加人体参数检测，注重生理感受及视觉感受模拟。让普通人感受到飞行体验，也让飞行员在训练中降低风险，节省国家培训成本。为保证迅速垂直爬升能力，在机械结构上明确机构分区先行，保证美观与舒适。通过设计提炼直升机大特征，提升包裹感，带给乘坐者安心舒适的体验。

This product is a VR experience module that simulates the flying experience of a real helicopter. On the basis of visual virtual reality technology, human parameter detection is added. In the man-machine experience, the product pays attention to the human body physiology feeling and the visual feeling simulation. It allows ordinary people to experience the real experience of helicopters, and also can reduce pilots'risks in flight training. In order to ensure rapid vertical climb, the mechanical structure is clearly defined to ensure the beauty and comfort of the partition. Through the design, helicopter's big feature was refined and package was also promoted. It brings a person more at ease and comfortable experience.

设计 DESIGN
大连大华中天科技有限公司
Dalian Dahuazhongtian Technology Co., Ltd.

沈阳智加问道科技有限公司
Shenyang ZCO Design Co.,Ltd.
生产 MANUFACTURE

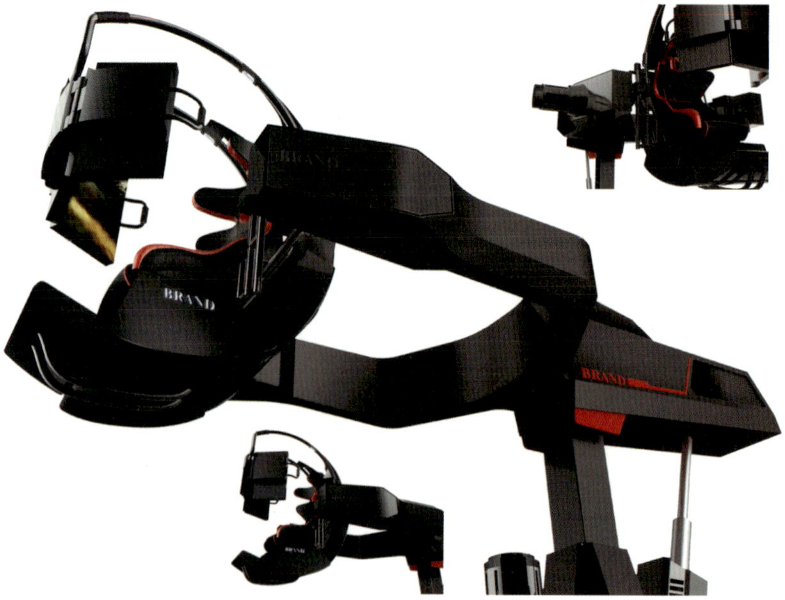

猛禽大型拖拉机
Raptor Large Tractor

“猛禽”大型拖拉机采用跨界思维方式，通过主流设计语言，构建创新产品。该产品通过发动机机罩空气导流设计，带走多余热量，降低能源消耗，提升工作效率与使用寿命。灯光系统采用 LED 光源，降低能耗；随动转向功能提高照射面积，使产品更智能。大尺寸驾乘空间，舒适易用。产品量产上市以来供不用求，帮助国内农机市场中的企业实现逆势上升。

Aptor Large Tractor adopts crossover ways of thinking, build and create new products through mainstream design language. Reasonable engine hood air guide design, quickly takes off the engine excess heat and reduces energy consumption to improve work efficiency and operation life. Lighting lamps are used to highlight LED lights, which significantly reduce energy consumption. The new lighting system, with the dynamic+K342K340 steering function, increasing the area of irradiation, is more intelligent. Large size driving space is comfortable and easy to use, since the production go public,the products sell very well, helping enterprises in domestic agricultural machinery market to buck up.

设计 DESIGN
山东鼎意工业设计咨询服务有限公司
Shandong Di.Design Consulting Co.,Ltd.

生产 MANUFACTURE
潍坊恒祥机械有限公司
Hengxiang Machinery Manufacturing Company

雷达物位计
Measuring Instrument

该产品是调频连续波原理的非接触式雷达的雷达物位计。产品具有超强信号处理能力，比传统物位计具有更强的测量有效性和重复性，可测量液体、浆体或固体的距离、液位和体积，可换接不同规格的天线，有很强的灵活性。通过设计使产品体积更加紧凑，节约安装空间。使用该产品的信号隔离器，可以达到精度高、性能稳定、抗干扰能力强的效果。

The product is innovative in the non-contract radar of a frequency modulated continuous wave principle. It has super strong signal processing ability and has stronger measurement validity and repeatability compared with traditional level meter. This radar can measure the distance, liquid level and volume of the liquid, slurry or solid, also allows connecting horn antenna in different specifications or spherical antenna in different sizes or materials.The design will make the product more compact and save installation space. Utilizing such signal separator can achieve high precision, stable performance and strong resistant to interference.

设计 DESIGN
武汉市本源造物设计咨询有限公司
Source Design

生产 MANUFACTURE
深圳万讯自控股份有限公司
Shenzhen Maxonic Automation Control Co., Ltd.

Freescan X5 系列手持三维扫描仪
Freescan X5 Series Handheld 3D Scanners

该产品是基于天远三维提出手持激光扫描仪概念和技术，开发出来国内最高技术水准的专业级产品。该产品兼顾体积便携和专业性能。应用在专业领域和各种复杂环境的测量任务。小巧轻便，可深入狭小空间单手长时间操作；无限制三维扫描。底座的设计方便产品放置，避免造成镜头损伤。该产品定位于中高端市场，构建了面向不同专业细分市场的完整产品线。

The product is developed on the basis of hand-held laser scanner ultra-convenient industrial 3D scanning concept and technology. It represents the highest technical standards of professional-grade products in the country. The product is convenient to carry and of professional performance, which can be applied in the measurement tasks of various professional areas and complex environments. It is small and lightweight, can be deep into the small space, single-handed operation for a long time. 3D scanning is almost without any restrictions. Large base design makes it convenient to put products and avoid the damage of lens.Freescan X5 series handheld 3D scanners are positioned in the mid and high-end markets,constructed for different market segments of professional a complete product line.

设计 DESIGN
诸暨瑞观工业设计有限公司
Zhuji Kcan Design Consulting Co.,Ltd.

生产 MANUFACTURE
北京天远三维科技股份有限公司
Tenyoun 3D Technology Co.,Ltd.

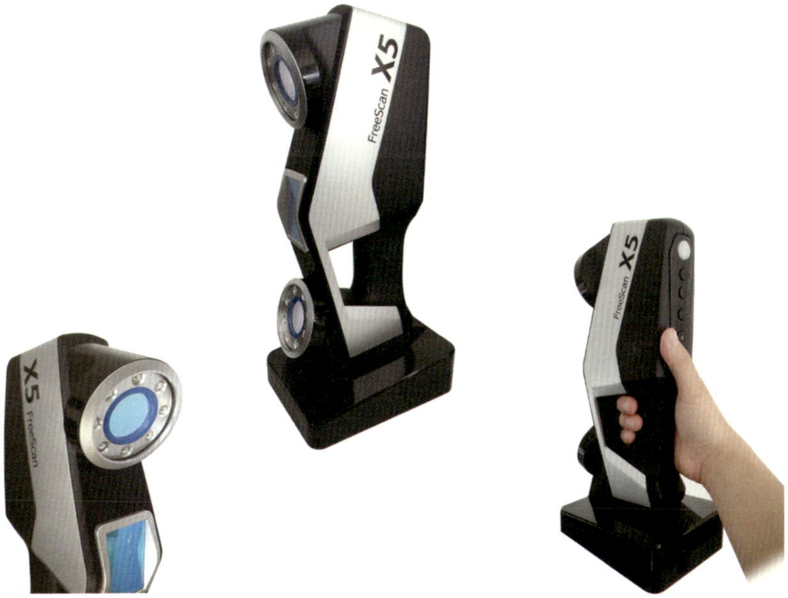

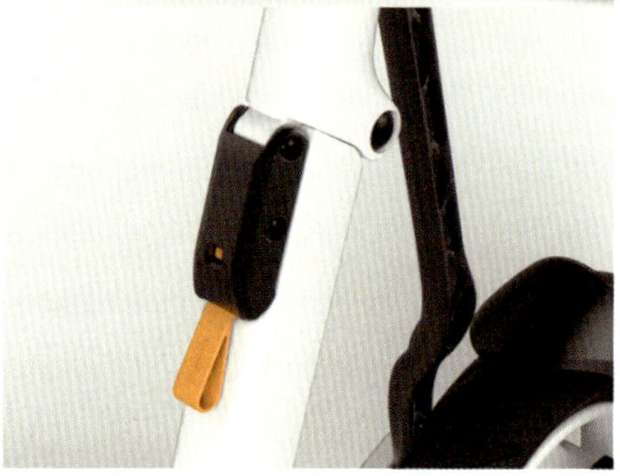

一英里光环微电折叠车
Halo City

该产品是一款个人出行的微电动折叠车。拥有 13 项国家专利，全车 98% 零件是自主研发和设计，创新整体连杆式一体折叠系统，满足城市便捷出行。独创 LED 行车灯，专业导光，节省能量。前后碟刹，避震坐杆，蝠形无弓鞍座。配备智能电池管理系统， 应用可连接车辆，查看信息。车身自带智能模组等多功能。致力于打造“城市移动 + 交通串联”的绿色生活方式。

Halo City is a personal folding E scooter for mobile travel . It has 13 national patent certification, more than 98% of the parts are independently researched and developed. The entire frame does not have a solder joint, making it more convenient for people in cities to go out. It has unique design of the integrated LED daytime driving lights and car professional level of light guide technology,saves energy. It has pioneered the front and back disc brake and suspension seat post. It has newly developed bat shaped non bow saddle, the structure of the saddle installed under the cushion. The smart battery management system will be equipped, the APP can connect to the scooter and check the information. The scooter itself also has intelligent modules and other functions. We will create a "mobile city + traffic series" green lifestyle.

设计
DESIGN
北京一英里科技有限公司
Beijing Onemile Technology Co.,Ltd.

生产
MANUFACTURE
北京一英里科技有限公司
Beijing Onemile Technology Co.,Ltd.

悬挂式单轨列车（空轨、空铁）
SMV（Suspended Monorail Vehicle）

该产品是中国首创悬挂式单轨列车。走行方式实现大部分工程工厂化制造，保证线路建设循环使用，现场安装简便，可持续发展，减少成本。首次采用铝骨架 + 复合材料蒙皮技术，实现列车轻量化。胶轮走行部件，爬坡能力强，震动小、噪音小。采用新一代大容量锂电池供电，环保可靠，绿色安全。可缓解紧张的城市地面空间，解决城市拥堵等问题。

It is the first SMV in China.The travel models mostly achieve industrial manufacturing, so that lines construction will be reused. Meanwhile, the line can be constructed quickly and removed easily for the purpose of cyclic utilization and sustainable development. Aluminum skeleton + composite enveloping is used for the first time, which reduces train weight. Rubber wheels running parts with strong gradeability are used, thus lowering noise and vibration. The train employs a new generation of high-capacity lithium battery, which is safe, reliable and friendly to environment.It allows efficient utilization of urban aboveground space and alleviates urban traffic jam.

设计
DESIGN
中车南京浦镇车辆有限公司
CRRC Nanjing Puzhen Co.,Ltd.

生产
MANUFACTURE
中车南京浦镇车辆有限公司
CRRC Nanjing Puzhen Co.,Ltd.

绅宝 X35
Senova X35

该产品是一款北汽汽车。继承了萨博品牌的设计标准和验证规范，延续北汽创新的车内空气质量控制技术，打造舒适安全的车内环境，全面领先国内行业水平。该款车型内饰采用多彩配色，运动时尚，并配备大尺寸全景天窗。实用配置丰富；多轮风阻优化；优化整车传动系统，传递效率提高，实现燃油经济性最佳。车型采用通用化设计，模块化生产工艺。

Senova X35 is baic car, not only inherited the SAAB brand design standards and test specification, also blended in baic stringent quality control concept, aiming at creating comfortable and safe environment inside attentively. The product is far leading in the national industry. The car's interior decoration uses unique and colorful color, sportss fashionable, and equipped with a rare large size at the panoramic sunroof.Multi-wheel wind resistance was optimized. Rectification system was optimized to increase vehicle transmission efficiency and save more fuel. The car adopts the generalized design and modularization production process.

设计
DESIGN
北京汽车股份有限公司汽车研究院
Baic Motor corporation Ltd. R

生产
MANUFACTURE
北京汽车股份有限公司
Baic Motor

乐卡儿童三轮车
Lecoco Children Tricycle

该产品让宝宝成为运动骑行家，专为辣妈辣爸设计。"C" 型轮毂设计，搭配车轮肌肉感纹理，整车活力十足、风格鲜明。该车身设计轻巧，推行便捷；一键折叠，轻松出行；后轮一键快拆；车轮采用密崎轮，避震耐磨，使用寿命长。产品设计人性化，拥有时尚、极简外观。车体采用碳钢、塑料件，安全无毒。采用椭圆截面管材，折弯后没有棱面，整体曲线更流畅。

The product is designed for the pursuit of fashion hot spicy mom and spicy dad, making every baby a sportsman. Unique "C" type wheel design, as well as muscle-like texture wheels make the vehicle full of vitality and distinctive style. The children tricycle has lightweight body design, is convenient to ride; It can also be folded and its real wheel can be released quickly. Wheels use dense battery wheel, which is suspension wear-resisting, good abrasion resisting and with long service life.The product is user-friendly, with more fashion and minimalism appearance. Car body is made of high quality carbon steel and plastic environmental protection, which is non-toxic. Unified use of elliptical cross-section of the pipe will cause no corner after bending, the overall curve is more smooth.

设计
DESIGN
周杰
Alex Zhou

生产
MANUFACTURE
宁波颖贝儿童用品有限公司
Ningbo Yingbei Children's Products Co.,Ltd.

特爱奇多功能电动滑板
Taq Multifunctional Electric Scooter

该产品是以猎豹进行仿生设计的多功能电动滑板。产品车座椅采用镂空活动索拉桥式架构，实现高效散热、重量轻、承载强效果；车把采用折叠和伸缩结合，使产品可依据场景需要、身高、驾驶习惯进行转换。该产品满足使用者的个性化追求。解决拥堵、停车难问题。有 3 道独立刹车系统，解决安全性问题，使用难度低。采用锂电池做动力源，实现零排放。

The product is a multi-function electric scooter simulated leopard's body appearance. The seat adopts a hollowed out movable bridge structure, which is characterized by high heat dissipation, light weight and strong weight bearing.The handlebar adopts folding and telescopic combination, so that the entire product can be adjusted on the basis of user scenarios, personal height and driving habits. There are 3 independent brake system to solve safety problem, and it's easy to operate.It uses lithium batteries as power source to realize zero exhaust emissions.

设计
DESIGN
孙龙
Sun Long

生产
MANUFACTURE
深圳市碰点时刻科技有限公司
Shenzhen Pengdian Time Technology Co.,Ltd.

名爵 ZS 城市互联网 SUV
MG ZS Urban Internet SUV

该产品是一款以年轻群体为主的潮流互联网车型。满足年轻人对首台运动型多用途汽车的需求，产品把用户核心需求延伸到功能布局上，不仅采用“蓝芯”高效动力科技；直喷涡轮增压发动机，功率大、油耗低；匹配多款变速器等配置，更搭载智能互联系统，区别同级产品，形成超高“品价比”，打破“配置多 + 低价格 = 好车”的思维定式。

The product is a fashionable SUV on the internet targeting young buyers, aiming at young people's demand for SUV multi functional cars. The product extends users' core demand into functional layout, not only adopting "Net Blue" high efficient dynamic technology, but also using direct nUzzling turbine-supercharging motor, which is of huge power and low oil consumption. Various types of speed changers are equipped and intelligent interlocking system carried. All these make it different from its counterpart and forms super high "quality price ratio". MG ZS broke the stereotype of "many layouts plus low price equals quality car".

设计 DESIGN
上海汽车设计中心
Saic Design

生产 MANUFACTURE
上海汽车集团股份有限公司乘用车分公司
Saic Motor Corporation Limited Passenger Vehicle Co.

全 TPE 健康汽车脚垫
Full TPE Healthy Car Mats

该产品是一款运用环保材料的汽车脚垫。解决脚垫材质散发有毒物质、清洗困难、不贴合导致行车安全等问题。产品采用热塑性弹性体材料，可回收利用、环保又安全。整块脚垫采用注塑模一次成型，无拼接、车缝线、针孔，三秒易清洗。设计上采用双层扣件，防滑更安全。产品首用专车三维立体扫描获得数据，精准匹配原车设计具有较强竞争优势。

Full TPE healthy car mats uses all environmentally friendly materials. Old car mats usually emit toxic substance, and is hard to clean, never fit the car. But the new product will solve these problems. The product uses recycled thermoplastic elastic materials, which can be safe and environmentally friendly. It take full TPE injection molding machine for one time molding, the whole piece of TPE is without any stitching, no car suture, no pinhole, and it's three seconds easy to clean. In design, it adopts double fastener to do anti-skid and safety. The product first uses 3D scan to obtain the car data and accurately match design of original cars. This makes the product more competitive.

设计 DESIGN
杭州未末工业设计有限公司
Hangzhou Wemore Industrial Design Co.,Ltd.

生产 MANUFACTURE
台州市黄岩震亚汽车用品有限公司
Huangyan Zhenya Auto Supplies Co.,Ltd.

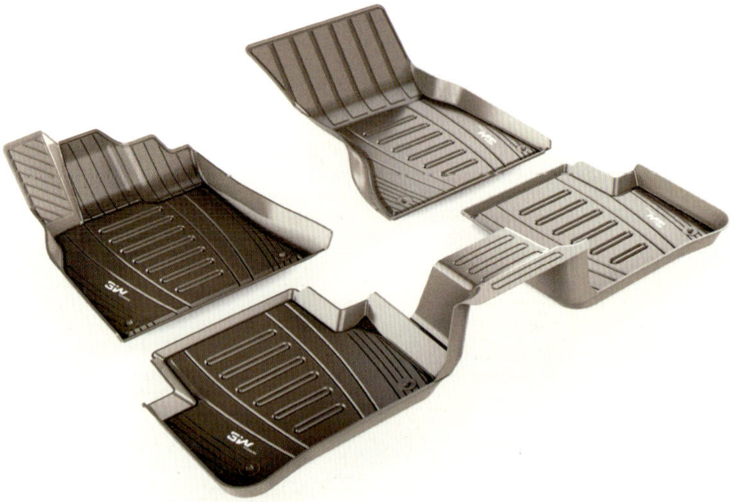

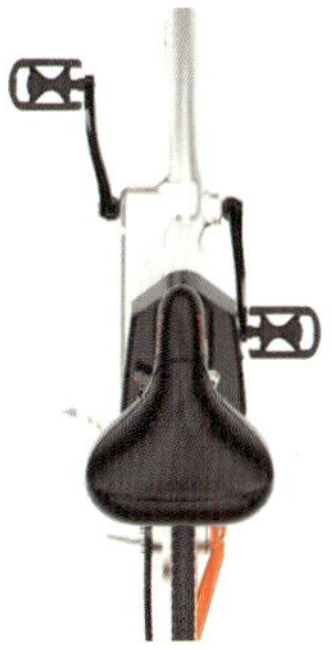

第二代经典版摩拜单车
Mobike2.0

该产品是在第一代基础上改进优化的第二代摩拜单车。产品改善齿轮比，骑行省力 30%；电磁刹电机升级为碟刹，骑行阻力小，转向更安全；升级随动刹，更易操控；利用轴承驱动，采用单摆臂技术，不会“掉链子”；车锁具备全球定位系统，全球移动通信系统，有防盗等功能。产品提供共享自行车服务，减少交通拥堵、环境污染，绿色出行。

The product is an improved andoptimized Mobike2. The new product improves gear ratio to save effort about 30%. Railing wheel uses disc brake in order to reduce resisitEnce and it's safer to change direction. The upgrades about Laura servo break has better control performance and is easy to control. The use of bearing driving and simple pendulum arm technology, the chains of the bikes won't drop so quickly. This lock has GPS, GSM, anti-theft and other functions. The product provides shared bike service, which will reduce traffic congestion and eliminate environmental pollution, making travel a trend.

设计 DESIGN 摩拜智造（无锡）物联科技有限公司 Mobike Intelligent Manufacturing(Wuxi) IOT Technology Co.,Ltd.

摩拜智造（无锡）物联科技有限公司 Mobike Intelligent Manufacturing(Wuxi) IOT Technology Co.,Ltd. **生产 MANUFACTURE**

巴西里约地铁四号线（奥运线）车辆
Vehicles of Brazil Rio Metro Line 4

该产品是服务于 2016 年里约奥运会期间的主要交通工具。该线路车辆由中国制造，首次在境外服务奥运会。有效缩短交通时间，方便市民往来。针对巴西治安环境，列车车窗、门等采用防爆材料；设置烟雾探测器，一旦检测到，新风口会自动关闭，防止烟气、毒气进入车厢；列车设置超速保护装置，当车辆速度达到或超过限速值，会进入相应状态，保证列车安全。

The product served as the main transportation tool in 2016 Rio Olympic Games. The vehicles in this line is manufactured by China and was firstly used to serve overseas Olympic games. This tool will effectively shorten the transportation time and makes it more convenient for citizens to go out. Considering the public security situations in Brazil, the explosion-proof polyester materials are used for the windows and the doors instead of glass for the first time. The air conditioning system for the trains is equipped with the smoke detection function, the fresh air inlet will close automatically once smoke is detected to efficiently prevent smoke and toxic gases from entering into saloons in case of a fire inside tunnels. The trains are also provided with over-speed protection devices which gives off buzz as pre-warning when the running speed of train reaches the preset limit speed values, and automatically enable the train into emergency brake status in case of exceeding the preset limit speed values to thereof guarantee safety of the train.

设计 DESIGN 中车长春轨道客车股份有限公司 CRRC Changchun Railway Vehicles Co.,Ltd.

王洪宝 Wang Hongbao **生产 MANUFACTURE**

荣威 i6 家用轿车
Roewe i6 Family Sedan

该产品是基于上汽平台设计的一款“互联网汽车”。搭载远程车控、语音控制等基础功能，还上线支付宝、美食地图等服务的智能互联系统，成为有开放属性、个性化的移动空间。产品采用蓝芯发动机，搭载直喷涡轮增压等国际先进技术，匹配 6 速手动、7 速双离合变速箱，满足强劲动力和低碳环保需求。并是首款以超低油耗获吉尼斯世界纪录认证的中国汽车。

The car is a "car on the Internet" based on the platform of SAIC. It carries basic functions such as remote car control and sound control. Alipay and foot road-map and other intelligent interlocking systems matched to make the product a personalized mobile space with open merit. The product is equipped with Net Blue motro, and carries direct nUzzling turbine-supercharging. It matches TST 7-speed dual-clutch/6-speed manual transmission,satisfying the requirement of strong dynamics and low carbon.It is the first Chinese car which won Guinness World Records for low fuel consumption.

设计 DESIGN 上海汽车集团股份有限公司乘用车分公司 Saic Motor Corporation Limited Passenger Vehicle Co.

上海汽车设计中心 Saic Design **生产 MANUFACTURE**

马来西亚机场线车辆
Vehicles of Malaysia Airport Line

该产品是基于马来西亚气候设计的动车组。该产品是铰接式市域车，实现小曲线通过，更轻量化和节能，提高平稳性和安全性。设有自动调光集中控制技术，地板采用防火隔离层，便于维护安全。设有能耗记录仪，记录列车能耗，能通过系统上传故障记录，提升检修效率。辅助逆变器是并网供电，如果失效，则单独为列车供电，无人工干预，具有更高冗余性。

The trainsets are based on Malaysian weather. It is an articulation urban vehicle with easily negotiating curves of small radii, lightweight and energy-saving,enhances the ride stability and safety of trainsets.The lighting system adopts fully auto-dimming LED central-controlled techniques and the floor uses fire-retardant layer to guarantee security. An energy-consumption recorder is provided to record energy consumption on trainsets. The recorded data of energy consumption can be uploaded via wireless train-borne control system, enhancing maintenance efficiency. Auxiliary inverters achieve synchronized power supplies via the medium voltage bus contactor box. The vehicles can be powered separately in case of failure of auxiliary synchronization. The redundancy is higher without human interference.

设计
DESIGN

中车长春轨道客车股份有限公司
CRRC Changchun Railway Vehicles Co.,Ltd.

许月勋
Xu Yuexun

生产
MANUFACTURE

3D 数字立体贴合汽车坐垫
3D Digital Stereo Seat Cushions

该产品是利用三维立体成型技术，采集座椅原数据设计的一款汽车坐垫。该产品解决了现有汽车坐垫易滑动、不贴合、不安全、不美观的缺点。利用三维软件对模型进行立体化分解；建立模型并加工成骨架；中层为海绵，韧性强、透气；表层为环保皮。该产品采用一车一模，无缝包裹两翼，最大限度贴合原车座椅。精准固定孔位设计，不滑动不移位更稳固。

3D digital stereo seat cushions are created through the using of 3D stereo technology and collecting of seat original data. The product solves the problem that the existing car seat cushion products have: easy to slide, unfit, unsafe and unsightly. It uses industrial design Three-dimensional software for the three-dimensional decomposition of the model, established the model and processed it into skeleton. The middle part is made of sponge, which is resilient and porous. The covering part is made of environmentally friendly leather. Stereo seat cushions use one mold for one car, seamlessly wrap wings and adhere to the original seat with largest advantage. Precise fixed hole design is adopted to ensure the seat from sliding and translocating and ensure the stability.

设计
DESIGN

台州宇森汽车用品有限公司
Taizhou Yusen Auto Accessories Co.,Ltd.

杭州未末工业设计有限公司
Hangzhou Wemore Industrial Design Co.,Ltd.

生产
MANUFACTURE

纳恩博独轮平衡车
Ninebot One Z

独轮平衡车是一种新型电动代步工具。这种去除控制油门的操控方式是颠覆性的，更简单直接。产品特别设计拉杆，在不骑行时可以推着走；提手设有传感器，检测到被提起，轮毂电机会停止转动，防止出现意外；可通过充气量调整胎型，用户更易学习操控；通过双备份控制器，保证骑行安全；采用纯电力驱动，对环境零污染。

Single wheel self-balance electric scooter is an innovative transportation tool. The controlling way of removing control throttle is revolutionary, which is simpler and more direct.Specially designed draw bar allows users to push the scooter like pushing a suitcase in any place not allowing riding. The sensor located at the handle will stop the hub motor's rotation to prevent accident while detecting that the balance vehicle is lifted up. The shape of tire can be adjusted through the aeration volume, which makes it easy for users to learn to control. We use the double backup controller to ensure the safety of riding. The scooter is fully electric power-driving, which will cause zero pollution to the environment.

设计
DESIGN

纳恩博（天津）科技有限公司
Ninebot (Tianjin) Tech Co.,Ltd.

李智星、刘磊
Li Zhixing, Liu Lei

生产
MANUFACTURE

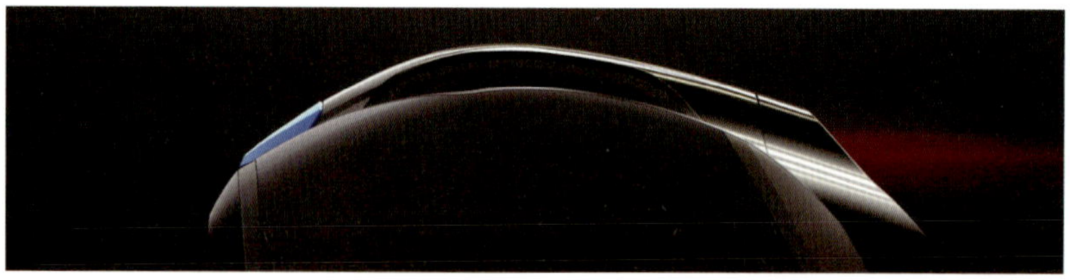

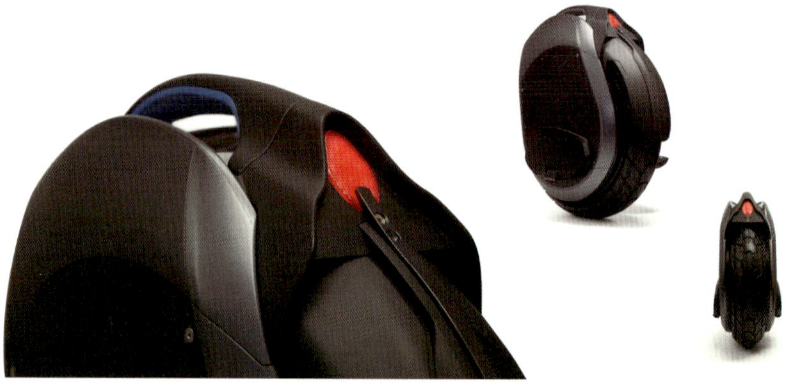

九号平衡车 Plus
MiniPlus

该产品是一款智慧平衡车。首次将军用级无线电定位技术应用于消费性产品，可实现自动跟随、用户遥控及拍摄等类机器人功能。产品拥有物理遥控器、比例式摇杆，一键召唤。内置语音音效包，可自定义录入，与他人互动。高附着力防滑胎，增强型镁合金底盘。35 公里续航，电池包防水，更安全出行。为人类环保出行提供一种创新方式。

Segway Plus is a smart balance vehicle. With the built-in radio positioning technology used in the consumer product for the first time in the world, it can realize a series of functions similar to a robot such as automatic tracking, user remote control and taking photos. The product owns physical remote control, proportional joystick and one button calling. With the built-in sound package, the users can record customized sound into the package and interact with others.Highly adhesive antiskid tire and strengthened magnesium alloy chassis are also included in the product. 35 km battery life and waterproof battery package can make travel safer. This provides an innovative way for green travel.

设计
DESIGN

刘晓影、刘磊
Liu Xiaoying, Liu Lei

生产
MANUFACTURE

纳恩博（常州）科技有限公司
Ninebot (Changzhou) Tech Co.,Ltd.

探梦者 Q3 双轮平衡车
Tomoloo Q3

该产品是从用户需求出发，采用独创物理性自平衡技术的双轮平衡车。这种技术让产品在不受外施扭力时，车身调整为自平衡状态，避免意外发生，降低学习成本，提升平稳性、操控性和安全性。同时产品实现手机蓝牙操控平衡车，增加趣味性。产品标准件的采用，让零部件可更换、回收，不会造成资源浪费。精心选择合适的材料，确保产品经久耐用。

Starting from the user requirements, the two-wheel balancing car uses the original physical self balancing technology. This kind of technology allows the vehicle to adjust itself as self-balancing status when the product is not influenced by wrestling power. This design avoids accident, greatly reduces the cost of learning, improving stability, control and safety. Phone Bluetooth controls the vehicle, making riding more interesting. The product also adopts standard parts, which will make all parts changeable and recyclable, wasting no resources. Great efforts are used to pick up proper materials to ensure durability of the product.

设计
DESIGN

深圳市木马整合设计有限公司
Shenzhen Moma Integrated Design Co.,Ltd.

生产
MANUFACTURE

深圳市四驾马车科技实业有限公司
Shenzhen Tomoloo Technology Industrial Co.,Ltd.

自由战士
Free Fighters

该产品是台铃自主研发的电动车。一键启动设计，集成了一键启停和三秒鞍座尾箱自动弹起功能；感应式尾箱灯，尾箱开启会自动点亮；创新一键修复技术，车辆故障时，一键自动修复故障单元，保障骑行；独创云动力模式，在特殊骑行路况时，实现动力瞬间加倍。原创液压前叉，起到更好的减震阻尼效果；产品动力来源采用储能电池的充放电。

Freedom Fighter is independent representatives of TAILG's own research and development. The latest one-button start design integrated a key to start and stop and three seconds automatic rebound function of tail box. Advanced induction tail case lamp will automatically turn on when tail box opens. When electrical fault occurs, the original one-button repair technology will automatically repair the fault unit to protect the ride.Unique cloud power pattern deal with climbing, acceleration, overtaking and special riding road conditions easily. Pressing the cloud power button, power output instantly doubled. From the technology in fork we reset the front fork damping method, change the spring shock for the hydraulic shock absorption, and inverted fork, to play a better role in reducing shock effect and damping. The energy resource of the product is from storage battery.

设计 DESIGN 天津深铃科技发展有限公司 Tianjin Shenling Technology Development Co.,Ltd.

天津深铃科技发展有限公司 Tianjin Shenling Technology Development Co.,Ltd. **生产 MANUFACTURE**

龙威二代
LongWin II

该产品是以科技人文主义为核心，更好实现智能化的电动车型。车辆驾驶舱布局、座椅舒适性等，都经过精准调校和优化。通过车联网、自动化驾驶技术、智慧云大数据平台，实现能化。产品完成 11 项安全改进，有多项领先于行业的安全配置，进行安全防护。产品采用磷酸铁锂电池，续航里程 320 千米，慢充 1 小时满电，解决里程、动力方面问题，起到节能减排作用。

The product takes science and technology humanism as the core to better realize intelligence. The layout of the cockpit, the comfort of the driver and passenger seat are all precisely adjusted and optimized.The vehicle intelligence can be realized through vehicle networking, automated driving technology and wisdom cloud large data platform. The product completes 11 security improvements, with a number of leading in the industry's security configuration, with a comprehensive proactive and passive security protection. The vehicle carries lithium iron phosphate batteries and has a 320Km life mileage. One-hour charge will reach the full power, so that the mile and energy problems will be solved. The product also helps save energy and reduce emission.

设计 DESIGN 厦门金龙联合汽车工业有限公司 Xiamen King Long United Automotive Industry Co.,Ltd.

厦门金龙联合汽车工业有限公司 Xiamen King Long United Automotive Industry Co.,Ltd. **生产 MANUFACTURE**

ARJ21-700 公务机内饰
Smart+

该方案遵循安全、经济、舒适和环保设计理念，为旅客提供舒适的环境以及便利的设备，同时采用最新科技营造独特的乘坐体验。在空间方面，设置大小储物间，来存放乘客使用物品。客舱整洁方面，采用无线充电设备，避免杂乱的电线。乘客操作方面，将常用操作按钮整合。设备选用轻量材料，减轻飞机重量，有效减少燃油使用，实现环保。

Adhering to the design idea of safe, economical, comfortable and clean, the solution aims at providing comfortable environment and convenient devices. At the same time, the latest technology is used to foster a unique ride experience. As about space, lockers with different sizes are designed to store passengers' stuff. Instead of electric wire, wireless charging devie will be used to make the cabin tidy.As for the operation, buttons that are frequently used will be integrated. Light materials are chosen to reduce plane's weight and effectively reduce the use of fuel oil, achieving environmental protection.

设计 DESIGN 中国商飞 COMAC

中国商飞上海飞机客户服务有限公司 工业设计所 COMAC Shanghai Aircraft Customer Service Co., Ltd. Industrial Design Institute **生产 MANUFACTURE**

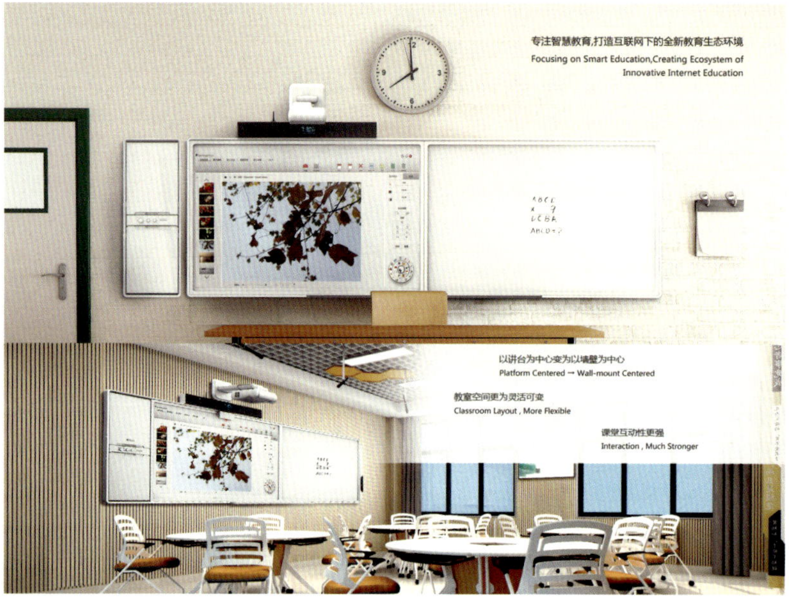

智慧助教云白板
Smart Edu Assistant Cloud Board

该产品是一款基于互联网下教育环境设计的智能云白板。产品涵盖教育云、无线传屏等技术，引领多项变革。该产品整合板书及多媒体，有随意批注、手写智能识别等功能。板面采用特殊材质，易擦拭，经久耐用。笔芯采用环保材料，保证师生健康。投影效果清晰护眼。大屏实时显示原板书，清晰可见；学生随意截取笔记，可专心听讲，让多媒体教室更智能。

The Smart Edu assistant cloud board is designed under the background of Internet education. The products include education cloud, wireless screen transmitting and other technologies that lead various revolution. It sets all the multimedia functions, such as random annotating and handwriting intelligent recognition. The page uses special materials that are easy to wipe, durable. Refills are made of green materials to ensure teachers' and students'health. The projection is clear and eyes protecting. Teachers' blackboard handwriting can be displayed on the big screen in real time. Students can screenshot notes and listen to teachers attentively, making the muitimedia room a more intelligent one.

设计 DESIGN
姚欣、陈立勋
Yao Xin, Chen Lixun

生产 MANUFACTURE
杭州迈杰教育科技有限公司
Hangzhou Maijie Educational Technology Co.,Ltd.

城市家具
City Furniture

该产品是一款放置在城市公共绿地的座椅。产品有两种设计，靠背椅放置在路旁，直椅放置在路中央，既可让两侧分别坐，也可躺下休息。座椅表面采用曲面设计，雨天不积水。这套公共设施座椅采取模具批量生产，数量多的情况下成本更低廉，也更易维修。设计灵感源于海鸥，将海鸥翅膀元素应用到产品造型上，更好地与环境融合。

This product is a chair that should set in a city's public area.The chair has two kinds of design. The back chair is put on the roadside and the straight chair can be placed in the center of the road. You can go both sides or lie down for a rest. The surface of the seat was designed with a curved surface so that in rainy days the water could flow along the both sides of the seat on the ground.This public facility is manufactured by mold so that the cost is lower when the quantity is considerable and easier to repair or maintain. The design of the public facilities was inspired by seagulls. The shape elements of gull wings were used in the design of public seats, in order to echo the overall atmosphere.

设计 DESIGN
高尚
Sandy Gao

生产 MANUFACTURE
上海壹生图文设计制作有限公司
Shanghai One Life Graphic Design Co.,Ltd.

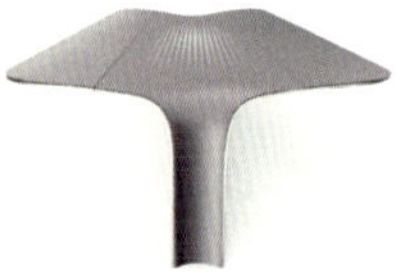

溪客度假屋
Seek Holiday House

大地溪客度假屋是低能耗可移动型原生态构筑屋。功能齐全的模块化设计，标准零件化的构建生产技术是产品核心。整体荷花外观，模块拼装的构筑方式。功能齐全，每套可容约 6 人居住。该屋 72 小时拼装完成，可直接使用，适应多地形条件安装。自带污水处理设备层，用来提供再生能源循环使用。该屋采用再生木材料、真空保温层，内外阻燃、安全性高。

Seek holiday house is a low energy consumption ecological construction of housing of movable type.The core of the product is that modularized design with comprehensive functions and manufacturing technology with standard components. The overall appearance looks like a lotus with module assembled construction.The house has multiple functions and could fulfill five to six tourists' needs in full size. The house could be completed in 72 hours and could adapt to various field requirements.The house has its pollution water treatment floor for energy recycling system.The holiday house take new recycled composite ecological wood and flame resistant vacuum insulation layer from inside to outside,which could promote house safety.

设计 DESIGN 北京大地溪客露营建筑科技有限公司 Beijing BES Seek Camping Architecture Technology Co.,Ltd.

生产 MANUFACTURE 北京大地溪客露营建筑科技有限公司 Beijing BES Seek Camping Architecture Technology Co., Ltd.

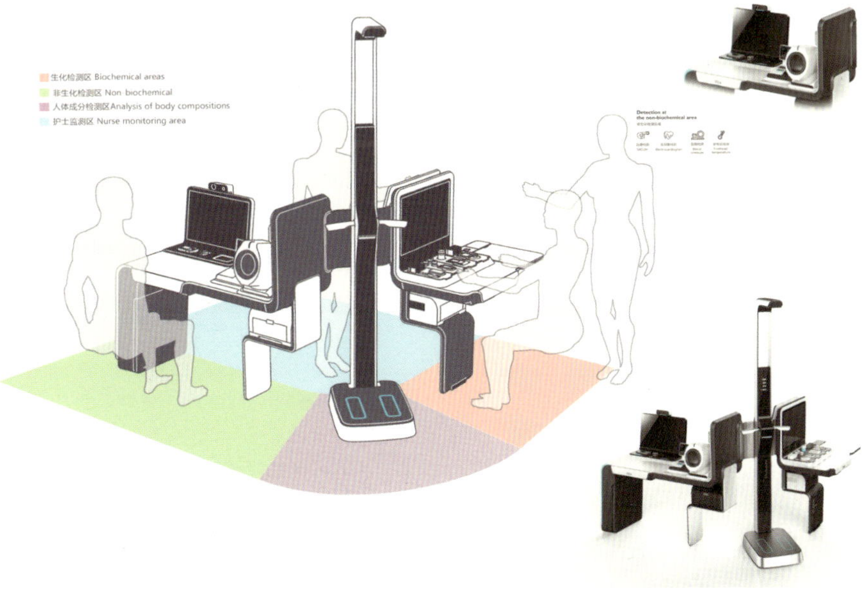

移动互联网医院
Mobile Internet Hospital

移动互联网医院作为连接枢纽，大限度整合医疗资源，将常规检查、健康咨询等在互联网医院解决，突发疾病、重大疾病等在实体医院解决，合理分配资源。解决看病难、服务差、社区医疗水平低问题。互联网医院无缝连接医患，可直接提供在线诊疗、专家服务、24 小时急诊，缓解医疗压力。模块化设计方式，可根据医院需要自由组合，节省购置成本。

As a connecting hub, the Internet Hospital integrate medical resources with great strength, letting routine checks and health consultation finished on the Internet hospital while serious diseases or surgeries can be treated in the entity hospital.In this way, resources are distributed reasonably to solve the problems such as difficulties in getting medical care, poor service attitudes and low medical treatment level in community. The Internet hospital connects patients seamlessly, can provide direct online diagnosis and treatment, specialists service and 24 hour emergency to alleviate medical pressure. Modular design can be combined freely according to hospitals' needs and thus saves purchase costs.

设计 DESIGN 深圳市柏斯工业设计有限公司 Shenzhen Perth Industrial Design Co.,Ltd.

生产 MANUFACTURE 深圳市柏斯工业设计有限公司 Shenzhen Perth Industrial Design Co.,Ltd.

多功能通道闸机
Multi-Function Channel Gates

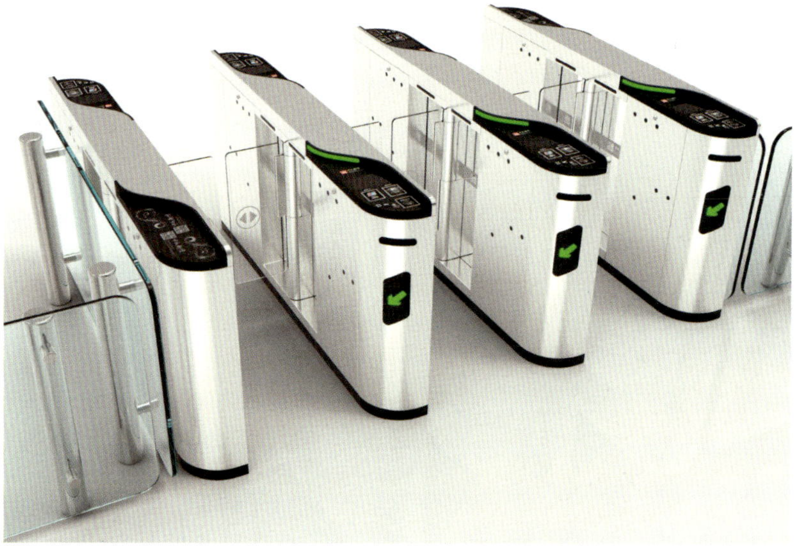

多功能通道闸机基于复杂内部结构，排布自主研发生产的元器件，使其实现多种方式获得通过许可。该产品不仅操作方式多样化，而且配有 7 寸显示屏，使用过程一目了然，提高便捷性、流通性。通过明确灯光、标识，使人们在操作上简单易懂。产品采用机械装置、门体位置、电流检测、通道传感器等技术，保证行人安全。可用于地铁、办公、景区等多种环境。

Under the premise of a compact complex inner structure，multi-function channel gates arranges independently researched and developed components, making it achieve a variety of ways to get through permission. The products not only owns diversified operation mode, but is also equipped with a 7-inch large display to display the whole operating process, raising convenience and liquidity. With simple and clear lights and logo, people can easily learn the operation. The mechanical devices, the door location, current detection and channel sensor quad are equipped to protect the pedestrian's security. And it can be used in the subway, office, scenic spot and so on.

设计 DESIGN
北京中成科信科技发展有限公司
Beijing Zhongcheng Technology and Trust Development Co., Ltd.

北京赛佳图工业设计有限公司
Beijing Saga Fig Industrial Design Co.,Ltd.
生产 MANUFACTURE

生态绿植墙空气净化系统
Ecological Green Wall Air Purification System

该产品通过植物与净化系统相互作用来提高办公、家庭等环境空气质量。整套空气净化系统是由绿植墙空气净化器、两个柜体净化器构成。两部分可同时使用，也可单独使用，降低空间限制。其可以代替墙体又有分离内外空间等作用。采用模块化设计，根据不同环境需求，设计不同的造型。整个绿植墙辅以灯光效果，可为植物生长提供光源，又美观。

This is a purification system aims at improving the office, family and other environmental air quality through the interaction of plants and purification systems. The system is consisted of green plants wall air purifier and two cabinet purifiers. These two parts can be used simultaneously or separately. Its own can replace the wall, but also can separate internal and external space. The modular concept is used according to the needs of different environments, different shapes can also be designed. The green wall with lighting effects, can provide a source for plant growth and can play a role in landscaping,

设计 DESIGN
北京生泰宝科技有限公司
ECO-BAO Co.,Ltd.

北京上品极致产品设计有限公司
Beijing Top Industrial Design Co.,Ltd.
生产 MANUFACTURE

DT-7000i58 小额现金循环机
DT-7000i58 Compact Cash Recycler

该产品是基于“银行—商户—厂商”三方合作管理模式设计的自动柜员机。由商户负责“清机、加钞、维护、推广”，解决银行基建、运营成本、资金占用问题。该产品采用定制化、模块化设计，拓展性、功能强。产品加载第三方支付业务，实现综合性服务平台，运行成本低、效率高。通过与商户合作，在终端增加不同内容，使用户在家门口就能享受综合金融服务。

I58 is an automatic teller machine based on the "bank - merchant - manufacturers" tripartite cooperation model. By introducing merchants to be responsible for the daily "cleaning, adding notes, maintenance, promotion", the product can help reduce and solve the bank infrastructure costs, operating costs, cash flow and other issues. It adopts customized and modular design concept to strengthen extensibility and functions. i58 is also able to load third-party payment method to achieve a comprehensive financial services platform, which makes it the lowest cost and the most efficient cash recycler.With the cooperation of merchants, the bank will increase terminals with different contents to allow users enjoy comprehensive financial service at their home.

设计 DESIGN
广州广电运通金融电子股份有限公司
GRGBanking Equipment Co.,Ltd.

广州广电运通金融电子股份有限公司
GRGBanking Equipment Co., Ltd.
生产 MANUFACTURE

公共智能宠物寄存柜
Smart Pet Storage Box

该产品是市面上第一款商用宠物托管监护机。解决出行过程中，禁止携带宠物场合的临时存放问题，以及宠物占大量宠物的照料管理问题。该产品具有手机应用，用来智能显示监测，用户可对宠物实时监测，能减少宠物与主人的距离感，减少人力看护成本，实现现代、智能化监测功能。集成宠物排泄物收集装置及处理工具，实现便捷流程化排泄物处理方式。

This is the first commercial pet custody guarding machine on the market, designed to solve the travel problems which may exist in the ban on pet occasions, as well as large numbers of pet care management issues on pet shops.This product has an APP to smartly display monitoring. That means users can monitor their pets in real time. It can also reduce the distance between the pet and the owner, and the cost of human care to achieve modernization, intelligent monitoring and control network. Integrated pet excreta collection device and processing tools can achieve a convenient process of excreta disposal.

设计 DESIGN 上海宠儿宠物用品有限公司 Petin China Co.,Ltd.

生产 MANUFACTURE 杭州奥格工业设计有限公司 AUG Hangzhou Industrial Design Co.,Ltd.

再生混凝土组合式透水地面砖
Recycled Aggregate Concrete Combined Water Permeable Ground Bricks

该产品是再生混凝土组合式地面砖。使用建渣做骨料，具有环保性。产品组合方式多样，适用于多种场地铺装。分为透水、非透水部分，采用普通砖体包围透水砖体形式，克服物理性能制约，提高强度，增强耐用性。砖体边缘设导水槽，加快雨水下渗。侧面设肋条，增加摩擦力，使两种砖型更贴合、稳固。砖体可使雨水回归地表，缓解城市热岛效应、内涝问题。

The product is a recycled aggregate concrete combined water permeable brick. Building debris are used as aggregate to be environmentally friendly. The combination of products are various and can be suitable for multiple sites' pavement. The product is divided into the permeable part and the impermeable part. The design of ecological combining water permeable brick system to the ordinary bricks overcomes the physical properties restriction and increases the strength and durability of the water permeable brick. The design of guiding gutter on the margins of the brick could speed up the rainwater infiltration; the rib strips on the sides of the bricks increase the force of friction which makesthe two kinds of bricks jointed more closely and the combined brick could be more stable. This combining mode increases the permeable rate and the strength at the same time, and the various paving modes are suitable for multiple sites.The bricks design will make rain go back to earth surface, which can help ease urban heat island effect and waterlogging.

设计 DESIGN 成都沙苑工业产品设计有限公司 Chengdu Shayuan Industrial Design Co.,Ltd.

生产 MANUFACTURE 成都沙苑工业产品设计有限公司 Chengdu Shayuan Industrial Design Co.,Ltd.

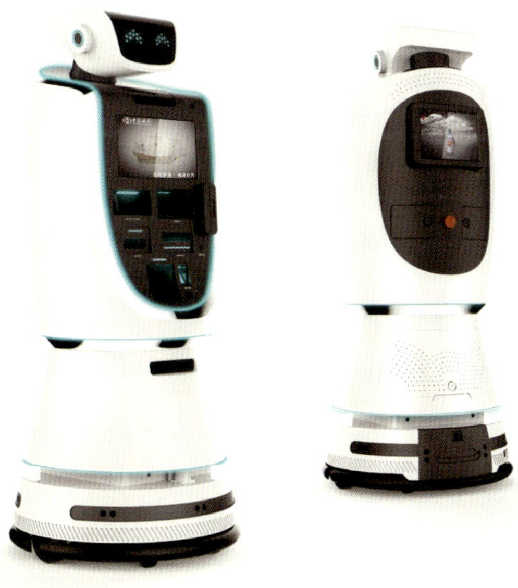

银行金融发卡机器人
Intelligent Financial Card Issuing Robot

该产品是一款首次将人工智能引入银行服务领域，实现无人化银行服务机器人。产品首创多项智能技术结合自助设备，通过激光、声呐、避碰传感器等，实现自主导航、避让。产品在现有业务基础上，具备引领服务功能，将企业宣传、产品介绍等信息置于产品，客户通过触摸屏互动，可获取信息，减少排队现象。当机器人电量低时，可自主充电。节约人力成本。

The intelligent financial card issuing robot is a product which first introduces the concept of artificial intelligence into bank service field, realizing unmanned bank service. It first combines multi-inntelligent technologies with self-service equipment to achieve self navigation and evasion through laser, sonar and evasion sensors. Information like enterprise promotion and products introduction are inserted in the product, but with the help of leading service function, clients can interact through touch screen and gain information, so that people don't need to wait in the long line for these. When the robot's battery is low, it can conduct self-charging and reducehuman costs.

设计 DESIGN 北京东方兴华科技发展有限责任公司 Beijing DFXH Orient Xinghua Technology Development Co.,Ltd.

生产 MANUFACTURE 北京智加问道科技有限公司 Beijing ZCO Design Co.,Ltd.

简约智慧路灯（星海系列）
Simple Intelligent Streat Lamp

该产品是集成照明、监控、无线网覆盖、天气监测、空气检测以及广告宣传、公共充电系统于一身的智能照明设备。产品采用多模块化组件系统，可使不同功能组合，或去除、更换组件，以适应不同街道环境需求，解决街道照明设备杂乱的情况。产品采用电源和太阳能双重供电系统，节约能源消耗。该产品高度集成一般照明设备的所有功能，节省财政投入。

Modern minimalist smart poles are intelligent lighting devices that integrate lighting, monitoring, WIFI coverage, weather monitoring, air detection, and advertising, public charging systems. At the same time multi-modular component system can make products have different functional combinations. Or to remove or change components to accommodate different streets environmental requirements, solving the problem of messy street lighting devices. The street light using power and solar dual power supply system, greatly saving the energy consumption. This product highly integrates all functions of other lighting devices, which can reduce financial input.

设计 DESIGN
四川能投光电有限公司
SCEI Optoelectronic Co.,Ltd.

上海木马工业产品设计有限公司
Shanghai Moma Industrial Product Design Co.,Ltd.
生产 MANUFACTURE

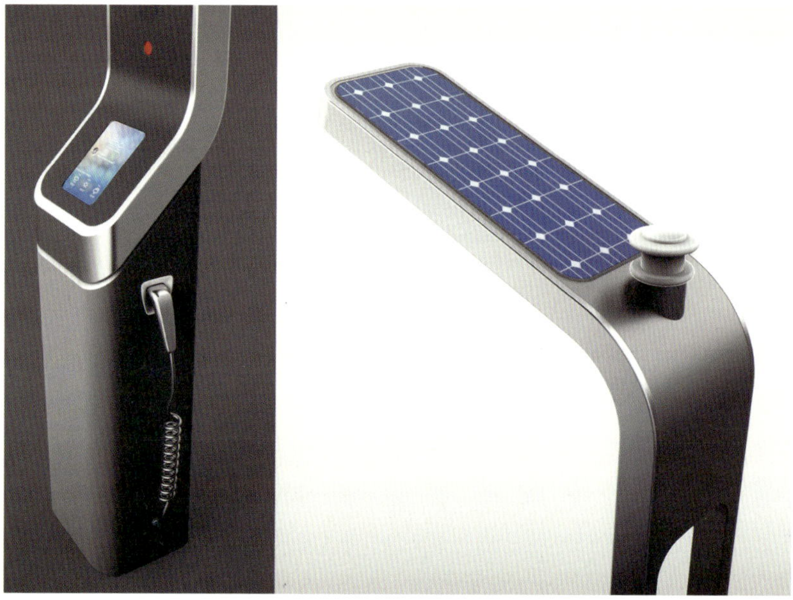

魔力伞
Molisan

该产品是基于现代化物联网开发的一种共享型雨伞设备。人们可通过手机找到最近共享处，快速借伞。每把伞内置电子标签，借还过程只需约 40 秒。产品放置机器可容纳 50 把伞，放置在人群密集的公共场所，服务范围广。产品采用共享理念，解决出行带伞不便，或是特殊天气没伞困境，旨在便利出行，降低社会公共资源浪费。

This product is based on a shared umbrella developed by the Internet of Things. People can find the nearest sharing places by mobile phones to borrow an umbrella timely. A digital label is set in every umbrella and it will only take 40 seconds to borrow or return an umbrella. Each machine can accommodate 50 umbrellas and the umbrellas are placed in crowded public places to have a wide service scope. This product has adopted the sharing ideas to solve the inconvenience of bring an umbrella or the situation where people go out without umbrella in sunny, rainy or snowy days.It aims at bring convenience to people going out and reduce the waste of public resources.

设计 DESIGN
上海艺升信息科技有限公司
Shanghai Yisheng Information Technology Co.,Ltd.

杭州汉点工业设计有限公司
Hangzhou Handot Industrial Design Co., Ltd.
生产 MANUFACTURE

2017
2017

12th

2017

红星原创奖银奖

Silver Award of Original Design Award

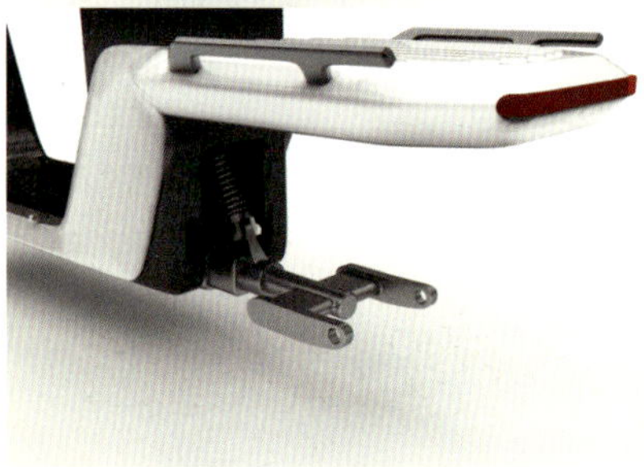

Eco-Motor 城市物流电动车
Express Eco-Motor

Eco-Motor 城市物流电动车是针对城市物流运输设计的专业摩托式运载工具。正三轮设计，可倾侧的前后车身，使该车辆比普通两轮车拥有更好的稳定性。小巧的车型设计更加灵活，双后轮和双载货区的设计带来 450 升大容量载货量，模块化可更换电池可以有效满足一天内长距离派送，大屏幕车载屏可以规划路线规避拥堵，并且能快速签收。Eco-Motor 城市物流电动车的设计能够对快递业面临的在复杂城市路况路网中下一站分发的难题：如何灵活地走街串巷，如何兼顾大容量负载，如何提升快递员的职业荣誉，更高效率的签收提出很好的解决方案，为广大快递员带来全新体验。

Express Eco-motor is a professional motorized vehicle, designed for urban logistics transportation. Tricycle design and tilted body make it more stable than ordinary two-wheeled vehicle. Small vehicle design makes it more flexible and the design of dual rear wheels and cargo area brings a large capacity of 450L. The modular replaceable batteries can meet the need of long distance delivery in one day. The large screen can plan a route to avoid congestion and quickly sign. The design of Eco-Motor can solve the problems of distribution for next station, facing the complicated city traffic network by the express industry, such as how to go through the city flexibly, how to balance the large capacity, how to promote the couriers occupation honor and propose a good plan for more efficient sign to bring a new experience for the majority of couriers.making both lighting effects and modeling change have stereoscopic sensation, and presenting a fantastic effect.

设计
DESIGN

周才致、张沙、李鸿佳
Zhou Caizhi, Zhang Sha, Li Hongjia

能量胶带
Energy Tape

能量胶带是一款可循环使用的太阳能胶带。在使用过程中根据不同的使用场景，用户可将胶带贴在任何物体的表面，任意形状，任意大小，让物体成为临时“发电站”。它能将吸收的能量储存于内置的电源内，以满足用户在户外的临时用电需求。设计者利用现有对太阳能获取技术的了解，与电子消费产品结合进行再创新设计，从其功能属性上满足用户对产品的基本要求，在考虑技术可行性方面较为成熟地进行了思考，从生产制造角度评估具有很强的可行性，从目前电能补充的需求角度出发，具有较大的市场空间，能支持项目的持续开展，以满足用户各类场景的使用需求。

Energy tape is a reusable solar cell designed as a tape. Users can stick the tape to any object's surface according to different situations, then the tape will make the object a temporary “power plant” regardless of its shape and size. It can store energy in a built-in power supply to meet users’ temporary electricity demand outdoors. The designers use the knowledge of the existing solar acquisition technology and combine it with consumer electronics products to make creative design. It meets the basic requirements of users in products’ functional attributes, in consideration of technical feasibility. It has strong feasibility from the point of production. From the perspective of current demand of electricity power, it has large market potential and could support the continuous development of the project to meet the using demands of users in various situations.

设计
DESIGN

林思安、杨磊、李承勇
Lin Sian, Yang Lei, Li Chengyong

交流的坐具
The Rattan Chair that Promotes Communication

交流的坐具是一款满足一人或多人舒适休息的躺椅，同时设计出了促进人们交流的结构。设计者通过研究寻找舒适的休息姿势，满足忙碌工作人群对放松舒适的需求，针对不同人的习惯找到不同的姿态，设计出符合这一姿势的曲面，满足多人使用，半包的背部曲线营造出空间感，使人放心地说出心里的烦恼的同时感到安全感。“交流的坐具”使用传统的藤条材料，充分利用藤条的物理特性和人文特性，创造出了与环境和谐的自然形态，和人与人之间回归自然的生活情境。该设计从传统材料出发，创造出了现代的形式表达，该设计在藤条的收口细节处，结构交代清晰，使用性合理。

A chatting chair that satisfies one or more people rests, at the same time, a structure that promotes communication. Through the study to find a comfortable rest posture, designers try to meet the needs of people to relax after busy work. Finding different gestures according to the habits of different people, this surface of this posture is designed to serve various people. The curve of the back creates a sense of space, making people feel safe to say inside worries. The chatting chair uses traditional rattan materials, fully making use of the physical and human characteristics of rattan and create a harmoniously natural form and the situation of life between people after getting back to nature. It starts from traditional materials to create modern expression. The design details in the closing of rattan is clear and reasonable.

设计
DESIGN

黄莹莹
Huang Yingying

KIWIGOGO 2-Way 奇异果双向智能车
KIWIGOGO 2-Way Electric Bicycle

KIWIGOGO 2-Way 双向智能车， 是一个可以在公路骑行电动车和双轮平衡车中间自由切换的交通代步工具。当在慢速封闭场合中它可以以平衡车姿态在 0-20 千米每小时的速度骑行，灵活便捷；当行驶到公路上时，它可以变形成公路电动车，以 20-40 千米每小时的速度快速骑行，高效安全。中央侧倾控制系统保证其在两轮平衡车行驶时的稳定性，以及在公路高速行驶时的良性侧倾。本设计在功能创新与使用场景设计上突破传统模式，设计方案完整，包含可实施的结构设计、模式切换方案、中央侧倾控制系统等。虽然仍处于概念阶段，但是结合目前的方案成熟度，后续工业设计优化，有进一步细化的可能性。

Kiwigogo is a two-way Electric Bicycle and is designed to be a new type of traffic tool，being able to transformed from a stand up urban electric bike to an bike balancing car. For slow speed and close quarter environments where an balancing car stance is more appropriate, the Kiwigogo can be ridden by 0-20km/h, flexible and convenient. When in urban roads, it could be transformed to road electric bike and ridden by 20-40km/h, high efficient and safe. It has a tilt adjustment mechanism to keep stable in double wheel stance and benign roll on the high speed ridding.

设计
DESIGN

青岛奇异果智能科技有限公司
Qingdao Supranatural Intelligent Science &Technology Co.,Ltd

2M 高峰快线
2M Peak Express

“2M 高峰快线”是具有高效运载乘客功能的地铁车厢设计。当早晚出行高峰时段来临时，位于每排座椅中间部分的四个座椅会定时折叠起来成为腰靠，而两端的弱势群体座椅则固定不变。且新增高低多样的立柱扶手设计，可满足更多乘客的需求。此外，内饰材质采用大量的木质复合材料与金属材质结合，一改往常单一冰冷的金属地铁色。“2M 高峰快线”设计提升了运载效率和乘坐体验，创新性地实现了高峰期地铁空间的弹性扩展，并且从情感上充分体现了社会人与人之间的和谐相处。

"2M peak express" design is the essence of the more efficient carrying passengers. When the morning and evening peak arrives, the four seats in the middle of each row of seats are regularly folded and lumbar, and the vulnerable seats at both ends are fixed. And the addition of high and low column handrail design meet the needs of more passengers. In addition, the interior material adopts a large number of wood composite materials and metal materials, a change in the usual cold metal subway color. "2M peak express" design enhances the carrying efficiency and ride experience, an innovative implementation of the expansion of the subway space in the peak period, and fully reflects the social harmony between people in the perspective of emotion.

设计
DESIGN

黄赫中、王喆义
Huang Hezhong, Wang Zheyi

空中消防车
Air Fire Engine

空中消防车是一款结合了无人机和消防储水车的消防设备。它最大的特点是：消防范围相比目前的消防设备提升了十倍之多，而成本只是目前设备的四分之一。消防员和消防车到不了的地方无人机都可以飞达，灭火面积更是之前的十倍之多。此外，杜绝了烈火、爆炸对消防员的威胁。该概念设计利用当下突飞猛进的无人直升机技术，创造地用于消防设备上，直接补足了现有高层建筑的消防设备的短板问题。该设计具有很强的经济性和强大的市场需求，相信经过一定的技术整合与落地，在未来将会成为对社会具有积极意义的现实装备。

This is a airfire engine which combines advantages of unmanned aerial vehicles and fire reservoir. The biggest feature of this equipment is that the scope of watering has enhanced ten times compared the current fire equipment, while the cost is only a quarter of the current equipment. Unmanned aerial vehicles can reach where firemen and fire engines could not be. The area of fire fighting is ten times as much as before. In addition, it puts an end to the threat of the fire and explosion of firefighters. The conceptual design using the unmanned helicopter technology progresses by leaps and bounds, creatively applies it to fire fighting equipment and directly make up the short of the existing problems of fire equipment of high-rise building. This design has a strong economy and market demand. It is believed that after a certain technology integration and fall to the ground, it will be reality equipment, being positive to the society in the future.

设计
DESIGN

范石钟
Fan Shizhong

2017

12th

优秀设计师奖

Best Designer Award of Original Design Award

2017

范石钟
Fan Shizhong

男，被美国杂志《福布斯》评为“中国最具发展潜力设计师”，受到国务院副总理刘延东接见。担任湖南大学 FANSTONE 设计工作室负责人，小狗设计咨询有限公司创始人，湖南佰意文化创意有限公司设计总监，武汉古龙桥文化创意有限公司首席设计顾问，美国工业设计师协会（IDSA）会员。获得国内外设计大奖 120 多项，成为湖南省年度教育新闻人物、晋江市第二类优秀人才（院士级）、中国大学生年度人物暨中国十佳大学生。设计作品登上《设计》杂志封面，受到英国《每日邮报》、中央电视台、湖南卫视、美国《商业周刊》等媒体报道。其设计的“空中消防车”荣获 2017 中国设计红星原创奖银奖。

Mr. Fan Shizhong is included in the list of “most promising designers” released by Forbes, and received by vice premier Liu Yandong. He is the person in charge of FANSTONE design studio of Hunan university, the founder of Puppy Design Consulting Co., Ltd. and the designer director of Design Director of Hunan Baiyi Culture & Creative Co., Ltd. He is also the Chief Design Consultant of Wuhan Cologne Culture & Creative Co., Ltd., and Member of American Industrial Designers Association (IDSA).He has won more than 120 domestic and international design awards, become one of the annual education news personalities in Hunan Province, and the second category of outstanding talent (academician) in Jinjiang City. He is also person of the year of Chinese college students and one of China's top ten college students. His design works have appeared on the front page of “Design” magazine cover. He has been in the news of the British Daily Mail, China Central Television, Hunan TV, American Business Week and other media. His design of the "Air Fire Engine" win the Silver Award in 2017 China Red Star Original Design Award.

如今是一个大设计时代、服务设计时代，“设计 +”是我所推崇的，任何事物都需要设计，且人人都是设计师。社会影响力、社会价值、商业价值是我的设计三要素。

Now it’s an era of “big design” and service design. What I admire is “design plus”. Anything can be designed and anyone can become a designer. The three elements in my design is social influence, social value and commercial value.

王谭
Vincent Wang

男，2009 年毕业于韩国东西大学工业设计专业，2016 年创办了青岛奇异果智能科技有限公司。在产品设计中，无论是对整体风格的把握，还是产品细节的雕琢，都有自己独特的风格和见解。潜心研究产品设计的颜色、材质与工艺（CMF）设计和人因工程，并应用在现有的产品设计上，取得了良好的效果。参与设计的项目涵盖了新能源车、游艇、智能家电、医疗设备等领域，优秀的设计风格，坚持原创设计的理念深得客户认可。设计的产品获得国内外知名奖项。其设计的“KIWIGOGO 2-Way 奇异果双向智能车”荣获 2017 中国设计红星原创奖银奖。

Mr. Vincent Wang, graduated from the East Korea University in 2009, his major is industrial design and, in 2016, he founded the Qingdao Kiwi Intelligent Technology Co., Ltd. He has his own unique style and insights in product design, whether it is the overall style or product details. He concentrated on the studies of product design in color, material and technology (CMF) and human factors engineering. He has applied these factors in product design, and achieved good results. The design projects he has participated include new energy vehicles, yachts, smart appliances, medical equipment and other fields. Clients voice their approval of his designer due to his excellent design style and adherence of original design. His design products have won famous domestic and international awards. The products he designs have won famous domestic and international awards. He has won the Silver Award of 2017 China Red Star Original Design Award because of "KIWIGOGO 2-Way Smart Car".

创新是通往未来的钥匙。

Innovation is the key to the future.

2017
2017

未来之星奖

Future Star Award of Original Design Award

杨磊
Yang Lei

男，致力于从交互设计到产品设计不同领域的跨界创新，获得了国内外设计奖项80多项。曾在华为用户体验设计部门、百度用户体验部门、清华美院服务设计研究所、清华 xLab 孵化器等机构和部门实习。2015 年 6 月担任北京洛可可设计集团服务设计师；10 月加入深圳岸泊信息科技有限公司，担任设计师；2016 年成立“一种感动”设计工作室。作品被 Designboom、Yanko design 等国内外知名设计平台报道，并在北京国际设计周、北京国际家具展展出。作为“新锐设计师”受邀出席全球顶尖设计师社区 Behance Shenzhen 线下分享活动。其设计的“能量胶带”获得 2017 中国设计红星原创奖银奖。

Mr. Yang Lei is dedicated to cross boundary innovationin different fields from interactive design to product design. He was once intern in Huawei user experience design department, Baidu user experience department, service design center of Tsinghua university, and Tsinghua xLab. He took up the position of service designer in Peking lkk design group since June 2015 and joined into Shenzhen Anbo Information Technology Co., Ltd as designer in October. In 2016, he founded “Touched” design studio. His designs have been displayed in Beijing International Design Week and Beijing International Furniture Fair and have been in the news of renowned local and international design platforms, Designboom, Yanko design included. As an “emerging designer”, he was invited to attend off-line sharing activities held by the Behance Shenzhen where top designers meet each other. The “energy tape” he designed has contributed to let him win the Silver Award in 2017 China Red Star Original Design Award.

在今后的设计创新里，将会加倍投身设计创意产业，锐意创新，不断进取，为促进经济发展，中国的创意产业贡献一份力量。

I will dedicate myself to creative design industry in the future and keep innovative and keep moving on to make contribution to boosting the economic development and China's creative design industry.

周才致
Zhou Caizhi

男，湖南大学设计艺术学院工业设计工程专业研究生。专业成绩年级领先，对设计抱有极大的热情，拥有 4 项专利，国家级专业技术人员认证。大学期间获得“IF 设计新秀奖”、全国大学生工业设计大赛国家级二等奖等国内外诸多设计奖项。被列入文化部文化产业创业创意库重点人才库，全国大学生年代代表人物候选人 200 名，创办芒果创客设计工作室，获“芙蓉学子—学术创新奖”等诸多荣誉。其组建团队设计的“Eco-Motor 城市物流电动车”获得 2017 中国设计红星原创奖银奖。

Mr. Zhou Caizhi is a postgraduate in design engineering in School of Design Art of Hunan University. He has a leading academic performance and shows great passion to design. He has four patents and certification of national professional and technical personnel. He has got "IF New Designer Award", state-class second prize in national collegiate industrial design contest and many other domestic and international design prizes. He is in the list of key talents of Culture Department of cultural industry creative library and top 200 nominees of annual representatives of national college students. He founded mango creator design studio and won "lotus student-academic innovation prize". "Eco-Motor", an urban logistic electric vehicle, helped him to win the Silver Award in 2017 China Red Star Original Design Award.

Eco-Motor 城市物流电动车有效解决了城市物流送慢、形象差、不安全等痛点。希望在今后的日子里不断努力将这款优秀的产品落到实处。

The urban logistic electric vehicle "Eco-Motor" can solve the problem of in "slow delivery, poor image, low security" in urban logistics. I will keep on trying to put this excellent product into practice.

2017

红星原创奖

Excellent Award of Original Design Award

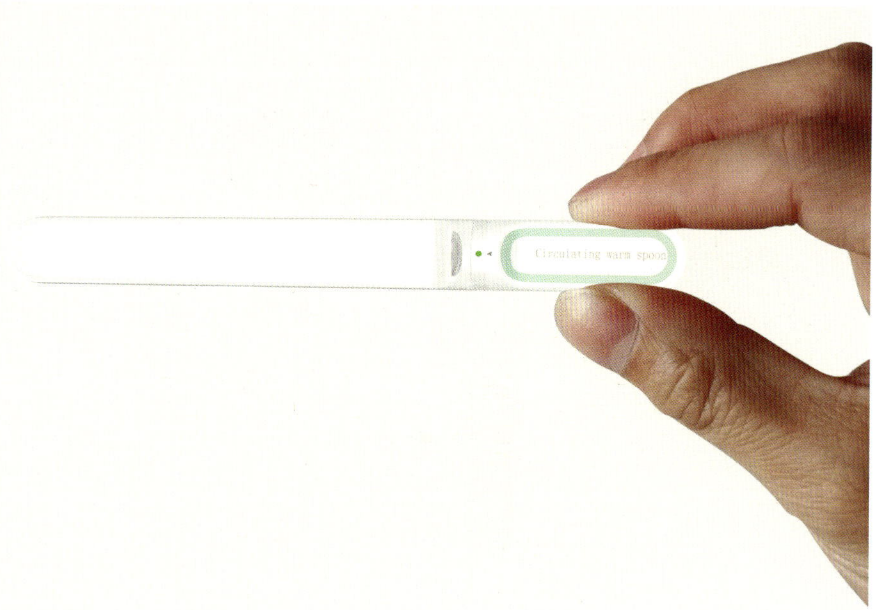

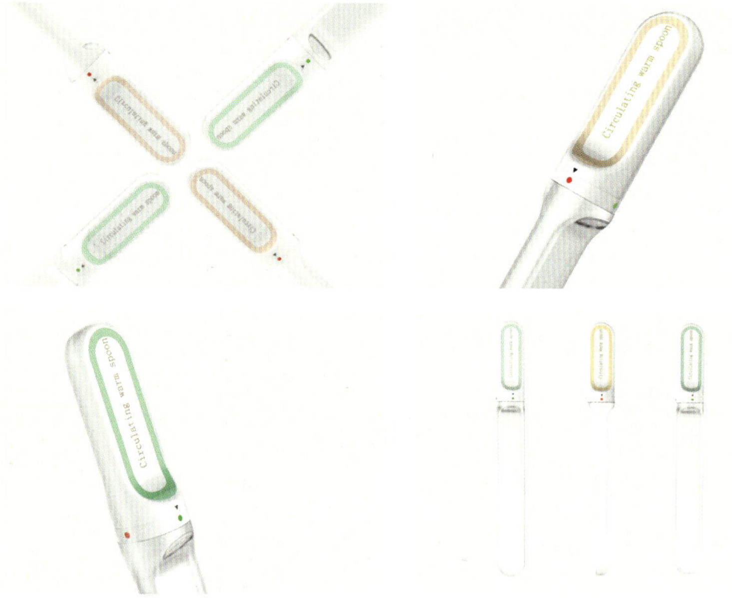

棒 —— 循环加热搅拌棒
BANG—Cyclic Heating Stir Bar

这款多功能搅拌棒集循环加热和可视化提示饮品冷热的功能。它针对人们喝咖啡牛奶等热饮料时，热饮料还没喝完就冷了的现状而设计。搅拌时，搅拌棒内无水醋酸钠受热发生可逆反应，吸收并储存热量；饮料冷却后旋转手柄可触发逆向反应释放热量，加热饮料，绿色环保，不影响口感。手柄上的色带可以显示饮品的冷热，可循环使用。

This multifunctional stirring bar combines the function of cyclic heating and visualization tips for cold and hot drinks. It is designed for the situation where hot drinks like coffee and milk get cool when they aren't finished. When stirring, anhydrous sodium acetate in stirring bar reacts reversibly when heated, absorbing and storing heat; When drinks get cool, twisting handle can trigger the reverse reaction to release heat and heating beverage, the process is green, environmental protection and do not affect the taste. The ribbon on the handle can show the hot and cold conditions of drinks, and can be recycled.

设计
DESIGN

孙建昆
Sun Jiankun

行李助手
Luggage Helper

行李助手为解决出行时选择行李箱大小苦恼而设计。它有三种形态，一是单层模式，体积只有普通行李箱的一半．适合短期出差旅行使用；二是双层模式，体积只有普通行李箱大小；三是推车模式，轮子可以拉伸出来变换成小推车的形态，有普通行李箱容量的两倍以上，更加轻松便捷。

The baggage assistant is designed to solve the problem of picking suitcase size when traveling. It has three forms, the first kind is the single mode, only half the volume of ordinary trunk, it is suitable for short-term travel; the second kind is the double mode, only the size of an ordinary suitcase; the third kind is the cart model, the wheels can be stretched out and transformed into the form of small cart, the capacity is two times more than that of ordinary luggage, it is more easy and convenient.

设计
DESIGN

师艳江、楚文宝、戴新宇
Shi Yanjiang , Chu Wenbao, Dai Xinyu

生命标记
Life Markers

生命标记是一款搜寻无人机设计，它可以节省救援的时间，提前使用无人机对废墟进行扫描，当探寻到生命迹象时，会由无人机携带的喷嘴喷出红色圆圈标记，方便救援人员赶到现场以后直接搜救，为救援争取时间。

Life markers is a design for unmanned aerial vehicle, it can save the rescue time and advance the use of drones to scan the ruins. When finding signs of life, the UAV carrying nozzle will spray the red circle to mark, which is convenient for rescue personnel rushed to the scene to rescue and save time.

设计
DESIGN

欧阳雪欣、徐文鑫、王子健
Ouyang Xuexin, Xu Wenxin，Wang Zijian

暖手拐杖
Warm Crutch

这是一款为老人冬天出行设计的暖手拐杖。老人冬天外出散步，经常需要携带暖手袋，行动不便的老人还要带上拐杖，造成不便。这款拐杖既可以给老人支撑，又可以提供暖手功能。内置太阳能芯片应急充电，通过太阳能转化为电能再转化热能；内置感应器，当外界温度低于 30 摄氏度时，自动启动加热功能，还设有急救按钮。

This is a warm crutch designed for the elderly in winter. When old people go out for a walk in winter, they often need to carry warm handbags, and those with mobile difficulty also have to bring crutches, causing inconvenience. The crutch supports the elderly and warms their hands. The built-in solar chip emergency charging can convert the solar energy into electric energy and then into the heat energy; the built-in sensor can automatically start heating function when the outside temperature is below 30 degrees. The crutch is also equipped with emergency button.

设计
DESIGN

深圳市韵博产品策划有限公司
Shenzhen Yunbo Product Planning Co., Ltd.

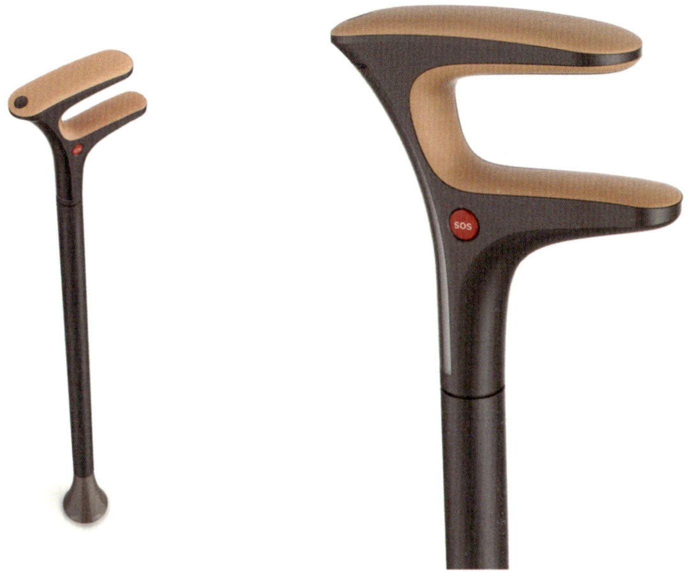

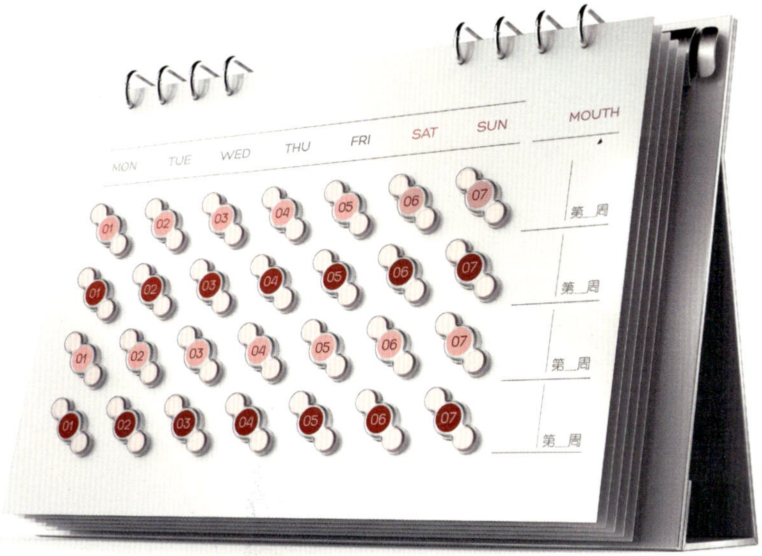

日历保健品包装
Health Care Products Packaging with Calendar

这是一款提醒人们按时服用保健品的包装设计。现代人由于压力较大，亚健康人群越来越多。需要服用保健品的人也越来越多，但由于较快的工作生活节奏，人们通常会忘记是否按时服用保健品。这款设计创新性地将药品包装和日历进行了结合，每到一天，就需要吃掉对应当天日期下面的保健品，这样有没有按时服用保健品就一目了然，让消费者能够按时按量地服用保健品。

The packaging design can remind people to take health care products on time. Because of the great pressure, more and more people are in sub healthy condition. More and more people need to take health care products, but because of the rapid pace of work and life, people usually forget to take health care products on time. The design combines the drug packaging and calendar innovatively. Every day, you need to eat the health care products under the date of that day, thus whether the health care products are taken or not is clear and unambiguous, so that consumers can take health care products of proper dosage at the right time.

设计
DESIGN

无限极（中国）有限公司
Infinitus(China)Company LTD

火灾应急水性口罩
Fire Emergency Water Mask

火灾应急水性口罩用于公共场合如地铁站的火灾应急逃生使用。基于口罩使用的最原始动作：“湿物蒙鼻，匍匐前进，防止浓烟呛入”进行设计，解决了在紧急时候人们往往难以寻找湿物阻隔浓烟的问题，给人们提供及时有效的帮助。

Fire emergency water masks are used for fire emergency escape in public places such as subway stations. The design is based on the original motion in using mask “covering the nose with wet things and creeping forward” to prevent from choking smoke, the problem that it is difficult for people to find the wet smoke barrier in an emergency is solved, providing timely and effective assistance to people.

设计
DESIGN

薛伟峰、祝灵洁
Xue Weifeng, Zhu Lingjie

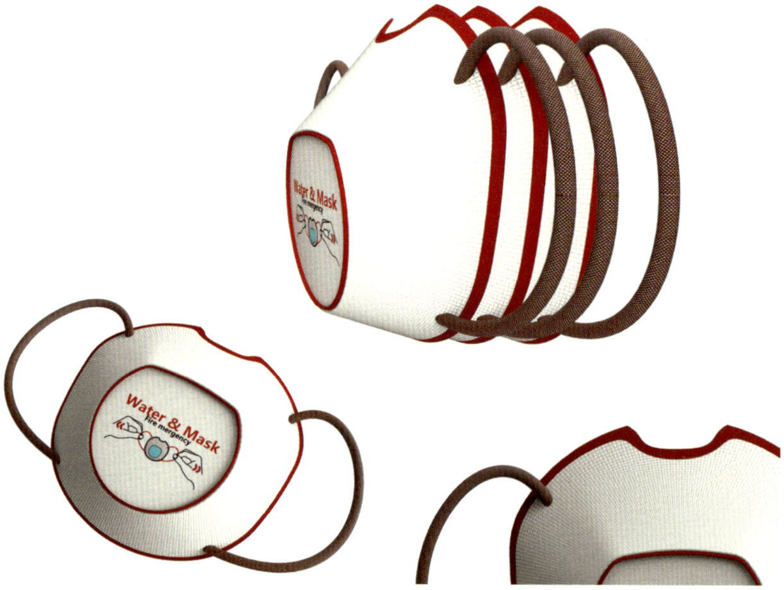

盲文电子书
Braille E-book

这是一款利用活字印刷术的原理为盲人设计的盲文电子书。
结合活字印刷与手感触摸感应科技，实时更换盲文电子书的页面文字。根据盲文的自身使用特点，电子书整体设计简洁，简化不必要的操作程序。健康人使用蓝牙传输电子书文件到电子设备，盲文电子书自动识别文件转换为盲文，手部感应触摸一页结束后自动更新新的内容，将新一页盲文中不需要的点隐藏。

This is a Braille book designed for the blind using the principle of movable type printing. With the combination of movable type printing and hand touch sensing technology, the page text of Braille books can be changed in real time. According to the characteristics of Braille itself, the overall design of e-book is simple, simplifying unnecessary procedures. Healthy people use Bluetooth to transmit e-book files to electronic equipment, then Braille e-book automatically recognize files and change them into Braille. After a page's hand sensing touch, the new content will be automatically updated and the needless points in the new page will be hidden.

设计
DESIGN

褚圣洁、沈颖颖、王思凝
Chu Shengjie, Shen Yingying, Wang Sining

雨天骑行听力结构
Rain Riding Listening

这是一款雨天骑行听力保护结构设计，适用于任何雨衣的改良型方案。利用简洁的内部结构处理达成，大雨时收紧面部防止进水的同时耳朵结构自动立起。同时也有效地解决了雨衣的面部收紧时头部的透气问题。

This is a rain riding hearing protection structure designed for any improved program of the raincoat, using the simple internal structure to achieve the effect. When tighten the face in heavy rain to prevent water, the ear structure will automatically erect. Meanwhile the ventilation problem is effectively solved when the raincoat face is tightened.

设计
DESIGN

肖博文、李嘉、孙淑娴
Xiao Bowen, Li Jia, Sun Shuxian

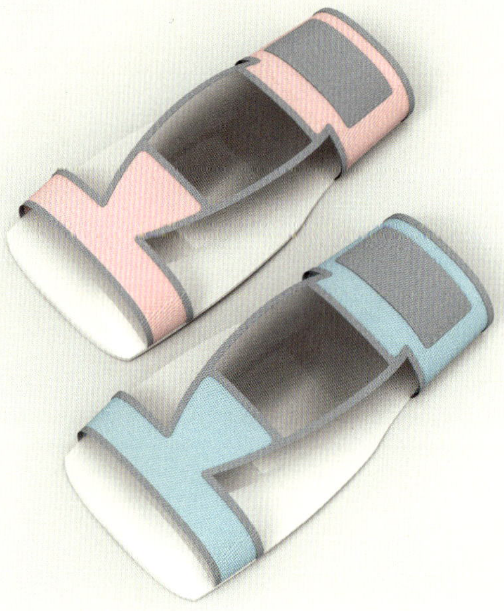

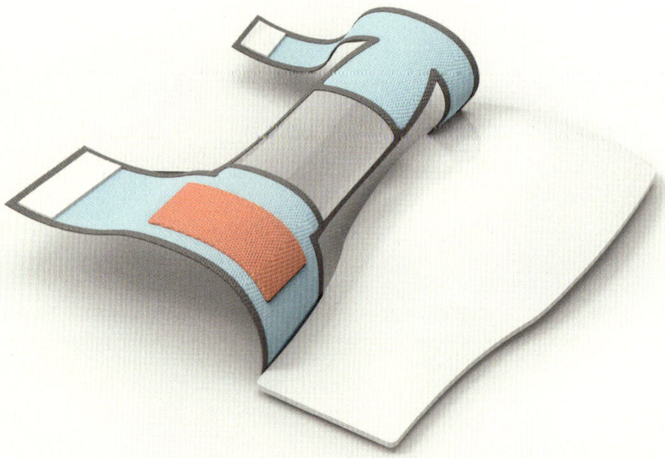

儿童输液加热固定板
Children Infusion Heating Fixed Plate

儿童输液加热固定板专为儿童设计。它由固定板、绑带、加热片组成。固定板设计为适合手部曲线的流线型，使患者在长时间输液的情况下保持舒适。绑带靠近皮肤的一侧可插入加热片，在输液过程中可以持续保持手腕的温度适中。减轻了儿童对输液的恐惧感，解决了儿童在输液中因好动而漏针的问题，缓解了输液药品过凉导致手腕酸疼与输液困难的问题。

Children infusion heating fixed plate is specially designed for children. It consists of a fixed plate, a bandage and heating plate. The fixed plate is designed to fit the streamline of the hand curve, allowing the patient to remain comfortable for extended periods of infusion. The bandage side closing to the skin can be inserted into the heating plate and helps to maintain the proper temperature of the wrist in the infusion process. Children's fear of transfusion is reduced, solving children's dropping stitching problem caused by restless, meanwhile, the wrist pain and transfusion difficulty caused by the cold temperature of infusion drugs.

设计
DESIGN

芦彬、裴雪原、龚诗雨
Lu Bin, Pei Xueyuan, Gong Shiyu

棒棒糖压舌棒
"Lollipop" Spatula

棒棒糖压舌棒解决了传统压舌棒的体验问题。压舌棒的前端由大米粉、小麦粉等原料制作而成，有多种果味选择，在孩子检测口腔时能让孩子尝到甜头，检测完后还可以让孩子带走食用，减缓了传统压舌棒在接触孩子口腔时给其带来冰冷的感受和害怕、抗拒的心理，让孩子就医的过程更加和谐。

Lollipop spatula solves the experience problems of the traditional one, the front part of the spatula is made of raw materials such as wheat flour and rice noodles. With a variety of fruit flavor selection, it can make children taste the sweetness in oral test, after the detection, children are allowed to take it away and eat. It slows down the feeling of cold, fear and resist psychological process that the traditional spatula brings when contacting with children's mouth, all these make children's process of seeing a doctor more harmonious.

设计
DESIGN

晏阳震
Yan Yangzhen

无限调色板
Unlimited Palette

这是一款方便清洁的调色板。在绘画时，清洗调色板是让人最头痛的一件事。画师要浪费大量的时间在清洗调色板上，且洗完回来时画意全无。油彩、丙烯等颜料要浪费大量的水资源才能清洗干净，尤其是在户外写生时，就更不方便了。而无限调色板，表面是由很多层透明薄膜组成，当需要清洁调色板时，只需要撕掉一层薄膜即可。便捷、高效、环保、节水。

This is a palette that is easy to clean. In painting, cleaning the palette is one of the biggest headache things. The artist will waste a lot of time in cleaning the palette, when he comes back after cleaning, he always don't want to paint any more. Painting, acrylic and other pigments usually waste a lot of water resources to clean, it is inconvenient especially in outdoor sketching. The surface of the infinite palette is composed of multi-layer transparent film. When you need to clean the palette, you only need to tear off a layer of film. It is convenient, efficient, environmental protection and water saving.

设计
DESIGN

蔺薛菲、范石钟
Lin Xuefei, Fan Shizhong

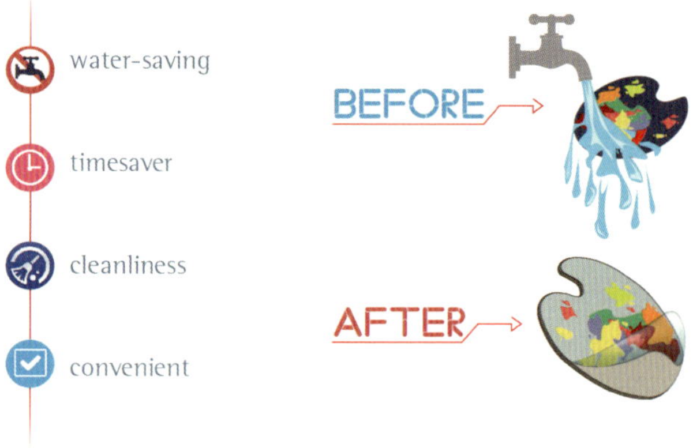

应急灾难门把手
Disaster Emergency Door Handle

灾害应急门把手是为灾害逃生而设计的应急物品。大门是人们逃生时的必然出口，该设计将应急包与门把手相结合。将门把手分为四个部分分别装有灾难中生存的必要物品。在人们逃生的关键时刻，不必再去花费时间翻找应急物品，浪费逃生时间。只要灾害一发生，就直接奔向逃生出口。在打开大门的瞬间，只需要 1 秒钟，轻轻往上一抬把手上带有明显标示的部分，就可快速将其卸下。带上应急物品快速逃生将灾害带给人们的伤害减少到最低。

The emergency door handle is an emergency article designed for disaster escape, and the gate is the necessary exit for people to escape. The design combines the emergency kit with the door handle. The door handle is divided into four parts, each containing the necessary items for survival in disaster. At the crucial moment of escaping, people do not have to spend time looking for emergency supplies. As soon as the disaster happens, they just go straight to the escape exit. When you open the door, it takes only 1 second to gently lift up the clearly visible part of the handle, it will be unload quickly. Bring emergency supplies to escape quickly can minimize the damage to people.

设计
DESIGN

张宏珅
Zhang Hongshen

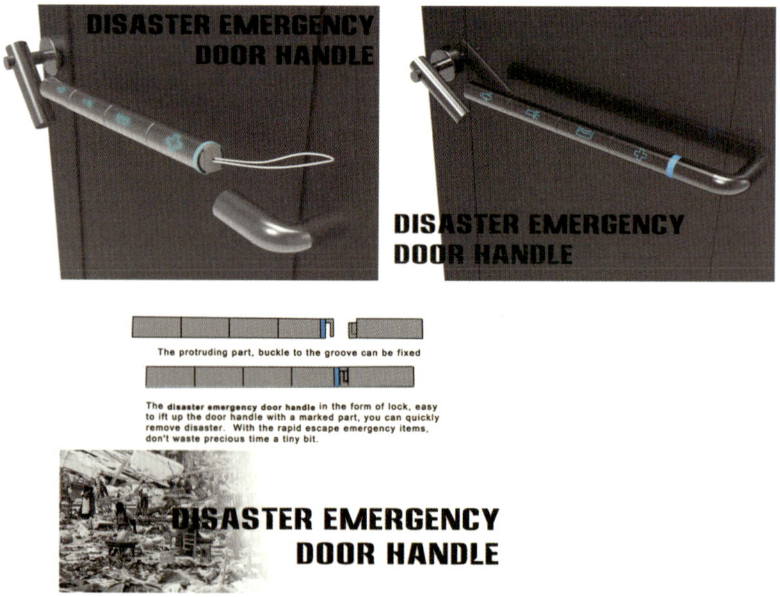

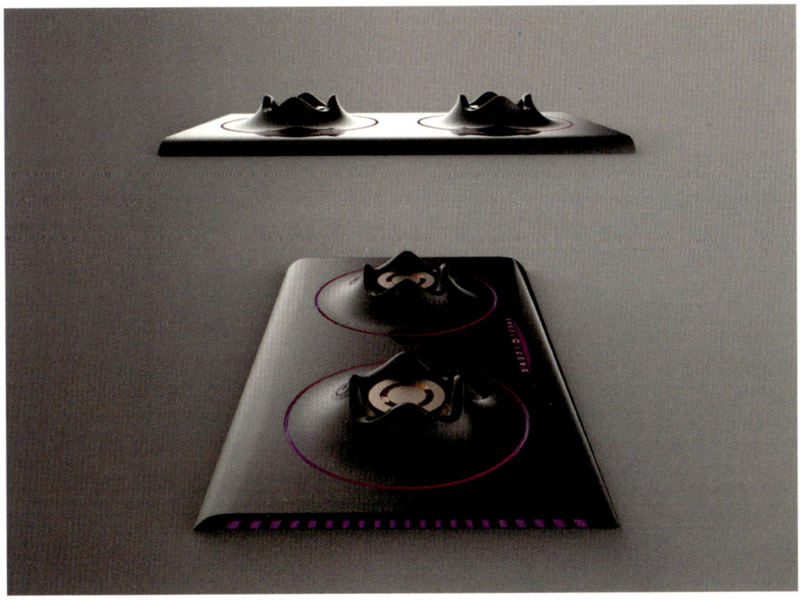

空气盒子燃气灶
AIRBOX GAS STOVES

空气盒子燃气灶灵感来源于传统燃气灶“油烟杀手”的痛点；它通过创造性地结合空气放大器技术，为燃气灶周围吹出一道风墙，从而有效隔绝炒菜时产生的油烟与热量，给家人带来健康与舒适的厨房体验。通过空气盒子燃气灶创新的空气放大器技术，向人们展示全新的健康厨房理念，运用富有责任心的创新理念赋能健康厨房。

The innovation of air box is inspired by pain points of "smoke killer" of traditional gas stove; through the creative combination of air amplifier technology, it blows out a wall for gas stove, thus effectively isolating the smoke and heat generated when cooking to bring your family healthy and comfortable kitchen experience. Through the innovative air amplifier technology of air box gas stoves, it shows people a new healthy kitchen concept, and the use of a responsible innovative idea makes kitchen healthy.

设计
DESIGN

黎泽锋
Li ZeFeng

即抛型注射器
Disposable Syringe

这款注射器设计为一次性使用型，杜绝了二次利用。工作原理是：针管中置有弹性橡胶组件，当药液被推出针管，橡胶组件回弹从而抵住活塞。多家媒体已披露了由注射器供应商引起的注射器二次使用案例，这款注射器可防止这些事件导致的不必要的医疗事故。

The syringe is designed to be disposable and eliminates the possible of a secondary use. The working principle is: there are elastic rubber components inside the needle, when the liquid medicine is introduced from needle, rubber components rebound to resist the piston. Several media outlets have disclosed the secondary use cases of syringes caused by syringes suppliers. This syringe can prevent unnecessary medical accidents from these medical malpractices.

设计
DESIGN

合肥鼎典工业设计有限公司
Hefei Designdo Industrial Design Co.,Ltd

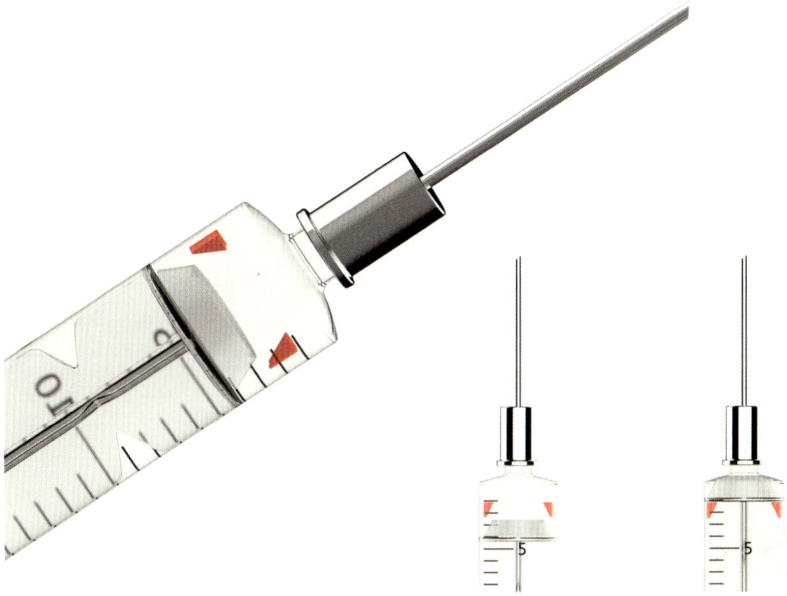

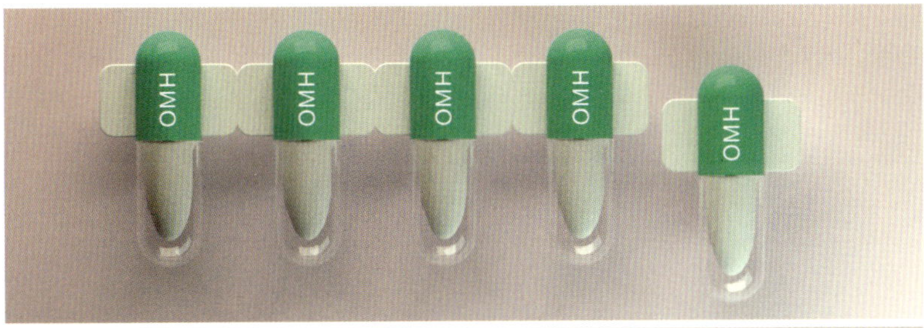

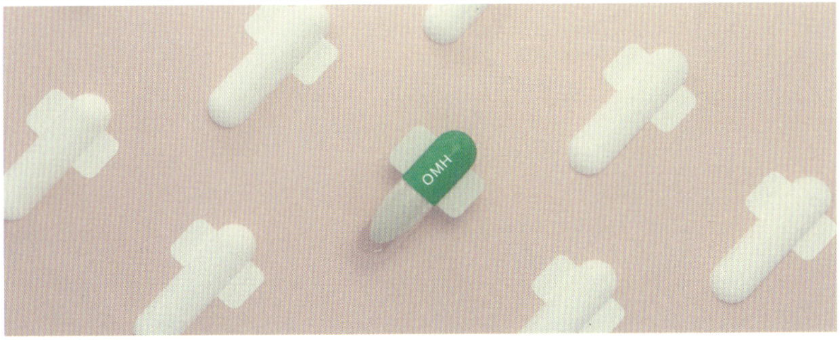

便携药丸棉
Portable Capsule Absorbent Cotton

这是一款方便卫生的棉签。生活中人们常用棉签去蘸取酒精，既不方便也不卫生，棉签的形态也不美观。这款棉签设计将酒精与消毒棉一体化，使用时只需轻轻按压，非常方便、卫生。药丸的形态设计，符合人们对医疗用品的形态认知，且不失美观。

This is a convenient and sanitary cotton swab. People often use cotton swabs to dip alcohol in ordinary life, which is neither convenient nor sanitary, and the form of cotton swabs is not pretty. The cotton swab is designed to combine alcohol with sterile cotton together. It only needs to be gently pressed when used. It is very convenient and sanitary. The form design of the pill conforms to the people's cognition of the form of the medical articles and does not lose its beauty.

设计
DESIGN

胡焱华
Hu YanHua

易用汤锅
Easy to Use Pot

这款汤锅整体采用六边形的造型设计，使汤锅从此易于倾倒食物，以及能轻松实现烹饪时的排气。此汤锅解决了用户在使用汤锅过程中的两大难题，没有增加任何成本，且外观造型美观、时尚，做到了功能与形式之间的统一。

The overall design of the pot is hexagonal, which makes the pot easy to pour food, and the exhaust can be easily achieved during cooking. This pot solves two major problems in the use, without any increase in cost, and the appearance is beautiful and fashion, achieving the unity between form and function.

设计
DESIGN

周鹏
Zhou Peng

雪地取水杯
Snowfield Collected Water Cup

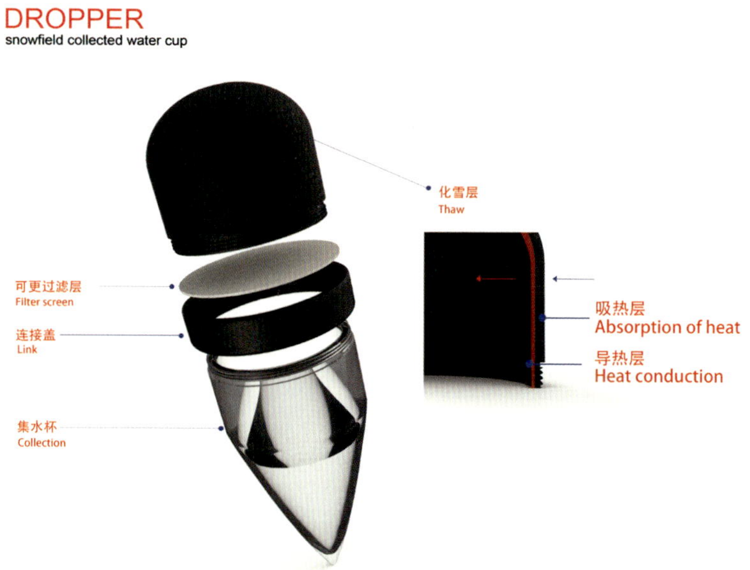

该设计为一款方便雪中取水的容器。整体采用食品级材料制造。瓶身为滴管型，方便登山者使用。运用黑色易吸热的物理原理，吸收雪地中的日照光线，加速雪球融化，通过瓶中可更换过滤层，去除水中杂质，即可安心饮用。并解决了登山爱好、雪地长时间工作者的饮水问题。

The product is a convenient design for extracting water from the snow. The whole product uses food-grade material, and the body of the bottle is dropper shape,convenient for the climers to use, By applying the physical principle that black absorbs heat more easily, the sunlight can be easily absorbed in the snow to accelerate the melting of snow. By changing bottle's filter, the impurities in water can be removed and you can feel free to drink the water. The product solves the problem of drinking water for climbing enthusiasts, workers who work in snow for a long time.

设计
DESIGN

何璐君
He Lujun

便携加热奶瓶
Heating Bottle

便携加热奶瓶是一个带有加热功能、适合便携使用的奶瓶。
带孩子出门，如何泡一杯温度适宜的奶一直是妈妈们最头疼的事。便携加热奶瓶的底部具有一个加热模块，且可以实时显示瓶内液体的温度。只需往奶瓶里加入纯净水，通过奶瓶加热到适合的温度，再倒入奶粉，一杯温度适宜的奶就冲泡好了。同时还具有一键保温功能。

Heating bottle is a bottle with heating function and is easy to carry.How to make a bottle of milk with appropriate temperature is always a hard issue for moms.
It comes with a heating module at the bottom, with that, the temperature of the liquid inside can also be displayed in a real-time. Just adding pure water into the bottle, the bottle will hea t the water to the appropriate temperature. Then pour in milk powder, a cup of milk with proper temperature is well brewed. The product also has the function of one-key heat preservation.

设计
DESIGN

厦门伊亚创新科技有限公司
Xiamen Yeeya Innovations Science and Technology Co., Ltd.

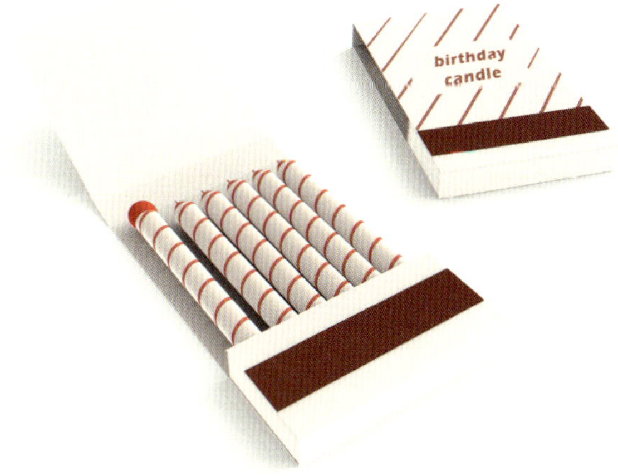

便捷生日蜡烛
Convenient Candles

这是一个便捷生日蜡烛的设计。每当过生日需要点蜡烛时，总是会苦恼找不到打火机。为了方便生日蜡烛的使用，所以将火柴的点火方式运用在生日蜡烛的设计上，利用蜡烛顶部的红磷与包装上的擦纸摩擦点燃蜡烛。该设计作品生产成本低廉，使用起来也更加环保。

The design makes it more convenient to light birthday candles. People always have the worry of finding out lighters when they need to ignite candles during birthday. In order to facilitate the use of birthday candles, the ignition method of the match is used in the design of birthday candles. The candle can be lit by rubbing the red phosphorus at the top of the candle and the abrasive paper on the package at the same time. This design has the advantage of simple process, low cost, and is more environmentally friendly to use.

设计
DESIGN

张田田、冉然
Zhang Tiantian, Ran Ran

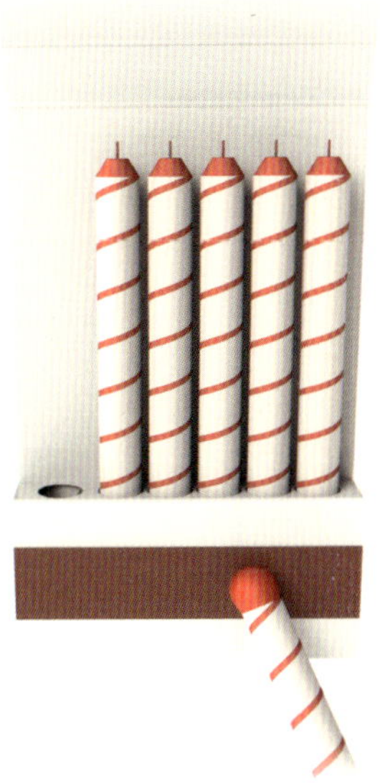

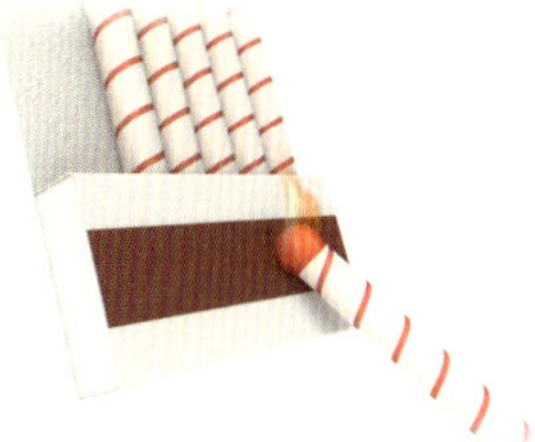

会呼吸的盲人记事本
Breathing Notepad

这是一款专门为盲人而设计的即时记事本。盲人在工作或日常生活中遇到需要记录信息的时候，通过按压“会呼吸的记事本”上的触点来记录想要保留的信息，用力按压“会呼吸的记事本”的两侧，触点通过空气的挤压恢复原状，从而能反复使用。

Breathing notepad is a notebook designed for the blind. During daily work or life, anytime the blind need to record information they can press the touch spots to keep records. The notepad can be used repeatedly. Just press both sides to discharge air, and the touch spots will be restored.

设计
DESIGN

何维翰、黎卓颖
He Weihan, Li Zhuoying

折叠式浴缸
The Folding Bathtub

这是一款利用折纸原理设计的折叠浴缸。平整的纸张折叠成立体的造型本就是一个奇妙的过程，可折叠的浴缸更是改变了现有家庭浴缸的稳定固有的感觉，利用三维与二维的不停转换，新奇而灵活。当展开完成时，它是一个舒适且弥漫着怀旧风情的浴缸，当使用过后它可转变为一个小巧的提包，充满乐趣还可以解决收纳问题，节省 20% 的空间。

The bathtub is designed in the use of origami principle. Folding the smooth paper into three-dimensional shapes is a wonderful process, and afoldable bathtub is to change the existing family bathtub stability and inherent feeling. The use of three-dimensional and two-dimensional continuous conversion is novel and flexible. When folded, it is a small, thick square paper bag, and when the expansion is completed, it is a bathtub which is comfortable and full of nostalgia. After using, it becomes a small bag which is interesting and also can help collect, saving 20%space.

设计
DESIGN

徐志刚、胡艺、高波
Xu Zhigang, Hu Yi, Gao Bo

定向激光尺
Directional Laser Ruler

这款设计解决了在大幅图纸作图时尺子太短，无法轻易确定两条直线的相互关系的问题。此直尺与激光笔结合，它延伸了尺子的功能界限，并使得两条线之间的关系视觉化，进而帮助使用者更好地运用自己的经验。增强了设计者在进行创造性思维时的流畅性，它也可作为激光笔使用。

When we are drawing large drawings, sometimes ruler is too short to easily determining the relationship
between the two straight lines. But the directional laser ruler solves the problem. The combination of ruler with a laser
pen extends the functional boundaries of the ruler and
makes the relationship between the two lines visualization
and thus help users to better use their own experience. It also enhances the users' fluency when they conduct innovation thinking. It can also be used as a laser pen.

设计
DESIGN

齐群波、王征、王永东
Qi Qunbo,Wang Zheng,Wang Yongdong

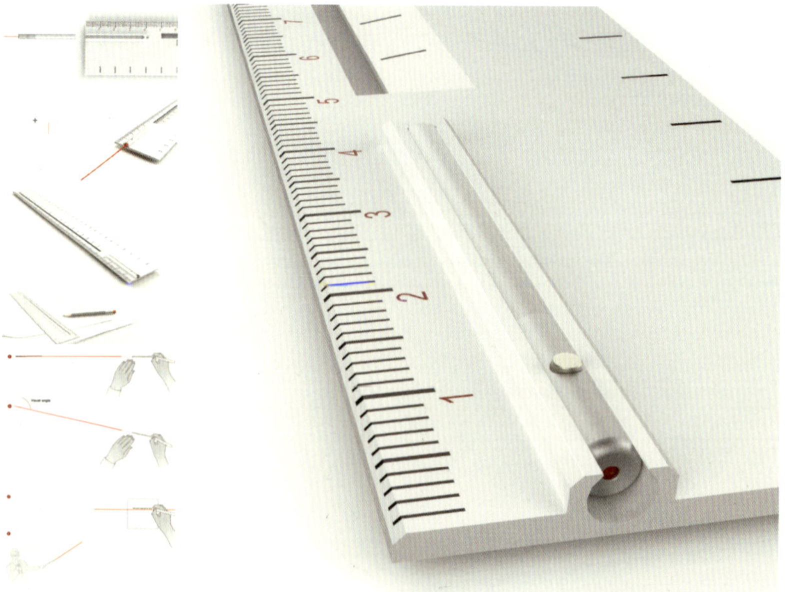

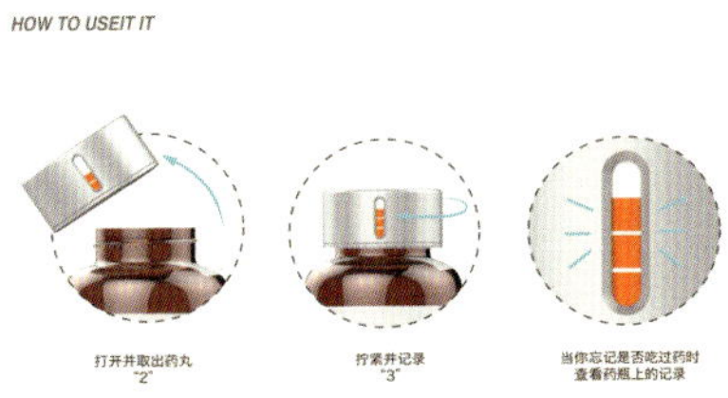

Don't Forget——直观记录的药瓶
Don't Forget — A Visual Record of Medicine Bottle

这款药瓶设计帮助病人记录吃药次数。许多慢性病患者或需要长期服药的人群一天要多次服药，他们经常会忘记自己在这一天中是否已经服过药或者已经服过几次药，导致用药不足或重复服药。"直观记录的药瓶"采用最简单的方式并且不增加任何多余步骤——每次吃药打开盖子后拧紧，盖子就会记录你的用药次数。用户完成当天用药次数，第二天再次使用时，药瓶将重新开始记录。

The design helps patients to record times of medicine taking. Many patients with chronic illness or people who need long-term medication have to take the medicine many times a day, and they often forget whether they have taken medicine or how many times they already taken pills, which results in insufficient medication or repeated medication. A visual record of medicine bottle takes the simplest way and not to add any additional steps (only the process of opening the lid and taking the medicine), which can record the times of taking medicine. The lid will record your medication times when you take medicine, open the lid and screw it down at a time. When the user completes the medication times on that day and reuses it in next day, the medicine bottle will start to record again.

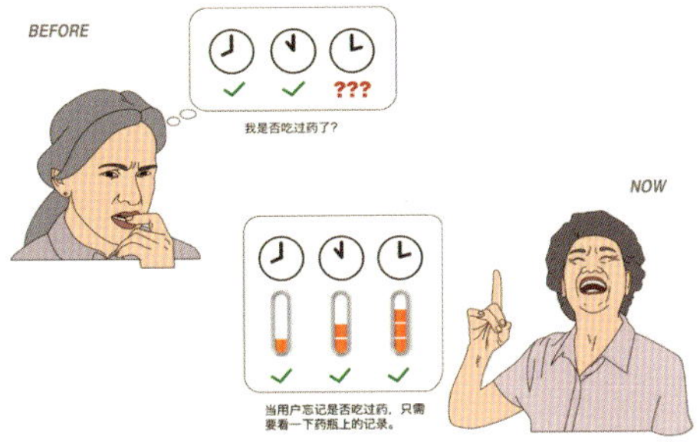

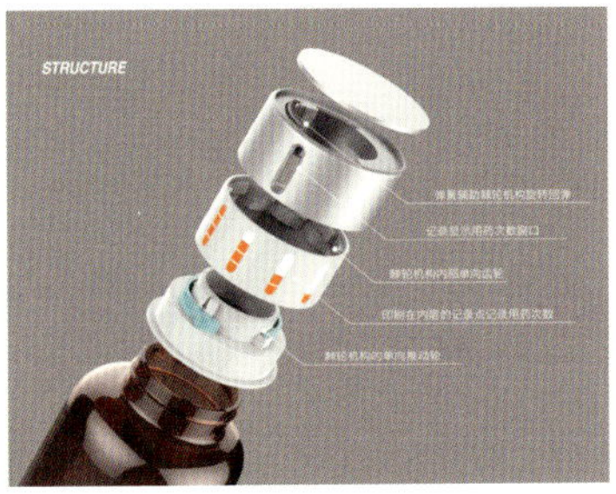

设计
DESIGN

麦培珊、竹科英
Mai Peishan,Zhu Keying

易清洁地漏
Fish-Clean

这款地漏设计从鱼骨造型中获取灵感，重新设计后使得原本困难、不卫生的清理工作变得简单便捷。避免了手部和肮脏的残留物接触带来的卫生隐患，只需用水冲洗即可清洗掉残留物。通过对生活细节的观察用简单有趣的方式解决生活中的不便，帮助人们提高生活质量的同时带来不经意的感动。

For [Fish-clean],the inspiration is obtained from the fishbone modeling.The originally difficult and insanitary cleanup work becomes easy and simple after redesign. As a result,hidden sanitary trouble brough by the dirty residues that the hand contacts is avoided.The residus can be rinsed with clean water. Through observation of the details of life,the inconvenience in life is solved through simple and interesting ways. People are casually moved while given the assistance to improve their living standard.

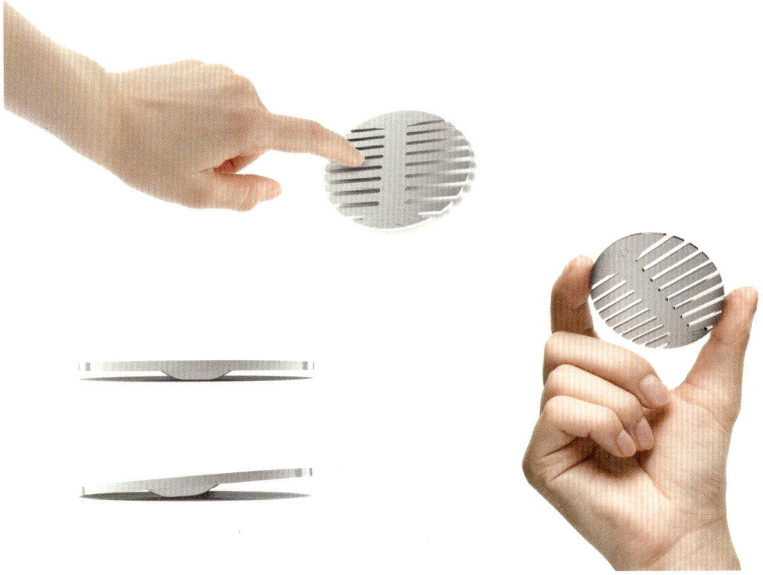

设计
DESIGN

李志强、鲁盛溧
Li Zhiqiang, Lu Shengli

山水之境
Habitat Landscape

山水之境这款水龙头利用了光线的折射效应。让水龙头流出来的水通过光线的折射，把水龙头的整体变得犹如一幅活山水画。山在水中游，山随水动。让使用者在山水动静之间，享受雨过色新的意境之美。山水之境，是一种美妙的物理效果，是一种若隐若现的山水之境。

The faucet uses the refraction effect of light. Using the refraction of the light, water coming from faucet turns into a live waters- and- mountains painting."The mountain seems to swim on the water, with the water moved surrounding the mountain". It is believed that it can allow the users enjoy the beauty of landscape with stable mountain and moving river. Habitat landscape is a wonderful physical effect as well as gleaming water and muntain scene.

设计
DESIGN

杨朝生、黄依琪、刘奕祈
Yang Chaosheng, Huang Yiqi, Liu Yiqi

“可撕”移植花盆
"Can Tear"Flowerports

“可撕”移植花盆是一款方便植物移植的纸质环保器皿，解决了人们在移植植物时会不小心把泥土散落或对植物本身的伤害。“可撕”花盆利用废纸压制而成，其外形仿照树的造型，更接近大自然，树枝处是为了方便拉伸花盆而设计。在移植植物时可以直接进行种植，不需要再把植物从花盆中移出，可在园林中大量使用。

Can-Tear Flowerports is an environmentally friendly paper pot convenient to plant transplant. When people transplanted plants,they often inadvertently scattered soil or hurt the plants. "Can Tear" flower ports are made of wast paper，their shapes are modelled after trees, which make them closer to the nature and the branches are designed to facilitate the stretching of flowerpots.Using the flowerport can be planted directly when transplanting plants, do not need to remove the plant from the port. Besides, this kind of port can widely use in garden.

设计
DESIGN

罗简妹
Luo Jianmei

竹篓木马
Bamboo Basket Horse

“竹篓木马”是将竹篓与木马结合的儿童玩具，赋予竹篓新的功能，当竹篓倒过来放时能成为一个竹木马。该设计作品希望可以帮助那些生活条件艰苦，从小无法像城市孩子一样享受优越成长条件的山区儿童，让他们享受快乐。该设计依托每个农村家庭的生活必需品——竹篓进行再设计，利用竹编工艺支撑起整个结构，具有强韧的特性，承受重物时平稳且不易变形。

The product is the combination of bamboo basket and wooden horse. When you turn the bamboo basket upside down, you get yourself a bamboo horse for kids to sit on to play and have fun. Life of children in mountainous areas is very tough; they don't have enough toys and can't enjoy the superior growing condition as the children in cities. We are aimed at letting the children in mountainous areas to entertainment themselves by the local materials and use the lowest cost to help them grow up happily.The whole framework is made by bamboo basketry, which makes it strong and malleable to carry heavy things smoothly and ametabolic.

设计
DESIGN

杨磊、林思安、李承勇
Yang Lei, Lin Sian, Li Chengyong

内窥镜手柄
Endoscope Handle

这是一款为医务工作者带来便利的内窥镜手柄。解决医生使用内窥镜长时间抬起手臂从而犯肩周炎的问题。普通市场上一个内窥镜重量约大半瓶水。这款新设计的手柄是让医生手臂尽可能保持自然下垂，这样可以减少肩膀的损伤，考虑了手臂的和全身的人机工程。

This endoscope handle will bring convenience for medical personnel. As before, the physicians need to keep their arms uplifted for a long time when using the endoscope. Long-term usage makes the physician vulnerable to scapulohumeral periarthritis.This design makes the users maintain natural status and makes their arms keep drooping as far as possible, meanwhile the ergonomics of the palm is complied as well.

设计
DESIGN

王秋波
Wang Qiubo

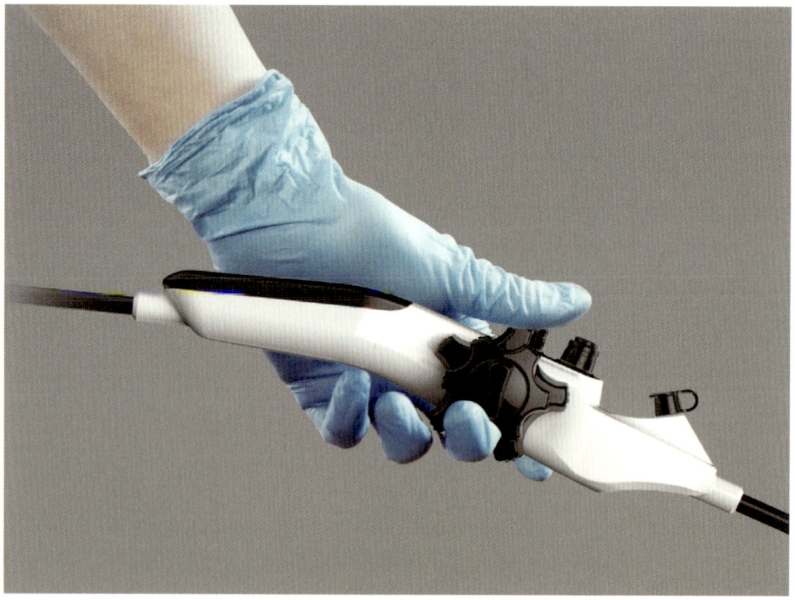

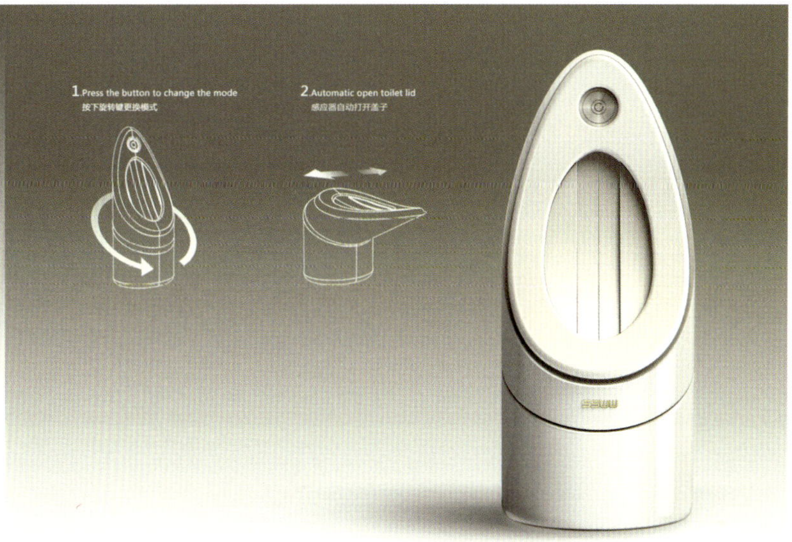

空间旋转式坐便器
Rotary Pedestal Pan

空间旋转式概念坐便器巧妙地运用浴室空间，能实现坐便器的空间收纳，同时拥有小便尿兜与坐便器两种模式的转换。满足了随着社会人口的增长、土地的缺乏，空间的使用也越来越讲究的趋势。

The rotary pedestal made use of bathroom space subtly to realize the space admission of the toilet. At the same time, urine pocket and toilet will obtain two modes of conversion. The design conform to the trend of exquisite use of space with the growing population and scarce land.

设计
DESIGN

陈志刚
Chen Zhigang

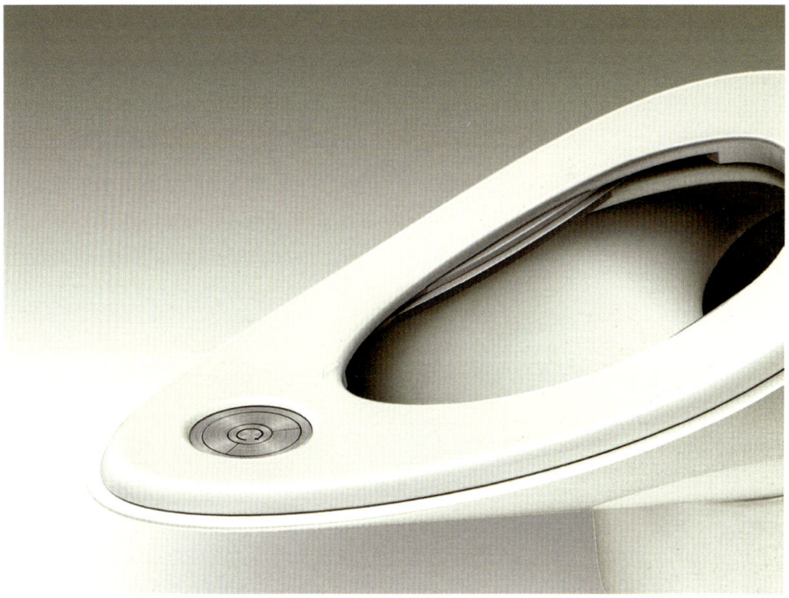

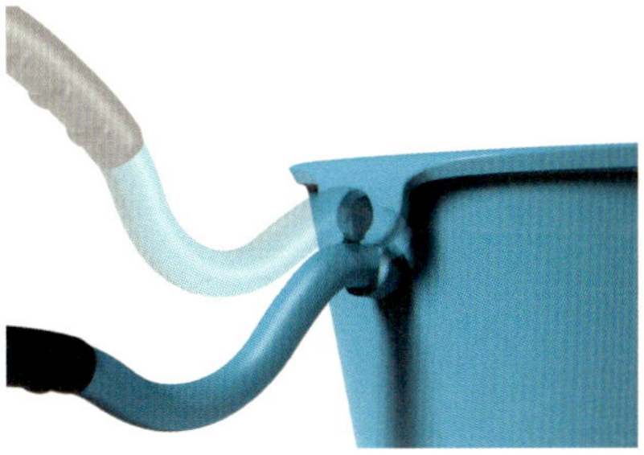

更方便的水桶
User-Friendly Bucket

这款设计巧妙将水桶与接水管合二为一。当人们在较高的洗水槽接水往往需要另外准备水管引流到水桶之中，该设计将水桶柄改为橡胶软管，软管的两端为坚硬的橡胶制成，其榫卯连接桶身。需要接水时，只需轻叩末端取下水管头弯曲连接水龙头便可接水，接满水后将软管叩回原处，即可转变成水桶柄将满桶水拎起。水桶柄巧妙的改变，方便了生活。

The design combines bucket with water tube wisely. The design changes the bucket handle into rubber tube, with its both ends made of hard rubber and connected with the bucket body through tenon and mortise joint. When people need to take water, they only have to knock at the ends of the handle slightly, remove the handle and bend it to drain water from the tap. When the bucket is full, the tube could be easily put into original place and turned back into the handle to carry the bucket. The clever design of the handle facilitates daily life.

设计
DESIGN

纪建宇、袁通、夏松杰
Ji Jianyu, Yuan Tong, Xia Songjie

与扇书台灯
Fantern

与扇书台灯是一款将折扇的造型和功能运用到人与灯光交互中的产品。双层圆形风车折扇扇面之间是光源灯体，人可以根据需求将扇面打开到不同角度从而调节亮度。灯光开启时，不论如何放置，其光影都会依灯与墙面的距离的远近，扇面打开的角度的大小，把扇骨的曲线和扇面的朦胧，叠射出不同层次的光影质感。产品既实现了人与灯之间新颖的交互方式，又能在光影变幻中传达出扇古朴柔美的文化属性。

Fantern is a people-lamp interactive product applying both the shape and function of curved fan. The light source body lies in double-decked circular windmill fan between the fan. According to the needs, fan can be opened to different angles to adjust the brightness. When the light is turned on, no matter how it is placed, its light and shadow will follow the distance between the lamp and the wall. The size of the fan opening angle reflects the fan curve and the fan surface of the hazy, stacked different levels of light and shadow texture. The product achieves a new way of interaction between people and lights, but also in the light and shadow changes in the fan to convey the ancient cultural attributes.

设计
DESIGN

郭雅文
Guo Yawen

成长——两用椅子
Dual-Purpose Chairs

儿童成长过快导致其相关产品寿命缩短，造成资源浪费。传统儿童餐椅受结构和尺寸限制功能单一，使用期短。为解决这一问题，成长椅将儿童餐椅设计成双种用途的椅子，通过翻转正面和反面实现两种功能，一端是儿童餐椅，另一端是成人椅子。椅子的整个框架可以采用木材或竹子材料，并与编制的麻纤维结合使用。

The rapid growth of children leads to the shortening of related product life and the waste of resources. Traditional children's dining chair is limited in structure and size and has a short life. In order to solve the problem, the chair is designed as a dual purpose chair for the children's dining chair. The two functions are realized by flipping the front and the back, one is the children's dining chair and the other is the adult chair. The entire frame of the chair can be made of wood or bamboo material and is used in combination with the preparation of hemp fiber.

设计
DESIGN

辽宁石油化工大学
Liaoning Shihua University

布袋边几
Cloth-Bag Side Table

这是一款有收纳功能的边几。它日常状态下就像套着桌布的静谧优雅的小桌，可呈现摆放在它上面的物品。当需要收纳放置，只需要将物品放在边几台面上，然后抓着桌布两边的提手向上一拉，此时桌布变成了一个可收纳物品的布袋子。这个设计更强调的是桌布转变为袋子那一瞬间传递的惊喜感，以及边几功能状态的转变。

This side table has storage function. It is like a quiet and elegant table with a tablecloth in daily life, and the objects are placed on it. When you need to gather and store something, just place them on the side-table tablecloth, and then pull up the handle of the tablecloth on both sides. Then you will find in surprise the tablecloth turns into a cloth bag that can contain goods. The design much more emphasizes instant feeling of surprise when the tablecloth turns into a bag and the transformation of functional status of side table.

设计
DESIGN

罗家杰
Luo JiaJie

随行智能吹风机
Accompany Smart Hair Dryer

为解决目前的吹风机噪音大、不够智能、不够便携、收纳不便、线的杂乱缠绕等困扰，设计者对吹风机做了全新的设计，收纳后它是一个完整的极简造型，电源线隐藏在手柄处，使用时只需将手柄旋转 180 度，将插头从手柄处分离，便可体验一次智能舒适的吹发体验。机身加入新型吸音材料，磁悬浮式电子马达，达到静音模式；吹风机同时搭载芯片微处理器，连接 APP 可检测监测发质与头发健康。

The designer made a new design of the hair dryer to solve the problems lying in the current product for it has loud noise and it is less intelligent, less portable and inconvenient in storage due to the tangled wire. After rearrangement, it is an integrated and much simpler shape. The wire is hidden inside the handle part and while using, you just need to rotate the handle to 180 degree and separate the plug from the handle and then you can enjoy a smart and cozy hair drying experience. The body part takes new acoustic material and magnetic electric motor to realize silent mode. With the assistance of the built-in microprocessor chip, it can connect with the App to help you to monitor hair quality and the health of scalp.

设计
DESIGN

范民轩
Fan Minxuan

落叶归根——生态环保护树池
Re-Leaf

落叶归根——生态环保护树池针对落叶而设计，为落叶提供了一个腐化空间，便于落叶和雨水充分接触进行腐化，从而变成自然肥料，供给树木养分。同时，这款设计采用了模块化的组合方式，通过将整个树池的 1/4 作为单元模块进行圆周阵列形成了最后的护树池，这个设计形态支持多种材料，便于生产和实际应用。

Fallen leaves return to the roots. The ecological tree pool is designed for fallen leaves by providing a rotten space to make fallen leaves have a better contact with rainwater so as to become natural fertilizer to provide nutrition for trees. At the mean time, this design adopted modularized way of combination, setting a quarter of the tree pool as a unit module to make circular pattern to form the final tree pool. This design shape supports varieties materials which is convenient to production and actual use.

设计
DESIGN

薛文凯、孙健、杜鹤菈
Xue Wenkai, Sun Jian, Du Heli

多功能婴儿椅
Dual-Purpose Chair

这是一款多功能用椅。当一个家庭迎来一个新生儿的时候，为了方便，会买一个婴儿椅。但是随着婴儿慢慢长大，婴儿椅失去了它的使用价值。两用椅可以同时给大人和婴儿使用。它有更广的使用范围和更长的使用周期。它不仅是给椅子增加了一个新的功能，还传递了一种保护环境的精神。

This is a multi-functional chair. When a family has a newborn, they will buy a baby chair for convenience. But as the baby grows up, the baby chair loses its value in use. The dual-purpose chair can be used by both adults and infants. It has a wide range of application and a longer life cycle. It not only adds a new function to the chair, but also conveys a spirit of environmental protection.

设计
DESIGN

北京极智创新设计
JZCX Design

输液安全系统
Guarded

输液安全系统主要解决用户在输液时不能及时注意到输液袋中的情况所造成的血液回流，以及输液的紧张感，医护不及时换液等问题。在输液袋或输液瓶口放置输液安全系统，运用非接触式光电探测技术，感测输液袋或输液瓶中是否有水，将信息显示在护士台的显示面板中，形成一套体系，做到实时汇报输液情况，让护士准确了解输液情况，减轻工作压力。

The infusion security system mainly solves problems like blood return in infusing for users cannot notice the infusion bag in time, the feeling of tension while infusing and the delayed change of medicine of medical staffs. By setting infusion security system on the infusion bag or the bottle of infusion, using the non-contact photoelectric detection technology to detect whether there is water in the infusion bag or infusion bottle and display the information on the display panel of nurse' s workstation, it forms a set of system to report the infusion situation on time and let the nurse know the situation precisely so as to release the working stress.

设计
DESIGN

张献哲、王娟娟
Zhang Xianzhe, Wang Juanjuan

车窗安全锤
Rescue More

这是一个巴士安全锤的改良设计，它能够同时击碎两块玻璃窗，目的是能够让车内的人在最短的时间内开放更多的逃生出口，让更多的人能够逃生而不用争抢。它比起普通的安全锤操作更简单和省力，利用弹簧的反向弹力击碎玻璃，两端各设有钢钉，当遇到紧急情况时，车内乘客先将其拉出，旋转 90 度后迅速松手，就可以通过回弹力击碎两面玻璃窗。让前后的乘客都可以更加快速有效地逃生而不用争抢，体现出一种互救的精神。

This is a improved design of bus emergency hammer which can break two pieces of glasses at the same time. It aims at being able to let people inside the bus open more exits in the shortest time and let more people escape without scrambling. Compared with common emergency hammer, it is easier and needs less strength to operate. It takes use of the reverse elastic force of the spring to break the glass. The two sides are set with steel nails, when emergency situation happens, the passengers in the bus can pull it out, rotate it to 90°and then loosen hands immediately to break the two pieces of glasses by elastic force. This enables the passengers to escape more quickly and efficiently without scrambling, reflecting a spirit of mutual-aid.

设计
DESIGN

杨磊、李承勇、林思安
Yang Lei, Li Chengyong, Lin Sian

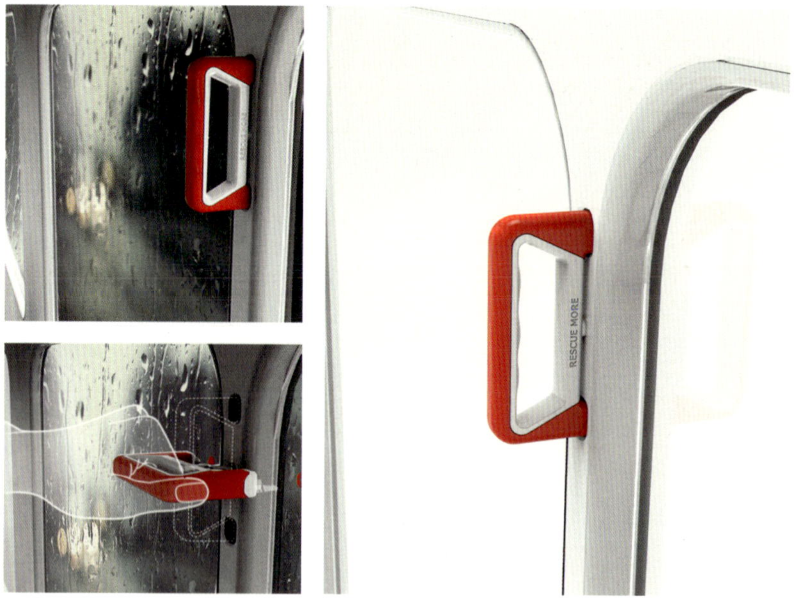

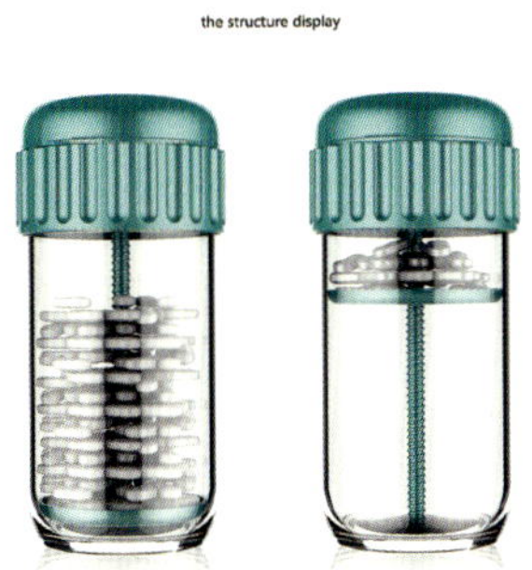

可升降易拿取保健品包装
Packaging Bottle with Rotatory Part for Ease Access of Tablets or Capsules

这款药瓶设计解决了传统的丸剂或胶囊包装常常会导致人们不小心倒出好多颗，从而再次装入瓶中导致原来瓶中的丸剂或胶囊可能会有卫生隐患的问题。通过全新的结构设计，在瓶中增加了一个旋转上升的空间，当需要服用丸剂或胶囊时，旋转瓶盖位置，即可将装药片的空间提升，这样无论瓶内还有多少丸剂或胶囊，都可以从顶部直接拿取，方便卫生。

People often pour out more tablets than they need by accident due to the traditional package of tablet or capsule, therefore the extra tablets or capsules maybe contaminated and cause some sanitation problems. This design of medicine solved this problem by a brand new design structure. It adds a rolling-up space and when taking tablets or capsules, you just need to turn the bottle cap to increase the space of tablets. Therefore, no matter how many tablets or capsules left, you can take from the top directly which is convenient and sanitary.

设计
DESIGN

无限极（中国）有限公司
Infinitus(China)Company LTD

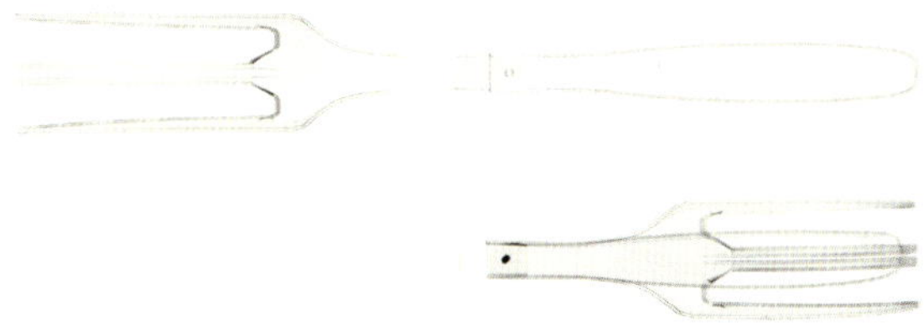

方便挤出酱料的叉子
Fork for Squeezing Sauce

吃泡面的时候，酱料包很难全部挤出，并且酱料经常会不小心蹭到手上。“方便挤出酱料的叉子”将叉子中间的两个叉齿的间距缩小，因此当酱料包穿过较小的缝隙时，酱料可以轻松又干净地被挤出来，避免了浪费，防止手上蹭上酱料，从而解决挤出酱料不方便、不彻底的问题。

When we are eating instant noodles, it is hard to squeeze completely all the sauce which always rubs against our hands. Fork for squeezing sauce shortens the distance between prongs in the middle. So you can squeeze the sauce between the narrow prongs, which avoid direct contact with hands and unnecessary waste. It completely solves the problem of extruding the sauce inconveniently and unthoroughly.

设计
DESIGN

黄龙跃
Huang Longyue

能够洗手的水龙头开关
The Faucet Switch

针对厨房洗手的二次污染，去除手上油污和异味的问题。洗手水龙头开关的设计将普通的厨房水龙头旋钮改造成可分离的肥皂，通过特殊打磨的不锈钢材料的磨砂表面与物体摩擦，释放出来的铁离子跟异味分子结合达到祛味的效果。洗手水龙头开关在洗手的同时也对开关旋钮进行了清洁，很好地解决了洗手过程中的二次污染问题，也免去了肥皂的使用，减少对资源的消耗。

Aiming to solve the secondary pollution of washing hands in the kitchen and the removal of oil stain and odor, the design of the faucet switch changes the knob of the common faucet into the separable soap. It makes the frosted surface with special polished stainless steel materials to rub against the objects, so the released iron ion will be combined with odor molecule so as to remove the odor. While washing hands, the switch knob is also cleaned by the faucet switch, which better solves the secondary pollution problem in the process of washing and also eliminates the use of soap to reduce the resource consumption.

设计
DESIGN

黄立清、张仲伟
Huang Liqing, Zhang Zhongwei

Freedom 水龙头
Freedom Faucet

Freedom 水龙头的设计解决了现有公共空间水龙头的 “点”状分布，参考长凳的设计，将现有水龙头设计从 “点” 变为 “线”。该水龙头下方有红外感应区，其前部有一排出水口。只需将手放在下方的感应区域，水就会从对应位置的出口流出。解决了公共卫生空间拥堵问题，减少排队时间，提高效率和用户体验。设计采用不锈钢材料，成本与现有龙头差异不大，水龙头感应方式比较卫生，且体验更有科技感，总体来看，值得推广使用，是一款非常好的设计。

The design of Freedom faucet solved the spotty distribution of the faucets in current public space. Referring to the design of bench, the faucet is designed from "point" to "line". There is an area of infrared sensors beneath the faucet and its front has a row of outlet. Users can put hands in the infrared sensing zone to make the water flow down. It solved the problem of crowd situation in public space, reduced the queue up time and improves efficiency and user's experience. The design takes stainless steel material which cost merely the same as the current product. The sensory is more sanitary and the sense of technology is more impressive. In an overall view, it is a good product that worth using widely.

设计
DESIGN

傅娇娇、董石羽、李然
Fu Jiaojiao, Dong Shiyu, Li Ran

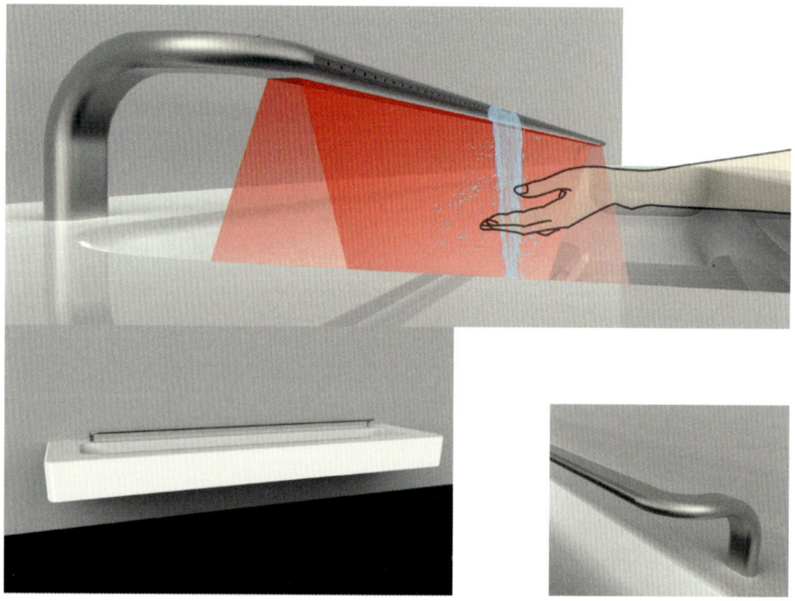

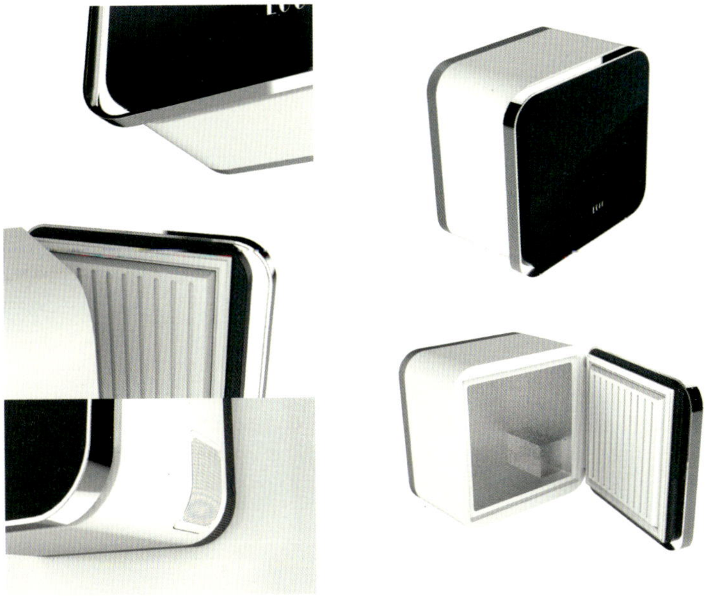

挂壁式冰柜
Wall Freezer

这款挂壁式家庭小冰柜，突破传统落地式冰柜，将冰柜设置在墙上，一来相对加大了家住面积，充分利用了墙面空间；二来一改以往的使用方式，不需要再弯腰或蹲下存取物品，只需根据用户的高度和使用习惯来安装，不仅家中大人使用方便，也防止了小孩因为调皮而改变冰柜内温度。

This wall-hanging type wall freezer breaks the traditional console mode freezer, setting it on the wall. It not only increases the living space and makes full use of the wall space, but also changed the way that people do not need to bend down or squat down to catch goods. It just needs to install according to user's height and using habit. It not only is convenient for the adults but also prevents the change of temperature because of children's naughty.

设计
DESIGN

廖秀雯
Liao Xiuwen

拼接方凳
Stitching Stool

本品为满足当代年轻人和普通消费者购买力不强但依然期望拥有一款有品质又好用的坐具的需求而设计。这款拼接凳的板材机械切割的加工方式极大地降低了成本。徒手拼接的安装方式让产品运输成本降低，同时便于携带。凳面的凹槽给了用户 DIY 的空间，可以按自己的喜好搭配坐垫甚至绘画。简约到极致的外观更符合年轻人的品位。

The original intention of creating this product is for the sake of contemporary young people and ordinary consumers. Their purchasing power may not be strong, but they still expect to have a seat that has good quality and is easy to use. The mechanical plate cutting joint stool greatly reduced the cost. The hand-made installation way reduced the transportation cost and it is also portable. The groove of the stool provides an opportunity for the young to decorating by themselves and they can match or paint cushion according to their preferences. The simplest appearance meets the taste of young people well.

设计
DESIGN

杨存园、邱品锦、钱哲
Yang Cunyuan, Qiu Pinjin, Qian Zhe

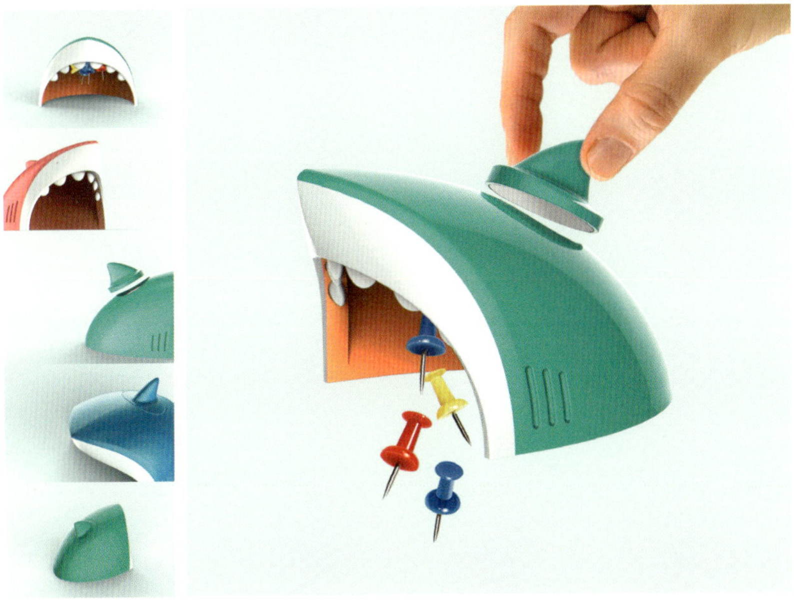

“大鱼吃小鱼”图钉收纳器
“The Shark” Pushpin Box

收，从来都是为了更方便地取。推动这款图钉收纳器在桌面上移动，就能将散落的图钉或其他金属小工具全“吃”进去。当你想要取出图钉时，将嵌入磁铁的“背鳍”拿开，就能将被“吃”掉的东西全“吐”出来了，避免了手伸入被刺伤。在外观设计上，在圆润的曲面中加入了硬棱线，保留了鲨鱼原生的锋利感，追求一种自然的视觉平衡。

To collect is always for easier to take out. The pushpin container can “eat” all the scattered pushpins or other small metal tools by pushing it along the table top. To take out the pushpins, you can remove the back fin embedded with magnet and then all the staff can be split out, which prevents hands from being stabbed. In terms of the appearance, the round hook face is added with some hard lines, which keeps the original sharpness of the shark and achieves a visual balance.

设计
DESIGN

深圳市矩阵工业产品设计有限公司
Shenzhen Matrix Industrial Product Design Co.,Ltd

智能交通警示机器人
Intelligent Traffic Warning Robot

交通事故中大部分车主没有合理设置好警示牌从而导致二次事故的发生。该设计采用了螃蟹的设计元素，生动醒目，识别性好。能沿道路上的白色车道分界线自走，不跑偏。结合定位系统功能，与手机同步定位，机主在不动的情况下，让它沿线移动到适当的安全距离，提前把道路安全状况反馈给车主，大大降低在设置警示牌过程中的危险系数。

Most of the owners in the traffic accident did not set up a good warning sign, which led to a second accident. The design uses the crab design element which is vivid and eye-catching with good recognition. It can walk along the rode on the white lane line and will not be off tracking. It is combined with GPS function and is synchronized with mobile phone. The owner can let it go along the line to the appropriate safe distance and make feedback of road safety state in advance without moving himself which greatly reduced the risk in setting the warning sign.

设计
DESIGN

区耀光
Ou Yaoguang

刻度钉子
Graduated Nails

该设计在现有钉子的基础上，标注了钉子长度和直径等刻度信息，有效地满足用户（如操作工、艺术家、设计师、建筑工、DIY 爱好者）打钉子时精确控制钉子长度的实际需求，同时也更加便于用户购买和识别所需要的钉子种类。该设计包含一系列不同长度和直径尺寸的钉子。

The design made scale information such as length and diameter of the nail on the basis of the existing nails. It effectively solved the actual needs for accurate length in driving nails of the users (such as operator, artist, designer, architect and DIY fan). It is also more convenient for the users to purchase and identify types of nails they need. The design contains a series of nails with different length and diameter dimensions.

设计
DESIGN

黄天杨
Huang Tianyang

最后一碟
The Last Ketchup

"最后一碟"是一个改良番茄酱瓶的设计。通常当瓶装的番茄酱剩下最后一点时，人们总是尝试各种各样的方法来把它用光。这个设计把底部变成一个可以拆卸的小碗，这样就可以解决问题了。当吃剩最后的番茄酱时，可以把瓶子的底部拧成一小盘番茄酱。瓶底是通过螺纹结构与瓶身相连，简单方便地解决了问题，并且易于使用。

The Last Ketchup is an improved ketchup bottle. When there is little ketchup left in the bottle, people always try various ways to run it out. This design changes the bottom of the bottle to a detachable small bowl which can solve the problem easily. When you reach the bottom of the ketchup, you can twist it to a small plate of ketchup. The bottom of the bottle connects the body part with thread structure which easily solved the problem and is conveniently to use.

设计
DESIGN

张剑、吕嘉纯、黄凯琪
Zhang Jian,Lv Jiachun,Huang Kaiqi

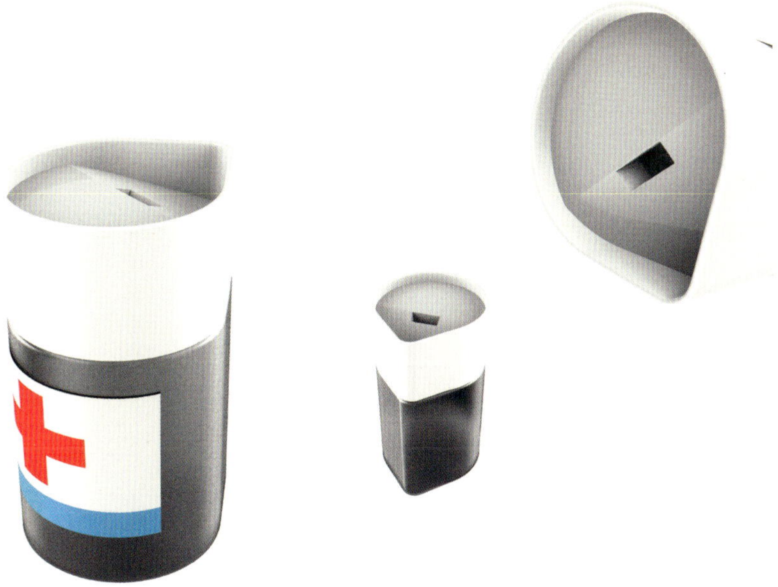

半片药瓶
Half a Pill

此药瓶解决了药片半片剂量问题以及半片药片拿取问题。帮助使用者单手掰开药片；瓶身的直角设计利于打开药瓶，瓶盖处的直角设计及斜坡设计利于药片的收取，药瓶的直角设计可以避免在包装中转动，瓶身的透明设计可直观地查看药片数量。

This medicine bottle solved the dosage of half pill and the take out problem of half pill. It helps users to break off the pill by hands. The right angle design of the body part makes it easy to open the medicine bottle. The right angle design and slope design of the bottle cap benefit the collecting of pills. The whole right angle design avoids the translocation in the package. And the transparent design of the bottle makes people look the quantity of the pills directly.

设计
DESIGN

李顺鑫
Li Shunxin

2017

12th

获奖名单
Winner List

2017

2017 中国设计红星奖获奖名单
Winner List of 2017 China Red Star Design Award

至尊金奖
Best of the Gold Prize

小牛电动 M1
Niu M1 smart escooter

设计 Design
小牛电动创新研发室
Niu Innovation Lab

生产 Manufacture
江苏小牛电动科技有限公司
Jiangsu Niu Electric Technology Co.,Ltd.

013

金奖
Gold Prize

米家激光投影电视
Mi Laser Home Cinema Projector

设计 Design
小米生态链工业设计团队
Mi Ecosystem Industrial Design Team

生产 Manufacture
峰米（北京）科技有限公司
Fengmi (Beijing) Technology Co., LTD

016

超薄小便器
Urinal

设计 Design
舒曼先生、刘惠锋
Schumann, Liu Huifeng

生产 Manufacture
九牧厨卫股份有限公司
Jomoo Kitchen&Bathroom Appliances Co.,Ltd.

019

小米 MIX 手机
Mi MIX

设计 Design
小米科技有限责任公司
Xiaomi Inc.

生产 Manufacture
小米科技有限责任公司
Xiaomi Inc.

022

机器人行李箱 R1
Cowarobot R1

设计 Design
黄定
Daniel Huang

生产 Manufacture
安徽酷哇机器人有限公司
Cowarobot Co., Ltd.

017

质子治疗系统
Proton Therapy System

设计 Design
北京智加问道科技有限公司
Beijing ZCO Design Co.,Ltd.

生产 Manufacture
合肥中科离子医学技术装备有限公司
Hefei CAS Ion Medical and Technical Devices Co.,Ltd.

020

小米米家电动滑板车
Mi Electric Scooter

设计 Design
小米生态链工业设计团队
Mi Ecosystem Industrial Design Team

生产 Manufacture
纳恩博（天津）科技有限公司
Ninebot Inc

023

比佛利净饮机
Beverly High-End Gas Water Dispenser

设计 Design
美的集团热水器事业部工业设计部
Industrial Design Center of Midea Group Water Heater Appliances

生产 Manufacture
美的集团热水器事业部
Midea Group Water Heater Appliances

018

魔碟灶
Rotatable-Burner Stove

设计 Design
何伟坚
He Weijian

生产 Manufacture
华帝股份有限公司
Vatti Corporation Limited

021

小牛电动 U1
Niu U1 smart escooter

设计 Design
小牛电动创新研发室
Niu innovation lab

生产 Manufacture
江苏小牛电动科技有限公司
Jiangsu Niu Electric Technology Co.,Ltd.

024

银奖
Silver Prize

管家机器人
Unibot

设计 Design

科沃斯机器人股份有限公司
Ecovacs Robotics Co.,Ltd.

生产 Manufacture

科沃斯机器人股份有限公司
Ecovacs Robotics Co.,Ltd.

028

XCA550 全地面起重机
XCA550 All Terrain Crane Truck

设计 Design

徐工集团 徐州重型机械有限公司 工业设计所
XCMG Xuzhou Heavy Machinery Co.,Ltd.Industrial Design

生产 Manufacture

徐工集团 徐州重型机械有限公司
XCMG Xuzhou Heavy Machinery Co.,Ltd.

029

微单 V1 锂电折叠自行车
V-danci V1 Lithium Folding Bike

设计 Design

北京洛可可科技有限公司
LKK Design Beijing Co.,Ltd.

生产 Manufacture

天津微驰科技有限公司
Tianjin V-Danci Co.,Ltd.

030

康复理疗车
Rehabilitation Wheelchair

设计 Design

杭州瑞德设计股份有限公司
Hangzhou R&D Design PLC

生产 Manufacture

浙江旺得福车业有限公司
Zhejing Wangdefu Motor Co.,Ltd.

031

传祺 GS8
Trumpchi GS8

设计 Design

广州汽车集团股份有限公司汽车工程研究院
Guangzhou Automobile Group Co., Ltd. Automotive Engineering Institute

生产 Manufacture

广州汽车集团乘用车有限公司
Guangzhou Automobile Group Motor Co.,Ltd.

032

米家全景相机
Mi Sphere Camera

设计 Design

小米生态链工业设计团队
Mi Ecosystem Industrial Design Team

生产 Manufacture

北京疯景科技有限公司
Fengjing Techonolgy Co.,Ltd.

033

ARJ21 国产支线喷气式客机
ARJ21 Regional Jet Plane

设计 Design

上海飞机设计研究院
Shanghai Aircraft Design and Research Institute

生产 Manufacture

上海飞机制造有限公司
Shanghai Aircraft Manufacturing Co.,Ltd.

034

光芒系列洗衣机
Radiant

设计 Design

惠而浦（中国）工业设计中心
Whirlpool (China) GCD

生产 Manufacture

惠而浦（中国）股份有限公司
Whirlpool (China) Co.,Ltd.

035

婴儿培养箱
Neonatal Incubator

设计 Design

钟琳琳
Zhong Linlin

生产 Manufacture

深圳市科曼医疗设备有限公司
Shenzhen Comen Medical Instruments Co.,Ltd.

036

最佳团队奖
Best Team Prize

小牛电动创新研发室
Niu Innovation Lab

039

最佳新人奖
Best New Designer Prize

赵自然
Zhao Ziran

041

红星奖
Excellent Prize

安旅盒子
Hotel Security Equipment

设计 Design

七百设计（深圳）有限公司
700 Design (Shenzhen)

生产 Manufacture

浙江公共安全技术研究院
Zhejiang Province Public Security Institute of Technology

044

火麒麟电脑机箱
Fire Kirin Computer Case

设计 Design

东莞市尚同工业设计有限公司
Dongguan Shangtong Industrial Design Co.,Ltd.

生产 Manufacture

广州耀众电子科技有限公司
Guangzhou Yaozhong Electronic technology Co., Ltd.

044

背包式 VR 一体机
Venus

设计 Design

何海洋、刘汶涓
Ocean He, Liu Wenjuan

生产 Manufacture

浙江大华技术股份有限公司
Zhejiang Dahua Technology Co.,Ltd.

045

“天鹅”智能云 POS
"Swan" Smart Cloud POS Equipment

设计 Design

胡源
Hu Yuan

生产 Manufacture

东软集团
Neusoft Corporation

045

4G 智能执法记录终端
Video Speaker Microphone

设计 Design
深圳意云设计有限公司
Shenzhen Eevin Design Co.,Ltd.
生产 Manufacture
深圳意云科技有限公司
Shenzhen Eevin Technology Co.,Ltd.

046

切割定位式光纤熔接机
Cutting and Positioning Type Optical Fiber Welding Machine

设计 Design
成都思睿工业产品设计有限公司
Chengdu Sirui Industrial Product Design Co.,Ltd.
生产 Manufacture
成都捷康特科技有限公司
Chengdu Jiekangte Technology Co.,Ltd.

048

GLXSS Pro 智能眼镜
GLXSS Pro Smart Glass

设计 Design
杨金超
Seed Yang
生产 Manufacture
北京亮亮视野科技有限公司
Beijing LLvision Technology Co.,Ltd.

050

远云网络云储存
Yuanyun Network Cloud Storage

设计 Design
广州大业产品设计有限公司
Guangzhou Daye Industrial Design Co.,Ltd.
生产 Manufacture
广州远云网络科技有限公司
Guangzhou Yuanyun Network Technology Limited Company

052

HPC 高性能服务器机柜
HPC Server Cabinet

设计 Design
浪潮电子信息产业股份有限公司
Inspur Electronic Information Industry Co.,Ltd.
生产 Manufacture
浪潮电子信息产业股份有限公司
Inspur Electronic Information Industry Co., Ltd.

046

多功能声级计
Multi-Function Sound Level Meter

设计 Design
杭州领跑者工业设计有限公司
Hangzhou LPZ Industrial Design Co.,Ltd.
生产 Manufacture
杭州爱华仪器有限公司
Hangzhou Aihua Instruments Co.,Ltd.

048

红米 Note 4X 手机
Redmi Note 4X

设计 Design
小米科技有限责任公司
Xiaomi Inc.
生产 Manufacture
小米科技有限责任公司
Xiaomi Inc.

050

联想 ideacentre 620s 型号计算机
Lenovo ideacentre 620s Mini PC

设计 Design
联想设计
Lenovo Design
生产 Manufacture
联想集团
Lenovo Group

052

华号智能安全路由器
Beacon Tower Intelligent Security Router

设计 Design
深圳市佳简几何工业设计有限公司
Shenzhen XIVO Design Co.,Ltd.
生产 Manufacture
大庆华号科技有限公司
Daqing Huahao Technology Co.,Ltd.

047

苹果手机 U 盘 U365
iPhone USB Flash Drive U365

设计 Design
杨晔
Yang Ye
生产 Manufacture
爱国者电子科技有限公司
Aigo Electronics Technology Co.,Ltd.

048

10G-PON 智能网关
10G-PON

设计 Design
武汉栎维道创意科技有限公司
Wuhan Liweidao Creative Technology Co.,Ltd.
生产 Manufacture
烽火通信科技股份有限公司
Fiberhome Telecommunication Technologies Co.,Ltd.

051

中兴锁屏系统应用
ZTE Locker System APP

设计 Design
中兴通讯股份有限公司
ZTE Corporation.Shenzhen,China
生产 Manufacture
中兴通讯股份有限公司
ZTE Corporation.Shenzhen,China

052

糖猫儿童手表 M2PRO
Teemo Children Watch M2PRO

设计 Design
北京搜狗网络技术有限公司
Beijing Sogou Network Technology Co.,Ltd.
生产 Manufacture
深圳比亚迪股份有限公司
BYD Company Limited

047

FPV 航拍微型摄像机
FPV Aerial Miniature Cameras

设计 Design
深圳市金标源创工业设计有限公司
Shenzhen King-Bill Design Company
生产 Manufacture
深圳市三锐智能技术有限公司
Sree Technology Co.,Ltd.

049

生物指纹终端采集器
Biometric Fingerprint Acquisition Termina

设计 Design
深圳市白狐工业设计有限公司
Shenzhen Bifoxs Industrial Design Co.,Ltd.
生产 Manufacture
深圳市白狐工业设计有限公司
Shenzhen Bifoxs Industrial Design Co.,Ltd.

051

指纹识别笔记本
Lockbook

设计 Design
深圳市麦锡工业产品策划有限公司
Maxypro Industrial Product Scheme Co.,Ltd.
生产 Manufacture
深圳指尖儿科技有限公司
FPlife Technology Co.,Ltd.

053

按键式加密 U 盘
Touch-Tone Encrypted USB Disk

设计 Design
深圳市点臻设计有限公司
Shenzhen a.Cus Design Co.,Ltd.
生产 Manufacture
深圳市艾尔卡特电子科技有限公司
Shenzhen Arycarter Electronic Technology Co.,Ltd.

047

深瞳人眼摄像机
DeepGlint Foveacam

设计 Design
成都意町工业产品设计有限公司
Chengdu Iding Industrial Design Co.,Ltd.
生产 Manufacture
北京格灵深瞳信息技术有限公司
Beijing DeepGlint Technology Limited

049

车喵 H8 智能后视镜
Carmew H8 Intelligent Rearview Mirror

设计 Design
杭州领跑者工业设计有限公司
Hangzhou LPZ Industrial Design Co.,Ltd.
生产 Manufacture
北京高科中天技术股份有限公司
Itonology Co.,Ltd.

051

小米米家对讲机
Mi Walkie-Talkie

设计 Design
小米生态链工业设计团队
Mi Ecosystem Industrial Design Team
生产 Manufacture
西安蜂语信息科技有限公司
Xi'an Fengyu Information Techonolgy Co.,Ltd.

053

CP200pro 老人定位手机
CP200pro The Aged Positioning Mobile Phone

设计 Design

四川长虹佳华信息产品有限责任公司
Changhong IT Information Products Co.,Ltd.

生产 Manufacture

四川长虹佳华信息产品有限责任公司
Changhong IT Information Products Co., Ltd.

054

飒途 600B 卫星通信系统
Sattour 600B Satellite Communication System

设计 Design

毕朝瑞、李志中
Echo, Dr.Lee

生产 Manufacture

航天恒星科技有限公司（503 所）
Space Star Technology Co., Ltd.

054

生活防水携带式硬盘
Diamond D30

设计 Design

邱美玲、王钟纬
Qiu Meiling, Wang Zhongwei

生产 Manufacture

广颖电通股份有限公司
Silicon Power

055

5G 通讯基站
5G Base Station

设计 Design

中兴通讯股份有限公司
ZTE Corporation.Shenzhen,China

生产 Manufacture

中兴通讯股份有限公司
ZTE Corporation.Shenzhen,China

055

小米电视 4
Xiaomi TV 4

设计 Design

王川、李宁
Wang Chuan, Li Ning

生产 Manufacture

北京小米电子产品有限公司
Beijing Xiaomi Electronics Co.,Ltd.

056

M1E 蓝牙运动耳机
M1E Sport Bluetooth Headset

设计 Design

深圳市科奈信科技有限公司
Shenzhen Cannice Technology Co.,Ltd.

生产 Manufacture

深圳市科奈信科技有限公司
Shenzhen Cannice Technology Co., Ltd.

056

VR 电脑
VR Computer

设计 Design

北京有初科技有限公司
Beijing Yochu Technology Co.,Ltd

生产 Manufacture

北京有初科技有限公司
Beijing Yochu Technology Co.,Ltd.

057

智能集尿器
Intelligent Urine Collector

设计 Design

慈溪大业工业设计有限公司
Cixi Daye Industrial Design Co.,Ltd.

生产 Manufacture

宁波新海医疗科技有限公司
Ningbo Xinhai Medical Technology Co., Ltd.

057

折叠二合一吸尘器
Rechargeable 2 in 1 Vacuum Cleaner

设计 Design

陈龙辉、陈立明
Chen Longhui, Chen Liming

生产 Manufacture

广东新宝电器股份有限公司
Guangdong Xinbao Electrical Appliances HoldingsCo., Ltd.

057

Skyworth W9 OLED 电视
Skyworth W9 OLED TV

设计 Design

深圳创维 -RGB 电子有限公司工业设计研究院
Shenzheng Chuangwei -RGB Electronics Co.,Skyworth Design

生产 Manufacture

深圳创维 -RGB 电子有限公司
Shenzheng Chuangwei-RGB Electronics Co.,Ltd.

058

Skyworth W8 OLED 电视
Skyworth W8 OLED TV

设计 Design

深圳创维 -RGB 电子有限公司工业设计研究院
Shenzheng Chuangwei -RGB Electronics Co.,Skyworth Design

生产 Manufacture

深圳创维 -RGB 电子有限公司
Shenzheng Chuangwei-RGB Electronics Co.,Ltd.

058

JBL Bar 3.1 家庭影院条形音箱系统
JBL Bar3.1

设计 Design

哈曼设计团队
Harman Design Center

生产 Manufacture

哈曼国际
Harman International Industries

058

JBL Boombox 便携式蓝牙音响
JBL Boombox

设计 Design

哈曼设计团队
Harman Design Center

生产 Manufacture

哈曼国际
Harman International Industries

059

创维 55G6D 电视
Skyworth 55G6D TV

设计 Design

深圳创维 -RGB 电子有限公司工业设计研究院
Shenzheng Chuangwei -RGB Electronics Co.,Skyworth Design

生产 Manufacture

深圳创维 -RGB 电子有限公司
Shenzheng Chuangwei-RGB Electronics Co.,Ltd.

059

健康高效原汁机
Healthy and Efficient Juice Machine

设计 Design

陈龙辉、刘鹏
Chen Longhui, Liu Peng

生产 Manufacture

广东新宝电器股份有限公司
Guangdong Xinbao Electrical Appliances Holdings Co., Ltd.

060

哈曼卡顿 Traveler 便携式蓝牙音响
Harman Kardon Traveler

设计 Design

哈曼设计中心
Harman Design Center

生产 Manufacture

哈曼国际
Harman International Industries

060

智能调节变频水泵
Intelligent Adjustment Frequency Conversion Pump

设计 Design

区要光、徐训军
Oson, Xu Xunjun

生产 Manufacture

森森集团股份有限公司
Sunsun Group Co.,Ltd.

061

Halomini 双目 AR 智能眼镜
Halomini Smart Glasses

设计 Design

深圳市想象力产品策划有限公司
Imagination Design Co.,Ltd.

生产 Manufacture

上海影创信息科技有限公司
Shadow Creator Information Technology Co.,Ltd.

061

老板 58G8 燃气灶
Robam-58G8 Gas Stove

设计 Design

老板电器工业设计中心
Robam Industrial Design Dept.

生产 Manufacture

杭州老板电器股份有限公司
Hangzhou Robam Applicances Co.,Ltd.

061

数码变频发电机（CH2000i）
CH2000i Digital Inverter Generator

设计 Design

刘渊博、徐乐
Liu Yuanbo, Xu Le

生产 Manufacture

苏州双马机电有限公司
Suzhou ERMA Machinery Co.,Ltd.

062

AW-S17G105 电热水壶 AW-S17G105 Electric Kettle

设计 Design
龙域设计
Loe Design

生产 Manufacture
浙江爱仕达生活电器有限公司
Zhejiang Aishida Household Equipment Co.,Ltd.

062

智能卧室风扇 Smart Bedroom Fan

设计 Design
郭玉强
Guo Yuqiang

生产 Manufacture
广东美的环境电器制造有限公司
GD Midea Environment Appliances MFG.Co., Ltd.

064

艾泡一起充电器 Ayepow Wireless Charging Station

设计 Design
深圳亮明月设计有限公司
IU+ Design Co.,Ltd.

生产 Manufacture
深圳市荣卓电子有限公司
Excel World International (Shenzhen) limited

066

PTC 暖风机系列 Series PTC Tower Haater

设计 Design
孟一郎
Meng Yilang

生产 Manufacture
广东美的环境电器制造有限公司
GD Midea Environment Appliances MFG. Co.,Ltd.

068

老板 5610 吸油烟机 Robam-5610 Range Hood

设计 Design
老板电器工业设计中心
Robam Industrial Design Dept.

生产 Manufacture
杭州老板电器股份有限公司
Hangzhou Robam Applicances Co., Ltd.

063

九阳无渣豆浆机 Q7 DJ13R-Q7 Soybean Milk Maker

设计 Design
沈健、李雁巢
Jack Shen, Jason Lee

生产 Manufacture
杭州九阳小家电有限公司
Hangzhou Joyoung Small Household Appliances Co.,Ltd.

064

暴风人工智能电视 65X5 ECHO

设计 Design
暴风设计团队
Baofeng Design

生产 Manufacture
深圳暴风统帅科技有限公司
Shenzhen Baofeng Leader Technology Co.,Ltd.

066

便携式咖啡机 Portable Coffee Machine

设计 Design
杭州九合形物工业设计有限公司
Hangzhou Johe Design Co.,Ltd.

生产 Manufacture
慈溪欧能电器有限公司
Cixi Owner Electrical Appliance Co.,Ltd.

069

Landroid 智能割草机 Landroid Robotic Mower

设计 Design
宝时得科技（中国）有限公司
Positec Technology (China) Co., Ltd.

生产 Manufacture
宝时得科技（中国）有限公司
Positec Technology (China) Co.,Ltd.

063

手机三轴稳定器 Smooth 3 3-Axis Smartphone Stabilizer Smooth 3

设计 Design
桂林智神信息技术有限公司
Guilin Zhishen Information Technology Co.,Ltd.

生产 Manufacture
桂林智神信息技术有限公司
Guilin Zhishen Information Technology Co.,Ltd.

065

佑美 Q1 跑步机 Umay Q1

设计 Design
杭州热浪工业产品设计有限公司
Hangzhou Hotdesign Co.,Ltd.

生产 Manufacture
浙江荣顺科技有限公司
Zhejiang Rongshun Techonlogy Co.,Ltd.

067

多功能电动刷 Multi-Function Electric Brush for Kitchen and Washroom

设计 Design
苏州轩昂工业设计有限公司
Suzhou Superdesign Industrial Design Co.,Ltd.

生产 Manufacture
苏州科比电器有限公司
Suzhou kvc Electric Co.,Ltd.

069

DF-EF0816V 循环扇 DF-EF0816V Air Circulation Fan

设计 Design
联创工业设计中心
Lianchuang Industry Design Center

生产 Manufacture
深圳市联创科技集团有限公司
Shenzhen Lianchuang Technology Group Co.,Ltd.

063

九阳厨下反渗透净水机 Water Purifier

设计 Design
张岩、李雁巢
Zhang Yan,Jason Lee

生产 Manufacture
杭州九阳小家电有限公司
Hangzhou Joyoung Small Household Appliances Co.,Ltd.

065

尚酷智能保险柜 Shangku Intelligent Safe

设计 Design
宁波市艺佳意工业设计有限公司
Ningbo 1and1 Industrial Design Co.,Ltd.

生产 Manufacture
宁波永发智能安防科技有限公司
Ningbo Yongfa Intulligent Security Technology Co.,Ltd.

067

坚果 R1 遥控器 JmGo R1 Remote Control

设计 Design
深圳市火乐科技发展有限公司
Shenzhen Holatek Co.,Ltd.

生产 Manufacture
深圳市火乐科技发展有限公司
Shenzhen Holatek Co.,Ltd.

069

棒米耳温计 Earmo

设计 Design
杭州奥格工业设计有限公司
AUG Hangzhou Industrial Design Co.,Ltd.

生产 Manufacture
杭州棒糖网络科技有限公司
Hangzhou Bangtang Network Technology Co.,Ltd.

064

亚都 KJ455G-S4D 双面侠 YADU KJ455G-S4D Double-Faced Purifier

设计 Design
北京千策良品工业设计有限公司
RCB Industrial Design

生产 Manufacture
北京亚都环保科技有限公司
Beijing Yady Environmental Science and Technology Co.,Ltd.

065

云音云锦蓝牙音箱 Cloud Sound Bluetooth Audio

设计 Design
马涛
Ma Tao

生产 Manufacture
江苏汇鸿国际集团中鼎控股股份有限公司
High Hope Zhongding Corporation

068

坚果 S1 激光电视 JmGo S1 Laser Television

设计 Design
深圳市火乐科技发展有限公司
Shenzhen Holatek Co.,Ltd.

生产 Manufacture
深圳市火乐科技发展有限公司
Shenzhen Holatek Co.,Ltd.

070

松下充电式无线手持吸尘器 Panasonic's Rechargeable Wireless Hand-HeldVacuum Cleaner

设计 Design

杭州汉度工业设计有限公司
Hangzhou HANDO Industrial Design Co.,Ltd.

生产 Manufacture

松下电器（中国）有限公司
Panasonic Corporation of China

070

电脑手绘板 Computer Hand Drawing Board

设计 Design

深圳市问鼎工业设计有限公司
Shenzhen Wing-id Co.,Ltd.

生产 Manufacture

深圳市绘王动漫科技有限公司
Shenzhen Huion Animation Technology Co.,Ltd.

072

FOXEER BOX 运动相机 FOXEER BOX Action Camera

设计 Design

深圳市万有引力工业设计有限公司
SZ-Gravity Design Co.,Ltd.

生产 Manufacture

深圳市鑫安泰视频技术有限公司
Shenzhen Xinantai Video Technology Co.,Ltd.

074

液态金属笔 Liquid Metal Pen

设计 Design

深圳市白狐工业设计有限公司
Shenzhen Bifoxs Industrial Design Co.,Ltd.

生产 Manufacture

云南中宣液态金属科技有限公司
Yunnan Yizhong Liquid Metal Technology Co.,Ltd.

076

JBL Free 真无线入耳式耳机 JBL Free

设计 Design

哈曼设计团队
Harman Design Center

生产 Manufacture

哈曼国际
Harman International Industries

070

"小幸熨"迷你蒸汽挂烫电熨斗 "Little Fortune Iron" – A Mini Steam Hanging Iron

设计 Design

孟一郎
Meng Yilang

生产 Manufacture

广东美的环境电器制造有限公司
GD Midea Environment Appliances MFG.Co., Ltd.

073

游戏鼠标 Gaming Mouse

设计 Design

深圳市问鼎工业设计有限公司
Shenzhen Wing-id Co.,Ltd.

生产 Manufacture

深圳富民微电子有限公司
Shenzhen Fmsemi Electronics Co.,Ltd.

074

净能达空气净化机 Full Function Air Cleaner

设计 Design

张可、李海涛
Zhang Ke, Li Haitao

生产 Manufacture

霍尼韦尔
Honeywell

077

JBL Soundgear 可穿戴式微型无线音箱 JBL Soundgear

设计 Design

哈曼设计团队
Harman Design Center

生产 Manufacture

哈曼国际
Harman International Industries

071

RO 智能净饮机 RO Smart Water Purifier

设计 Design

宁波明锐工业产品设计有限公司
Ningbo Meanew Industrial Design Co.,Ltd.

生产 Manufacture

宁波轩畅电器有限公司
Ningbo Xuanchang Electric Appliance Co.,Ltd.

073

N910 智能 POS 终端 N910 Smart POS Terminal

设计 Design

福建新大陆支付技术有限公司
Fujian Newland Payment Techenology Co.,Ltd.

生产 Manufacture

宏泰机电科技（漳州）有限公司
Kingtronics Corporation of Elec.&Mech.Techenology (Zhangzhou) Co.,Ltd.

075

WOW!dea 奇点 M PLUS 模块化多功能无线音响 WOW!dea M Plus Modular Wireless Speaker

设计 Design

北京元隆雅图文化传播股份有限公司
Beijing Yuanlong Yato Culture Dissemination Co.,Ltd.

生产 Manufacture

北京元隆雅图文化传播股份有限公司
Beijing Yuanlong Yato Culture Dissemination Co.,Ltd.

077

JBL Grip 500 无线入耳式运动耳机 JBL Grip 500

设计 Design

哈曼设计团队
Harman Design Center

生产 Manufacture

哈曼国际
Harman International Industries

071

V58 变频除湿机 V58 Frequency-Conversion Dehumidifier

设计 Design

宁波明锐工业产品设计有限公司
Ningbo Meanew Industrial Design Co.,Ltd.

生产 Manufacture

宁波德业日用电器科技有限公司
Ningbo Deye Electrical Appliance Tech.Co.,Ltd.

073

美型带线移动硬盘 Armor A62

设计 Design

蔡卉柔、许砚翔
Cai Huirou, Xu Yanxiang

生产 Manufacture

广颖电通股份有限公司
Silicon Power

075

CHiQ Q5S 系列电视 CHiQ Q5S TV

设计 Design

四川虹微技术有限公司、合肥长虹实业有限公司
Homwee Technology (Sichuan) Co.,Ltd., Hefei Changhong

生产 Manufacture

合肥长虹实业有限公司
Hefei Changhong Industry Co.,Ltd.

077

美菱宅·酷单门冰箱 Meiling Z. Cube Refrigerator

设计 Design

四川虹微技术有限公司、合肥美菱股份有限公司
Homwee Technology (Sichuan) Co.,Ltd., Hefei Meiling Co.,Ltd.

生产 Manufacture

合肥美菱股份有限公司
Hefei Meiling Co.,Ltd.

072

凡帝罗法式四门冰箱 BCD-532WGPZV Vandelo French-Style Four-door Refrigerator

设计 Design

美的冰箱工业设计中心
Midea Refrigerator Industrial Design Center

生产 Manufacture

合肥美的电冰箱有限公司
Hefei Midea Refrigerator Co.,Ltd.

074

看尚 iCAN 影院 P1 智能投影仪 iCAN P1 Smart Projector

设计 Design

成都浪尖工业设计有限公司
Chengdu Artop Industrial Design Co.,Ltd.

生产 Manufacture

环球智达科技（北京）有限公司
Universal Wisdomtech.(Beijing) Co.,Ltd.

076

无线自组网通信设备 Wireless AD-Hoc Communication Device

设计 Design

成都浪尖工业设计有限公司
Chengdu Artop Industrial Design Co.,Ltd.

生产 Manufacture

成都奥特为通讯有限公司
Chengdu OTT for Communications Co.,Ltd.

078

Netvue Belle 人工智能门铃
Netvue Belle

设计 Design
深圳市天和荣科技有限公司
Netvue Technologies Co.,Ltd.
生产 Manufacture
深圳市天和荣科技有限公司
Netvue Technologies Co.,Ltd.

078

万家乐 X7 家用中央热水燃气热水器
Macro X7 Domestic Center Hot Water Gas Water Heater

设计 Design
广东顺德东方麦田工业设计有限公司
East-Innovation Shunde GD Co.,Ltd.
生产 Manufacture
广东万家乐燃气具有限公司
Guangdong Macro Gas Appliance Co.,Ltd.

080

西蒙 i7 智能温控器
Simon i7 Thermostat

设计 Design
上海犀科环境科技有限公司
Shanghai Seekco Environmental Tech Co.,Ltd.
生产 Manufacture
西蒙电气（中国）有限公司
Spain Simon （China） Ltd.

082

婴儿用品消毒器
Baby Accessory Sterilizer

设计 Design
合肥方块工业设计有限公司
Square Industrial Design Co.,Ltd.
生产 Manufacture
安徽匠造物科技有限公司
An Hui Artisan Creator Technology Co., Ltd.

084

HQ5 电热水器
HQ5 Electric Water Heater

设计 Design
美的集团热水器事业部工业设计部
Industrial Design Center of Midea Group Water Heater Appliances
生产 Manufacture
美的集团热水器事业部
Midea Group Water Heater Appliances

078

万家乐“mate3 智联烟灶锅”烹饪套装
Macro mate3 Smart Cooking Appliance Suit

设计 Design
广东顺德东方麦田工业设计有限公司
East-Innovation Shunde GD Co.,Ltd.
生产 Manufacture
广东万家乐燃气具有限公司
Guangdong Macro Gas Appliance Co.,Ltd.

081

海信 Ta 空间冰箱
Hisense Ta Sapce Refrigerator

设计 Design
海信集团工业设计中心
Hisense Industrial Design Center
生产 Manufacture
海信（山东）冰箱有限公司
Hisense (Shandong) Refrigerator Co.,Ltd.

082

三宝家庭机器人
Sanbot Family Robot

设计 Design
广州大业产品设计有限公司
Guangzhou Daye Industrial Design Co.,Ltd.
生产 Manufacture
旗瀚科技有限公司
Qihan Technology Co., Ltd.

084

智能净化系统
A-box

设计 Design
杭州亿智智能科技有限公司
Hangzhou YSAE Design
生产 Manufacture
杭州亿智智能科技有限公司
Hangzhou YSAE Design

079

联想 ThinkVision P27q 显示器
Lenovo ThinkVision P27q Monitor

设计 Design
联想设计
Lenovo Design
生产 Manufacture
联想集团
Lenovo Group

081

比佛利高端燃热系列
Beverly High-End Gas Water Heater Series

设计 Design
美的集团热水器事业部工业设计部
Industrial Design Center of Midea Group Water Heater Appliancesv
生产 Manufacture
美的集团热水器事业部
Midea Group Water Heater Appliances

083

气泡智能音箱
Bubble Smart Speaker

设计 Design
叶菲梓、陈焕鹏
Ye Feizi, Chen Huanpeng
生产 Manufacture
北京智能管家科技有限公司
Intelligent Steward Co.,Ltd.

085

MINI 声波洁面仪
Perfectclean MINI Sonic Facial Cleansing Device

设计 Design
深圳可思美科技有限公司
Shenzhen Cosbeauty Technology Co.,Ltd.
生产 Manufacture
深圳可思美科技有限公司
Shenzhen Cosbeauty Technology Co.,Ltd.

079

立达信智能家居系列
Leedarson Home Automation Series

设计 Design
立达信工业设计中心
Leedarson IDC
生产 Manufacture
厦门立达信绿色照明集团有限公司
Leedarson Group

081

海尔 U5 净水器
Haier U5 Water Purifier

设计 Design
广州大业产品设计有限公司
Guangzhou Daye Industrial Design Co.,Ltd.
生产 Manufacture
海尔施特劳斯水设备有限公司
Haier Strauss Water Equipment Co.,Ltd.

083

储能式电暖器
Thermal Energy Storage

设计 Design
武汉市本源造物设计咨询有限公司
Source Design
生产 Manufacture
北京凯昆广胜新能源电器有限公司
Beijing Kaikunguangsheng New Energy Electric Appliance Co.,Ltd.

085

燃气热水壁挂炉 / 冷凝炉
Gas Hot Water Wall Hanging Boiler/ Condensing Furnace

设计 Design
珠海格力电器股份有限公司
Gree Electric Appliances,Inc.of Zhuhai
生产 Manufacture
珠海格力电器股份有限公司
Gree Electric Appliances,Inc.of Zhuhai

080

新一代多联机 sk6
New Generation of VRF sk6

设计 Design
珠海格力电器股份有限公司
Gree Electric Appliances,Inc.of Zhuhai
生产 Manufacture
珠海格力电器股份有限公司
Gree Electric Appliances,Inc.of Zhuhai

082

爱米优系列双向快充移动电源
OUHUO Two-Way Fast Charging Mobile Power Series

设计 Design
北京华新意创工业设计有限公司
Beijing Ideas Design Co.,Ltd.
生产 Manufacture
北京隆通科技有限公司
OUHUO

083

ASNAP 手机夜拍补光灯
ASNAP Fill-in Light for Smartphones

设计 Design
杭州正负极工业设计有限公司
Hangzhou Pmuse Industrial Design Co.,Ltd.
生产 Manufacture
深圳宗匠科技有限公司
Accompany Tech. Co.,Ltd.

085

I90-TWS 对吸蓝牙耳机
TWS-H2

设计 Design
深圳市恩佳产品策划有限公司
Shenzhen N Plus Product Planning Co.,Ltd.

生产 Manufacture
广州海蔚特科技有限公司
Guangzhou Havit Technology Co.,Ltd.

086

摇滚之星蓝牙音箱
Rockstar Bluetooth Speaker

设计 Design
深圳市麦锡工业产品策划有限公司
Maxypro Industrial Product Scheme Co.,Ltd.

生产 Manufacture
君伍科技（北京）有限公司
Dreamwvae Audio USA,LLC

088

天使与恶魔保温杯
Angel and Devil Cup

设计 Design
广州市可莓日用品有限公司
Guangzhou Kemei Daily Necessities Co.,Ltd.

生产 Manufacture
广州市可莓日用品有限公司
Guangzhou Kemei Daily Necessities Co., Ltd.

091

反向汽车安全伞
Reverse Safety Umbrella

设计 Design
李若权
Li Ruoquan

生产 Manufacture
惠州市鑫和丰雨伞制品有限公司
Huizhou Xinhefeng Umbrella Products Co.,Ltd.

093

热辐射电暖器
Heat Radiator

设计 Design
郭玉强
Guo Yuqiang

生产 Manufacture
广东美的环境电器制造有限公司
GD Midea Environment Appliances MFG.Co., Ltd.

086

中兴蓝牙麦克风
ZTE Bluetooth Microphone

设计 Design
中兴通讯股份有限公司
ZTE Corporation.Shenzhen,China

生产 Manufacture
中兴通讯股份有限公司
ZTE Corporation.Shenzhen,China

088

无畏旅行商务背包
Backpack for Business Trips Wuwei Co

设计 Design
胡庆峰
Hu Qingfeng

生产 Manufacture
重庆传梵服装设计工作室
Chongqing Creative Fashion Design Studio

091

LED 条形灯
LED Shop Light

设计 Design
季剑辉、白云飞
Winston Ji, Charly Bai

生产 Manufacture
上海顿格电子贸易有限公司
Dangoo Electronics

093

巧克力电视
Chocolate TV

设计 Design
微鲸工业设计部
Whaley Technology ID Team

生产 Manufacture
微鲸科技有限公司
Whaley Technology Co., Ltd.

086

单手快拔电源插头
Single Hand's Power Plug

设计 Design
苗亮
Miao Liang

生产 Manufacture
绍兴市锦涛电子有限公司
Shaoxing Jintao Electron Co.,Ltd.

90

早先生组合式枕头
Mr.Z Modular Pillow

设计 Design
广州早尚创意文化有限公司
Guangzhou Mrz Creative Culture Co.,Ltd.

生产 Manufacture
广州市欧亚床垫家具有限公司
Guangzhou Eurasia Mattress & Furniture Co., Ltd.

092

曲智系列
Quzzi

设计 Design
浙江科尔卡诺办公家具有限公司
Kano.Cn

生产 Manufacture
浙江科尔卡诺办公家具有限公司
Kano.Cn

094

布丁豆豆智能机器人
Pudding BeanQ Smart Robot

设计 Design
叶菲梓、郑斌
Ye Feizi, Zheng Bin

生产 Manufacture
北京智能管家科技有限公司
Intelligent Steward Co.,Ltd.

087

踢踢桶
Kick Bin

设计 Design
许坤南、吴康松
Xu Kunnan, Wu Kangsong

生产 Manufacture
米巢（厦门）信息技术有限公司
Micasa (Xiamen) Info Technology Co.,Ltd.

090

贝壳餐椅
Lord Chair

设计 Design
柴晓东
Alex Chai

生产 Manufacture
杭州科沃工业设计有限公司
Gradodesign

092

梦旅人
Picnic

设计 Design
李快
Li Kuai

生产 Manufacture
越甲科技（北京）有限公司
Yuejia Technology (Beijing) Co., Ltd.

094

“X7PRO 家用中央热水”燃气热水器
"X7PRO Domestic Centr Hot Water" Gas Water Heater

设计 Design
广东顺德东方麦田工业设计有限公司
East-Innovation Shunde GD Co.,Ltd.

生产 Manufacture
广东万家乐燃气具有限公司
Guangdong Macro Gas Appliance Co.,Ltd.

087

Hello 焖烧罐
Hello

设计 Design
合肥行言产品设计有限公司
Hefei Xingyan

生产 Manufacture
合肥颂智商贸有限公司
J&V (Hongkong) Industrial Limited

091

嗒嗒桌
Dada Table

设计 Design
柴晓东
Alex Chai

生产 Manufacture
杭州科沃工业设计有限公司
Gradodesign

092

珂莱浴室龙头
Kola Basin Mixer

设计 Design
黄彩云
Huang Caiyun

生产 Manufacture
广州海鸥卫浴用品股份有限公司
Guangzhou Seagull Kitchen and Bath Products Co.,Ltd.

095

智能足球鞋
Smart Football Shoes

设计 Design
福建省莆田市双驰智能信息技术有限公司
Fujian Putian Semsx Information Technology Co.,Ltd.
生产 Manufacture
双驰实业股份有限公司
Shuangchi Industrial Co.,Ltd.

095

折纸椅
Bend Chair

设计 Design
柴晓东
Alex Chai
生产 Manufacture
杭州格度家具设计有限公司
Gradodesign

097

国人迷你打蛋器
Mini Egg Whisk

设计 Design
宁波江东矩成创意产品设计有限公司
Ningbo Galachy Creative Product Design Co.,Ltd.
生产 Manufacture
宁波市鄞州立翔塑胶有限公司
Ningbo Yinzhou Lixiang Plastic Co., Ltd.

099

儿童趣味手工皂——极地系列
Children Handmade Soap - Polar Series

设计 Design
唐雅、徐霍成
Tang Ya，Xu Huocheng
生产 Manufacture
兜宝（上海）教育衍生品科技发展有限公司
Doubao (Shanghai) Technology Development Co.,Ltd.

101

脉诊仪
Instrument of Pulse

设计 Design
沈阳创新设计服务有限公司
Shenyang Innovation
生产 Manufacture
辽宁瓦基机器人科技有限公司
Liaoning Wakirobot

095

宝护片智能婴幼儿体温监护仪
BHP Intelligent Infant Body Tempesrature Monitor

设计 Design
北京宝护科技有限公司
Beijing Baohu Technology Co.,Ltd.
生产 Manufacture
富士康精密组件（北京）有限公司
Foxconn International Holdings Co.,Ltd.

097

乐摇筛筛盆
Leyao Sieve Basin

设计 Design
陈涛
Chen Tao
生产 Manufacture
宁波海嘉塑料有限公司
Ningbo Haijia Plastic Co.,Ltd.

099

卷挑桌
Roll Picking Table

设计 Design
张永和
Zhang Yonghe
生产 Manufacture
曲美家居集团股份有限公司
Qumei Home Furnishings Group Co.,Ltd.

101

李宁超轻 13 跑鞋
Li-Ning Superlight 13 Running Shoes

设计 Design
孙京颐
Sun Jingyi
生产 Manufacture
李宁（中国）体育用品有限公司
Li- Ning (China) Sports Goods Co., Ltd.

096

节能过滤器
Green Filter

设计 Design
张桃燕
Zhang Taoyan
生产 Manufacture
厦门建霖工业有限公司
Xiamen Runner Industrial Corporation

098

极致净水龙头
Slim Drinking-Water Faucet

设计 Design
珠海普乐美厨卫有限公司
Primy Corporation Limited
生产 Manufacture
珠海普乐美厨卫有限公司
Primy Corporation Limited.

100

黛尔花洒
Slight Nod Shower

设计 Design
张桃燕
Zhang Taoyan
生产 Manufacture
厦门建霖工业有限公司
Xiamen Runner Industrial Corporation

102

蒙斯书盒
Mons

设计 Design
厦门松霖家居有限公司
Solux Home Lifestyle Co.,Ltd.
生产 Manufacture
厦门松霖家居有限公司
Solux Home Lifestyle Co.,Ltd.

096

滑背椅
Imove

设计 Design
佛山市米朗工业设计有限公司
Foshan Milon Industrial Product Design Co.,Ltd.
生产 Manufacture
佛山市谷腾家具有限公司
Goodtone Furniture Co.,Ltd.

098

20V 高压清洗机
20V High Pressure Washer

设计 Design
宝时得科技（中国）有限公司
Positec Technology (China) Co.,Ltd.
生产 Manufacture
宝时得科技（中国）有限公司
Positec Technology (China) Co., Ltd.

100

小巨蛋 T6
Mini Tea Set T6

设计 Design
百伦设计
Balance Design
生产 Manufacture
厦门沿喜科技有限公司
Xiamen Pertouch Co.,Ltd.

102

施陶芬实木软垫扶手椅
Fantasy

设计 Design
厦门松霖家居有限公司
Solux Home Lifestyle Co.,Ltd.
生产 Manufacture
厦门松霖家居有限公司
Solux Home Lifestyle Co.,Ltd.

096

手绘椅
Sketch Chair

设计 Design
柴晓东
Alex Chai
生产 Manufacture
杭州科沃工业设计有限公司
Gradodesign

099

20V 智能枪钻
20V AI Drill

设计 Design
宝时得科技（中国）有限公司
Positec Technology (China) Co., Ltd.
生产 Manufacture
宝时得科技（中国）有限公司
Positec Technology (China) Co.,Ltd.

100

格调
Style

设计 Design
曲美设计中心
QM Design Center
生产 Manufacture
曲美家居集团股份有限公司
Qumei Home Furnishings Group Co.,Ltd.

103

23 平方米 LOFT 变身七居室 停车库也能搬回家 Transformable Smart Home

设计 Design

张海翱
Zhang Haiao

生产 Manufacture

上海华都建筑规划设计有限公司
Shanghai Huadu Aechitectural Design Limited

103

天元智能宠物喂食机 Tianyuan Intelligent Pet Feeder

设计 Design

杭州热浪工业产品设计有限公司
Hangzhou Hotdesign Co.,Ltd.

生产 Manufacture

杭州天元宠物用品股份有限公司
Hangzhou Tianyuan Pet Products Co.,Ltd.

105

易用定时器 Easy Timer

设计 Design

公牛集团工业设计团队
Gongniu Design Team

生产 Manufacture

公牛集团有限公司
Gongniu Group Ltd.

107

智能多功能电动执行器 Intelligent Mutual Function Circuit Actuator

设计 Design

温州先临左岸工业设计有限公司
Wenzhou Shining Left Bank Industrial Design Co.,Ltd.

生产 Manufacture

浙江澳翔自控科技有限公司
Zhejiang Aoxiang Auto-Control Technology Co.,Ltd.

109

微烹宝 2 Microwave Cooking Pot

设计 Design

王晓作、吴涛
Wang Xiaozuo, Wu Tao

生产 Manufacture

台州优家塑业有限公司
Uka Home Production Co.,Ltd.

103

智能电子锁设计 Intelligent Electronic Lock Design

设计 Design

北京赛佳图工业设计有限公司
Beijing Saga FIG Industrial Design Co.,Ltd.

生产 Manufacture

安钥（北京）科技股份有限公司
An Key (Beijing) Technology Co., Ltd.

105

沁宝 650 Atmobot 650

设计 Design

科沃斯机器人股份有限公司
Ecovacs Robotics Co.,Ltd.

生产 Manufacture

科沃斯机器人股份有限公司
Ecovacs Robotics Co.,Ltd.

107

G28 连框开关 G28 Grid-Type Switches

设计 Design

严熙银、田发文
Yan Xiyin, Tian Fawen

生产 Manufacture

宁波公牛电器有限公司
Ningbo Gongniu Electric Co.,Ltd.

109

智能主动降噪助听器 Intelligent Active Noise Reduction Hearing Aid

设计 Design

深圳市知行创新工业设计有限公司
Shenzhen Thinkdo Design Co.,Ltd.

生产 Manufacture

深圳航天金悦通科技有限公司
Shenzhen Aerospace Golden Shine Technology Co., Ltd.

104

蜂巢插座 Comb Socket

设计 Design

成都意町工业产品设计有限公司
Chengdu Iding Industrial Design Co.,Ltd.

生产 Manufacture

成都白云互动科技有限公司
Magicwe Technologies (Chengdu) Limited

106

HDE5001T 智能连体坐便器 HDE5001T Smart Toilet

设计 Design

惠达卫浴研发中心
Huida R

生产 Manufacture

惠达卫浴股份卫浴有限公司
Huida Sanitary Ware Co.,Ltd.

107

LED 灯带 The LED Lights Bring

设计 Design

宁波公牛光电科技有限公司
Ningbo Gongniu Optoelectronic Technology Co.,Ltd.

生产 Manufacture

宁波公牛光电科技有限公司
Ningbo Gongniu Optoelectronic Technology Co.,Ltd.

109

“视界”签字笔 Wide Vision Signature Pen

设计 Design

晨光文具大众品牌中心工业设计部
M&G R&D Center

生产 Manufacture

上海晨光文具股份有限公司
Shanghai M.G Stationery Inc.

104

双层沥水篮 Double Drain Basket

设计 Design

杭州热浪工业产品设计有限公司
Hangzhou Hotdesign Co.,Ltd.

生产 Manufacture

义乌市品沐电子商务有限公司
Yiwu Pinmoo Electronic Commerce Co.,Ltd.

106

旱博士养花器 Hydro-Box Flower Pot

设计 Design

刘豪、胡越强
Liu Hao, Hu Yueqiang

生产 Manufacture

浙江泰索科技有限公司
Zhejiang Taisuo Technology Co.,Ltd.

108

智立方插座（F1330/F1331） PowerDock

设计 Design

公牛集团工业设计团队
Gongniu Design Team

生产 Manufacture

公牛集团有限公司
Gongniu Group Ltd.

110

种植栓 Seed Capsule

设计 Design

马鞍山三卅工业设计有限公司
Ma'anshan Sansa Industrial Design Co.,Ltd.

生产 Manufacture

马鞍山三卅工业设计有限公司
Ma'anshan Sansa Industrial Design Co., Ltd.

104

H1 多功能拉杆箱 H1-Hybrid Luggage

设计 Design

马涛
Ma Tao

生产 Manufacture

江苏汇鸿国际集团中鼎控股股份有限公司
High Hope Zhongding Corporation

106

微波烧烤锅 Microwave Grill Pot

设计 Design

苏州奔马厨具有限公司
Suzhou Benm Kitchen Appliance Co.,Ltd.

生产 Manufacture

苏州奔马厨具有限公司
Suzhou BenM Kitchen Appliance Co.,Ltd.

108

米格 S LED 台灯 Mi-Ge S LED Desk Lamp

设计 Design

欧普照明全球研发中心
Opple Lighting Global R&D Center

生产 Manufacture

欧普照明股份有限公司
Opple Lighting Co.,Ltd.

110

free lady 哑铃杯
Free Lady Dumbbell Cup

设计 Design
杭州领跑者工业设计有限公司
Hangzhou LPZ Industrial Design Co.,Ltd.
生产 Manufacture
杭州领跑者工业设计有限公司
Hangzhou LPZ Industrial Design Co.,Ltd.

110

安全瓜刨
Peeler S

设计 Design
叶晋豪
Ye Jinhao
生产 Manufacture
阳江市爱立德实业有限公司
Yangjiang Ailide Industries Co.,Ltd.

113

物理防烫吸管
Anti-Scald Straw

设计 Design
合肥为先产品设计有限公司
Hefei Weixian Product Design Co.,Ltd.
生产 Manufacture
合肥为先产品设计有限公司
Hefei Weixian Product Design Co., Ltd.

114

Mini 艾灸器
Mini Moxibustion

设计 Design
深圳市融一凤巢设计发展有限公司
Shenzhen Rone Phoenix Nest Design Development Co.,Ltd.
生产 Manufacture
广州绿源堂健康科技有限公司
Guangzhou Green Yuan Hall Health Technology Co., Ltd.

117

必迈全程马拉松跑鞋
MILE 42K

设计 Design
刘铮
Axis Liu
生产 Manufacture
北京必迈体育用品有限公司
Bmai Sports

111

提篮几
Tii Table

设计 Design
周安彬
Zhou Anbin
生产 Manufacture
广州一起住家具有限公司
Guangzhou Living Together Furnither Co.,Ltd.

113

老人马桶升降辅助器
Protected-Toilet Seat Lifting Equipment

设计 Design
董平莉、吴冬
Dong Pingli，Wu Dong
生产 Manufacture
九牧厨卫股份有限公司
Jomoo Kitchen&Bathroom Appliances Co.,Ltd.

115

红壹佰厂矿灯
Red100 Factory Lamp

设计 Design
马鞍山金马工业设计有限公司
Ma'anshan Jinma Industrial Design Co.,Ltd.
生产 Manufacture
红壹佰照明有限公司
Red100 Lighting Co.,Ltd.

117

畅流 反冲洗前置过滤器
Flow Backwash Pre-Filter

设计 Design
彭江明、林细勇
Peng Jiangming, Lin Xiyong
生产 Manufacture
日丰企业集团有限公司
Rifeng Enterprise Group Co.,Ltd.

111

随心控厨房龙头
Free Control Kitchen Faucet

设计 Design
林纪巧、卢玲
Lin Jiqiao， Lu Ling
生产 Manufacture
九牧厨卫股份有限公司
Jomoo Kitchen&Bathroom Appliances Co.,Ltd.

113

暖言一人食器
For One

设计 Design
刘培清、陈文
Liu Peiqing, Chen Wen
生产 Manufacture
杭州膳佳家居用品有限公司
Hangzhou Shanjia Lifestyles Co.,Ltd.

115

艺术椅
Artchair

设计 Design
深圳卓瑞文化礼品有限公司
Shenzhen Greensong Design Consultant Co.,Ltd.
生产 Manufacture
广州艾彻艺术品有限公司
Guangzhou Artchair Artwork Co.,Ltd.

117

家居两用刷
Dual-use Brush

设计 Design
义乌市浪尖工业设计有限公司
Yiwu Artop Design Co.,Ltd.
生产 Manufacture
义乌市良舍家居用品有限公司
Yiwu Liangshe Household Articles Co.,Ltd.

112

分装奶粉盒
Formula Container

设计 Design
李曼、向华
Li Man，Shine Xiang
生产 Manufacture
德珂（上海）母婴用品有限公司
Decobebe (Shanghai) Co.,Ltd.

114

儿童坐便器
Baby Potty

设计 Design
李曼、向华
Li Man，Shine Xiang
生产 Manufacture
德珂（上海）母婴用品有限公司
Decobebe (Shanghai) Co.,Ltd.

116

小鹿按摩棒
Baby Deer Massage Stick

设计 Design
杭州木马商务咨询有限公司
Hangzhou Moma Business Consulting Co.,Ltd.
生产 Manufacture
山东丽波电子科技有限公司
Shandong Wave Electronic Technology Co., Ltd.

118

折叠收纳盒
Folding Storage Box

设计 Design
叶晋豪、麦结恩
Ye Jinhao, Mai Jie'en
生产 Manufacture
阳江市爱立德实业有限公司
Yangjiang Ailide Industries Limited

112

铠甲舰队 V505A PLUS
V505A PLUS

设计 Design
麦克英孚（宁波）婴童用品有限公司，研发部
Max-inf (Ningbo) Baby Product Co.,Ltd. R
生产 Manufacture
麦克英孚（宁波）婴童用品有限公司
Max-inf (Ningbo) Baby Product Co., Ltd.

114

全景天窗锅具
Panorama Pan

设计 Design
梁佳、李华民
Liang Jia，Li Huamin
生产 Manufacture
上海嘉通电子科技有限公司
GreenTec Enterprise Limited

116

超薄一体智能坐便器 AKB1197
Ultra - Thin One Intelligent Toilet AKB1197

设计 Design
箭牌卫浴
ARROW
生产 Manufacture
佛山市乐华恒业卫浴有限公司
Foshan Lehua Hengye Sanitar Co.,Ltd.

118

中国象棋
Chinese Chess

设计 Design
杭州本来工业设计有限公司
Beladesign

生产 Manufacture
杭州提格科技有限公司
Hangzhou Teague Technology Co.,Ltd.

127

大碗茶情怀
Big Bowl Tea

设计 Design
焦哲
Kurt Jiao

生产 Manufacture
老舍茶馆
Laoshe Teahouse

128

寻见自然 超有机亚麻籽油
Xunjianziran

设计 Design
青岛知行天下品牌策划有限公司
China Kdc Brand Design Co.,Ltd.

生产 Manufacture
青岛知行天下品牌策划有限公司
China Kdc Brand Design Co.,Ltd.

128

铝合金触感签字笔
Aluminium Alloy Sensual Pen

设计 Design
南京可可青工业设计有限公司
Co-Green Design Consultants

生产 Manufacture
南京坦途机械制造有限公司
Nanjing Tantu Machinery Manufacturing Co.,Ltd.

128

益涂纳米书写膜
Hipaint Nano-Tech Writing Shield

设计 Design
程思祺
Cheng Siqi

生产 Manufacture
境洁环保科技（上海）有限公司
Jingjie Environment Technology（Shanghai）Co.,Ltd.

129

岛城头条
Daochengtoutiao

设计 Design
青岛知行天下品牌策划有限公司
China Kdc Brand Design Co.,Ltd.

生产 Manufacture
青岛即东鲞山湾食品有限公司
Qingdao Jidong Food Co., Ltd.

129

时光隧道辉光管时钟
Time Pipeline Clock

设计 Design
杨帆
Yang Fan

生产 Manufacture
北京腾达万喜科技有限公司
Beijing Tengdawanxi Technology Corporation

130

"伏笔"书写工具
Full-Pen

设计 Design
刘松
Liu Song

生产 Manufacture
嵘器（北京）创意设计有限公司
Rongqi(Beijing) Creative Design Co., Ltd.

130

可平置的酒瓶
X-Sir

设计 Design
张剑
Zhang Jian

生产 Manufacture
北京最红科技有限公司
Beijing Zuihong Technology Co.,Ltd.

131

龙先生强化维生素饮料
Mr.Long Fortified Vitamin Drinks

设计 Design
上海奎燕广告有限公司
Shanghai Key Advertising Co.,Ltd.

生产 Manufacture
佛山市三水区隐雪食品有限公司
Foshan Sanshui District Hidden Snow Food Co.,Ltd.

131

十六岁石榴水
Pomegranate Fruit Drinks

设计 Design
上海奎燕广告有限公司
Shanghai Key Advertising Co.,Ltd.

生产 Manufacture
武汉天喔茶庄饮料有限公司
Wuhan Tenwow Tea Company Beverage Co., Ltd.

131

药梨膏
Yao Li Gao

设计 Design
上海奎燕广告有限公司
Shanghai Key Advertising Co.,Ltd.

生产 Manufacture
上海梨膏糖食品厂
Shanghai Pear Sugar Food Factory

132

演艺系列纪念腕表
A Souvenir Watch of Acting Collection

设计 Design
深圳市雷诺表业有限公司
Shenzhen Rarone Watch Industry Co.,Ltd.

生产 Manufacture
深圳市雷诺表业有限公司
Shenzhen Rarone Watch Industry Co.,Ltd.

132

缩变的立方体
Shrinking Cube

设计 Design
北京上品极致产品设计有限公司
Beijing Top Industrial Design Co.,Ltd.

生产 Manufacture
北京交通大学
Beijing Jiaotong University

132

月时陶瓷月相灯
Moonii

设计 Design
庞鸣、郑鑫鑫
Pang Ming，Zheng Xinxin

生产 Manufacture
上海墨睿工业设计有限公司
Shanghai Moori Design Co.,Ltd.

133

海宴品牌全案策划设计
The Design of The Whole Package of Sea Feast Brand

设计 Design
青岛悟本正奇广告有限公司
Qingdao is now the odd advertising Limited

生产 Manufacture
青岛十三月餐饮管理有限公司
Qingdao March Food Management Co.,Ltd.

133

斗拱探秘
Dou Gong Confidential

设计 Design
马珺
Ma Jun

生产 Manufacture
北京菁草堂文化艺术中心
Beijing Jingcaotang Art&Design Center

134

剑脊·直尺
Jianji·Ruler

设计 Design
乔安琪、汤懿
Qiao Anqi, Tang Yi

生产 Manufacture
什物计画文化创意有限公司
Shiwujihua Cultural Creative Company Limited

134

智存
Cyber

设计 Design
谢磊、林帆
Xie Lei, Lin Fan

生产 Manufacture
上海文采实业有限公司
Shanghai KACO Industrial Co.,Ltd.

135

品致
Square

设计 Design
林帆
Lin Fan

生产 Manufacture
上海文采实业有限公司
Shanghai KACO Industrial Co.,Ltd.

135

大内咪探 AR 画册 AR Picture Album of The Imperial Palace Cat

设计 Design

北京洛可可科技有限公司
LKK Design Beijing Co.,Ltd.

生产 Manufacture

北京洛可可科技有限公司
LKK Design Beijing Co.,Ltd.

135

知竹快客杯 Zhizhu Quick Cup

设计 Design

崔建赟
Cui Jianyun

生产 Manufacture

北京新绎爱特艺术发展有限公司
Beijing Ovation Art Development Co.,Ltd.

136

俏 / 花器 Qiao/Flower

设计 Design

彭钟
Peng Zhong

生产 Manufacture

北京汉今国际文化发展有限公司
Beijing China Today International Culture Co., Ltd.

136

人看花 花看人 People See Flowers and Flowers See People

设计 Design

彦辰设计
Iseead Design

生产 Manufacture

彦辰设计（深圳）有限公司
Iseead Design Co.

136

月老红绳戒 Goddess

设计 Design

杨朝生
Yang Chaosheng

生产 Manufacture

上海品漫网络科技有限公司
Shanghai Pinman Network Technology Co.,Ltd.

137

Tapole T 系列 Tapole Series T

设计 Design

丁栋
Ding Dong

生产 Manufacture

深圳图谱人文科技有限公司
Tapole Co.,Ltd.

137

吉香居榨菜真芯 True Heart

设计 Design

希杰（青岛）食品有限公司
CJ(Qingdao) Foods Co.,Ltd.

生产 Manufacture

四川省吉香居食品有限公司
Jixiangju Food Co.,Ltd.

138

nubia Z17 智能手机包装 nubia Z17 Smartphone Packaging

设计 Design

努比亚技术有限公司
Nubia Technology Co.,Ltd.

生产 Manufacture

努比亚技术有限公司
Nubia Technology Co., Ltd.

138

竹叶青 Bamboo Liquor

设计 Design

水星组
Mercury Team

生产 Manufacture

深圳市柏星龙创意包装股份有限公司
Shenzhen Baixinglong Creative Packaging Co.,Ltd.

139

文化茶 Wenhua Tea

设计 Design

深圳市麦锡工业产品策划有限公司
Maxypro Industrial Product Scheme Co.,Ltd.

生产 Manufacture

深圳市字在文化传播有限公司
Zizai Culture Communication Co., Ltd.

139

五色本草 Tie-Dye Teaching Kit

设计 Design

林泓魁、李岩
Lin Hongkui, Li Yan

生产 Manufacture

北京泓羽文化艺术有限公司
Beijing Hongyu Culture and Arts Co., Ltd.

139

七轴协作机器人 Seven Cooperative Robot

设计 Design

沈阳创新设计服务有限公司
Shenyang Innovation

生产 Manufacture

新松机器人自动化股份有限公司
SIASUN

140

蜂鸟 Hummingbird

设计 Design

胡益丹、王群
Hu Yidan，Charlie Wang

生产 Manufacture

惠州市卡儿酷科技有限公司
Huizhou Carku Technology Co.,Ltd.

140

西门子 SOMATOM go. CT 扫描平台 Somatom go.

设计 Design

Designaffairs 设计公司
Designaffairs

生产 Manufacture

西门子医疗
Siemens Healthcare GmbH

141

物证勘查仪 Material Evidence Exploration Instrument

设计 Design

艺可意工业设计（北京）有限公司
Ecoe Industrial Design （Beijing）Co.,Ltd.

生产 Manufacture

艺可意工业设计（北京）有限公司
Ecoe Industrial Design（Beijing） Co.,Ltd.

141

掘进机 TBM

设计 Design

沈阳创新设计服务有限公司
Shenyang Innovation

生产 Manufacture

北方重工集团
NHI

141

超声药物导入治疗仪 Ultrasonic Medicine Import Therapeutic Apparatus

设计 Design

上简设计（武汉）有限公司
Up Design(Wuhan)

生产 Manufacture

安徽省玉林医药有限公司
Anhui Yulin Pharmaceutical Co.,Ltd.

142

DZ931 系列塑壳断路器 DZ931 Series Moulded Case Circuit Breaker

设计 Design

杭州木马商务咨询有限公司
Hangzhou Moma Business Consulting Co.,Ltd.

生产 Manufacture

常熟瑞特电气股份有限公司
Changshu Ruite Electric Co.,Ltd.

142

压裂车 Fracturing Truck

设计 Design

沈阳创新设计服务有限公司
Shenyang Innovation

生产 Manufacture

北方重工集团
NHI

142

易操作省空间生物质自动化锅炉 Easy to Use and Saving Space Automatic Biomass Boiler

设计 Design

广东顺德东方麦田工业设计有限公司
East-Innovation Shunde GD Co.,Ltd.

生产 Manufacture

河北鑫华新环保科技有限公司
Hebei Xinhua New Environmental Technology Co., Ltd.

143

ST858 破拆机器人
ST858 Broken Robot

设计 Design
马鞍山飞渡工业设计有限公司
Ma'anshan Feel Do Industrial Design Co.,Ltd.

生产 Manufacture
惊天智能装备股份有限公司
Giant I-Equipment Co.,Ltd.

143

Gray Sculpture 麻醉工作站
Gray Sculpture Anaesthetic Workstation

设计 Design
李俊杰
Leo Li

生产 Manufacture
北京思瑞德医疗器械有限公司
Beijing Siriusmed Medical Device Co.,Ltd.

145

医用压缩雾化器 - FC08-W（启泰）
Medical Compression Atomizer

设计 Design
张俊生
Johnson Zhang

生产 Manufacture
英华融泰医疗科技股份有限公司
ENTIE Medical PLC

147

儿童脑瘫治疗仪
Pediatric Cerebral Palsy Treatment Apparatus

设计 Design
杭州汉度工业设计有限公司
Hangzhou Hando Industrial Design Co.,Ltd.

生产 Manufacture
浙江新丰医疗器械有限公司
Zhejiang Xinfeng Medical Instrument Co.,Ltd.

149

GT20-S 工程机器人
GT20-S Machine Robot

设计 Design
马鞍山市安工大工业技术研究院有限公司
Ma'anshan, Anhui University of Technology Industrial Technology Research Institute Co.,Ltd.

生产 Manufacture
惊天智能装备股份有限公司
Giant I-Equipment Co.,Ltd.

143

PUE0810 履带式破碎机
Tracked Mobile Plants

设计 Design
江苏徐州工程机械研究院工业设计中心
ID Center of Xuzhou Construction Machinery Group Co.,Ltd.

生产 Manufacture
徐州工程机械集团有限公司
ID Center of Xuzhou Construction Machinery Group Co.,Ltd.

145

"辽"矢量多旋翼无人机
Woozoom Tandem Wing Tilt Rotor UAV

设计 Design
沈阳无距科技有限公司
Woozoom

生产 Manufacture
沈阳无距科技有限公司
Woozoom

147

XYGC800 手持式动力切割机
XYGC800 Cutting Machine

设计 Design
杭州源骏工业产品设计有限公司
Hangzhou Runite Industry Design Co.,Ltd.

生产 Manufacture
星月集团有限公司
Xingyue Group Co.,Ltd.

149

生物质链条热水锅炉
Biomass Chain Hot Water Boiler

设计 Design
郑州一诺工业产品设计有限公司
Zhengzhou Enor Industrial Product Design Co.,Ltd.

生产 Manufacture
河南绿探集团
Henan Green Agent Group

144

QT-216 型智能语音导盲服
QT-216 Intelligent Voice Guide Clothing

设计 Design
周萍
Zhou Ping

生产 Manufacture
北京绮彤子姗服装有限责任公司
Beijing Qitong Children's Clothing Co., Ltd.

146

军用四旋翼（折叠翼）无人机
Military Four-Rotor UAV

设计 Design
北京赛佳图工业设计有限公司
Beijing Saga FIG Industrial Design Co.,Ltd.

生产 Manufacture
山东蜂巢航空科技有限公司
Honeycomb Aerospace Tecnologies (Shandong) Co., Ltd.

148

DOBOT Magician 智能机械臂
DOBOT Magician

设计 Design
吴志文
Wu Zhiwen

生产 Manufacture
深圳市越疆科技有限公司
Shenzhen Yuejiang Technology Co.,Ltd.

150

GMC2040 定梁龙门式加工中心
GMC2040 Fixed Beam Gantry Machining Center

设计 Design
区耀光、吕慧彬
Oson, Lv Huibin

生产 Manufacture
山东威达重工股份有限公司
Shandong Weida Heavy Industry Co.,Ltd.

144

GMC-2015 数控龙门加工中心
GMC-2015 CNC Gantry Machining Center

设计 Design
重庆道合工业设计有限公司
Chongqing Daohe Industrial Design Co., Ltd

生产 Manufacture
南通聚田机电科技有限公司
Nantong Jutian Electrical and Mechanical Technology Co., Ltd.

146

全自动核酸检测仪
Automatic Nucleic Acid Detector

设计 Design
杭州汉度工业设计有限公司
Hangzhou Hando Industrial Design Co.,Ltd.

生产 Manufacture
杭州杰毅麦特医疗器械有限公司
Hangzhou Gene-Meta Medical Device Co., Ltd.

148

双子塔智能加油机
Twin Towers Intelligent Oiling Machine

设计 Design
广州易用设计有限公司
Ease Design Guangzhou Co.,Ltd.

生产 Manufacture
珠海市贝林加油设备有限公司
Zhuhai Beilin Fueling Equipent Co.,Ltd.

150

YSF 全身健康扫描系统
YSF Full-Body Health Scanning System

设计 Design
郑州一诺工业产品设计有限公司
Zhengzhou Enor Industrial Product Design Co.,Ltd.

生产 Manufacture
河南恒东医疗器械有限公司
Henan Hengdong Medical Instrument Co.,Ltd.

144

可视插管软镜
Video Flexible Intubationscope

设计 Design
李兰华
Lory Li

生产 Manufacture
珠海迈德豪医用科技有限公司
Zhuhai Mindhao Medical Technology Co., Ltd.

147

红外温热治疗仪
Optical Instrument

设计 Design
北京上品极致产品设计有限公司
Beijing Top Industrial Design Co.,Ltd.

生产 Manufacture
北京斯丹姆赛尔技术有限公司
Beijing Adams Damm Purcell Technology Co.,Ltd.

148

汽油数码变频发电机组（GS950i）
Gasoline Inverter Generator

设计 Design
天津爱谷工业设计有限公司
Tianjin I.Co Industrial Design Co.,Ltd.

生产 Manufacture
浙江星月实业有限公司
Zhejiang Xingyue Industry Co., Ltd.

150

LERA S1 62V 锂电吹风机
LERA S1 Series 62V Lithium Electric Blower

设计 Design
杭州源骏工业产品设计有限公司
Hangzhou Runite Industry Design Co.,Ltd.

生产 Manufacture
宁波动一电器有限公司
Ningbo Lera Electric Appliance Co.,Ltd.

151

NUX 折叠电子鼓
NUX Foldable Digital Drum

设计 Design
邱剑锋、王琳
Kevin Qiu, Wang Lin

生产 Manufacture
深圳市蔚科电子科技开发有限公司
Cherub Technology Co.,Ltd.

152

重离子治疗床
KJTJ Heavy Ion Medical Bed

设计 Design
杭州领跑者工业设计有限公司
Hangzhou LPZ Industrial Design Co.,Ltd.

生产 Manufacture
兰州科近泰基新技术有限责任公司
Lanzhou Kejintaiji Co.,Ltd.

155

新松柔性手臂机器人
Siasun Flexible Arm Robots

设计 Design
杭州领跑者工业设计有限公司
Hangzhou LPZ Industrial Design Co.,Ltd.

生产 Manufacture
沈阳新松机器人自动化股份有限公司
Shenyang Siasun Robot&Automation Co.,Ltd.

156

LERA S1 62V 锂电链锯
LERA S1 Series 62V Lithium Electric Chain Saw

设计 Design
杭州源骏工业产品设计有限公司
Hangzhou Runite Industry Design Co.,Ltd.

生产 Manufacture
宁波动一电器有限公司
Ningbo Lera Electric Appliance Co.,Ltd.

151

多功能扫路机
Multi-Function Sweeper

设计 Design
邓扬、吕志涛
Dong Yang, Lv Zhitao

生产 Manufacture
长沙中联重科环境产业有限公司
Zoomlion

153

智能物流机器人
Intelligent Logistic Robot

设计 Design
北京乐品乐道科技有限公司
Beijing Ledao Thenaropin Technology Co.,Ltd.

生产 Manufacture
北京极智嘉科技有限公司
Beijing Zhijia Science and Technology Co.,Ltd.

155

银河（GALAXY）系列高清显示租赁屏
(GALAXY) Series HD Display Rental Screen

设计 Design
深圳市木马整合设计有限公司
Shenzhen Moma Integrated Design Co.,Ltd.

生产 Manufacture
深圳市威尔科视光电有限公司
Shenzhen Weier Christie Photoelectric Co.,Ltd.

157

“无距”串列翼倾转旋翼无人机
Woozoom Series of Wings Tilting The Rotor

设计 Design
沈阳无距科技有限公司
Woozoom

生产 Manufacture
沈阳无距科技有限公司
Woozoom

151

四轴码垛机器人
Four-Axis Palletizing Robot

设计 Design
广东顺德潜龙工业设计有限公司
Chinno Design Co.,Ltd.

生产 Manufacture
广州数控设备有限公司
Guangzhou CNC Equipment Co., Ltd.

153

近红外荧光成像系统
Near-Infrared Fluorescence Imaging System

设计 Design
迟崇巍、毛亚敏
Chi Chongwei, Mao Yamin

生产 Manufacture
北京数字精准医疗科技有限公司
Beijing Digital Precision Medical Technology Co.,Ltd.

155

自动缠绕机
Automatic Winding Machine

设计 Design
苏州上品极致产品设计有限公司
Suzhou Top Industrial Design Co.,Ltd.

生产 Manufacture
江苏小黄蜂智能科技有限公司
Smart Wasp Intelligent Technology(Suzhou) Co.,Ltd.

157

40V 高压清洗机
40V High Pressure Washer

设计 Design
蒋祥军、孙山虎
Sky Jiang，Tiger Sun

生产 Manufacture
浙江亚特电器有限公司
YAT Electrical Appliance Co., Ltd.

152

新松床椅一体化机器人
Siasun Bed-Chair Integrated Robot

设计 Design
杭州领跑者工业设计有限公司
Hangzhou LPZ Industrial Design Co.,Ltd.

生产 Manufacture
沈阳新松机器人自动化股份有限公司
Shenyang Siasun Robot&Automation Co., Ltd.

154

体感假肢机器人
The Upper Limb Exoskeleton Rehabilitation Robot

设计 Design
上简设计（武汉）有限公司
Up Design(Wuhan)

生产 Manufacture
武汉与木造物工业设计有限公司
Wuhan and Wooden Industrial Design

156

工业用防护口罩
Industrial Protective Respirator

设计 Design
北京智加问道科技有限公司
Beijing ZCO Design Co.,Ltd.

生产 Manufacture
北京华创矿安科技有限公司
Beijing Huachuangkuangan Technology Co.,Ltd.

158

无人机干扰器
UAV Scrambler 300

设计 Design
成都意町工业产品设计有限公司
Chengdu Iding Industrial Design Co.,Ltd.

生产 Manufacture
四川益丰电子科技有限公司
Sichuan Yifeng Electronics Science & Technology Co.,Ltd.

152

无溶剂凹版印刷机
Solvent Free Intaglio Press

设计 Design
广东顺德潜龙工业设计有限公司
Chinno Design Co.,Ltd.

生产 Manufacture
中山松德印刷机械有限公司
Zhongshan Sotech Printing Machinery Co.,Ltd.

154

手术缝线推结器
Surgical Suture Pusher

设计 Design
日照工业设计中心有限公司
Rizhao Industrial Design Center Co.,Ltd.

生产 Manufacture
山东贝诺斯医疗器械有限公司
Shandong Bainus Medical Instrument Co.,Ltd.

156

阿帕奇 VR 直升机模拟器
Apache VR Helicopter Simulator

设计 Design
沈阳智加问道科技有限公司
Shenyang ZCO Design Co.,Ltd.

生产 Manufacture
大连大华中天科技有限公司
Dalian Dahuazhongtian Technology Co., Ltd.

158

ARJ21-700 公务机内饰
Smart+

设计 Design
中国商飞上海飞机客户服务有限公司 工业设计所
COMAC Shanghai Aircraft Customer Service Co., Ltd. Industrial Design Institute

生产 Manufacture
中国商飞
COMAC

166

多功能通道闸机
Multi-Function Channel Gates

设计 Design
北京赛佳图工业设计有限公司
Beijing Saga Fig Industrial Design Co.,Ltd.

生产 Manufacture
北京中成科信科技发展有限公司
Beijing Zhongcheng Technology and Trust Development Co., Ltd.

170

银行金融发卡机器人
Intelligent Financial Card Issuing Robot

设计 Design
北京智加问道科技有限公司
Beijing ZCO Design Co.,Ltd.

生产 Manufacture
北京东方兴华科技发展有限责任公司
Beijing DFXH Orient Xinghua Technology Development Co.,Ltd.

171

智慧助教云白板
Smart Edu Assistant Cloud Board

设计 Design
姚欣、陈立勋
Yao Xin, Chen Lixun

生产 Manufacture
杭州迈杰教育科技有限公司
Hangzhou Maijie Educational Technology Co.,Ltd.

168

生态绿植墙空气净化系统
Ecological Green Wall Air Purification System

设计 Design
北京上品极致产品设计有限公司
Beijing Top Industrial Design Co.,Ltd.

生产 Manufacture
北京生泰宝科技有限公司
ECO-BAO Co.,Ltd.

170

简约智慧路灯（星海系列）
Simple Intelligent Streat Lamp

设计 Design
上海木马工业产品设计有限公司
Shanghai Moma Industrial Product Design Co.,Ltd.

生产 Manufacture
四川能投光电有限公司
SCEI Optoelectronic Co.,Ltd.

172

城市家具
City Furniture

设计 Design
高尚
Sandy Gao

生产 Manufacture
上海壹生图文设计制作有限公司
Shanghai One Life Graphic Design Co.,Ltd.

168

DT-7000i58 小额现金循环机
DT-7000i58 Compact Cash Recycler

设计 Design
广州广电运通金融电子股份有限公司
GRGBanking Equipment Co., Ltd.

生产 Manufacture
广州广电运通金融电子股份有限公司
GRGBanking Equipment Co.,Ltd.

170

魔力伞
Molisan

设计 Design
杭州汉点工业设计有限公司
Hangzhou Handot Industrial Design Co., Ltd.

生产 Manufacture
上海艺升信息科技有限公司
Shanghai Yisheng Information Technology Co.,Ltd.

172

溪客度假屋
Seek Holiday House

设计 Design
北京大地溪客露营建筑科技有限公司
Beijing BES SEEK Camping Architecture Technology Co.,Ltd.

生产 Manufacture
北京大地溪客露营建筑科技有限公司
Beijing BES SEEK Camping Architecture Technology Co.,Ltd.

169

公共智能宠物寄存柜
Smart Pet Storage Box

设计 Design
杭州奥格工业设计有限公司
AUG Hangzhou Industrial Design Co.,Ltd.

生产 Manufacture
上海宠儿宠物用品有限公司
Petin China Co.,Ltd.

171

移动互联网医院
Mobile Internet Hospital

设计 Design
深圳市柏斯工业设计有限公司
Shenzhen Perth Industrial Design Co.,Ltd.

生产 Manufacture
深圳市柏斯工业设计有限公司
Shenzhen Perth Industrial Design Co.,Ltd.

169

再生混凝土组合式透水地面砖
Recycled Aggregate Concrete Combined Water Permeable Ground Bricks

设计 Design
成都沙苑工业产品设计有限公司
Chengdu Shayuan Industrial Design Co.,Ltd.

生产 Manufacture
成都沙苑工业产品设计有限公司
Chengdu Shayuan Industrial Design Co.,Ltd.

171

2017 中国设计红星原创奖获奖名单
Winner List of 2017 China Red Star Original Design Award

红星原创奖银奖
Silver Award of Original Design Award

Eco-Motor 城市物流电动车
Express Eco-Motor

设计 Design
周才致、张沙、李鸿佳
Zhou Caizhi, Zhang Sha, Li Hongjia

176

能量胶带
Energy Tape

设计 Design
林思安、杨磊、李承勇
Lin Sian, Yang Lei, Li Chengyong

177

交流的坐具
The Rattan Chair that Promotes Communication

设计 Design
黄莹莹
Huang Yingying

178

KIWIGOGO 2-Way 奇异果双向智能车
KIWIGOGO 2-Way Electric Bicycle

设计 Design
青岛奇异果智能科技有限公司
Qingdao Supranatural Intelligent Science &Technology Co.,Ltd

179

2M 高峰快线
2M Peak Express

设计 Design
黄赫中、王喆义
Huang Hezhong, Wang Zheyi

180

空中消防车
Air Fire Engine

设计 Design
范石钟
Fan Shizhong

181

优秀设计师奖
Best Designer Award of Original Design Award

范石钟
Fan Shizhong

184

王谭
Vincent Wang

185

未来之星奖
Future Star Award of Original Design Award

杨磊
Yang Lei

188

周才致
Zhou Caizhi

189

红星原创奖
Excellent Award of Original Design Award

棒——循环加热搅拌棒
BANG—Cyclic Heating Stir Bar

设计 Design
孙建昆
Sun Jiankun

192

行李助手
Luggage Helper

设计 Design
师艳江、楚文宝、戴新宇
Shi Yanjiang , Chu Wenbao, Dai Xinyu

192

生命标记
Life Markers

设计 Design
欧阳雪欣、徐文鑫、王子健
Ouyang Xuexin, Xu Wenxin，Wang Zijian

193

暖手拐杖
Warm Crutch

设计 Design
深圳市韵博产品策划有限公司
Shenzhen Yunbo Product Planning Co., Ltd.

193

日历保健品包装
Health Care Products Packaging with Calendar

设计 Design
无限极（中国）有限公司
Infinitus(China)Company LTD

193

火灾应急水性口罩
Fire Emergency Water Mask

设计 Design
薛伟峰、祝灵洁
Xue Weifeng Zhu Lingjie

194

盲文电子书
Braille E-book

设计 Design
褚圣洁、沈颖颖、王思凝
Chu Shengjie, Shen Yingying, Wang Sining

194

雨天骑行听力结构
Rain Riding Listening

设计 Design
肖博文、李嘉、孙淑娴
Xiao bowen, Li jia, Sun shuxian

194

儿童输液加热固定板
Children Infusion Heating Fixed Plate

设计 Design
芦彬、裴雪原、龚诗雨
Lu Bin, Pei Xueyuan, Gong Shiyu

195

棒棒糖压舌棒
"Lollipop" Spatula

设计 Design
晏阳震
Yan Yangzhen

195

无限调色板
Unlimited Palette

设计 Design
蔺薛菲、范石钟
Lin Xuefei, Fan Shizhong

196

应急灾难门把手
Disaster Emergency Door Handle

设计 Design
张宏珅
Zhang Hongshen

196

空气盒子燃气灶
AIRBOX GAS STOVES

设计 Design
黎泽锋
Li ZeFeng

197

即抛型注射器
Disposable Syringe

设计 Design
合肥鼎典工业设计有限公司
Hefei Designdo Industrial Design Co.,Ltd

197

便携药丸棉
Portable Capsule Absorbent Cotton

设计 Design
胡焱华
Hu YanHua

197

易用汤锅
Easy to Use Pot

设计 Design
周鹏
Zhou Peng

198

雪地取水杯
Snowfield Collected Water Cup

设计 Design
何璐君
He Lujun

198

2017

12th

主办及专家委员会
Organizer & Jury Committee

2017

中国设计红星奖委员会主席
Chairman of China Red Star Design Award Committee

朱焘
Zhu Tao

中国设计红星奖专家委员会
Jury Committee of China Red Star Design Award

柳冠中
Liu Guanzhong

中国
China

清华大学美术学院责任教授，博士生导师，享受政府津贴学者
Professor & doctoral supervisor of Academy of Arts & Design, Tsinghua University, with governmental subsidies

何人可
He Renke

中国
China

湖南大学设计艺术学院院长、教授
Dean & Professor of School of Design, Hunan University

Peter Zec

德国
Germany

红点设计奖主席
President of Red Dot Design Award

Ralph Wiegmann

德国
Germany

iF 国际设计论坛首席执行官
CEO, iF International Forum Design GmbH

Brandon Gien

澳大利亚
Australia

澳大利亚国际设计奖主席
Chair of the Australian International Design Awards

喜多俊之
Toshiyuki Kita

日本
Japan

日本优良设计大奖（G-Mark）评委会前主席
Former Chairperson of the Jury of G-Mark Award

鲁晓波
Lu Xiaobo

中国
China

清华大学美术学院院长、教授
Dean & Professor of Academy of Arts & Design, Tsinghua University

Arturo Dell'Acqua Bellavitis

意大利
Italy

意大利米兰三年展主席
President of the Triennale Design Museum

Mugendi K. M'Rithaa

肯尼亚
Kenya

世界设计组织主席（2015—2017）
President of World Design Organization(2015-2017)

童慧明
Tong Huiming

中国
China

广州美术学院工业设计学院前院长
Former Dean of College of Industrial Design, Guangzhou Academy of Fine Arts

Michael Young

英国
UK

迈克尔·杨工作室创始人
Founder & Director of Michael Young Studio

陈冬亮
Chen Dongliang

中国
China

北京工业设计促进中心主任
Director of Beijing Industrial Design Center

Tapani Hyvönen

芬兰
Finland

海德海沃恩设计首席执行官
CEO of Hyde-Hyvonen Design Ltd.

Orrin Shively

美国
USA

美国迪士尼交互传媒集团艺术和设计资深总监
Senior Director of Art & Design, Disney Interactive, Disney Interactive Media Group

陈文龙
Chen Wenlong

中国台湾
China Taiwan

浩汉设计总经理
General Manager of Nova Design

刘小康
Freeman Lau

中国香港
China Hong Kong

香港设计中心副主席
Vice Chairman of Hong Kong Design Center

辛向阳
Xin Xiangyang

中国
China

国际交互设计会议（ICID）学术委员会主任
Director of International Conference on Interaction Design Academic Board

石大宇
Jeff Shi

美国
USA

清庭设计中心创办人暨创意总监
Dragonfly Design Center Founder and Creative Director

娄永琪
Lou Yongqi

中国
China

同济大学设计创意学院院长
Dean of College of Design & Innovation, Tongji University

许平
Xu Ping

中国
China

中央美术学院教授
Professor of China Central Academy of Fine Arts

Andrej Kupetz

德国
Germany

德国设计委员会主席
General Manager of German Design Council

David Jonathan Waterman

英国
UK

伟易达通讯设备有限公司高级设计总监
Senior Design Director of AT&T/VTECH Telecommunications

徐伯初
Xu Bochu

中国
China

西南交通大学人机环境系统设计研究所所长
Director of the Institute of Design and Research for Man-Machine-Environment Engineer System, Southwest Jiaotong University

Christian Schwamkrug

德国
Germany

保时捷设计工作室设计总监
Design Director of Porsche Design Studio

刘传凯
Carl Liu

中国台湾
China Taiwan

牛电科技设计副总裁
Vice President for Design, Niu Technologies Group Limited

Francois Lenfant

法国
France

通用电气医疗全球设计经理
Global Design Manager for Europe & Middle-East (EMEA), GE Healthcare

曾辉
Zeng Hui

中国
China

北京国际设计周组委会办公室副主任
Deputy Director of Beijing Design Week Organizing Committee

Tim Flattery

美国
USA

美国艺术中心设计学院娱乐设计系主任
Chair of Entertainment Design at Art Center College of Design

邱丰顺
Kumo Chiu

中国台湾
China Taiwan

1925 文创品牌创始人
Founder of 1925

Robert Sachon

德国
Germany

博世家电全球设计总监
Global Design Director, BOSCH

应放天
Ying Fangtian

中国
China

中国工业设计协会副会长兼秘书长
Vice President & Secretary of China Industrial Design Association

蔡军
Cai Jun

中国
China

清华大学美术学院工业设计系教授
Industrial Design Professor of Art College of Tsinghua University

李淳寅
Lee Soon In

韩国
Korea

世界设计组织主席（2011—2013）
President of World Design Organization [2011-2013]

Axel Thallemer

德国
Germany

新加坡国立大学设计与环境学院工业设计教授
Deputy Head(Research], Professor, Division of Industrial Design, School of Design and Environment, National University of Singapore

殷正声
Yin Zhengsheng

中国
China

同济大学设计创意学院教授
Professor of Design Innovation College of Tongji University

Alpay Er

土耳其
Turkey

伊斯坦布尔技术大学工业产品设计系主任、教授
Chair and Professor, Dept. of Industrial Product Design, Istanbul Technical University (ITU]

Harald Leschke

德国
Germany

梅赛德斯奔驰汽车集团设计总监（1978—2007）
Head of Mercedes-Benz Advanced Desig(1978—2007)

渡边慎二
Shinji Watanabe

日本
Japan

日本千叶大学设计系主任
Professor, Chair of Design, Chiba University

林衍堂
Lam Yanta

中国香港
China Hong Kong

香港理工大学设计学院副主任
Professor of Design & Associate Head school of Design, the Hong Kong Polytechnic University

严扬
Yan Yang

中国
China

清华大学美术学院工业设计系教授
Professor of Industrial Design Department of Academy of Arts & Design, Tsinghua University

陈汗青
Chen Hanqing

中国
China

上海视觉艺术学院副院长
Vice President, Shanghai Institute of Visual Art

Duncan Trevor-Wilson

澳大利亚
Australia

通用电气医疗集团先进概念全球设计总监
Global Design Director for Advanced Concepts at GE Healthcare

马春东
Ma Chundong

中国
China

大连民族大学设计学院院长
Dean of Design School, Dalian Minzu University

Andy Ogden

美国
USA

美国艺术中心设计学院工业设计系研究生院主任
Chair of Graduate Industrial Design at Art Center College of Design

叶宇轩
Yeh Yu-Hsuan

中国台湾
China Taiwan

北京耶爱第尔设计公司（YEHIDEA）品牌创始人
Founder of Beijing YEHIDEA Design

Mathis Heller

荷兰
Netherlands

中国汽车工程研究院有限公司设计顾问
Automotive Design Consultant of China Automotive Engineering Research Institute

陈江
Chen Jiang

中国
China

广州美术学院工业设计学院院长
Dean of College of Industrial Design, Guangzhou Academy of Fine Arts

Dimitri Vicedomini

意大利
Italy

华晨汽车集团华颂前设计总监
Former Design Director of Huasong, Brilliance-Auto Shenyang

朱小杰
Zhu Xiaojie

中国
China

澳珀家具艺术总监
Art Director of Opal Furniture

李凤朗
Li Fenglang

中国
China

联想消费 PC 设计前高级总监
Former Executive Director of PC Department of Lenovo

Severin Filek

奥地利
Austria

奥地利设计协会总经理
Managing Director, Design Austria

朱长岭
Zhu Changling

中国
China

中国家具协会理事长
President of China National Furniture Association

Borjana Lambreva

德国
Germany

大众汽车集团（中国）战略规划与研究部模块与技术战略主管
Head of Module and Technology Strategy Group Strategy Planning and Research at Volkswagen Group China

杨明洁
Jamy Yang

中国
China

杨设计创始人
Founder of Yang Design

温浩
Wen Hao

中国
China

广州美术学院家具研究院院长
The Institute of Furniture Design, Guangzhou Academy of Fine Arts

李剑叶
Li Jianye

中国
China

锤子科技（北京）有限公司工业设计副总裁
Vice President of Industrial Design, Smartisan Digital

Edna dos Santos-Duisenberg

巴西
Brazil

联合国贸易和发展会议创意经济项目前主任
Former Chief of Cabinet of the Secretary General of UNCTAD

Jorge Teixeira

葡萄牙
Portugal

葡萄牙设计师协会会员
Member of Portuguese Association of Designers

Jeroen Raijmakers

荷兰
Netherlands

飞利浦医疗全球设计总监
Global Design Director of Healthcare at Philips

田中一雄
Kazuo Tanaka

日本
Japan

GK 设计株式会社总裁
President of GK Design Group Inc.

周佚
Zhou Yi

中国
China

上海指南工业设计有限公司创始人、总经理
Founder & General Manager, S Point Design

邱丽梅
Leimei Julia Chiu

日本
Japan

武藏野美术大学教授
Professor of Musashino Art University (MAU)

王昀
Wang Yun

中国
China

中国美术学院设计艺术学院副院长
Vice president, Design Art College of China Academy of Art(CAA)

叶慧儿
Amy Ip

中国香港
China Hong Kong

峡湾设计集团设计总监
Group Design Director of Fjord Design

王日华
Wang Rihua

中国
China

上海工业设计协会会长
President of Shanghai Industrial Design Association

吴剑
Wu Jian

中国
China

海尔创新设计中心总经理
General manager of Haier Innovation Design Center

中国设计红星奖组织机构
Institutes of China Red Star Design Award

项目支持 / **Support**
北京市科学技术委员会
Beijing Municipal Science & Technology Commission

主办单位 / **Organizer**
中国设计红星奖委员会
China Red Star Design Award Committee

发起单位 / **Sponsor**
中国工业设计协会
北京工业设计促进中心
国务院发展研究中心《新经济导刊》杂志社
China Industrial Design Association
Beijing Industrial Design Center
New Economy Weekly

承办单位 / **Host**
北京工业设计促进中心
Beijing Industrial Design Center

工作站 / **Work Station**
上海工业设计协会
广东省工业设计协会
深圳市设计联合会
中国光谷楚创空间
合肥市工业设计协会
洛客
Shanghai Industrial Design Association
Guangdong Industrial Design Association
Shenzhen Industrial Design Association
China Optics Valley Chu Innovation Space
Hefei Industrial Design Association
LKKER

协办单位 / **Co-organizer**
北京光华设计发展基金会
北京工业设计促进会
天津市工业设计协会
重庆工业设计协会
黑龙江省艺术设计协会
江苏省工业设计学会
湖南省工业设计协会
四川省工业设计协会
陕西省工业设计协会
广州工业设计促进会
宁波市工业设计联合会
青岛市工业设计协会
绍兴市工业设计协会
顺德工业设计协会
Dragon Design Foundation
Beijing Industrial Design Promotion Organization
Tianjin Industrial Design Association
Chongqing Industrial Design Association
Heilongjiang Province Artistic Design Association
Jiangsu Industrial Design Association
Hunan Industrial Design Association
Sichuan Industrial Design Association
Shaanxi Industrial Design Association
Guangzhou Industrial Design Association
Ningbo Industrial Design Union
Qingdao Industrial Design Association
Shaoxing Industrial Design Association
Shunde Industrial Design Association

战略合作伙伴 / **Strategic Partner**
阿里巴巴集团
视觉中国
苏州图书馆
横琴国际知识产权交易中心
中国设计智造大奖
花瓣网
Alibaba Group
China Visual Group
Suzhou Library
Hengqin International Intellectual Property Exchange Co.,Ltd
Design Intelligence Award
huaban.com

合作伙伴 / **Partner**
京东金融
北京国际设计周
杭州国际设计周
中国（深圳）国际工业设计周
元美传媒
上海品三谛信息技术有限公司
JD Finance
Beijing Design Week
Hangzhou International Design Week
China(Shenzhen) International Industrial Design Week
Yami media
PIN3D

报道媒体 / **REPORTING MEDIA**
人民日报
中央电视台
经济日报
科技日报
环球时报
中国科学报
中国艺术报
北京日报
北京晚报
北京电视台
北京青年报
北京商报
消费日报
设计
设计通讯
趋势
创意世界
新华网
千龙网
中国网
中国新闻网
凤凰网
国际在线
光明网
新浪家居
网易家居
腾讯网
搜狐数码
中国文艺网
视觉同盟
意大利 DESIGNBOOM
Billwang
设计癖
Hi 设计
格物者
People's Daily
CCTV
Economic Daily
Science and Technology Daily
Global Times
China Science Daily
China Art
Beijing Daily
Beijing Evening News
Beijing Television Station
Beijing Youth Daily
Beijing Business Today
Consumption Daily
Design
Design Communication
Trend
Creativity
news.cn
qianlong.com
China.org.cn
Chinanews.com
ifeng.com
cri.cn
gmw.cn
jiaju.sina.com.cn
home.163.com
qq.com
digi.sohu.com
cflac.org.cn
visionunion
designboom
billwang.net
shejipi.com
hisheji.cn
52gewu.com

鸣谢（排名不分先后）
Acknowledgement (Listed in no particular order)

北京市西城区人民政府
中关村科技园西城园管委会
北京市通州区科学技术委员会
武汉市城乡建设委员会
中创红星设计创业投资基金
北京科技大学
袈蓝公社
都市时报
Xicheng District People's Government of Beijing Municipality
Administrative Committee of Zhongguancun Xicheng Science Park
Tongzhou District Science and Technology Commission of Beijing Municipality
Wuhan Urban And Rural Construction Commission
China Innovation Design Red Star and Creative Industry Entrepreneurship Investment Fund
University of Science & Technology Bejing
SYN Architects
City Times

中国设计红星奖委员会

主席 朱焘
执行主席 黄武秀、陈冬亮

委员
刘晖、刘宁、左倩、楼晓红、王海宁、邢雷、崔立祥、陈孝超、张锡、张震甫、何人可、宋慰祖、周佳奇、杨为渝、胡启志、聂熙睿、许世虎、王日华、刘振、樊超然、齐宽明

CHINA RED STAR DESIGN AWARD COMMITTEE

CHAIRMAN Zhu Tao
EXECUTIVE CHAIRMAN Huang Wuxiu / Chen Dongliang

MEMBERS
Liu Hui / Liu Ning / Zuo Qian / Lou Xiaohong / Wang Haining / Xing Lei / Cui Lixiang / Chen Xiaochao / Zhang Xi / Zhang Zhenfu / He Renke / Song Weizu / Zhou Jiaqi / Yang Weiyu / Hu Qizhi / Nie Xirui / Xu Shihu / Wang Rihua / Liu Zhen / Fan Chaoran / Qi Kuanming

红星奖办公室

楼晓红、谢迪、万菊、陈宇、张芸皓、栾一丞、刘雨茜、杨馨媛、黄艺欣、方艺润、冯硕

CHINA RED STAR DESIGN AWARD OFFICE

Lou Xiaohong / Xie Di / Wan Ju / Chen Yu / Zhang Yunhao / Luan Yicheng / Liu Yuxi / Yang Xinyuan / Huang Yixin / Fang Yirun / Feng Shuo

GOOD DESIGN
韩国好设计奖
Korea
Good Design

GOOD DESIGN AWARDS
澳大利亚国际设计奖
Australia
International Design Award

奖项互认

2010 年和 2012 年，红星奖分别与韩国“好设计奖”、澳大利亚“国际设计奖”实现了标准互认。

中国设计红星奖与韩国好设计奖的互认，部分选定产品可以使用红星奖与好设计奖的标志。

中国设计红星奖与澳大利亚国际设计奖的互认，部分选定产品可以使用红星奖与澳大利亚国际设计奖和澳大利亚好设计奖的标志。

Mutual Recognition

In 2010 and 2012, Red Star has respectively realizes the mutual recognition with "Good Design" from Korea and "International Design Award" from Australia.

Selected entries shall be allowed to carry a jointly branded design label with China Red Star Design Award and GD Award as the conclusion of mutual recognition between Red Star and GD.

Selected entries shall be allowed to carry a jointly branded design label with China Red Star Design Award and Australian International Design Award™ and Australian Good Design™ as the conclusion of mutual recognition between Red Star and AIDA.

2017

12th

不忘初心 · 砥砺前行

Never forget why you started, and forge ahead

2017

2006-2011
红星照耀中国 是创新的中国
Red Star over China – Innovative China

2012
红星照耀中国 是美丽的中国
Red Star over China – beautiful China

2013
全球视野 国家利益
Global Vision National Interest

2014
设计为人民
Design for People

2015
中国好设计
China Good Design

2016
中国精工 —— 好设计 • 新供给
Precision Manufacturing of China —— Good Design • New Supply

2017
创新设计 中国智造 服务人民
Innovation design Made by China People oriented

2018
设计让生活更美好
Design makes a better life

2006 年，举行新闻发布会
2006, news release conference

2006 年，为评委颁发聘书
2006, granting certificate to Jury members

2011 年，参展韩国设计展
2011, participating Design Korea

2011 年，参展中国台北世界设计大会国际设计博览会
2011, participating the World Design Conference International design EXPO, China Taipei

2014 年，首次在法国巴黎联合国教科文组织（UNESCO）总部举办展览，UNESCO 总干事博科娃参观
2014, Red Star's first UNESCO exhibition held in Paris, France. Director-General of UNESCO Mrs. Irina Bokova visited the exhibition

2014 年，联合国教科文组织总部工作人员体验获奖产品
2014, officer of UNESCO Headquarter was experiencing one awarded product

2012 年，创立中国设计红星奖博物馆
China Red Star Design Award founded in 2012.

2012 年，颁奖典礼设计师与盲童登台互动
2012, communication between designer and blind child on the award ceremony

2015 年，颁奖典礼颁发至尊金奖
2015, awarding Best of the Gold Prize on the ceremony

2015 年，大众参观颁奖典礼展览
2015, public enjoying the ceremony exhibition

2016 年，评审现场
2016, screening site

2016 年，执行主席与评委合影
2016, group photo of Red Star Executive Chairman and jury

2016 年，参加在东莞举办的中国加工贸易产品博览会
2016, exhibition at China Processing Trade Products Fair in Dongguan, Guangdong

2016 年，颁奖典礼来宾与获奖产品互动
2016, interaction between the ceremony guests and awarded product

2016 年，颁发未来之星奖
2016, awarding Future Star Awards

国际组织
International organizations

热烈祝贺！
Warm congratulations!

联合国前秘书长布特罗斯·布特罗斯－加利
Former Secretary-General of United Nations, Boutros Boutros-Ghali

祝贺在联合国教科文组织举办了一场如此令人难忘的展览。
Congratulations on organizing such a memorable exhibition at UNESCO.

联合国教科文组织助理总干事汉斯·道维勒
Assistant Director-General for Strategic Planning of UNESCO, Hans D'orville

行业协会
Industry associations

红星奖提出的口号都是对国家发展理念的践行。红星奖的诞生和发展是中国传统生产模式转向新的生产发展模式、理念的过程，所以它是中国创新走向国际的一个最亮丽的符号和最强的声音。

The slogan proposed by the China Red Star Design Award is the practice of the concept of national development. The birth and development of the China Red Star Design Award is a process in which China's previous mode of production and development shifted to a new mode of production and development. Therefore, it is one of the most beautiful symbols and strongest voices of China's innovation toward internationalization.

中国工业设计协会会长刘宁
President of China Industrial Design Association, Liu Ning

红星奖的产品质量有了很大的提高，种类更丰富，内容更有深度。一些设计的改动可能并不是很大，但增加了趣味和功能，让我们与生活更加贴近了。透过红星奖可以看出，中国设计水平这些年在快速提高。

In regard of the product, we can clearly find that they are substantially improved, being richer than the past, and products su bmitted for assessment, what I mean is the depth of their content, is deepened than before. For my experience, on the whole, and through Re d Star Design Award, holistic Chinese design has gained rapid development. Through all of these, I can find that our overall product l evel is increasing rapidly.

中国家具协会副理事长陈宝光
Vice President, China National Furniture Association, Chen Baoguang

工业设计对产品品质的提升有着决定性的作用。产品首先是满足使用功能的需要。而今天，生活的需求基本都能够得到满足，这就要求我们把设计的更多细节做得更到位，满足对生活品质和精神的需求。

Industrial design has a decisive role in product quality improvement. First, the product is to meet the needs of the function of use, but today, life has already come to this premise, where all the basic needs can be met, which requires us to design more perfect details to meet the quality of life and spiritual needs.

广东省工业设计协会秘书长周红石
Secretary-General of Guangdong Industrial Design Association, Zhou Hongshi

通过红星奖产品能够感受到很多设计师都注意
察生活。生活因设计更精彩、更美好。特别是我
到很多设计能关注到少年儿童和老年人，非常人
化。我为红星奖能为设计师搭建这么好的一个平
而感到骄傲。

Through the products of Red Star, I feel th
many designers are good at observing life, s
life is much better because of design. I find ma
designs pay attention to children and the elder
which are very people oriented. I'm proud of th
Red Star platform which provides such a goo
platform for the designers.

上海工业设计协会会长王日
President of Shanghai Industrial Desig
Association, Wang Rihu

红星奖的产品整体质量高，同时更加生活化和实
化，表现了现在设计师不再是以浮夸的造型为主，
而是更加实用和更加贴近生活、走进生活的一个
向。设计始终是以生活为本的。

The overall quality of China Red Star Desig
Award-winning products is high, at the sam
time, they are closer to life and more practica
This shows one of the direction designers toda
that is, their direction is no longer based o
exaggerated style, but more practical and close
to life, which can entry into life. Design is alway
life-based.

深圳市设计联合会秘书长刘
Secretary-General of Shenzhen Industria
Design Association, Liu Zhe

红星奖安徽站正式落地中国（合肥）工业设计城，
志着"自主创新设计"被提升到新的高度，自主创
设计也将通过红星奖这个专业化和国际化的平台
到最大程度的推广和转化，以实际成果推动工业
计发展。

Anhui Station of China Red Star Design Awar
officially landed in China (Hefei) Industria
Design City, marking the 'independent innovatio
design' was elevated to a new level, independen
innovation design will also get the maximall
promotion and conversion through the Chin
Red Star Design Award--this professional an
international platform, with the actual results t
promote industrial design and development.

合肥市工业设计协会秘书长王正
Secretary-General of Hefei Industria
Design Association, Wang Zhengron

星奖产品让我印象深刻，无论是 10000 件的参评数量还是极高的水平。比如一些产品拥有优雅的设计语言，同时兼顾环境保护。我们看到高水平的中国设计正在推动"中国制造"走向"中国创造"。世界设计正关注着中国领导力，而红星奖所代表的中国设计令人瞩目，这也将带动世界其他地区关注创新、设计和创意，提升生活品质。

his year's entries have really impressed me. n terms of the numbers, in terms of quantity ver 10,000 entries as well as the quality which s of an excellent level. Some products take are of the environment and we need to look at ssues like climate change and the sustainable evelopment goals. The kind of quality of designs oming out of China moving from "Made in hina" to "Created in China". The world design ooking at China for that kind of leadership and what's coming out of China through the Red Star s actually very impressive. So it's becoming a atalyst to other regions to also start look at nnovation and design and creativity. So as to ontribute to people's a quality of life.

世界设计组织主席（2015—2017）穆根迪·瑞塔
President of World Design Organization(2015—2017), Mugendi K. M'Rithaa

我认为中国设计红星奖对提升设计标准起到了很大的作用。它为中国的设计师、生产者和企业设定了基准：这就是优秀设计。

think the China Red Star Design Award has layed a big role in improving design standards. t sets the benchmark for Chinese designers, roducers and enterprises: This is good design.

澳大利亚国际设计奖主席布兰顿·基恩
Chairman of Australian International Design Award, Brandon Gien

红星奖产品种类之多、数量之大难以想象，这是令人惊叹的。希望邀请红星奖获奖产品到米兰三年展进行展出，如此之好的产品应该在更国际化的舞台上崭露头角。

It is unimaginable that there are many types and numbers of China Red Star Design Award-winning products, which is amazing. I hope to invite Star Award-winning products to be exhibited at the Triennale de Milan, and such good products should emerge in a more cosmopolitan arena.

意大利米兰三年展主席拜拉维提斯
President of the Triennale Design Museum, Arturo Dell'Acqua Bellavitis

现在有很多尖端行业都应用了设计的手段，让人看到了中国设计发展的突破，为产业发展带来巨大进步。

Nowadays, there are many cutting-edge industries that have applied the means of design, to let people see the breakthrough and tremendous progress of China's industrial development and industry development.

清华大学美术学院责任教授柳冠中
Professor of Academy of Arts & Design, Tsinghua University, Liu Guanzhong

今年是红星奖第 12 年，这 12 年不仅见证了设计的发展，而且见证了中国发展轨迹。红星奖产品越来越多元化，有更多高科技产品，比如高铁和大飞机，这些都体现了国家在各方面重要的发展。

This year is the 12th year of China Red Star Design Award, during the past 12 years, we have not only witnessed the development of the design, but also witnessed the development of China.The works are more diversified. There are more high-tech products in the award-winning products, such as high-speed rail and large aircraft, which reflect the important development of the country in all aspects.

湖南大学设计艺术学院院长何人可
Dean of School of Design, Hunan University, He Renke

作为中国设计人，乐见红星奖提升中国创新设计能力的同时，也希望看到更多的社会公众能够参与到围绕红星奖展开的系列活动中，了解并学会运用设计思维中所体现出来的人本思想、生态观念以及解决复杂问题的协调能力，并越来越多地享受到创新设计在信息、服务乃至公共事务管理等领域的成果。

As a Chinese designer, I am very pleased to witness the China Red Star Design Award to enhance China's innovative design capabilities, but I also want to see more of the public can participate in a series of activities around the China Red Star Design Award. The public understands and learns to use the humanistic ideas, ecological concepts and coordination of complex issue, and they can also enjoy more benefits of innovative design in the areas of information, services and public affairs management.

江南大学设计学院教授辛向阳
Professor of Design Institute, Jiangnan University, Xin Xiangyang

红星奖能够关注弱势群体让我十分感动。太阳花LED 灯、盲文点读机和空巢老人呼叫器等等这些设计关注的是我们生活中最常忽略的。一个小小的设计创新会使我们的生活变得很好。

I am very touched that the China Red Star Design Award can focus on vulnerable groups. These designs are the most often overlooked in our lives, such as sunflowers, braille point readers and pagers for empty nesters elders and so on. A little design innovation will make our life better.

观复博物馆创办人、馆长马未都
Founder & Director of Guanfu Museum, Ma Weidu

我们的团队是一个非常年轻、充满活力、非常有创造力的优秀设计队伍，连续三年获得了国内设计界最有国际影响力的红星奖金奖。其中，2014年一款出口土耳其的不锈钢地铁，结合了当地民族文化，成为解决当地交通出行的重要轨道交通工具。

Our team is a very young, energetic, very creative outstanding design team, we won the gold medal of the most influential international China Red Star Design Award in the domestic design industry for three consecutive years. Among them, there is a stainless steel subway exported to Turkey in 2014,combined with local ethnic culture, and it became an important orbital vehicle for local traffic trips.

中车株洲电力机车有限公司
CRRC Zhuzhou Locomotive Co., Ltd.

我们将继续积极响应总书记的号召，不忘初心，砥砺前行，坚持弘扬“工匠精神”，忠诚履行好“让祖国的大飞机早日翱翔蓝天”的光荣使命，以实际行动贯彻落实党的十九大精神。

We will continue to respond positively to the call of the General-Secretary Xi. We will never forget the original intention, persevere in carrying forward the "craftsmanship" and faithfully discharge the glorious mission of "letting the big motherland fly soaring into the sky as soon as possible". We will take concrete actions to implement the spirit of 19th National Congress of the Chinese Communist Party.

中国商用飞机有限责任公司
Commercial Aircraft Corporation of China, Ltd.

红星奖的广度和深度为更多行业的原创设计提供了展示平台，非常感谢红星奖及各位评委对工程机械工业设计的认可和支持。

The breadth and depth of the China Red Star Design Award provides a display platform for original design in more industries. We appreciate the recognition and support for the industrial design of engineering machine from China Red Star Design Award and the judges.

徐工集团
XCMG Group

我们坚信一款好的产品除了在设计中下足功夫，还需通过实现技术与功能完美结合，给用户带来出色的使用体验。在未来，产品智能化服务将以用户为轴心，辐射至其生活周边，打造由出行工具所引领的生活方式闭环。

We firmly believe that a good product not only must do all efforts in design, but also must through the perfect combination of technology and function, to give users an excellent user experience. In the future, the intelligent product service will take users as its axis, radiating the periphery of its life and creating a closed-loop lifestyle led by tools.

小牛电动创新研发室
Niu Innovation Lab

我们要从系统、用户体验、生活方式来看一个设计，这些会变成一种无形资产，虽然看不见，但是在未来这些会成为核心的部分。

We look at design from system, user experience and lifestyle, design will become an intangible asset that, although invisible, it will become central part of the future.

海尔集团
Haier Group

想于 2006 年第一届红星奖获得至尊金奖，十年之
再获此殊荣。这个奖项是奖励给中国原创设计的，
谢红星奖！设计的目的是为了提升人们的生活品
，设计师要回归到初心和感受生活。一个设计师
社会责任就是以设计营造一个和谐的社会关系。

enovo, as the winner of Best of the Gold Prize the first session of in 2006, is the re-winning ompany ten years later. This award is rewarded the original design of China, thanks to the hina Red Star Design Award! The purpose of e design is to improve people's quality of life, esigners should return to the original intention nd feel life. A designer's social responsibility is create a harmonious social relations.

联想消费 PC 设计高级总监李凤朗
Executive Director of PC Department of Lenovo, Li Fenglang

盲文点读机仅有卡片般大小，机身与按键分别使用
橡胶与塑料，可以清楚分辨按键的位置，提供简单
的盲文自学方法。希望产品能够增加盲童的学习乐
趣，缩短学习时间。充满爱的设计才是真正美的设
计！

raille reader only has a card size. The fuselage nd the keys are used separately rubber and lastic, you can clearly distinguish the location f the keys to provide a simple method of braille elf-learning. We hope that products can ncrease the fun of learning for blind children nd shorten the study time. Design full of love is real design of beauty.

和硕设计总监郭文祺
Design Director, Pega Design, Guo Wenqi

我们希望当我们的产品出现在生活里的时候，没有任何门槛，每个普通人都可以使用它。同时和周围环境非常和谐一致。设计既能让产品质量变得更好，又能为生活品质带来提升。

We hope that when our products appear in the life, an ordinary person can use it without any threshold, while the surrounding environment is very harmony. We hope to make the product quality better, and it can bring improvement to the quality of life.

小米科技生态链产品总监夏勇峰
Product Director of Ecological Chain, Mi Technology, Xia Yongfeng

红星奖是国内同类奖项的代表，在国际上也是日益彰显其影响力。参评奖项是产品附加值的一种体现也是对设计者价值的认可。

The China Red Star Design Award is the representative of similar awards in China and is increasingly showing its influence in the world. The participation of award is a manifestation of product' s added value, but also a recognition of the designer value.

北京谊安医疗工业设计总监孙家明
Industrial Design Director, Beijing Aeonmed Co,.Ltd. Sun Jia-ming

快舒尔医疗设计生产的一款无针注射器获得 2015 年中国设计红星奖金奖后受到社会各界关注，这让这款好设计收获更多消费者的信任与认可，为更多患者减轻病痛，带去幸福。

QS-M needleless syringe was designed and manufactured by Kuaishuer Medical. After being awarded the Golden Prize of China Red Star Design Award in 2015, it received the attention of all sectors of society. This makes this good design reap the trust and recognition of more consumers, relieve the pain and bring happiness to more patients.

北京快舒尔医疗技术有限公司陈苏宁
Beijing QS Medical Technology Co.,Ltd. Chen Suning

大众点评
Public comment

好设计让我的家人减轻了病痛。奶奶以前用针头注射，她老花眼，看不太清胰岛素吸入量，用完了还得把针头放起来，怕扎到谁。无针注射器使用简单，可以直接选择注射量，也不怕扎到别人，也没有疼痛感。

Good design alleviated the pain of my family member. My grandma used to have a needle for injection. She had presbyopia and she did not look too clear, when she was taking insulin. When it's done, she has to put the needle up for fear of reaching somebody. Needle-free syringe is easy to use, you can directly select the amount of injection, do not have to be afraid to tie others, there is no pain.

糖尿病患者家属
Family member of a patient with diabetes

有了盲文点读机以后，我觉得生活更丰富多彩了，我的学习也变得非常的快乐方便。它可以读中文、拼音和英语字母，使用它我觉得特别开心。

With this braille reading machine, I feel that life is more colorful, my study has become very happy and convenient. It can read Chinese, pinyin and English letters, I feel very happy to use it.

盲童
Blind child

新时代女性要兼顾家庭与工作，好设计和好产品可以让做家务变得格外幸福。

In the new era, women should consider both family and work. Good design and good products can make housework extra happy.

职场女性
Office lady

红星奖产品种类丰富，从小家电到高铁飞机。而且很多产品都针对生活中的实际问题而设计，也有一些以前没见过的产品，为我们的生活提供了更多的可能性。

The products of China Red Star Design Award are rich in variety, you can see the products from small appliances to high-speed rail and aircraft, and many products are designed for practical problems in life, there are some products have not seen before, providing more possibilities for our life.

大众评审投票者
Voter of the public screening

许多展品贴近人们的日常生活，通过设计的方法解决社会的突出问题。比如智能轮椅，使行动不便的群体可以生活更加独立，提高生活的舒适度。

Many exhibits are close to the daily life of people and are designed to solve outstanding social problems. Such as intelligent wheelchairs, make accessible to people with limited mobility to live more independently, improve the comfort of life.

2017 红星奖精品展观众
Visitor of selected products exhibition of China Red Star Design Award

体
edia

)06 年至 2017 年十二年来红星奖的发展过程，是
中国设计发展历程的回顾，也呈现出设计和科技
展对生产和生活方式带来的改变。

ne development process of the China Red Star esign Award in the 12 years from 2006 to 2017, a review of the development history of China's esign. It also shows the changes to production nd life style, brought by the development of esign and technology.

新华网
Xinhuanet

设计生发，在红星奖的感召和带动下，企业开始
考如何为社会发展做出自身努力。红星奖不仅表
优秀设计和创新企业，更着眼鼓励人们发现需求，
决问题。

roduced and developed by design, inspired nd led by the China Red Star Design Award, ompanies began to think about how to make neir own efforts for social development. The hina Red Star Design Award not only recognizes utstanding design and innovative businesses, ut also focus on encouraging people to find eeds and solve problems.

人民网
People.cn

作为中国唯一盘点和展望中国社会、产业、经济的设计大奖，红星奖以一贯鲜明的态度影响着人们对设计的认知和行为。“民众的幸福感”“经济的品质运行”“美丽中国”“创新驱动”等关键词，既是设计精神回归本质的追求，也是红星奖表彰优秀设计的出发点。

As the only design award in China for counting and looking forward to China's social, industrial and economic issues, the China Red Star Design Award has always influenced people's perceptions and behaviors in design. The key words such as "people's happiness", "quality of economy", "beautiful China", and "innovation-driven", are the pursuits of return to the essence of the design, but also the starting point why China Red Star Design Award would like to commend outstanding design.

腾讯
Tencent

红星奖获奖项目中既有通过设计提升产业竞争力的典范，也有不少关注民生的人性化作品，其中获得红星奖原创奖的多是那些方便实用、构思精巧的小设计。

Among the China Red Star Design Award -winning projects, there are both models that enhance industrial competitiveness through design, and many people-oriented works that focus on people's livelihood. Among them, most of the original award-winning products of China Red Star Design Award are small designs, which are convenient and practical, sophisticated design.

新浪
Sina

红星奖的发展趋势，一方面体现了中国制造业逐步走向全球的中心位置，另一方面也体现了中国设计红星奖服务国家战略、引领未来前沿的导向作用。

The development trend of the China Red Star Design Award shows that, on the one hand, China's manufacturing industry has gradually moved toward the global center; on the other hand, it also embodies the guiding role of China Red Star Design Award for serving the national strategy and leading the cutting edge of the future.

网易
Netease

中国设计红星奖委员会执行主席　陈冬亮

Chen Dongliang, Executive Chairman of China Red Star Design Award Committee

设计让生活更美好

Design makes a better life

党的十九大为设计指明了未来发展方向

举世瞩目的中国共产党第十九次全国代表大会胜利召开，习近平新时代中国特色社会主义思想为决胜全面建成小康社会，夺取新时代中国特色社会主义伟大胜利，为实现中华民族伟大复兴的中国梦指明了前进方向。

中国特色社会主义进入新时代，我国社会主要矛盾已经转化为人民日益增长的美好生活需求和不平衡不充分的发展之间的矛盾。这一科学的论断是关系全局的历史性变化，对我们今后的工作提出了许多新要求。作为设计从业者和促进者的我们，要重新审视和思考如何在继续推动发展的基础上，更好满足人民在衣、食、住、行、用等各方面对美好生活日益增长的要求。

新时代设计将发挥全新的价值与作用

设计是促进产品与服务品质提升的重要抓手

面对新时代社会主要矛盾及消费需求的变化，人民日益增长的美好生活，需要更好品质和质量的产品与服务。设计作为创新发展的重要环节，在提升产品美观、性能、品质等方面发挥了核心作用，不仅催生出了新中装、新国服、智能家居、共享单车等新兴消费品类的产品，同时也助推了以中国高铁等为代表的中国创造品牌塑造及传播。设计正在强化提升市场主体的创新力和竞争力，努力创造新需求，实现新价值，通过不断推进供给侧改革，为社会提供更加满足人民美好生活的产品和服务，使设计真正成为促进经济建设、城市发展、市民生活共融共生的助推器，成为实现“创新引领、开放包容、充满活力、富有魅力”美好幸福“中国梦”的重要引擎。

设计是展现文化魅力和实现创新发展的重要手段

文化作为一个国家综合国力的重要组成部分，是满足人民过上美好生活的新期待所必须提供的精神食粮。设计不仅是构成文化内涵的核心要素，也是文化魅力的表现形态。设计作为肩负着承上启下重要使命的工具，不仅是加强文物保护利用和文化遗产保护传承的重要手段，也是支撑“讲好中国故事，弘扬中华优秀传统文化”精神的核心力量。设计还是促进文化科技融合的重要手段，通过创新发展，不断推动云计算、互联网 +、大数据等先进、创新技术在新闻出版、影视传媒、文化演艺等文化领域的应用，可有效促进传统业态升级，催生新兴文化业态，不断提高国家文化软实力。

设计是促进科技创新成果转化的战略工具

设计是科技服务业的高端环节，是打通科技成果转化最后一公里，是将科技优势转化为社会经济发展新优势的重要途径。通过设计手段，可以有效促进科技与文化融合，弘扬传统优秀文化，将文化优势资源转化为文化产业、文化事业发展优势的重要手段。随着我国在互联网、大数据、人工智能等领域科技成果不断涌现，设计作为科技创新成果转化链条的关键环节，是加快科技成果转移转化，打通科技与经济结合的通道，是形成新的生产力的重要引擎。作为国内唯一一家能够自主生产数字化 G 型臂 X 光机（Ⅲ型）的厂家，北京东方惠尔图像技术有限公司是拥有国际领先的 X 光双向同步控制技术、实时成像技术的基础上，通过导入“产品定位、用户诉求、人机交互及品牌内涵”等环节的设计，极大地提升产品的创新力和竞争力，成为更好满足人们需求的实用产品，为开拓市场奠定了良好基础。

设计是促进城市人居环境改善的核心支撑

人民日益增长的美好生活的需求还体现在了对优美生态环境和城市现代化发展的需要。设计作为战略工具可以提供更多优质的产品和服务，推进城市的可持续发展。通过对构成城市人居环境的各项实质单元，如住宅、商店、工厂、学校、交通设施，以及公园绿地等公共场所等的创新创意设计，使其满足人们在生活、社会、经济以及美观、性能、便捷等方面的需求。另外还可以通过内容、形式、技术等设计手段，加强城市交通、公共空间、社区、老城改造的合理性规划和建设，不断提升城市环境的宜居性和可持续性，有效满足了人民对美好生活环境畅想和城市生态文明建设的需求。

设计是推动农村社会发展改善民生的动力引擎

“产业兴旺、生态宜居、生活富裕”是新时期农村社会发展的新需求，设计通过创新农村旅游、改良农业产品、进行能力建设等手段实现绿水青山就是金山银山的美好愿景。通过设计农村创新旅游产品，在保证生态环境基础上充分调动与发挥农村的文化旅游资源，吸引更多游客，提高农村人民收入。通过设计改良农业生产方式，加快推进农业现代化，用更人性化的科技化、机械化的手段提高农业生产效率，提供更多绿色农业产品，满足消费者高端化、个性化、多样化的需求。通过对农村从业者进行能力培训，授人以渔，提升其手工艺技能和设计能力，扩大就业范围，增加收入，实现精准扶贫。设计能有效提升农村人民的获得感、幸福感、安全感，让农村人民过上更加美好幸福的新生活。

设计是更好满足“美好生活需求”的发力点

在推进设计产业发展过程中，按照十九大报告精神，主要应从以下四个点发力。

一是全面落实新理念。以新的发展理念引领和推动设计产业发展，通过设计推进供给侧改革，充分发挥设计在科技创新成果的转化作用，不断提高产品的质量，推动产业升级和提质增效。**二是不断对接新需求**。根据人民群众日益增长的对美好生活的物质产品和精神文化需求，发挥设计在产品与服务创新中的重要作用，不断创新产品与服务的内容、形式、方式和手段，提升和完善适合人民群众需求的产品和服务，促进物质和文化消费品质提升。**三是积极培育新动能**。发挥设计在科技创新成果转中化的战略工具作用，推进科技文化融合，积极培育创新业态，激发产业发展内生动力，强化辐射带动作用，培育发展新动能。**四是努力拓展新领域**。不断融入全球创新网络，发挥联合国教科文组织创意城市网络的作用，吸引国际高端创新机构、全球顶尖人才和团队来华发展，提升本土设计水平和国际影响力。同时不断强化设计在推动文化旅游、拉动消费、形成特色品牌活动，践行“设计为人民”创新理念。

The 19th National Congress of the Communist Party of China indicated the future direction of development for the design.

The 19th National Congress of the Chinese Communist Party, which attracted worldwide attention, was successfully held, Xi Jinping's socialist thoughts with Chinese characteristics in the new era have described the future in building a well-off society in an all-round way, seizing the great victory of socialism with Chinese characteristics in a new era, carrying forward the Chinese Dream of great rejuvenation of the Chinese nation.

"Socialism with Chinese characteristics has entered a new era in which the major social contradiction in our country have been translated into the contradiction between the ever-growing demand for a better life and the unbalanced and insufficient development". This scientific thesis is a historic change that has a bearing on the overall situation and sets forth many new requirements for our future work. As practitioners and promoters of design, we must re-examine and reflect on how to better meet the ever-increasing demands of a better life, on the basis of continuing development, to promote people's livelihood in all aspects, such as clothing, food, habitat, transportation and use.

Design will play a new role and value in the new era.

Design is an important starting point to improve the quality of products and services.

Faced with the major social contradictions in the new era and the changes in consumer demand, the people's growing good life requires products and services with better character and quality. As an important part of innovation and development, design plays a key role in improving the product appearance, performance, quality and so on. Design not only spawned products of emerging Chinese consumer goods such as new Chinese clothing, new national clothing, smart household and sharing bicycle, but also promoted the creation and dissemination of brand in China represented by China High Speed Rail. Design is strengthening the innovation and competitiveness of market players, striving to create new needs and realize new values. By promoting supply-side reform, we will provide society with products and services that better meet the people's needs for good life. This will truly make the design a booster to promote economic construction, urban development and communal living together, and become an important engine for achieving the beauty and happiness of "Chinese Dream" full of "innovation, open and inclusiveness, vitality and charm".

Design is an important means to show the charm of the culture and realize the innovation and development.

As an important part of a country's overall national strength, culture is the spiritual food that must be provided to meet the new expectations of the people for a better life. Design is not only a core element that constitutes cultural connotation, but also a manifestation of cultural charisma. Design, as an important tool to shoulder the important task of supporting and opening up, is not only an important means to strengthen the inheritance and protection of cultural relics and the protection of cultural heritage, but also the core force that supports the spirit of " telling a good story of China and promoting the fine Chinese traditional culture." Design is also an important means of promoting the integration of culture and science and technology. Through innovation and development, the design promotes the application of advanced and innovative technologies such as cloud computing, Internet+, and big data in cultural fields such as press, publishing, film and television media and cultural performing arts to effectively promote the upgrading of traditional formats, to give birth to emerging cultural formats, and continue to improve the national cultural soft power.

Design is a strategic tool to promote the transformation of achievements of scientific and technological innovations.

Design is the high-end link of the science and technology service industry. Design is the last mile to get through the transformation of scientific and technological achievements, which transforms the advantages of science and technology into an important way for the new advantages of social and economic development. By means of design, it can effectively promote the integration of science and technology and culture, carry forward the traditional fine culture and transform the resources of cultural superiority into the important means for the development of cultural industries and cultural undertakings. With the continuous popularization of scientific and technological achievements in the fields of Internet, big data and artificial intelligence, design as the key link in the chain of transformation of scientific and technological innovations, is an important engine for speeding up the transfer and transformation the scientific and technological achievements, opening up channels for the intergration of science and technology with the economy, and forming a new productive force. As the only manufacturer in China, who can independently produce digital G-arm X-ray machine (III type), Beijing Oriental Whirlpool Image Technology Co., Ltd. has the world's leading X-ray bidirectional synchronous. On the basis of real-time imaging technology, it greatly improves the innovation and competitiveness of products by introducing such aspects as "product positioning, customer appeal, human-computer interaction and brand connotation". It becomes a practical product that better meets people's needs, which laid a good foundation for market development.

Design is the core support to promote the improvement of urban living environment.

The growing needs of the people are also reflected in the needs for a beautiful ecological environment and urban modernization. As a strategic tool, design can provide more quality products and services to promote the sustainable development of the city. By optimizing the design of the real various units that make up the urban living environment, such as residences, shops, factories, schools, parks and green spaces, it meets the needs of people in life, society, economy, beauty, performance and convenience. In addition, we can also strengthen the rational planning and construction of urban transport, public space, community and the renovation of the old city through the means of design in contents, forms and technologies,so as to enhance the livability and sustainability of the urban environment. This effectively meets the people's desire for a beautiful living environment and the construction of urban ecological civilization.

Design is the engine of power to promote rural social development and improve people's livelihood.

"Prosperous industry, ecological livability, rich life" is the new demand for rural social development in the new era. Design, through innovative rural tourism, improved agricultural products, capacity-building and other means, can achieve a beautiful vision of "Beautiful scenery is the gold and silver mines" . Through the design of rural innovative tourism products, on the basis of ensuring the ecological environment, we should fully mobilize and give play to the cultural tourism resources in rural areas to attract more tourists and raise the incomes of rural people. Through the design, it can improve the mode of agricultural production, speed up the modernization of agriculture, improve the efficiency of agricultural production with more humane and mechanized means, provide more green agricultural products and meet the needs of consumers with high-end, individuality and diversification . Through capacity training for rural practitioners, it can empower people with designing skills, upgrade their handicraft skills and design capabilities, expand their employment scope, and increase their income and achieve precise poverty alleviation. Design can effectively enhance the rural people's sense of acquisition, happiness and security, so that rural people live a more beautiful and happy new life.

Design is the force to better meet the needs of a better life.

In promoting the development of the design industry, in accordance with the spirit of the report on the 19th National Congress of the Communist Party of China, there are four force points as follows.

First, we should fully implement the new concept. We should guide and promote the development of the design industry with a new concept of development. We will promote supply-side reform through design, give full play to the role of design in the transformation of scientific and technological innovations, continuously improve the quality of products, and promote industrial upgrading and quality improvement. **Second, we should continue to meet new needs.** According to the masses' growing material and spiritual needs for a better life, we must give full play to the important role of design in the innovation of products and services, continuously innovate the contents, forms, ways and means of products and services, so as to improve and perfect the products and services that meet the needs of the people and promote the improvement of the quality of material and cultural consumption. **Third, we should actively cultivate new momentum.** We will give full play to the role of design as a strategic tool for the transformation of scientific and technological innovations, promote the integration of science and technology and culture, actively cultivate innovative formats, stimulate the industrial development of endogenous power, enhance the role of radiation and cultivate new momentum for development. **Fourth, we should strive to expand new areas.** We will continue to integrate ourselves into the global innovation network and give play to the role of UNESCO Creative City Network. We will attract international high-end innovation organizations, world-class talents and teams to come to China for development and upgrade local design standards and international influence. At the same time, we will continue to strengthen the design in promoting cultural tourism, stimulating consumption, forming distinctive brand activities and practicing innovative ideas of "design for people".

12th

创新设计 Innovation design

中国智造 Made by China

服务人民 People oriented

2017